INTERACTIVE LECTURING

INTERACTIVE LECTURING

A Handbook for College Faculty

Elizabeth F. Barkley and Claire Howell Major

JB JOSSEY-BASS™
A Wiley Brand

Published by Jossey-Bass
A Wiley Brand
One Montgomery Street, Suite 1000, San Francisco, CA 94104-4594—www.josseybass.com

Jossey-Bass books and products are available through most bookstores. To contact Jossey-Bass directly call our Customer Care Department within the U.S. at 800-956-7739, outside the U.S. at 317-572-3986, or fax 317-572-4002.

Wiley publishes in a variety of print and electronic formats and by print-on-demand. Some material included with standard print versions of this book may not be included in e-books or in print-on-demand. If this book refers to media such as a CD or DVD that is not included in the version you purchased, you may download this material at http://booksupport.wiley.com. For more information about Wiley products, visit www.wiley.com.

Library of Congress Cataloging-in-Publication Data

Names: Barkley, Elizabeth F., author. | Major, Claire Howell, author.
Title: Interactive lecturing : a handbook for college faculty / Elizabeth F. Barkley, Claire Howell Major.
Description: San Francisco, CA : Jossey-Bass ; Hoboken, NJ : John Wiley & Sons, 2018. | Includes bibliographical references and index.
Identifiers: LCCN 2017046228 | ISBN 9781119277453 (pdf) | ISBN 9781119277446 (epub) | ISBN 9781119277309 (pbk.)
Subjects: LCSH: College teaching–Aids and devices. | Lectures and lecturing–Handbooks, manuals, etc.
Classification: LCC LB2331 .B365 2018 | DDC 378.1/25–dc23 LC record available at https://lccn.loc.gov/2017046228

Cover Design: Wiley
Cover Image: © saicle/Shutterstock

Printed in the United States of America
FIRST EDITION
PB Printing 10 9 8 7 6 5 4 3 2 1

We dedicate this book to Maryellen Weimer. She is a teacher-scholar who has been a great source of support and encouragement for us over the years and a generous advocate of all of our books in the College Teaching Techniques series. She also offered us sound advice and guidance that pushed our thinking during the development of this book.

CONTENTS

ACKNOWLEDGMENTS

We are grateful to several individuals who supported the work of this project. We thank Shonteria Johnson for her assistance during the initial research phase. We also thank Carla Blakey for her help with bibliography development, manuscript management, and proofing. Thanks are also due to our three anonymous reviewers, who offered in-depth and thoughtful comments and suggestions that helped us shape the manuscript. We learned after the review process that these three reviewers were Kevin Kelly, Mark Maier, and Michael Palmer. Ted Major was a great support throughout the process but particularly during the final stages of the work; he read and edited the penultimate draft and offered practical suggestions based on his own classroom experience. Additionally, we continue to be grateful to K. Patricia Cross, whose pioneering work with classroom assessment and handbooks for college teachers laid the foundation for—and now bind together—the entire College Teaching Techniques series.

ABOUT THE AUTHORS

Elizabeth F. Barkley is professor of music at Foothill College, Los Altos, California. With over four decades as an innovative and reflective teacher, she has received numerous honors and awards, including being named California's Higher Education Professor of the Year by the Carnegie Foundation for the Advancement of Teaching, formally recognized by the California State Legislature for her contributions to undergraduate education, selected as "Innovator of the Year" in conjunction with the National League for Innovation, presented with the Hayward Award for Educational Excellence, and honored by the Center for Diversity in Teaching and Learning in Higher Education. In addition, her "Musics of Multicultural America" course was selected as "Best Online Course" by the California Virtual Campus. She was also named a Carnegie Scholar in the discipline of music by the Carnegie Foundation in conjunction with the Pew Charitable Trusts.

Beyond her academic discipline of music history, her interests include engaging students through active and collaborative learning; transforming face-to-face and online curriculum to meet the needs of diverse learners, especially those from new and emerging generations; contributing to the scholarship of teaching and learning; and connecting learning goals with outcomes and assessment. Barkley holds a BA and MA from the University of California, Riverside, and a PhD from the University of California, Berkeley. She is coauthor with Claire Howell Major of *Learning Assessment Techniques: A Handbook for College Faculty* (Jossey-Bass, 2016). She is coauthor with Claire Howell Major and K. Patricia Cross of *Collaborative Learning Techniques: A Handbook for College Faculty,* 2nd ed. (Jossey-Bass, 2014); author of *Student Engagement Techniques: A Handbook for College Faculty* (Jossey-Bass, 2010) and several music history textbooks, including *Crossroads: The Music of American Cultures* (Kendall Hunt, 2013), *World Music: Roots to Contemporary Global Fusions* (Kendall Hunt, 2012), *Crossroads: The Roots of America's Popular Music,* 2nd ed. (Prentice Hall, 2007); and coauthor with Robert Hartwell of *Great Composers and Music Masterpieces of Western Civilization* (Kendall Hunt, 2014).

Claire Howell Major is professor of higher education at the University of Alabama in Tuscaloosa. She teaches courses on college teaching, technology in higher education, reading research in the field of higher education, and qualitative research methods. Her research interests are in the areas of faculty work, pedagogical approaches, technology for teaching, and online learning. She also focuses on issues of higher education in popular culture and higher education as a field of study. She typically draws on qualitative methods to answer her research questions. Major holds a BA from the University of South Alabama, an MA from the University of Alabama at Birmingham, and a PhD from the University of Georgia. She has authored and coauthored several books, including *Teaching Online: A Guide to Theory, Research, and Practice* (Johns Hopkins University Press, 2015); *Collaborative Learning Techniques: A Handbook for College Faculty,* 2nd ed., with Elizabeth F. Barkley and K. Patricia Cross (Jossey-Bass, 2014); *The Essential Guide to Qualitative Research: A Handbook of Theory and Practice* with Maggi Savin-Baden (Routledge, 2013); *An Introduction to Qualitative Research Synthesis: Managing the Information Explosion* with Maggi Savin-Baden (Routledge, 2011); and *Foundations of Problem-Based Learning* with Maggi Savin-Baden (Open University Press, 2004). Major also publishes her work in leading education journals and presents at national and international conferences.

PART ONE

A CONCEPTUAL FRAMEWORK FOR INTERACTIVE LECTURING

Introduction

In classrooms around the country, college teachers work hard to engage students in the kind of learning that will prepare them to meet the demands of an increasingly complex world. Some professors lecture, others use a variety of approaches that fall under the banner of active learning. All want students to learn. But what is the most effective way to help students learn? For decades, many educators have been caught up in a debate arguing which approach is best, but what if we reframed the debate and instead looked for ways to maximize the benefits of both pedagogies?

What if college teachers who lecture used a little more active learning? Would instruction be more effective if students spent some of their class time participating in discussions or engaging in group projects instead of spending all of their class time listening? Alternately, what if college teachers who now use only active learning strategies spent a little more time in engaging modes of telling? Would instruction be more effective if students spent some of their class time listening to professors directly share knowledge about the disciplines and fields that they love instead of students having to discover everything on their own? We believe that the answer to all of these questions is yes.

In Part 1 of this book, we present the *conceptual framework* for blending engaging lectures and active learning methods. In so doing, we lay out the key assumptions, concepts, and research related to the interactive lecturing model. It is a representation of the essential elements of the model and relationships between them. We have organized our framework into two chapters:

Chapter 1. Lecture versus Active Learning: Reframing the Debate. Here we describe the ongoing debate between educators who are at odds with each other over whether lecture or active learning is the better instructional method, and we suggest that we reframe the issue.

Chapter 2. Integrating Lectures and Active Learning. In this chapter, we present our model for interactive lecturing and share the research that underpins the model.

CHAPTER 1

Lecture versus Active Learning: Reframing the Debate

Educators today would be hard-pressed to identify a teaching technique more heartily maligned than the lecture. Lectures are boring: "Some people talk in their sleep. Lecturers talk while other people sleep" (Albert Camus[1]). Lectures are ineffective: "A lecture is a process in which information passes from the notes of the lecturer into the notes of the student without passing through the minds of either" (Mark Twain[2]). Lectures are pointless: "Lectures were once useful; but now, when all can read and books are so numerous, lectures are unnecessary" (Samuel Johnson). Lecturing is currently considered to be so bad that one author imagines a future when universities are required to issue a warning to students that "lectures may stunt your academic performance and increase risk of failure" (Dawson, 2016). The list of criticisms continues and includes charges such as old-fashioned, overused, obsolete, and even unfair (see, for example, Abrams, 2012; Jensen & Davidson, 1997; Lambert, 2012; Paul, 2015; Segesten, 2012; Wieman, 2014).

Most of us have experienced listening to a lecture in which the speaker droned on and on; our minds wandered, our bodies fidgeted, and we would have dashed for the door had that been an option. One student expressed a similar sentiment: "I was so bored, I feared all the blood had left my head and I would pass out in the aisle" (El-Shamy, 2004, p. 24). Despite the surfeit of disparagements, research indicates that most college and university faculty members still lecture.[3] Lectures have remained popular for many reasons, including that they serve several important instructional purposes. Furthermore, lectures don't have to be dreary and mind-numbing. We—and students—have encountered situations in which we sat transfixed as we listened to a particularly captivating lecture. Indeed, a colleague recently shared that these kinds of lectures were the transformative events of his undergraduate education.

Although most college professors continue to lecture, researchers have also found that few today rely on the lecture entirely;[4] instead, they use lecture in combination with a variety of other teaching techniques, such as small-group work, case studies, discussion, and problem-solving—strategies that fall under the banner of "active learning." Active learning is a pedagogical approach that puts into practice over a half-century of research that demonstrates that, to truly learn, we need to make new information our own by working it into our personal knowledge and experience. As attractive as active learning is conceptually, however, many college teachers struggle with promoting it in practice. For example, assigning students to group work is a popular active learning pedagogy, yet teachers know that it is not safe to assume that students who are talking to each other are learning and that it is equally risky to conclude that students are learning when they are listening to other students talking. Furthermore, although lectures can leave some students disengaged, active learning strategies can engender full-blown resistance. We once overhead a student passionately protest, "Today was awful! My teacher . . ." [with our curiosity piqued, we waited for her to complete her complaint so that we could hear what terrible thing the professor had done] "assigned us to group work!"

Thus lecturing and active learning strategies have potential pitfalls, and although neither method is perfect, neither is despicable. Yet currently there is a fierce debate that sometimes intimates otherwise. This either-or dispute sets educators against each other in ways that we propose are unproductive. In this book, we aim to move past the premise that instructors must choose one or the other approach and suggest instead that faculty members can *combine* lectures with active learning to create a vibrant instructional environment that capitalizes on the benefits while minimizing the constraints of each. Our approach, a form of interactive lecturing, helps professors navigate the process of integrating lectures and active learning into a seamless whole that promotes deep learning.

We begin in Part 1 of this book by establishing our conceptual framework, which is grounded in research evidence. In this chapter, we answer the following questions:

- What is a lecture, and what is it good for?
- What is active learning, and what purposes does it serve?
- What are the main points of contention in the lectures versus active learning debate?
- Why is this debate problematic? And how can we reframe the basic proposition?

The Lecture

The word *lecture* comes from the Latin word *lectare,* which translates roughly into "to read" aloud, whereas the term *lecture* means "that which is read." To ancient Greeks, a lecture was the primary method of transmitting knowledge and information (Brown & Atkins, 1988), and this understanding served as the foundation for later developments. About the sixth century CE, scholars traveled hundreds of miles to European monasteries to hear monks read a book aloud from a lectern; as the monk read, scholars copied down the book verbatim (Exley & Dennick, 2004). With the establishment of universities in the Middle Ages, lectures persisted. Lecturing continued to be a core pedagogy as European higher education expanded during the subsequent centuries, and these traditions were transplanted to the colonies. By the mid-nineteenth century, lecturing was firmly established as the primary method of instruction in the American college classroom (Garside, 1996). But what exactly is a lecture?

Definitions of the Lecture

Bligh (1999) suggests a working definition of a lecture as "a more or less continuous exposition by a speaker who wants the audience to learn something" (p. 4). The literature is replete with similar definitions, such as the following:

- A lecture is an educational talk to an audience, especially to students in a university or college (*Oxford Dictionary,* n.d.).
- Lecture is a method of teaching in which the instructor gives an oral presentation of facts or principles to learners, who are responsible for note-taking (Good & Merkel, 1959).
- [A lecture is when] a teacher is talking and students are listening (Singh, 2006).

These definitions rely on a view of the lecture as a method of transmitting information. This model of lecturing became the prevalent pedagogy because it provided an essential method for conveying and spreading knowledge, especially in the centuries before the printing press facilitated widespread publication of books.

Purposes of the Lecture

Lectures have remained popular because they serve several important purposes. We summarize those purposes in Exhibit 1.1.

Exhibit 1.1 The Purposes of Lecture

Teachers use lectures to . . .

- Present information otherwise unavailable to students
- Present a synthesis of information from across multiple sources
- Organize information into a logical structure
- Share important background and contextual information and ideas
- Highlight similarities and differences
- Clarify confusing concepts, principles, and ideas
- Help learners consolidate information
- Model higher-order thinking strategies and skills
- Convey enthusiasm for the content
- Communicate why content is worth learning

Active Learning

Despite the trend of describing it as modern, active learning—similar to the lecture—has a long history in education. In 1852, John Henry Newman proposed that true learning consists "not merely in the passive reception into the mind of a number of ideas" but rather "in the mind's energetic and simultaneous action upon and towards those new ideas . . . and making the objects of our knowledge subjectively our own" (from *Idea of a University*). Page (1990) traces the origins of active learning back to the eighteenth and nineteenth centuries as found in the work of Rousseau, Pestalozzi, Dewey, Kilpatrick, and Piaget. She describes four common themes associated with active learning, including rejection of traditional teaching methods, belief in the cognitive learning paradigm, faith in the ability of the student, and belief in the importance of the relationship of school to society. Although active learning's roots run deep, the actual term *active learning* wasn't popularized until the late twentieth century with the publication of Bonwell and Eison's (1991) ASHE-ERIC Report titled *Active Learning: Creating Excitement in the Classroom.* But what exactly is active learning?

Definitions of Active Learning

Whereas definitions for the lecture seem relatively focused and straightforward, descriptions of active learning are broad and imprecise:

- Anything that involves students in doing things and thinking about the things they are doing (Bonwell & Eison, 1991)
- A process whereby students engage in activities, such as reading, writing, discussion, or problem-solving, which promote analysis, synthesis, and evaluation of class content (University of Michigan, Center for Research on Learning and Teaching, 2016)
- A method of learning in which students are actively or experientially involved in the learning process (Weltman & Whiteside, 2010)
- A process of learning through activities and discussion in class, as opposed to passively listening to an expert; it emphasizes higher-order thinking and often involves group work (Freeman et al., 2014)

Thus active learning is typically characterized by attempts to clarify what it *is*—a process or method of doing—as well as by what it *is not*—listening to a lecture.

Purposes of Active Learning

Active learning provides a means for students to apply knowledge in ways that achieve a variety of learning goals, as summarized in Exhibit 1.2.

Exhibit 1.2 The Purposes of Active Learning Methods

Teachers use active learning methods to . . .

- Reinforce content, concepts, and skills
- Help students deepen their subject matter knowledge
- Help students develop higher-order thinking skills
- Provide students with the opportunity to think about learning
- Provide students with an opportunity to apply learning through discussion and other activities
- Improve student engagement in learning
- Increase enthusiasm for a topic
- Improve student motivation
- Improve classroom climate and sense of community

The Debate: Lecture versus Active Learning

The debate over which method college instructors should use—lectures or active learning—is intense, with both sides claiming to have *the* correct claim. The key proposition in the debate is this: *professors should not lecture; they should instead engage students in active learning activities.* Let us explore the fundamental assertions of each side of this debate.

Arguments against the Lecture

Lecture critics proclaim that "the lecture is dead" and argue that the development of new theories of learning, new instructional approaches for engaged and active learning, and new learning technologies can (and should) take their place in college classrooms (see, for example, Abrams, 2012; Allain, 2017; Gross-Loh, 2016; Lambert, 2012; Segesten, 2012; Talbert, 2016a, 2016b). Critics of the lecture are united on several core contentions.

Contention 1: Students Are Passive Learners in Lectures

Perhaps the most common reproach to lecturing is that students are passive. This critique is so pervasive that educators have dubbed the lecture a "passive learning" pedagogy. The teacher stands in front of an audience of students and delivers a formal, structured presentation while students listen and take notes. Lecture critics suggest that students are passive in these lecture-based classes because teachers spend too much time lecturing, have too much back-to-the-class and face-to-the-board time, miss opportunities for student activities or engagement, and neglect to provide sufficient ongoing assessment, which means in turn that students receive little feedback on their learning.

Freire and others call this the *banking model.* In his *Pedagogy of the Oppressed* (1968, p. 58), Freire describes the banking model in this way:

> Instead of communicating, the teacher issues communiqués and makes deposits which the students patiently receive, memorize, and repeat. This is the "banking" concept of education, in which the scope of action allowed to students extends only as far as receiving, filing, and storing the deposits.

Thus in this view of lecturing, faculty members try to deposit information into the minds of students who store it so that they can call the information up later, when the bill comes due in the form of a test.

Contention 2: Lectures Do Not Offer Students Authority and Control over Their Own Learning

Lecture critics suggest that to truly engage with their own learning, students need to have some say in what they do and how they do it. Some educators argue that lecture is too teacher-centered and that we should allow students to have some input into the way in which they learn. The concern is that lecturers are too taken with their own roles as the center around which the rest of the classroom revolves to allow students to take control of their learning, whereas active learning provides students this opportunity. As Weimer (2015), a teaching and learning expert, puts it:

> Those of us who shake up the classroom with active learning see value in teacher and student activity. We're committed to students asking questions, attempting explanations, and testing ideas. We want them doing the hard, messy work of learning while we're there to help, support, and yes, correct. We don't feel that our expertise is eroded when teaching and learning happen elsewhere in the classroom. Rather, this dynamic fills the learning space (physical or virtual) with more promise and possibility than we can provide on our own.

Contention 3: Research Documents That Lectures Are Not the Best Approach

Lecture critics have been emboldened by a host of research studies that indicate the lecture is not the most-effective pedagogy for improving student learning. There have been hundreds of experimental and quasi-experimental studies over the past couple of decades that document this finding (see, for example, the well-known study by Deslauriers, Schelew, & Wieman, 2011). Several authors have written excellent research reviews describing these works (see, for example, Hake, 1998; Michael, 2006; Prince, 2004). Moreover, through a process of combining results from several meta-studies to determine an effect size, researchers have confirmed that transmission-based lectures are not the best approach to improving student learning in a college classroom. In particular, a widely publicized, useful meta-analysis by Freeman et al. (2014) compares student outcomes in lectures versus active learning in undergraduate STEM courses through a meta-analysis of 225 studies. The researchers found that when instructors used active learning strategies, student exam scores increased significantly and student failure rates decreased significantly when compared to instructors who used lecture methods alone. Educators have been quick to pick up on this particular meta-study, declaring active learning the "winner" of the pedagogy contest and questioning the very integrity of those who choose to continue to use lectures in the face of such evidence (Felten, 2014). Eric Mazur, the prominent Harvard physicist and educator, for example, stated, "This is a really important article—the impression I get is that it's almost unethical to be lecturing if you have [these] data." Mazur goes on to state that the meta-analysis presents "an abundance of proof that lecturing is outmoded, outdated, and inefficient" (quoted in Bajak, 2014). Nobel laureate Carl Wieman argues further that "lectures are about as effective as bloodletting" (quoted in Westervelt, 2016).

Contention 4: There Are Too Many Challenges to Learning in Lectures

Critics of the lecture also cite research related to challenges to student learning in lectures, pointing out the multiple potential problems researchers have identified. First, students often are not sufficiently prepared to participate in a lecture. They may come to learning with misconceptions that influence their ability to learn and that are resistant to change during direct instruction (Dunbar, Fugelsang, & Stein, 2007). Alternately, they may have such novice understandings of the content that it negatively influences their ability to integrate new learning (Hrepic, Zollman, & Rebello, 2007; Schwartz & Bransford, 1998). Second, the human attention span is limited, which interferes with attention during full-length transmission lectures. Critics of the lecture refer to several studies that have found that student attention wanes after a time during a lecture (Farley, Risko, & Kingstone, 2013; Risko, Anderson, Sarwal, Engelhardt, & Kingstone, 2012; Scerbo, Warm, Dember, & Grasha, 1992). Moreover, students who engage in task-switching behavior (sometimes called *multitasking*), particularly when using computers and especially when choosing unrelated tasks, lose attention as well (Aguilar-Roca, Williams, & O'Dowd, 2012; Hembrooke & Gay, 2003; Kraushaar & Novak, 2010; Mueller & Oppenheimer, 2014; Wood et al., 2011). Third, the limits of working memory can be a challenge for student learning in lectures. If the cognitive load of the information is too high and not been managed appropriately, students will not be able to process the information in ways that result in learning (Hattie, 2016). The constraints to working memory also can affect student ability to take good notes, which deprives them of a valuable record to refer to after the lecture. Fourth, student motivation can be a challenge to lecture learning, and students with lack of interest in the lecture will learn less (Bolkan, Goodboy, & Kelsey, 2016). Furthermore, students are motivated by varied instructional strategies, and teachers who only lecture are not able to capitalize on such motivation (Komarraju & Karau, 2008). Exhibit 1.3 summarizes the challenges to learning using transmission lectures.

Exhibit 1.3 Challenges of Transmission Lectures

The challenges with these lectures are that they . . .

- Imply that they function as a complete learning experience
- Rely on professorial presentation skills
- Require the teacher to make assumptions about students (what they know or don't, what they have or haven't experienced, what they might or might not find confusing)
- Rely on student preparation and readiness to attend to and understand information
- Rely on the limited human attention span
- Rely on student working memory
- Rely on student intrinsic motivation and interest in the topic
- Create opportunities for students to be passive
- Function as if all students learn at the same pace
- Prevent personalized instruction, which may be of particular benefit to marginalized learners

Arguments in Support of Lecture

Just as there are lecture critics, so there are lecture proponents. Lecture advocates argue that if the lecture were so terrible, it would not have endured as the dominant pedagogy for almost a millennium and that well-done lectures can be a powerful pedagogy. Proponents propose that educators imagine if orators such as Abraham Lincoln, Martin Luther King Jr., or Steve Jobs had assigned audience members to gather in groups to talk to each other instead of giving some of the greatest speeches in history. Defenders of lectures also point to the phenomenal success of TED Talks as evidence of the enduring appeal of good lectures. Proponents also suggest that although students understandably deplore poor lectures, they also recognize the value of good lectures. Strauss (2009), for example, notes that in the many course evaluations he has read, "students love pointed, provocative well-delivered lectures. They appreciate and respect a master narrative . . . ." Some proponents of lectures even see active learning as just "another in a long line of educational fads" (Prince, 2004, p. 1). Defenders of the lecture base their arguments on several key contentions.

Contention 1: Students Can Be Active Learners during Lectures

Proponents point out that a good lecture is not simply the recitation of facts but rather can take any number of valuable narrative formats that inspire and engage students in learning. For example, a lecture can be a careful construction of an argument that skillfully connects facts and captures the content and critical thinking of the discipline. Or it can provide students with a model of expert thinking or problem-solving. It can also be a captivating story or even a performance, and use tone, emphasis, and pacing to communicate an emotional vitality difficult to convey through other mediums. Live lectures also provide the opportunity for teachers to check in with students "in the moment" and clarify, delve deeper, or change direction as needed.

Lecturing also helps students learn three important ancillary skills, all of which require them to be active learners during lectures. First, students listening to lectures can learn to take good notes. Good note-taking skills involve not simply recording verbatim what one hears but also learning to be attentive and analytical as one reduces what is being said to its essentials. Second, paying attention for a sustained amount of time is a skill that students need to learn. Helping students move beyond the habit of multitasking and instead learn to focus attention teaches them mindfulness and how to "be present," abilities that are recognized as increasingly important in a culture in which many of us feel distracted and overwhelmed. Third, listening to good lectures requires students to grapple with complex, challenging ideas. Being able to invest the mental energy to absorb a long, intricate argument is hard, active work, and practicing this skill helps students learn to listen more critically. This struggling with multifaceted, substantive content teaches students to be wary of the seductive simplicity of sound-bites and tweets. This, in turn, prepares them to be more responsible and thoughtful workers, citizens, and community members.

Contention 2: Professors Are Experts and There Is a "Time for Telling"

The idea of a professor assuming the role "sage on the stage" rather than "guide on the side" (King, 1993) has been taken to task so vigorously that the very idea that professors might tell students anything rather than letting them discover everything for themselves has almost become taboo. Worthen (2015), for example, suggests that "in many quarters, the active learning craze is only the latest development in a long tradition of complaining about boring professors, flavored with a dash of that other great American pastime, populist resentment of experts." Proponents of the lecture, however, argue that the professor *is* an expert. They also believe, as Schwartz and Bransford (1998) suggest, that there is a "time for telling." These times include when students need direct answers, when they lack prior knowledge and need to be told what they need to know, when there are conflicting cases and they need information, and so forth. Furthermore, they argue, not all college professors have the skills, especially in terms of facilitation, to ensure active learning assignments are effective, whereas after years of training in their disciplines or fields, they do have the knowledge they need to offer a lecture.

Contention 3: Support and Research on Active Learning Is Based Primarily in the Sciences

Many proponents of the lecture point out that the research demonstrating the efficacy of active learning is predominantly based in the sciences and not in other disciplines, such as arts, humanities, or social sciences. They question the inherent assumption that a pedagogical approach that works well in the sciences necessarily works well in other disciplines. Defenders of lectures point out that lectures are part of a time-honored tradition in disciplines other than the sciences. For example, lecture combined with discussion is essential for teaching the basic skills of the humanities. These skills, which include comprehending and then creatively and critically thinking about big, complex ideas, have been at the heart of a liberal arts education since ancient Greece because their value extends beyond the classroom and prepares learners to be good citizens. Lecture advocates further suggest that we educators acknowledge and value different instructional methods, so why not acknowledge the value of lecturing as an important tool in an expanded repertoire of teaching strategies? Worthen (2015), particularly, is critical that the push for active learning in all disciplines is an attempt "to further assimilate history, philosophy, literature and their sister disciplines to the goals and methods of the hard sciences—fields whose stars are rising in the eyes of administrators, politicians, and higher-education entrepreneurs."[5]

Contention 4: There Are Cognitive Benefits to Lecture-based Learning in Comparison to Active Learning Methods

Countering the claim that there are too many challenges to learning in lectures, some educators argue that the lecture provides important cognitive scaffolding for students. Specifically, as a form of direct instruction, lectures can be particularly helpful to novices by providing them with the cognitive structuring they need to stay alert and active. Lecturing can help learners acquire foundational knowledge in efficient ways that prepare them to apply this knowledge productively. However, "minimal guidance" instructional methods, they argue, are not the most-effective instructional approach. The basic premise is that active learning ignores human cognitive architecture, the limits of working memory, issues of cognitive load, and expert-novice differences (Kirschner, Sweller, & Clark, 2006). For example, students with limited prior background on a topic simply do not have the knowledge they need to participate effectively in active learning assignments such as discovery learning, small-group discussion, or casework. As a result, they waste time and energy on unimportant details or, worse, learn or reinforce inaccurate information. Furthermore, attempting to participate in activities that ask them to apply concepts they don't yet even understand leaves them bewildered and frustrated. Thus active learning methods are not without their challenges, as we illustrate in Exhibit 1.4.

Exhibit 1.4 Challenges of Active Learning Methods

The challenges with active learning methods are that they . . .

- Do not *guarantee* high levels of student engagement in learning
- Can hinge on professors' pedagogical knowledge to do well
- Can rely on professors' facilitation skills to get students to higher levels of engagement
- Can depend on students' existing knowledge, which can vary by student
- Require student willingness to participate
- Can rely on student engagement in the activities
- Challenge student expectations of what being taught means
- Can make some students anxious, particularly if they are unprepared or unable to participate
- Can be more challenging to promote in large classes
- Can be less efficient than "telling"

Reconsidering the Debate: How We Frame It Matters

It appears that those who favor active learning are against lectures and vice versa (Paff, Weimer, Haave, & Lovitt, 2016). But is this really the case? If you look more closely at the arguments, you see that those who argue for the lecture almost always talk about the activities they incorporate into their lectures. Alternately, you see that almost all of those calling for the death of the lecture admit that they do some "telling" in their classes. If you examine surveys and observations of faculty practice, you find that most faculty members are incorporating varying degrees of lecturing and active learning (see, for example, Eagan et al., 2014; Ebert-May et al., 2011; Goffe & Kauper, 2014; Hora, 2015; Macdonald, Manduca, Mogk, & Tewksbury, 2005; Mathematics Association of America, 2013; National Survey of Student Engagement, 2015; Smith & Valentine, 2012). Finally, if you drill down into the research, very few of the research studies are of 100 percent lecture compared to 100 percent active learning. Rather, they are investigating classes with almost continuous exposition by an instructor compared to classes with *some* active learning to *some* exposition.

Thus, part of the problem with the current debate is that we have not yet settled on a common language to describe what happens in a college classroom, particularly when it comes to these two pedagogies. We say that active learning is better than "the lecture," but that ignores that "the lecture" is not a single monolithic thing. Bruff (2015), for example, proposes that there is a challenge in the terminology because *lecture* does not mean the same thing to all people; however, he notes that to many, it implies continuous exposition by the instructor. We agree with this contention and suggest several different dimensions across which lectures can vary, which we describe more fully in our Tip 10: *Select-a-Structure*. The two most important variables for this discussion, however, are how long a lecture lasts and how interactive it is, as we illustrate in Table 1.1.

Thus lecture formats can vary, but researchers have not delved deeply into the different approaches to lecture. What we do know is that a full-length, one-way lecture is not as effective as a mix of lecturing and active learning. For this reason, we argue that researchers need to be asking more nuanced questions about the lecture. When is a lecture useful? How much lecturing is too much? What kind of lecture is best? What supports are most effective?

Similarly, educators also have a tendency to talk about "active learning" as if it is a single monolithic thing. Yet educators include a host of instructional activities or techniques as

Table 1.1 Lecture Duration and Interactivity

Duration	**Full-session lecture.** The full class period in continuous exposition of content **Lecturette.** Approximately fifteen to twenty minutes, often linked with other lecturettes **Mini-lecture.** A brief, focused content presentation that lasts about five to fifteen minutes in length **One-minute lecture.** Approximately one minute of focused content; also termed *micro-lecture* when designed for online delivery
Interactivity	**One way.** Little interactivity, with questions entertained at the conclusion of the lecture **Two-way, limited.** Occasional interactivity initiated by instructor **Two-way, negotiated.** Occasional interaction initiated by instructor or students **Participatory.** Students involved in varied exchanges, initiated by instructor and students

Table 1.2 Examples of Active Learning Methods

Active Learning Technique Examples	Active Learning Pedagogy Examples
Think-aloud pair problem-solving. Partners solve problems aloud to try out their reasoning on a listening peer, which emphasizes process (not product) and helps them identify process errors. **Three-step interview.** Partners interview each other and report what they learn to another pair, which helps students network and improve communication skills. **Think-pair-share.** Students think individually for a few minutes and then discuss and compare their responses with a partner before sharing with the entire class, which prepares students to participate more fully and effectively in whole-class discussions. **Snapshots.** The instructor poses a single question or two, and students respond individually. They then try to convince their assigned partners that their responses are correct. The instructor provides the answer so students can assess whether they were correct.	**Cooperative and collaborative learning.** Students work together to solve a problem, complete a task, or create a product. **Team-based learning.** This is a specialized form of collaborative learning teaching strategy designed for units of instruction, known as *modules,* which are taught in a three-step cycle: preparation, in-class readiness assurance testing, and application-focused exercise. **Problem-based learning.** This is an approach in which students learn about a subject by working in groups to solve an open-ended problem. **Flipped classrooms.** This is a pedagogical model in which the typical lecture and homework elements of a course are reversed. Short video lectures are viewed by students at home before the class session, and in-class time is devoted to exercises, projects, or discussions.

well as more elaborate pedagogies under the banner of active learning. We illustrate just a few examples drawn from a very large pool of techniques and pedagogies in Table 1.2.

Although there is some research comparing different pedagogies against the full-class lecture (e.g., project-based learning [PBL], cooperative learning, team-based learning [TBL], and so forth), we don't know the particular features of these approaches that improve learning most.[6] Thus, what we don't know is what kinds of active learning are best for promoting what kinds of learning in what kinds of disciplines and fields. We simply need more research into what really works with which students in what educational contexts.

Conclusion

We propose that the debate between lecturing and active learning has become acrimonious and unhelpful, partly because it perpetuates a false dichotomy. Whether to lecture or not to lecture is not the question. Whether to use active learning or not use active learning is not the question. Teachers use lectures *and* active learning in their classrooms, and most don't stress over the distinctions between the two; they are simply teaching students. The real question is how to do this well. It is time to set aside our differences, adopt a common language so that we can better communicate, and get on with the art and craft of teaching students. In short, we need to reframe the current conversation and engage in a more-productive discussion about teaching and learning in higher education. We believe that a start to breaking down this fallacy is seeing that lectures and active learning can be combined in ways that capitalize on the benefits of each and minimize the challenges. The purpose of this book is to help our fellow college teachers find methods to integrate lecture and active learning in ways that best promote student learning and engagement.

Notes

1. According to *Harvard Magazine* (2013), the author of this adage is actually Alfred Capus, a well-known French journalist, and attributes the difference to a typo.
2. Some attribute this adage to Fulton J. Sheen, perhaps quoting Thomas Aquinas (Dawson, 2016). There is also a similar adage attributed to George Leonard: "[Lecturing is the] best way to get information from teacher's notebook to student's notebook without touching the student's mind" (Strauss, 2017).
3. In surveys of students in which they are asked about their classroom activities—such as the National Survey of Student Engagement (NSSE) or those conducted by the Mathematics Association of America (MAA)—responses indicate that the proportion of faculty members who lecture is somewhere between 60 and 75 percent. Surveys of faculty members show a lower but still impressive percentage. For example, the Higher Education Research Institute's survey of faculty (HERI) indicates that over 50 percent of faculty members report that they lecture "extensively" (Eagan et al., 2014). However, direct observation of faculty teaching suggests that the percentage may be higher. For example, Ebert-May et al. (2011) surveyed faculty members after completing a weeklong active learning workshop and determined that although 89 percent of instructors reported that they were employing active learning, when observed, 75 percent were still heavily dependent on the lecture. Clearly many college professors continue to rely on the lecture as their primary pedagogical tool.
4. The Faculty Survey of Student Engagement (FSSE) (http://fsse.indiana.edu/pdf/2014/FSSE%202014%20Faculty%20Time%20-%20Teaching%20Related%20Activities.pdf) estimates that faculty members spend nearly 40 percent of their time on lecturing, which in a fifty-minute class would mean about twenty minutes. Direct observation of instruction supports this report. Hora's (2015) observational study, for example, found that most faculty members lectured for periods of twenty minutes or less.
5. Although much of the research is based in sciences, there are some signs of change. Gasper-Hulvat (2017), for example, reviewed research on active learning in art history and found that active learning improves student-learning outcomes. Mello and Less (2013) looked across disciplines traditionally taught in arts and sciences and found gains of active learners to be significantly higher than their counterparts; in addition, active learners showed less variability in gains in academic performance than their counterparts.
6. However, there are some signs of change on this front. Strevler and Meneske (2017) have examined features of active learning that appear to be more effective. They have found that interacting with others and creating new information and content are related to even greater gains in student learning.

CHAPTER 2

Integrating Lectures and Active Learning

Conceptions of what constitutes effective college teaching and learning have changed dramatically in recent decades, raising expectations for teachers and students alike. No longer are college professors expected simply to stand in front of a classroom and transmit knowledge to an attentive but passive audience. Instead, today's teachers are challenged to engage diverse learners while developing students' abilities to apply thinking and problem-solving skills to rapidly changing social and workforce conditions. No longer are students expected primarily to progress through a sequence of steps designed to help them master a relatively stable storehouse of knowledge. Instead, today's students must grapple with complex content, demonstrate their learning through increasingly proficient performance, and learn how to learn in more powerful and efficient ways.

This book, at its most fundamental level, is about good teaching that is intentionally directed toward improved student learning. It's about finding effective, efficient, and engaging ways to share knowledge with students. It's about creating an instructional approach that fosters interaction among students and instructors. It's about promoting students' sense of agency and helping them develop the skills and abilities they need to be successful in and beyond a single course. It's about communicating high expectations and providing students with feedback on their learning so that they can improve. In short, it's about how best to teach students in ways that enable them to manage the demands of today's changed workforce and cultural context and engage in deep learning. In particular, this book is about integrating lectures *and* active learning to create a "pedagogy of engagement" (Edgerton, 2001).

We have titled our particular approach *interactive lecturing,* which we see as a unified integration of engaging lecture presentations and active learning methods. We draw from research findings as we provide faculty members with a practical guide on how to combine the two seamlessly to create a dynamic learning environment that encourages students to invest the energy and attention required to achieve deep learning. In this chapter, we answer the following questions:

- What is *interactive lecturing*?
- How can faculty members make lecture presentations more engaging?
- What active learning methods best support student learning during lectures?

The Interactive Lecturing Model

Interactive lecturing is the process of combining engaging presentations with carefully selected active learning methods to achieve intended learning goals. Our model builds on that of those who have suggested active and interactive lectures previously (e.g., Bonwell, 1996; Middendorf & Kalish, 1996; Silver & Perini, 2010; Sokoloff & Thornton, 1997; Steinert & Snell, 1999) but offers a more explicit approach of combining engaging presentation and active learning techniques. During an interactive lecture, the class session is structured into segments of presentation *combined with and punctuated by* segments of student activity. Interactive lecturing provides students with a way to prepare for the lecture, a format for active listening during the lecture, an opportunity to use information from the lecture, and an assessment of their learning after the lecture.

Interactive lecturing is useful for college teachers who not only want or need to lecture but also aim to do more than transmit information. Rather than simply presenting material, college teachers embed a well-planned, engaging presentation within a sequence of activities that help students understand, process, apply, and retain new information. Instead of simply "covering content," college teachers create conditions that empower students to take greater responsibility for their own learning. Thus college teachers can use interactive lectures to help students engage in a structured and supportive learning environment that ensures students are active participants before, during, and after the lecture. We illustrate our model in Figure 2.1.

Interactive lecturing is the product rather than the sum of the two components because engaging presentation and active learning strategies must be included and because combined they can work together to produce a powerful pedagogy greater than the sum of its parts. Blended together, engaging presentations and active learning methods result in something more than the simple conjoining of two instructional approaches. Indeed, our choice of the term *interactive* is rooted in the idea that engaging presentation and active learning methods can interact synergistically. We now turn our attention to the two core components of the model: engaging presentations and active learning methods. We begin each section with a description of the concept and an overview of the research that underpins our model, and we conclude by demonstrating the relationship of research to the Tips and Techniques in Parts 2 and 3 of this book.

Figure 2.1 Interactive Lecturing

Engaging Presentations

In an interactive lecture, an engaging presentation is a core component within a carefully constructed process designed to ensure learners are active participants in their learning. During the presentation, the instructor has the opportunity to share with students a wealth of knowledge honed over time. The knowledge may be explicit, when it is possible to articulate and codify, or it may be tacit, when it is more difficult to verbalize. Effective college teachers share their knowledge with students in ways that make students want to learn it. When teachers share knowledge in a "telling" situation (rather than having students access information on their own), good professors strive for engaging presentations. What counts as engaging probably varies by the learner. However, we propose that in general, engaging presentations are those in which the teacher does the following:

- Sparks the learner's curiosity and then maintains interest throughout
- Speaks with enthusiasm and expertise
- Respects the learners
- Uses language economically and effectively
- Shares content in a manner that is well-organized and unfolds logically
- Proceeds at a comfortable pace
- Concludes in a way that leaves listeners satisfied that their time listening was well spent.

Educational research provides useful information about what constitutes an effective lecture presentation, such that the presentation itself is related to improvements in student learning.

Research on Presentation Elements

We provide an overview of engaging presentation elements organized into five key themes: focus, format, supports, climate, and communication.

Focus

Educational research documents that creating and sharing clear learning goals is critical to effective teaching. Hattie (2011, p. 130), for example, conducted a synthesis of more than eight hundred meta-analyses about teaching and learning and concluded that "having clear intentions and success criteria (goals)" is one of the key strategies that "works best" in improving student achievement in college and university courses. Thus, we can help students learn more from lectures if we provide them with a clear indication of the intended purposes and desired learning achievements of the presentation.

Most educators will agree that lecturers can improve student comprehension of presentation material when they deliver content in ways that communicate a well-defined and logical structure, and educational research supports this idea. In a longitudinal study on the relationship between instruction and student learning outcomes, Wang, Pascarella, Nelson-Laird, and Ribera (2015) found that clear, organized instruction was related to improvements in deep learning and higher-order thinking skills. Loes and Pascarella (2015, p. 1) in turn found that "student perceptions of instructor clarity and organization are associated with student gains in . . . critical thinking, academic motivation, persistence . . . [and] likelihood of obtaining a college degree." Furthermore, researchers have found that teachers who are clear and organized contribute to students' development of cognitive and critical thinking skills and also influence college student departure decisions in a positive way (Braxton, Bray, & Berger, 2000; Pascarella, Edison, Nora, Hagedorn, & Terenzini, 1996; Pundak, Herscovitz, Shacham, & Wiser-Biton, 2009).

Format

Most of us intuitively understand that while students are listening to a lecture, they need to be able to concentrate on what the lecturer is saying. Sustained attention is necessary to make connections to the material and to store it in short-term memory. Yet several studies show that student attention wanes during long lectures (see, for example, Farley, Risko, & Kingstone, 2013; Risko, Anderson, Sarwal, Engelhardt, & Kingstone, 2012; Scerbo, Warm, Dember, & Grasha, 1992). These findings suggest that shorter lecture segments will be more effective than longer lectures.

Research also indicates that the specific type of lecture format a lecturer chooses may also influence student learning. Researchers have found, for example, that lecture demonstrations are beneficial to student learning (Balch, 2012). Others have found that storytelling and performance lectures also improve student learning (Glonek & King, 2014; Short & Martin, 2011). What these studies suggest is that lectures that are based on a format that students can easily recognize and process and that have some narrative sense and connectivity can improve learning.

Furthermore, students are oftentimes novices in our disciplines; thus, they may have a more difficult time distinguishing what is core content in a lecture and what is an interesting aside. Identifying and communicating the most essential points to students is critical. Researchers have found that too many details can distract student attention from the most important points in a lecture. Harp and Maslich (2005), for example, found that when students listened to a lecture with numerous details, their recall and problem-solving were hindered compared to when they listened to a lecture with fewer details.

Supports

Slides or no slides? That is the question that many lecturers today face, and several researchers have investigated the relationship between student learning in lecture classes and presentation slides. The general consensus seems to be that students *like* having slide-supported presentations and may feel that teachers who use them are more effective (Nouri & Shahid, 2008). Even though students may prefer slides, however, most studies indicate that these audiovisual supports do not necessarily correlate with improved learning. Indeed, some studies show that slide presentations with irrelevant information lead to poorer performance (Bartsch & Cobern, 2003) supporting Harp and Maslich's (2005) conclusion that distracting details can be a barrier to learning. Although the research on audiovisual supports is mixed, it generally suggests that presentation support materials that are clear and relevant contribute positively to lectures. Research also indicates that other kinds of supports, such as lecture outlines or note-taking frameworks that students fill in during the lecture, have improved student performance (Austin, Lee, & Carr, 2004; Raver & Maydosz, 2010).

Climate

Ambrose, Bridges, DiPietro, Lovett, and Norman (2010, p. 170) define classroom climate as "the intellectual, social, emotional, and physical environments" in which students learn. Weimer (2010), drawing on Fraser, Treagust, and Dennis (1996), defines classroom climate as "a series of psycho-social relationships that exist between faculty and students collectively and individually." Climate is determined by a constellation of factors that include faculty member–student interaction, the tone instructors set, instances of stereotyping or tokenism, course demographics, student-student interaction, and the range of perspectives represented in the course content and materials. Researchers have shown that a negative or uncivil climate can hinder student success (Hirschy & Braxton, 2004). They have also shown that instructors can make efforts to establish a positive climate that contributes to student success (Dallimore, Hertenstein, & Platt, 2006).

Communication

The very term *professor* suggests that communication is an important part of the job. Derived from Latin, the term means "one who professes." And although the term over time has come to mean a specific academic rank, communication is still key. Educational researchers have documented that instructor communication and interaction with students is critical to effective teaching. Umbach and Wawrzynski (2004, p. 21) found that faculty members' "behaviors and attitudes affect students profoundly, which suggests that faculty members play the single most important role in student learning" and retention. In particular, instructor caring, enthusiasm, and expressiveness are related to improvements in student learning (Dachner & Saxton, 2014; Hodgson, 1984; Murray, 1997).

Synthesis of the Research on Presentation Elements

The key themes in the literature suggest that instructors who plan to present should focus on several elements to improve student learning: focus, format, supports, climate, and communication. Shifting from a transmission lecture that tends to foster passivity to an interactive lecture designed to promote active learning requires teachers to adopt a different orientation as they attend to each of these elements, as illustrated in Table 2.1.

Tips for Engaging Presentations

An engaging presentation is an essential element of the interactive lecture. Although we acknowledge that some teachers seem to be naturally skilled at delivering lecture content in ways that listeners find inherently interesting, many of us who teach in the trenches of academe are not. Furthermore, some of the content we must deliver simply lacks luster. Yet regardless of our personal style or the challenges of the content, we can ensure we make the most of what we have. The Tips in Part 2 of this book provide concise, research-based

Table 2.1 Contrasting Transmission and Interactive Lecturing Presentations

	Transmission Lecturing	Interactive Lecturing
Focus	• Transferring information • Lecture as cause of learning • Cognitive focus • Concern to get the material "out" • Lecture as truth or opinion	• Engaging minds • Lecture as support of learning • Cognitive, affective, interpersonal • Concern to get knowledge "in" • Lecture as narrative
Format	• Instructor talks for the full period • Lecture only • Breadth of coverage • Objective or subjective • Linear structure	• Instructor talks with periodic pauses • Intermingling of various activities • Depth of coverage • Human (intersubjective) • Linear and nonlinear structure
Supports	• Oration only • Focus on vocalized information	• Body as pedagogy • Audiovisual supports as appropriate
Climate	• Climate determined by tradition • Tacit rules of behavior	• Climate established with intentionality • Explicit goals for participation
Communication	• Detached persona • Rhetorical questioning • Monologue • One-way communication • Minimal "interruptions"	• Engaged persona • Questions requiring response • Dialogue • Two-way communication • Intentional interactions

Informed by the research and inspired by Eison (2010) and Light and Cox (2001).

pointers for designing and implementing lecture presentations that promote meaningful learning and in ways that student learners will find engaging. They are organized on the key themes in the research and represent the factors faculty members should intentionally incorporate when crafting interactive lectures. We illustrate these interlinking elements in Figure 2.2.

The Tips are organized into five categories that loosely correspond to the five engaging presentation elements. The Tips correlate as well as to the stages of preparing for and then delivering lecture content. We illustrate the connections between presentation elements and Tips in Table 2.2.

The engaging presentation Tips are intended to offer guidance on various aspects of lecturing so that you can maximize the effectiveness of your content presentation.

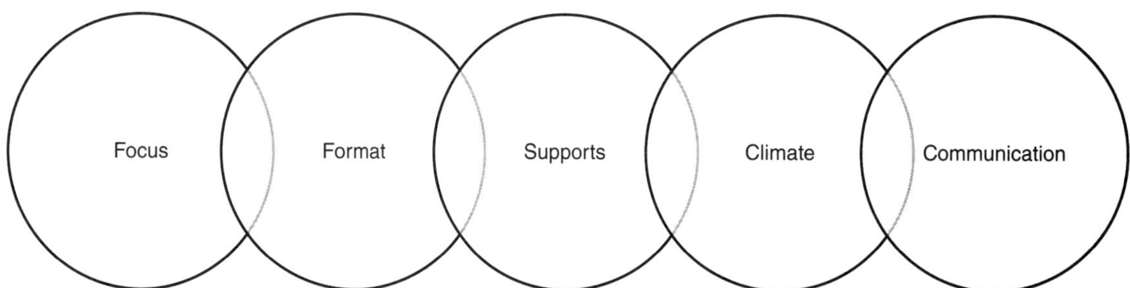

Figure 2.2 Engaging Presentation Elements

Table 2.2 Engaging Presentation Elements Correlated to the Engaging Lecture Tips

Presentation Element and Tip Category	These tips help you to . . .	Corresponding Chapters
Focus	Think through the overarching purpose and broad qualities that will shape your lecture	3. Setting Goals 4. Creating Content
Format	Organize and express more precisely lecture content and structure	5. Structuring the Session 6. Leveraging the Language
Supports	Produce the materials that will support presenting and understanding lecture content	7. Designing Effective Audiovisuals 8. Crafting Handouts and Supplements
Climate	Ensure you are prepared and primed for the lecture, addressing the social side of the lecture, and carrying out the session efficiently and effectively	9. Demonstrating Readiness 10. Generating Enthusiasm and Interest 11. Managing the Session
Communication	Use professional practices for speaking, taking questions, and wrapping up the session	12. Presenting Like a Professional 13. Asking and Answering Questions 14. Signaling the Takeaways

Active Learning

The second key component of interactive lecturing is active learning methods. In previous books in the College Teaching Techniques series, we argued for a broader understanding of active learning than simply associating the term with an instructional approach, activity, or technique. We suggested that active learning involves making students dynamic participants in their own learning in ways that require them to integrate new information into their personal knowledge and experience. As with what constitutes an engaging presentation, we suspect that what promotes active learning is different for different learners, but in general we suggest that active learning happens when students are engaged in their learning in one or more of the following ways:

- Use sophisticated learning strategies
- Seek deep, conceptual understanding rather than surface knowledge
- Use learning strategies with personal relevance
- Use self-regulatory and metacognitive strategies
- Seek to share personal perspectives
- Seek to understand others' perspectives
- Demonstrate curiosity, interest, and enthusiasm
- Offer input or suggestions
- Seek out additional and further opportunities for learning

Although active learning can happen anywhere and at any time, we propose that when identifying an approach to promote active learning in a college course, teachers should consider two components: a learning task and a goal for the level of activity involved. By *learning task,* we mean an academic activity that an instructor has intentionally designed for students to *do* to help them meet important learning outcomes. By *level of activity,* we mean students' mental investment and the strategies they use to reflect on and monitor the processes and the results of their learning.

Level of activity is a discrete component because one type of learning task does not necessarily demand more mental investment than another; rather, each type of learning task can require more or less mental activity depending on the individual learner as well as the content and design of the specific task. For example, although some educators argue that students who are listening to a lecture are *necessarily* learning more passively than those who are solving problems, consider the following problem: $X + 3 = 5$. Most college students can solve this problem without too much mental activity. However, college students who are listening carefully to a lecture can have high levels of mental activity, including focused attention, curiosity, empathy, critical thinking, and so forth. Thus students can have low to high levels of mental activity in any given learning task *and* any given learning task can require and result in more or less active learning from students. We offer our own conception of the active learning continuum for several key learning tasks in Table 2.3.

Viewed in this way, the term *active learning* can and should include the learning that can occur when students are listening to a lecture. If students learn something during a lecture, they have been mentally active, whether through listening, remembering, questioning, contemplating, or other. They likely have also been involved in activities such as note-taking, and in our model of interactive lectures, they will participate in additional activities, such as discussing and problem-solving. The challenge, then, is to help students move from level 1 (low) to level 3 (high) on the continuum in terms of their mental activity, whatever the learning task happens to be.

Table 2.3 The Active Learning Continuum for Several Key Learning Tasks

	Levels of Mental Activity ⟵⟶		
Learning Task	**1 Low**	**2 Moderate**	**3 High**
Listening	Listens for facts and information	Maintains concerted attention while trying to understand the message and to formulate questions about the message	Expresses interest and enthusiasm; attempts to critique and evaluate the message; monitors own attention
Problem-solving	Solves the problem	Recognizes the underlying structure of the problem	Considers the processes for solving the problem and self-monitors efforts and progress
Reading	Seeks facts and information	Seeks structural understanding	Seeks meaning and monitors own reading engagement; investigates related readings and resources
Discussing	Relays facts	Conveys ideas and concepts and encourages others	Shares personal perspectives and seeks to understand others; argues and evaluates concepts; self-monitors participation
Writing	Describes and defines	Explains and applies; expresses personal perspectives; seeks out references	Critiques, evaluates, and creates; seeks to express personal perspectives and connect with others' ideas; monitors progress and assesses quality

The techniques in Part 3 of this book are designed to help teachers assist students in moving to higher levels of mental activity. The techniques are grounded in research that documents that there are specific activities that support student learning in lectures, thereby addressing some of the constraints of learning associated with transmission lectures.

Research on Active Learning

We summarize the research on active learning that supports lectures along four themes: for preparation, for attention, for application, and during closure.

Preparation

Many of us who lecture think of our presentation as the starting point of a learning unit, but research suggests that engaging students *prior* to presenting new information can improve student learning from the lecture. Such prior preparation makes a lecture more effective because it provides students with the necessary background to understand new information, rather than relying on students' entering understandings of concepts, which may differ widely. Thus interactive lecturing involves starting the learning unit prior to the lecture session. Assigning pre-instructional tasks and stimulating student interest in the topic are two ways to prepare students for upcoming information.

Pre-instructional Assignments Researchers have investigated the effects of pre-instruction materials and modules and have found positive relationships to student learning. For example, in just-in-time-teaching (Marrs & Novak, 2004; Novak, Patterson, Gavrin, & Christian, 1999), students prepare for class through accessing online resources and completing assignments that the instructor reviews a few hours before class starts and then adapts the class session as needed. Another approach, interteaching (Boyce & Hineline, 2002; Saville, Zinn, & Elliott, 2005; Saville, Zinn, Neef, Norman, & Ferreri, 2006; Saville et al., 2014), has the instructor create an online preparation guide that includes five to ten items students must complete. In class, students first hear a brief clarifying lecture. They then pair up and spend the remaining class time discussing their individual responses to the preparation guide and completing a record in which they indicate items they would like the teacher to review in more detail. The teacher then uses this to create the next preparation guide. In team-based learning, students demonstrate their preparation through readiness assurance tests (Michaelsen, Davidson, & Major, 2014). Other researchers (see, for example, Chen, Stelzer, & Gladding, 2010; Moravec, Williams, Aguilar-Roca, & O'Dowd, 2010; Nevid & Mahon, 2009) have investigated similar uses of pre-instruction tutorials and quizzes and have found that such activities not only deepened student understanding and enhanced performance on exams but also that students appreciated the activities and believed that the activities aided in their understanding of course material.

Interest and Prior Knowledge Stimulators One challenge to transmission lectures is that students often come in thinking about outside interests and have very little to help them set those aside and focus attention to a lecture. Interest stimulators attract students' attention to an upcoming topic and entice them to want to learn about it. Researchers have found that offering a stimulus such as an intriguing graphic, quotation, poem, game, or puzzle that elevates interest can increase student learning. For example, Rosegard and Wilson's (2013) investigation of using hooks prior to lectures demonstrated that students in the stimulus group outperformed those in the control group on knowledge retention. In addition, Moukperian and Woloshyn (2013) found that providing and then activating prior knowledge improved student learning.

Attention

It makes sense that students who are focused and attentive during a lecture learn more than those who aren't. Researchers have examined the kinds of activities that students can do either throughout the lecture or at some point within the lecture to help them pay attention and have found several strategies that can help improve student learning. We have used this research as the foundation for our techniques, but here we focus on summarizing key studies on guided note-taking and on asking students questions.

Guided Note-Taking Students are often poor note-takers, and many need scaffolding to be effective at this important skill. Researchers have identified strategies teachers can use to help guide students to take better notes. For example, providing an outline or other partial structure that students fill in during note-taking has improved student performance (Austin et al., 2004; Raver & Maydosz, 2010). These partial structures help students engage with the material and, if provided in a form of a handout, prompt students to handwrite the lecture's most essential concepts (see Maier, 2016; Mueller & Oppenheimer, 2014; Weimer, 2016, for research findings on the importance of handwritten notes).

Some lecturers use cues so that students can create better notes, and research suggests that this strategy can improve learning. Titsworth and Kiewra (2004), for example, found that cues increased the number of organizational points and details students recorded in their notes and that it raised student achievement. Scerbo and others (1992) found that students who were given spoken cues recorded more information and retained it better. Rather than cues that directed students to a lecture's organization, Hackathorn and others (2010) used cues that prompted students to connect the lecture material to their own personal stories and found that this increased students' depth of learning.

Not surprisingly, prompting students to revise their notes, and providing them with opportunities to do so, improves student learning. Luo, Kiewra, and Samuelson (2016), for example, investigated the relationship between notes revision and student performance and found three effects across two experiments: (1) students who revised their notes recorded more additional notes and achieved somewhat higher scores on relationship items than those students who simply recopied their notes, (2) students who revised their notes during pauses outperformed those who revised after the lecture, and (3) students who revised notes with partners recorded more original notes than those revising alone.

Asking Students Questions Asking students questions during and after lectures has long been a popular teaching strategy. The trouble is that questions can be used ineffectively, with instructors providing too little time for students to think, too few students volunteering answers, and so forth. Research supports questioning, but it also suggests that a structured and intentional approach is best. Mazur (1997), for example, created a method he calls *peer instruction* to make lectures more interactive and to get students intellectually engaged with the lecture material. In this method, the instructor asks students to consider individually their response to a carefully constructed question and then discuss it with a peer, after which they respond again. Several studies have documented the effectiveness of this approach (Crouch & Mazur, 2001; Fagen, Crouch, & Mazur, 2003). Mazur and others now use automated response systems (clickers) to record student responses, and a flurry of literature evaluating the use of these systems generally shows that, when done well, clickers improve student learning (Bruff, 2009; Bunce, Flens, & Neiles, 2010; Duncan, 2005; Keough, 2012; McDermott & Redish, 1999).

Use

The time between presentation segments of an interactive lecture can be used for a variety of learning activities that ask students to apply and use the information they have just gained. Here we provide a brief overview of research on discussion and small-group work as examples of ways in which students can apply what they have learned.

Discussion Student discussions are frequently used in college courses, in part because small-group or pair discussions can be implemented effectively in many different class sizes. In an early empirical investigation of the discussion method used in a college classroom, Axelrod, Bloom, Ginsburg, O'Meara, and Williams (1949) studied differences between student learning in full-lecture classes and in lecture-discussion classes. The researchers found that students who experienced lecture and discussion were generally more satisfied with their learning than those in transmission lecture classes. Later studies (for example, DiVesta & Smith, 1979; Garside, 1996) upheld Axelrod and others' findings. More recent research also seems to confirm the early results. Jones (2014), for example, studied how the addition of in-class discussion groups related to student interest and engagement in the course, critical thinking, application skills, and satisfaction with the course. Jones found that the addition of discussion groups was related to increased learning outcomes and student understanding and engagement with new ideas and information.

Small-Group Work Many professors have organized students into small groups to complete a number of different activities, such as problem-solving, reciprocal teaching, and academic games. Researchers have investigated small-group learning, whether using cooperative, collaborative, or peer learning, for several decades. Research reports have consistently documented a positive relationship between use of small-group work and student learning outcomes (Barkley, Major, & Cross, 2014; Davidson & Major, 2014). For example, Johnson, Johnson, and Smith (2014) documented learning gains in several key areas, including knowledge development, critical thinking, problem-solving, and affective skills such as teamwork and self-confidence. Studies that focus on different types of group learning show increases in learning as well (Doymus, Karacop, & Simsek, 2010; Karacop & Doymus, 2013; Maden, 2010; Youdas, Krouse, Hellyer, Hollman, & Rindflesh, 2007).

Closure

Researchers have examined the effects on learning of various strategies that are typically implemented following student access to content. We next look at the research on quizzes and their impact on retrieval, retention, and transfer as well as research on the influence of metacognitive activities such as reflection.

Quizzes An essential component of the learning process is the ability to access and retrieve information when needed. Requiring students to spend some of their learning time on retrieving the information you want them to remember has been found to increase long-term retention of information. The testing effect indicates that frequent quizzing or testing improves learning. Multiple studies over time have identified the positive influence on learning that results from frequent quizzing (see, for example, Fitch, Drucker, & Norton, 1951; Gaynor & Millham, 1976; McDaniel, Anderson, Derbish, & Morrisette, 2007; McDaniel, Roediger, & McDermott, 2007). A growing line of research has also documented indirect benefits of quizzing and testing for learning transfer (Pastötter & Bäuml, 2014; Roediger, Putnam, & Smith, 2011; Szpunar, McDermott, & Roediger, 2008). Thus the research generally shows that frequent quizzing enhances students' ability to learn and retain information long term.

Metacognitive Reflection Asking students to reflect on their learning has become a more common teaching strategy, given the rise of interest in metacognition and self-regulation. Flavell (1976, 1979) distinguished two characteristics of metacognition: knowledge of cognition (what Fink (2013) refers to as *learning about learning*) and self-regulation of cognition (what Fink (2013) refers to as *self-directed learning*). Nilson (2013) argues that metacognition is an important component of self-regulation, but the self-cognition is the larger concept:

> . . . self-regulation encompasses the monitoring and managing of one's cognitive processes as well as the awareness of and control over one's emotions, motivations, behavior, and environment as related to learning. (p. 5)

There is a growing body of research studies that indicate that activities such as planning how to approach a given learning task, monitoring comprehension, and evaluating progress toward the completion of a task play a critical role in successful learning in college and university courses. Zhao, Wardeska, McGuire, and Cook (2014), for example, documented that metacognitive activities helped students move beyond surface approaches of memorization to deeper learning. Kauffman, Ge, Xie, and Chen (2008) examined how self-reflection improved students' capacity to solve problems and found that students who received prompts wrote with more clarity than those who did not. And Cacciamani, Cesareni, Martini, Ferrini, and Fujita (2012) found that ample opportunities for metacognitive reflection in an online class fostered higher levels of agency for sharing ideas and working with others.

Synthesis of the Research on Active Learning

The research suggests four main areas of active learning that require students to engage in lectures. In Table 2.4 we illustrate the differences in learner stances between transmission lectures and interactive lectures.

Table 2.4 Contrasting Learner Stances and Roles in Transmission and Interactive Lectures

	Transmission Lectures	Interactive Lectures
Prepare	• Study what they have to • Don't prepare or prepare minimally • Indiscriminately highlight text from reading assignments	• Study to learn • Prepare with intentionality • Think ahead about what to expect and what questions to ask
Attend	• Take notes verbatim • Distracted by daydreaming, non-course-related technology, and so forth	• Translate information into synthesized notes • Stay focused and formulate questions
Use	• Take all information as new • Accept all information as accurate • Isolate college learning from other knowledge	• Connect information to prior knowledge • Explore, question, and reflect on information • Connect information to the world
Assess	• Cram • Study highlighted tests • Reread notes • Rereads test • Memorize facts	• Reflect • Self-question • Write study questions • Consult other sources • Self-test

Techniques for Promoting Active Learning

The techniques in Part 3 of this book are intentionally designed active-learning activities that encourage specific forms of student engagement during a lecture session. They are not active learning activities for active learning's sake but rather are active learning activities carefully crafted for the purpose of lecture engagement. Our techniques help faculty members minimize the constraints to learning in the transmission lecture by offering teachers ways to help students be better involved in the lecture classroom. Our proposal for implementing the theoretical interactive lecture into practice involves thinking about the lecture process as consisting of four phases, each with a specific learning goal designed to ameliorate the constraints to learning of the transmission-model lecture, as illustrated in Figure 2.3.

We subdivide each of these four phases into subprocesses that support achievement of that phase's learning goal. For the third phase, the word *use* is chosen because it includes a wide range of learner processes such as apply, synthesize, and create.

The techniques in Part 3 of this book scaffold student learning through the use of activities that correlate to these four phases, as identified in Table 2.5.

The interactive lecture techniques help students to be better participants in the lecture classroom by encouraging students to think ahead, focus on new information, apply this information, and then self-assess their knowledge and learning. In this way, students are not passive but instead are active participants throughout the lecture session.

Figure 2.3 The Four Phases of Active Learning during the Interactive Lecture

Table 2.5 Active Learning Phases Correlated to the Active Learning Techniques

Active Learning Phase and Technique Category	*Helps students to . . .*	Corresponding Chapters
Prepare	Prepare to receive presented material through working ahead, accessing prior knowledge, or using that knowledge to anticipate lecture content	15. Actively Preparing 16. Anticipating and Predicting New Information
Attend	Focus their attention and listen actively to the lecture or create a meaningful record of information they learn in the lecture	17. Listening for Information 18. Taking Notes
Use	Use content, ideas, and information in ways that give it significance through rehearsal or application	19. Rehearsing Information 20. Applying Information
Assess	Check as well as reflect on their understanding	21. Checking Understanding 22. Reflecting and Metacognition

Conclusion

Interactive lectures combine engaging presentations with activities that promote active learning. In so doing, they help today's college teachers create a dynamic learning environment that weaves together multiple pedagogical approaches to improve student learning. An interactive lecture entails creating engaging presentations that motivate students to invest the energy to learn. It then embeds this presentation within a carefully crafted sequence of activities that help students receive, understand, process, and retain presentation content.

Engaging lecture Tips and active learning Techniques help teachers implement the interactive lecture. The Tips provide teachers with a range of practical and concise pointers on what they can do to design and give engaging presentations. The Techniques provide teachers with specific learning activities that they can implement in conjunction with their lectures that have an abundance of theoretical grounding to support their efficacy in the learning process. Thus the Tips provide guidance on what *teachers* can do, whereas the Techniques offer guidance on what teachers can assign *students* to do to support their learning. Together, the Tips and Techniques offer a clear and practical blueprint for creating class sessions that implement the interactive lecturing model, thereby addressing the learning constraints of the transmission lecture and capitalizing on what we know works from research on student learning.

PART TWO

ENGAGING PRESENTATION TIPS

Introduction

Interactive lecturing uses an engaging presentation as a core component within a carefully constructed process designed to ensure students are active participants in their learning. Here in Part 2, we focus our attention on the *engaging presentation* element of the model. Our engaging lecture Tips provide you with practical advice on how to craft and deliver presentations that will motivate students to invest the energy and attention required to learn from your lecture. The Tips are concise, research-based pointers that will help you design and implement presentations that promote meaningful learning and in ways that learners will find appealing. Thus Tips provide guidance on what *you* can do to make your presentation more effective.

Organization of the Engaging Presentation Tips

We present the fifty-three engaging lecture Tips in five key sections—focus, format, supports, climate, and communication—which are further subdivided into chapters, as illustrated in Figure P2.1.

We begin each Tip by providing a basic introduction to the general idea and then we highlight the key idea in a pullout for easy reference. This is followed by practical advice for implementing the Tip. Finally, we offer an example of the Tip in practice and highlight the key references we consulted while developing it.

Focus. This section is based in research that suggests that a central and clear purpose along with specific goals can help faculty members organize more-effective and focused lecture presentations. Here we provide practical advice about establishing a clear focus for the presentation segment of interactive lectures.

Chapter 3. Setting Goals. In this chapter, we present several methods for setting goals that can help direct the presentation segment of the interactive lecture.

Chapter 4. Creating Content. Here, we describe ways faculty members can brainstorm and organize presentation content.

Format. For the format section of this part of the book, we suggest that faculty members take into account research that suggests the particular ways they can go about presenting lecture content so that students can best understand it.

Chapter 5. Structuring the Session. Here we describe ways that faculty members can plan for fully interactive lecture sessions that intentionally embed presentations within an active learning environment.

Chapter 6. Leveraging the Language. In this chapter, we describe several uses of language that can help students understand the format of the content more clearly.

Supports. In this section of Part 2, we describe the supports that faculty members can use during the presentation portion of the interactive lecture to make their messages clearer and more memorable.

Chapter 7. Designing Effective Audiovisuals. In this chapter, we describe effective use of slides as well as other visual aids.

Chapter 8. Crafting Handouts and Supplements. Good handouts are an art form, and in this chapter we argue for treating them as such, rather than simply printing and handing out slides, to support the presentation portion.

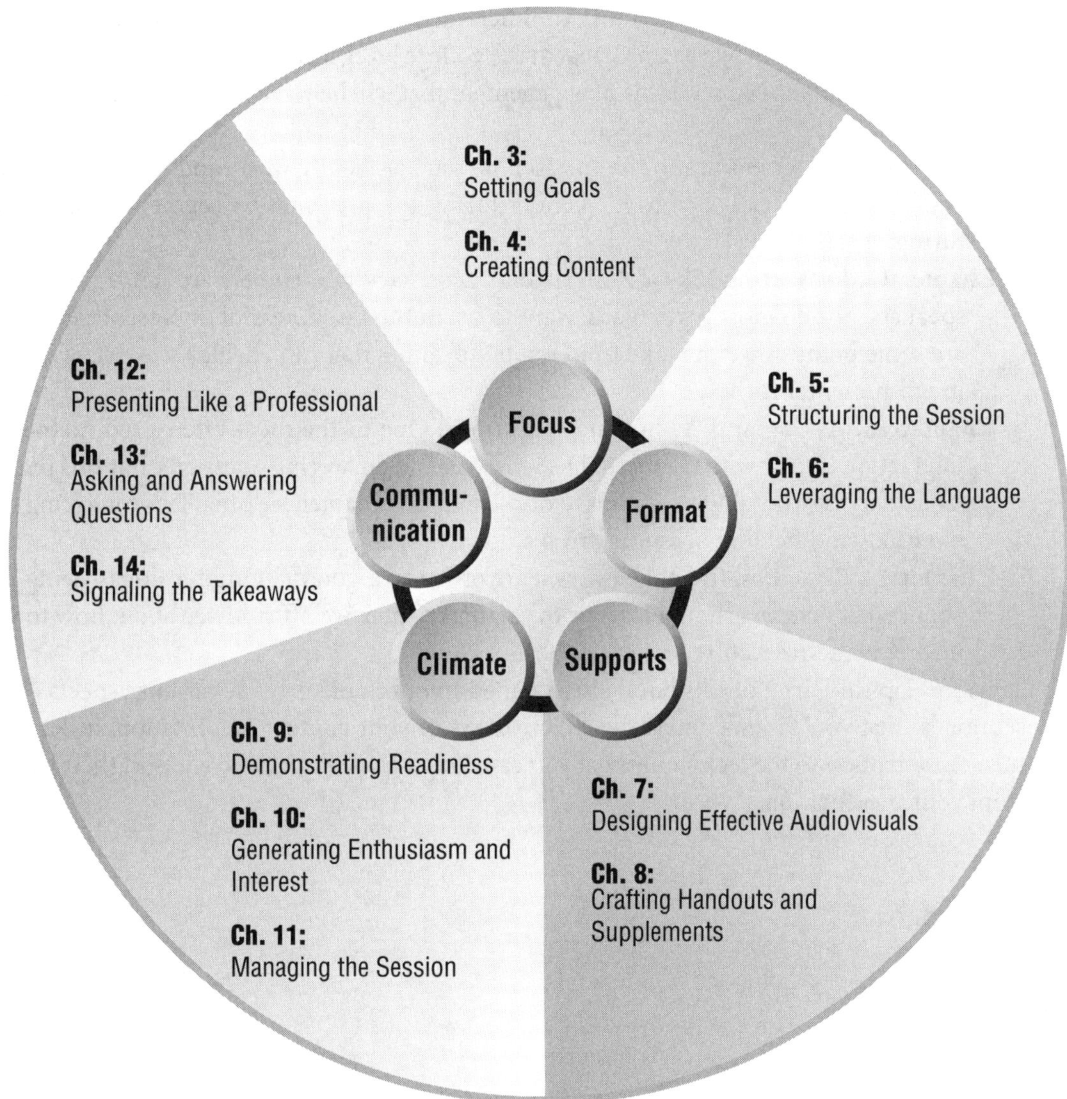

Figure P2.1 Organization of Engaging Presentation Elements and Tips

Climate. Classroom climate has demonstrable connections with student success, but it is often an afterthought in lecture courses, with the implicit assumption that students know how to be participants in lectures. This is not always the case, however, and in this section, we offer guidance on how faculty members can foster positive climates.

Chapter 9. Demonstrating Readiness. One of the ways that faculty members can set the bar for the classroom climate is to demonstrate professionalism and caring about the course. In this chapter, we offer Tips about how to do that.

Chapter 10. Generating Enthusiasm and Interest. Students don't always have the same level of interest in our topics that we do, and by investing some time and energy in demonstrating the importance of generating student interest we can improve student learning.

Chapter 11. Managing the Session. An inherent part of a good climate is classroom management, even if we like to think that at the college level, it should not be much of an issue. Faculty members can set terms of engagement that will help the interactive lecture session flow smoothly.

Communication. Communication is an essential part of faculty work, and in this section, we provide Tips for effective communication during the presentation segment of interactive lecturing.

Chapter 12. Presenting Like a Professional. Most faculty members are not trained public speakers, nor do most particularly want to be. But to be successful in presentations, there are some pointers we can take from public speaking that can enable us to perform better in our presenter roles.

Chapter 13. Asking and Answering Questions. One of the most-often-used methods of interaction to pair with presentations is asking and answering questions, but this particular activity is surprisingly difficult to do well. In this chapter, we offer Tips for asking good questions and fielding questions from students.

Chapter 14. Signaling the Takeaways. Part of being a good communicator is being clear about what listeners should leave with. In this chapter, we offer advice about how to wrap up an interactive lecture session.

Thus the Tips in Part 2 of this book are intended to offer guidance on various aspects of presenting so that you can maximize the effectiveness of your content presentation. In Part 3 we turn our attention to the techniques that you can assign *students* to do to support their learning from your presentation.

CHAPTER 3

Setting Goals

Goal setting involves developing an action plan that can guide you toward achievement of the goal. Setting goals is an important part of teaching effectively because it requires teachers to think through why they are doing what they are doing when they design their course's learning environment. The backwards design movement, popularized in Wiggins and McTighe's (1988) *Understanding by Design,* makes the case that instructors should identify learning goals as the very first step when planning a course. The authors suggest that teachers start by specifying the knowledge and skills that students should have when they leave the course. After faculty members have determined these learning goals, then they should consider what evidence will help them ensure the goals have been met. Thus it is not until after goals (and assessment) are established that faculty members should begin to make decisions on how to teach content, including choosing whether or not to share knowledge with students through a lecture presentation.

We agree that identifying significant learning goals is a fundamental first step in good teaching, and for this reason we provide detailed guidance on how to do this well in *Learning Assessment Techniques: A Handbook for College Faculty* (Barkley & Major, 2016). From that book, we have included information on our Learning Goals Inventory (LGI) and included it here in Tip 2: *SMART Lecture-Learning Goals.* In addition to identifying learning goals, there are other aspects of goal setting that are relevant to crafting good lecture presentations. These elements include articulating the purposes for your presentation, gathering relevant data regarding student characteristics so that you can be more effective in tailoring your presentation to meet learners' needs, and attending to the persona you project so that you can deliver more-focused and credible lecture presentations. Being intentional about elements such as these will help you construct and deliver more-effective presentations and also situate your presentation within the other activities in your interactive lecture session. In this chapter, we have identified Tips that we believe will help you to identify goals for the presentation segment of your interactive lecture. The Tips are summarized in Exhibit 3.1.

Exhibit 3.1 Setting Goals Tips

This Tip . . .	Provides guidance on how to . . .	It is particularly useful for . . .
Tip 1: *Big Why, Little Why*	Articulate a general purpose (*Big Why*) and a specific purpose (*Little Why*) for your presentation	Establishing a solid foundation on which you will build the content and organization of your lecture presentation
Tip 2: *SMART Lecture-Learning Goals*	Use the SMART acronym (**s**ignificant, **m**easurable, **a**ttainable, **r**elevant, and **t**ime-bound) to craft learning goals	Providing a simple structure to establish effective learning goals
Tip 3: *Student Characteristics Analysis*	Investigate pertinent student traits, including readiness and contextual factors	Crafting the most-suitable and appropriate presentation given your audience
Tip 4: *Presentation Persona*	Use presentation archetypes to better understand who you are as a speaker	Delivering more-authentic, unique, and credible lecture presentations

References

Barkley, E. F., & Major, C. H. (2016). *Learning assessment techniques: A handbook for college faculty.* San Francisco, CA: Jossey-Bass.

Wiggins, G., & McTighe, J. (1998). *Understanding by design.* Alexandria, VA: Association for Supervision and Curriculum Development.

ENGAGING LECTURE TIP 1

Big Why, Little Why

Every presentation has a communication purpose. Thinking through the general and the specific purposes of an upcoming talk is a critical step because these purposes can direct the presentation's shape and form, providing guidance during the planning process. Keeping your purposes at the forefront of your mind as you craft and communicate your message helps you identify the most important content and forgo unessential or less essential content. Crafting *Big Why, Little Why* statements can help you to shape the organization and sequencing of your message and to frame it in a way that aligns with your goals.

Knowing your whys will enable you to craft your message for the particular group of students who will hear it, to find a better match between your goals and the students' goals, and to better manage student expectations as well as better meet students' needs. (Students bring their own whys with them. See Tip 3: *Student Characteristics Analysis* for how to help identify students' whys.)

Key Idea

Planning a successful presentation is dependent on understanding its real purpose. Articulating a general purpose (*Big Why*) and a specific purpose (*Little Why*) provides the solid foundation on which you will build the content and organization of an interactive lecture session. Without this solid foundation, the structure of your session is less stable and its impact less powerful.

The *Big Why* involves identifying the main reason for choosing to share information through a lecture instead of another medium. In most college lectures, the *Big Why* is to provide students with information they do not already have, but you might also want to persuade and even to entertain. Although you may be wary of these secondary purposes, they are playing a greater role in today's higher education classrooms. For example, many college teachers see their roles as advocates of social justice. Also, many instructors are increasingly aware of the importance of being interesting, perhaps even entertaining, to the students who are listening in order to capture their attention and thus facilitate deeper learning. Your *Big Why* should not only be related to course goals and objectives, but it should also identify the greater purpose of lecturing. A few possible reasons include the following:

- To share your enthusiasm for a topic you care about
- To provide an alternative point of view or different approaches to the subject, concepts, or theories than the one(s) presented in readings
- To help students develop important skills, such as critical listening and effective note-taking

Articulating the *Big Why* creates the larger framework for the lecture and is an important first step in planning an effective presentation. The *Little Why* is the reason you have chosen to offer a presentation on a particular subject, at a particular time, to a particular group of students. Consider the following questions: What gets you excited about this topic? Why do you want students to learn about this topic? A few possible reasons include the following:

- To focus on a difficult point, concept, or theory and to provide explanation and details that will benefit students
- To place course material in context
- To interpret the text
- To address or demonstrate problems not presented in the text
- To provide essential information necessary for students to understand information to come

The *Little Why* provides a more direct lecture purpose.

Your *Big Why* and *Little Why* combine to form a statement that can guide the intent, scope, and direction of your talk and present a plan about the development of the argument. It can be useful to explain to students your *Big Why* so that they understand you are choosing to lecture with intentionality and purpose. It can also be useful to help students understand the purpose of a particular presentation (the *Little Why*). To craft your statement, write a single declarative sentence that summarizes the specific topic and goals of your lecture for the *Big Why* and *Little Why.*

- *Big Why.* The purpose of lecturing is to . . .
- *Little Why.* The aim of this particular lecture is to . . .

Big Why, Little Why encourages not only thinking about pedagogy but also articulating your general and specific purposes for offering a presentation. Your *Big Why* and *Little Why* should be important and worthy for you to craft the lecture and for students to listen to the lecture.

Example

A professor teaching a course on college teaching, mainly for her university's teaching assistants, was planning a lecture on cognitive load. She crafted her *Big Why, Little Why* statements as follows:

- *Big Why.* I choose to lecture because it enables me to share knowledge I have synthesized from sources of information I have read over decades in the hopes that it will help you to be better teachers at our university and better faculty members in your future careers.
- *Little Why.* The aim of this particular lecture is to share information with you about cognitive load theory so that you will understand cognitive principles that can influence student learning, which is foundational to understanding adult learning.

Key References and Resources

Ford, N., McCullough, M., & Schutta, N. T. (2012). *Presentation patterns: Techniques for crafting better presentations.* Boston, MA: Addison Wesley.

Sproat, E., Driscoll, D. L., & Brizee, A. (2013, March 1). *Purposes.* Retrieved from https://owl.english.purdue.edu/owl/resource/625/06/

University of Hawaii. (n.d.a). *Specific purpose statements.* Retrieved from www.hawaii.edu/mauispeech/html/your_purpose.html

University of Wisconsin. (2014). Thesis or purpose statements. *Writers handbook.* Retrieved from http://writing.wisc.edu/Handbook/Thesis_or_Purpose.html

ENGAGING LECTURE TIP 2

SMART Lecture-Learning Goals

Although a purpose is an overarching drive, goals are the concrete results you are trying to reach. Identifying learning goals is becoming increasingly important in higher education with the rise of assessment and accountability mandates, and thus it most often refers to what you hope to achieve regarding student learning. This focus has typically been on setting learning goals for a full course, but it is also helpful to identify learning goals for each class session and each lecture presentation. The acronym *SMART* provides a useful structure for the process of articulating goals, standing for the following concepts:

S Significant

M Measurable

A Attainable

R Relevant

T Time-bound

Setting *SMART Lecture-Learning Goals* can help you determine what knowledge students need to acquire, which can guide you in crafting lecture content. The goals can help you establish a direction for a lecture presentation by suggesting what content is most essential and what is detail. It can also help you spot potential distractions in content that can lead you astray or, worse, lead students astray as they seek to understand your message.

The primary advantage of setting *SMART Lecture-Learning Goals* is that they are easy to understand, and it is likewise easy to determine when they have been accomplished. With clearly defined *SMART Lecture-Learning Goals,* you can see and take pride in student progress and goal achievement over time. *SMART* goal setting can also improve your self-confidence as an instructor as you recognize your own ability and competence in helping students to achieve the learning goals.

Key Idea

Setting learning goals for each lecture session can help you find a focus and ultimately ensure that you have presented the concepts that students need to master in ways that can be assessed. The acronym *SMART* provides a structure for thinking through the process of setting learning goals.

S—Significant

This criterion suggests that learning goals should be important and worthy of the time and attention that it will take for students to achieve them. Setting *SMART Lecture-Learning Goals* is about identifying the most important ideas, concepts, and facts of a given lecture. To begin thinking through significant learning goals, we recommend taking our LGI, which is based on Fink's "Significant Learning Taxonomy" (2013). The LGI provides faculty members with a tool to self-assess their learning goals. It has broad goals and more-specific objectives. For example, within the taxonomic domain of "foundational knowledge," there are broad goals, such as helping students to understand and recall key facts, principles, ideas, and concepts, as well as more specific goals, such as helping students to recognize the difference between fact and opinion related to the subject area. Thus this is a useful starting place for considering goals.

The LGI is available in several formats:

- To see the LGI in print, along with information about survey validation, see our book *Learning Assessment Techniques: A Handbook for College Faculty* (Barkley & Major, 2016).
- To download a paper copy of the LGI, sign up for supplemental information at www.collegeteachingtechniques.com/learning-assessment-techniques/ (e-mail address required).
- To take the inventory online, go to https://bit.ly/CTTLGI.

From the LGI results, you can develop a significant and specific goal for a single lecture. This means the goal is related to your broader, more noteworthy learning goals and it is also clear and unambiguous. For example, you might have the significant learning goal of developing students' critical thinking skills while having a specific lecture goal that focuses on helping students to distinguish between fact and opinion in a given text. This more-specific goal addresses exactly what students should master as a result of listening to that particular lecture.

M—Measurable

The second criterion in the *SMART* acronym recommends identifying tangible criteria for measuring student progress toward goal attainment. The underlying idea is that if a goal is not measurable, it is impossible to know whether students have achieved it. For example, verbs such as *understand, know,* and *comprehend* are vague and difficult to observe or measure. Measurable goals typically involve something the learners can *do* as a result of having listened to the lecture. The following list presents selected examples of verbs that typically are measurable.

Answer	Generate	Provide
Compare	Identify	Record
Complete	Label	Retell
Contrast	List	Say
Define	Name	Select
Differentiate	Organize	Speak
Explain	Outline	Summarize

A—Attainable

The third criterion of the *SMART* acronym stresses the importance of goals that are realistic and thus reasonable. For this criterion, consider students' characteristics, such as entering level of knowledge and skills, and strive to match the message to their level (see Tip 3: *Student Characteristics Analysis* for additional information). If learners are not ready, then no matter how good your lecture is, learners will not receive and understand it. This concept relates to Vygotsky's zone of proximate development (ZPD), which is the difference between what a learner can do without help and what he or she can do with help. If you target content to students within the ZPD, it is hypothesized that students will be more ready and able to grasp it.

R—Relevant

The fourth criterion indicates the importance of choosing goals that are appropriate and pertinent. In considering whether the goal is relevant, you might ask whether the goal supports or aligns with other goals, such as the overall course goals, the program or department goals, and even the institution's goals. In considering whether the goal is relevant for students, you might consider whether it will be important to their future careers or responsibilities as ethical citizens.

T—Time-bound

The fifth criterion highlights the importance of grounding goals within a specific time. Commitment to a deadline helps students achieve the goals. To do a short-term goal, ask yourself, "What can I help students learn from the lecture today?" For a longer-term goal, you might ask, "What can students learn from this lecture that helps them achieve the learning goals for this module?"

Example

The professor of a qualitative research methods course took the LGI and identified a goal in the "application" domain of the significant learning taxonomy: students would be able to select a qualitative design appropriate to answering a specific question. **(S)**

This goal would be measured by students' abilities to select a research design that would be appropriate for answering a range of research questions. **(M)**

The instructor determined that the goal should be attainable given the students' levels of existing knowledge and skills. Most students were doctoral students, and most had taken an introductory research design course prior to the qualitative methods course. **(A)**

She deemed the goal relevant because most of the students in the course were doctoral students who had chosen to take the course because they would be writing a dissertation that would most likely involve qualitative studies. Students needed to know how to choose an appropriate design given their specific phenomena of interest for their dissertations. **(R)**

The professor set the time frame for the learning: during the second session of her weekend course, students met for three hours on Friday night and then eight hours on Saturday. She would do lecturettes with brief application exercises interspersed to ensure that students had achieved the goal by the end of this session. **(T)**

Key References and Resources

Barkley, E. F., & Major, C. H. (2016). *Learning assessment techniques: A handbook for college faculty.* San Francisco, CA: Jossey-Bass.

Doran, G. T. (1981). There's a S.M.A.R.T. way to write management's goals and objectives. *Management Review, 70*(11), 35–36.

Fink, L. D. (2013). *Creating significant learning experiences: An integrated approach to designing college courses.* San Francisco, CA: Jossey-Bass.

Piskurich, G. M. (2015). *Rapid instructional design: Learning ID fast and right.* Hoboken, NJ: John Wiley & Sons.

ENGAGING LECTURE TIP 3

Student Characteristics Analysis

A truism in good pedagogy and effective public speaking is that it is important to know one's audience. Students have intellectual, social, and emotional characteristics that bear on their learning, and knowing about these prior to offering an interactive lecture session helps ensure a good match with the goal, the message, and the learners. Thus to craft and deliver the best presentation possible, it helps to know not only who students are but also where they stand on a given topic prior to a given lecture. As Brookfield (2006, p. 74) comments:

> We may exhibit an admirable command of content, and possess a dazzling variety of pedagogical skills, but without knowing what's going on in our students' heads, that knowledge may be presented and that skill exercised in a vacuum of misunderstanding.

A *Student Characteristics Analysis* is a method for learning who students are, what they are thinking, and how you might best reach them. A *Student Characteristics Analysis* done in advance of the lecture can help you improve the experience for you and for students. Gathering information about students prior to the lecture will, for example, help you discover information that enables you to build common ground between you and them. If done well, a *Student Characteristics Analysis* can provide you with information and insights to help you focus your message, select the best content and visuals, and tailor your presentation to suit the needs of a particular group of students. In addition, being prepared will help you feel more confident in giving a lecture, which can help you do a better job of it.

Key Idea

Analyzing student characteristics can help you know your audience and thus best target your message. A *Student Characteristics Analysis* involves investigating pertinent student traits that may be related to a topic of study. It creates a clear, credible, and detailed picture of the students.

Demographic and Psychographic Factors

When you decide to do a *Student Characteristics Analysis,* there are several factors that may be relevant to the lecture. For example, depending on your topic and message, you might want to consider demographic factors. Thus consider the following questions (likely to be answered once at the start of a new course):

- How old are the students?
- What genders are represented in the class?
- Are students members of a certain race, culture, or ethnicity?

- Do students share a common primary language? Do you share it?
- What are their religious and spiritual beliefs?
- What is their educational level?
- What are their personality types? Are they introverts or extroverts?
- What other qualities relevant to your lecture do they possess? Are they married? Cell phone users? Avid readers? Runners?

Readiness Factors

Instead of (or in addition to) demographic characteristics, you might also consider whether certain readiness factors are relevant in general on the subject area or on a particular topic. A large part of students' abilities to process new information that they might gain through listening to a course lecture depends on the amount and quality of prior knowledge they bring with them to the given lecture. That is, an individual's ability to learn is contingent on readiness to do so. Two aspects of preparation seem to be particularly powerful influences on the quality of any individual student's learning experience: misconceptions and novice conceptual understanding and ability.

Misconceptions

Many students enter college courses with preexisting ideas and information about the topics to be covered during the academic term, but, unfortunately, many of their conceptions are incomplete or even inaccurate. The literature that documents misconceptions is most often from the sciences disciplines, but it also appears in other fields such as sociology (Goldsmith, 2006) and preservice teacher training (Longfield, 2009; Yip, 1998), and it is likely that students in most fields enter with some misinformation. Researchers have examined college student misconceptions and have found that they are exceedingly resistant to change. If new information is insufficient to really challenge existing misconceptions, students will simply memorize material to pass a test but continue to believe what makes the most sense to them, even if it is inaccurate. One familiar study investigated students' misconceptions of why seasons change and found that student beliefs remained unaltered even with video lectures and explanations that corrected the misinformation (see Dunbar, Fugelsang, & Stein, 2007). Because it is well established that an individual's prior knowledge influences learning (Bransford & Johnson, 1972; Resnick, 1983; Vygotsky, 1978), clearly misconceptions present a challenge for student learning in college, whether the instructor uses lecture or active learning or some combination. Indeed, although many educators suggest activating prior knowledge, doing so can be problematic if students do not have sufficient domain knowledge in the first place (Schwartz & Bransford, 1998), which intimates there may in fact be "a time for telling."

Novice Conceptual Understanding and Ability

In addition to entering with misconceptions, most students also enter a given course with a novice conceptual understanding. Because students have novice conceptual understanding, they receive and process information in different ways and at different rates than the instructor might anticipate. Lecturers are typically experts in their fields, and when they lecture to students with novice conceptual understanding, they can believe they have successfully "delivered" information, whether or not students have "received" it. Research supports this assertion. Hrepic (2007), for example, asked experts (physics instructors) and novices (students) to examine a videotaped lecture to indicate whether a set of questions had been answered during a lecture. By and large the experts felt that the questions had been answered, but the novices indicated that some questions remained unanswered. In addition, experts believed the questions were answered more thoroughly than the novices. The experts' assessments agreed with the lecturer's, underscoring the mismatch between the information the instructor believed was delivered and what the students actually perceived.

As Ausubel (1968, p. vi) says in the preface to his book *Educational Psychology: A Cognitive View*: "The most important single factor influencing learning is what the learner already knows. Ascertain this and teach him accordingly." Moreover, it is important for students and instructors to be aware of contradictions in prior understandings. Consider the following:

- What do students already know about the topic? Want to know? Need to know?
- Is there specialized terminology they need to understand in advance in order to grasp the significance of the lecture?
- What relevant concepts, processes, or skills are students familiar with?
- Have they had recent experiences that are related to the topic?
- What misunderstandings or misconceptions might they have about the topic?
- What is their openness toward the subject area? What preexisting beliefs do they have?
- Are students neutral, or are they predisposed to agree or disagree with your ideas?
- What do they expect to gain from the lecture?

Contextual Factors

You may also wish to consider the most important contextual factors. What are the circumstances surrounding your lecture? Perhaps it would be useful to have answers to the following questions:

- What have the students been going through in the days or weeks prior to your lecture?
- What factors might encourage students to engage with the lecture?
- What obstacles or distractions could influence students' ability to engage with the lecture?

There are many ways to gather information for a *Student Characteristics Analysis*. You may gather existing information, such as major field of study, level of education, and so forth, which is available through your institution's student information system. You can also gather information from other instructors. For example, if your course has a prerequisite, you could contact the professor(s) who taught the preceding course(s) for additional information about the student group. There are several ways to solicit information from students themselves. You could, for example, develop a short survey. You could also conduct a straw poll at the beginning of class by simply phrasing questions to elicit yes or no responses and ask for a show of hands in response. You could gather information from students by connecting this Tip with Tip 32: *Meet and Greet* in which you chat with students as they come in the door. The information you glean from this informal dialogue may provide you with a quick read on the level of knowledge they have about a given topic of the day. Although you might not have a chance to change your lecture much at this point, you can acknowledge that some students already have knowledge in certain areas.

Example

A professor was preparing a unit on US immigration and knew that students were likely to have strong personal opinions on the topic. She decided to implement an anonymous survey in order to get a better sense of where students stood on key issues. From a quick online search, she was able to locate an existing survey (www.isidewith.com/polls) that she could adapt and then administer online two days prior to the lecture. In addition to using survey responses to help her anticipate students' emotional reactions to her lectures and target her central message, she used the survey results as a prompt for a follow-up discussion. She concluded the session by displaying to students how they as a class compared with national responses to the same questions. Following is a sample of questions from her survey.

Part 1: Demographics

1. What is your age?
   - 18–20
   - 21–22
   - 23–25
   - 26–35
   - 36–45
   - Older than 46
2. What is your gender?
   - Man
   - Woman
   - Gender queer
   - Gender fluid

Part 2: Beliefs Related to Immigration

3. Should immigrants be deported if they commit a serious crime?
   a. Yes
   b. No
   c. Yes, but after they have finished their sentence
   d. Yes, as long as it is safe to return to their country
   e. No, only if they have entered the country illegally
4. Should the United States build a wall along the southern border?
   a. Yes, but make it a high-tech surveillance barrier instead of a physical one
   b. Yes, and Mexico should pay for it

(Continued)

(*Continued*)

c. No, this would be too costly and ineffective
d. No, but increase our military presence along the southern border
e. No, and we should adopt an open-border policy

5. Should illegal immigrants have access to government-subsidized health care?
   a. Yes
   b. No
   c. Yes, if they pay taxes
   d. Yes, but only for life-threatening emergencies or infectious diseases
   e. Yes, and grant them citizenship
   f. Yes, but they should be deported after treatment
   g. No, but they should be allowed to purchase private health care
   h. No, but their children should have access
   i. No, and we should deport all illegal immigrants
   j. No, and the government should never subsidize health care

Part 3: Contextual Considerations

6. Do you plan to attend the next class session, which focuses on immigration?
   - Yes
   - No
7. If you answered yes to question 6, what is the most important reason you will attend class?
   - Because attendance is required
   - Because I would like to learn more about immigration issues
   - Because I have strong feelings about immigration issues
8. If you answered no to question 6, what is the most important reason you will not attend class?
   - Because I am not required to come
   - Because I am not interested in immigration issues
   - Because I have a personal conflict with the issue
   - Other ______________________________

Key References and Resources

Ausubel, D. P. (1968). *Educational psychology: A cognitive view.* New York, NY: Holt, Rinehart, and Winston.

Bransford, J., & Johnson, M. (1972). Contextual prerequisites for understanding: Some investigations of comprehension and recall. *Journal of Verbal Learning and Verbal Behavior, 11,* 717–726.

Brookfield, S. D. (2006). *The skillful teacher: On technique, trust, and responsiveness in the classroom* (2nd ed.). San Francisco, CA: Jossey-Bass.

Carnegie Mellon University, Eberly Center on Teaching Excellence and Educational Innovation. (n.d.b). *Recognize who your students are.* Retrieved from www.cmu.edu/teaching/designteach/design/yourstudents.html

Dunbar, K. N., Fugelsang, J. A., & Stein, C. (2007). Do naïve theories ever go away? Using brain and behavior to understand changes in concepts. In M. C. Lovett & P. Shah (Eds.), *Thinking with data: 33rd Carnegie Symposium on Cognition* (pp. 193–205). Mahwah, NJ: Erlbaum.

Goldsmith, P. (2006). Learning to understand inequality and diversity: Getting students past ideologies. *Teaching Sociology, 34,* 263–277.

Hrepic, Z. (2007). Utilizing DyKnow software and pen-based, wireless computing in teaching introductory modern physics. In *Proceedings of 30th Jubilee International Convention MIPRO, Conference on Computers in Education, May* 22–26, Opatija, Croatia.

Longfield, J. (2009). Discrepant teaching events: Using an inquiry stance to address students' misconceptions. *International Journal of Teaching and Learning in Higher Education, 21*(2), 266–271.

Resnick, L. B. (1983). Mathematics and science learning: A new conception. *Science, 220,* 477–478.

Schwartz, D., & Bransford, J. (1998). A time for telling. *Cognition and Instruction, 16*(4), 475–522.

Vygotsky, L. S. (1978). *Mind in society: The development of higher psychological processes.* Cambridge, MA: Harvard University Press.

Yip, D. Y. (1998). Identification of misconceptions in novice biology teachers and remedial strategies for improving biology learning. *International Journal of Science Education, 20*(4), 461–477.

ENGAGING LECTURE TIP 4

Presentation Persona

Part of being an effective teacher is being comfortable with yourself, knowing who you are, and identifying how you can best convey that to students; in short, it is helpful to know your teaching persona and how best to share it with students. A *teaching persona* is the aspect of your character related to your role as a teacher that you present to students. Students will perceive some of your persona—for example, your age, gender, level of fitness—without your attempts to convey it. Similarly, your choices of what to wear, the number and size of your bags and carrying cases you bring to class, whether you choose to use technology or not, how you address the students, and so forth also convey persona to students.

A *Presentation Persona* is a subset of a teaching persona. It is who you are as a speaker, a lecturer. It should flow naturally from your teaching persona and should also guide you in your decisions as a presenter. Your *Presentation Persona* should be something that is authentic and unique to you. Identifying a clear *Presentation Persona* can help you deliver better, more-focused, and more-credible lecture presentations. It can also signal students as to your intent.

Key Idea

Being aware of your *Presentation Persona* can help you better focus your message.

There are several presenter archetypes in public speaking literature that can help you think about who you are as a teacher-presenter. For example, are you a data scientist? An inventor? A storyteller? A coach? Other? In Figure 3.1, which we adapted from Teteak (2013), we offer a way to get started on thinking about who you are as a presenter.

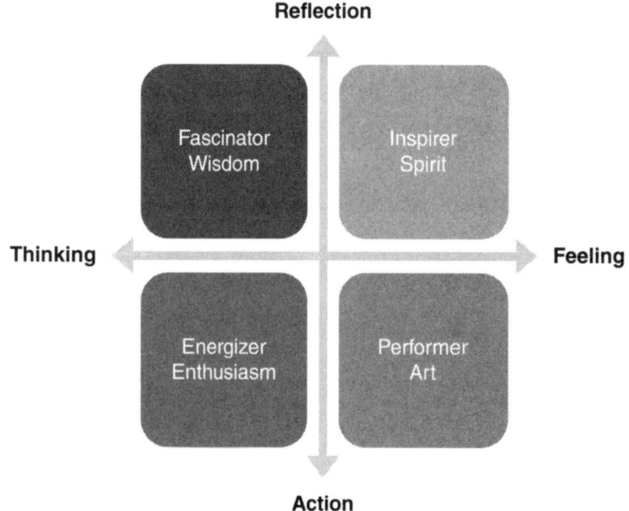

Figure 3.1 Presenter Archetypes

Aspects

You can begin to consider who you are as a speaker by considering where you think you fall along two different continua.

Thinking-Feeling. You may have an idea of your stance on this aspect from a Myers-Briggs inventory. Are you motivated by your thinking mind, the one that likes to use logic, weigh evidence, and consider pros and cons? Or are you more motivated by your feeling mind, the one prompted by values, compassion, and idealism?

Reflection-Action. Reflection refers to your preference for having time to think before reacting or for moving quickly into action and doing, for example, hands-on activities.

Archetypes

You can also consider whether you fall into one of the following archetypes:

Fascinators. Fascinators share wisdom and information, convincing and reassuring students that they are reliable sources. They enjoy sharing important information as well as trivia and are prepared and often anticipate audience questions. Examples of fascinators include Sir Ken Robinson, Temple Grandin, and Susan Cain.

Inspirers. Inspirers convey their enthusiasm and spirit and are often storytellers, who use stories to make a point. They are empathetic, caring, and like people, which makes an audience feel safe. They work to build credibility and rapport, often sharing their feelings rather than leaving them for the audience to guess. Examples of inspirers include Martin Luther King Jr., Barack Obama, and Jill Bolte Taylor.

Energizers. Energizers endear with their enthusiasm, building the audience's confidence and firing them up with energy to go out and do something. They welcome competition and challenges. They are passionate and have leadership qualities and a strong presence. Examples of energizers include Tony Robbins and Erin Gruwell.

Performers. Performers entertain their audiences. They enjoy the spotlight and use body language, their voices, and their words to model key concepts and explanations. They enjoy and feed off of the audience's energy. Examples of performers include Bill Clinton and Angelina Jolie.

In practice, we are typically a combination of different archetypes. For example, most college lecturers will likely identify with the fascinator role—if we are lecturing, we are probably trying to share our knowledge and wisdom with others. But we also want to inspire students to achieve, maybe even to energize them into carrying on their studies in our field or to go forth to make a difference in the world. We also likely want that information to be interesting, and although we might resist the idea that a college lecture should be entertaining, good speakers recognize that part of effective lecturing is in fact performance; a great lecture is a work of art. Whatever qualities constitute your preferred presentation persona, recognizing and refining them can help you deliver your lectures more effectively.

Example

> A professor in a small department had a very popular colleague who was well-known for his flamboyant personality and entertaining lectures. Recognizing that his own introverted personality did not support his lecturing in a similarly extroverted style, he decided to adopt a more personally authentic presentation persona and exploit and refine its unique attributes. After careful reflection, he decided he was an inspirer and that he would use his lectures to emphasize his ability for empathy and caring. Over time, he found that he was no longer intimidated by or felt competitive with his dynamic colleague but rather he became more comfortable with his own style and he had developed a loyal student following who appreciated the way he focused on their needs.

Key References and Resources

Grabowski, P. (2016, January 28). How to deliver an unforgettable pitch by finding your presentation style [Web log post]. Retrieved August 18, 2016, from https://attach.io/blog/deliver-an-unforgettable-pitch-by-finding-your-presentation-style/

Teteak, J. (2013, October 21). *Find your presentation style.* Retrieved from http://ruletheroom.com/find-your-presentation-style/

CHAPTER 4

Creating Content

Creating lecture content is a responsibility about which many of us can feel ambivalent. As college professors, most of us chose our academic discipline because we found it fascinating. We can therefore "geek out" about certain areas of content or methodology, captivated with the intricacies of the ideas and their interrelations. We are also oftentimes creative individuals who enjoy making things, either through writing or designing experiments or other forms of productive expression. For all of these reasons, creating content for lectures can be an enjoyable task.

Content creation for the purpose of lecturing can also be challenging. It sometimes can be frustrating to try to figure out how to make the information relevant and accessible to students. It can be difficult, especially in classes with widely diverse learners, to identify ways for students to make connections between new information and what they already know. It can be tough trying to determine the best examples, illustrations, analogies, and so forth that will enable students to comprehend our message. In this chapter, we have identified Tips for content creation that will help you identify the central and most important ideas, and we summarize these Tips in Exhibit 4.1. Using these Tips in turn will help you make the focus of the content and its organization clear to students.

Exhibit 4.1 Creating Content Tips

This Tip . . .	Provides guidance on how to . . .	It is particularly useful for . . .
Tip 5: *Sticky Note Diagrams*	Generate and organize ideas for a lecture	Identifying common themes among the ideas and then sorting and organizing the ideas to develop lecture content
Tip 6: *Brainstorming*	Produce content in ways that help you think outside the box and look at the topic from the perspective of others	Helping you get unstuck so that you can come up with new ideas
Tip 7: *Logical Patterns*	Determine effective ways to structure and present information	Organizing information in ways that students will recognize, understand, appreciate, and remember
Tip 8: *Rule of Three*	Use a three-part structure to organize elements of lecture content	Making the core ideas clear and memorable to students

ENGAGING LECTURE TIP 5

Sticky Note Diagrams

Sticky Note Diagrams enable you to generate and then organize a large number of ideas into their natural relationships. Similar to an affinity grouping, which is done in groups (see Barkley Major, & Cross, 2014), *Sticky Note Diagrams* are completed by individuals. When applied to preparing for a lecture presentation, this approach can be a powerful method not only for producing and capturing ideas but also for managing and making sense of a large body of facts or concepts. *Sticky Note Diagrams* help individuals discover previously unseen connections that link common things of a group together, thereby understanding information in new ways. It can also be effective for seeing the "forest in the trees." Thus it is useful when issues seem too large and complex to fully grasp or, alternately, when seemingly countless facts or ideas result in apparent chaos. *Sticky Note Diagramming* involves generating ideas for the lecture, identifying common themes among the ideas, and then sorting and organizing the ideas and themes accordingly in ways that can make the content more accessible for students.

Key Idea

You can use *Sticky Note Diagrams* to generate ideas for a lecture, identify common themes among the ideas, and then sort and organize the ideas to develop and organize lecture content.

To work through the process of *Sticky Note Diagrams* you will need the following materials: sticky notes or index cards, pens or pencils, and a large surface to work on, such as a wall, table, or floor. *Sticky Note Diagrams* have four main phases: idea generation, idea sorting, idea selection and discarding, and idea group labeling.

- **Idea generation.** Think of as many ideas as possible related to the lecture content, expressing each idea in a single word or a short phrase that you write on a separate sticky note or card.
- **Idea sorting.** Randomly spread notes on the work surface so that all of the notes are visible. Next, look for ways to group the individual notes. Start small, selecting just two ideas that seem to be related in some way and then placing the sticky notes side by side. Repeat the matching process, grouping several notes together into a pile. The purpose is to engage in a process of constant comparison of ideas to look for association, kinship, or likeness, all of which are synonymous with affinity. The grouping continues until you have placed all of the notes in their appropriate spots. (It's okay to have loners that don't seem to fit a group. You can decide in the next step if these are critical parts of the content.)
- **Idea selection and discarding.** Instructors have a tendency to include everything and to be reluctant to discard favorite details. However, research shows that having too many details can be distracting for students and can harm their learning. When you have created groups, it is easy to see which ideas are the most central—they are the ones that have the most sticky notes. Consider keeping those and discarding piles with very few notes.

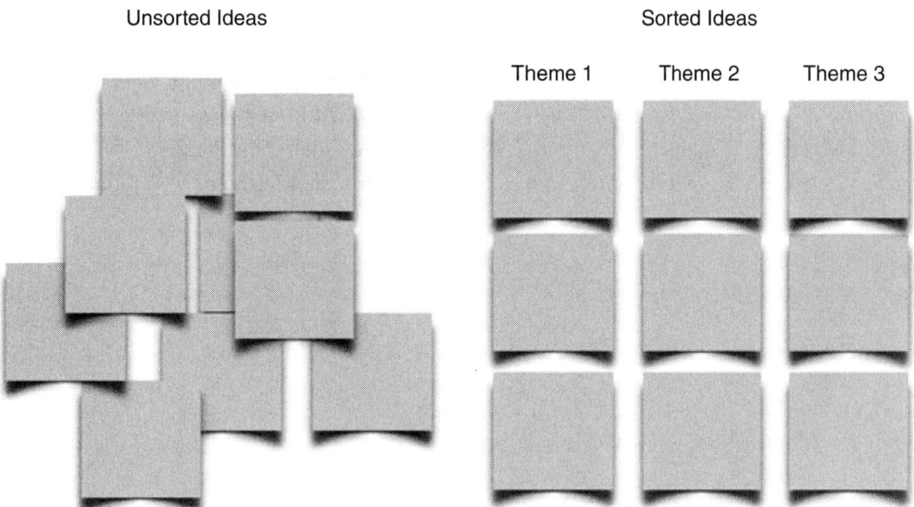

Figure 4.1 Idea Group Labeling Example

- **Idea group labeling.** Select a heading for each group by looking for a note in each grouping that captures the meaning of the group. If no such note exists, write one. When you have found an appropriate title for the collection, place it at the top of the group. Some shifting of notes during this phase is common, so recombine note groupings as appropriate. The notes might look something like that shown in Figure 4.1.

Although as described this technique involves physically handling the ideas, there are several online mind-mapping and note-taking tools that can make doing this technique directly on a computer an option, such as Memosort, Popplet, and Bubbl.us. You could also use the Smart Art graphic tool in Word or PowerPoint.

Example

A professor teaching a science fiction course was planning a new lecture on the novel *Ender's Game.* Because it was the first time she would be offering this particular lecture, she knew she needed to spend some time researching and brainstorming the topic. She decided to use *Sticky Note Diagrams* to help her generate and organize her ideas.

She gathered several essays and book reviews of the novel and read through them while reading the novel again. During her reading, she jotted ideas onto sticky notes, using one note per idea. She took all of the individual sticky notes and placed them on a wall in a long hallway. From there, she started sorting them into related piles and then named each pile as a separate theme. She organized her lecture on the key topics that she generated through her sorting technique.

Key References and Resources

Barkley, E. F., Major, C. H., & Cross, K. P. (2014). CoLT 19 affinity grouping. *Collaborative learning techniques: A handbook for college faculty*. San Francisco, CA: Jossey-Bass.

Brassard, M. (1989). *The memory jogger II*. Methuen, MA: Goal/QPC Press.

King, R. (1989). *Hoshin planning: The developmental approach*. Methuen, MA: Goal/QPC Press.

ENGAGING LECTURE TIP 6

Brainstorming

Brainstorming is an approach to idea generation. The goal is to produce as many ideas as possible by deferring judgment and remaining open to them all, from the mundane to the outrageous. Although brainstorming was first conceived as a group technique, brainstorming done by a single individual can also be a powerful process, and indeed, in some cases, individual brainstorming appears superior to group brainstorming. The challenge with individual brainstorming, however, is that it can become too inwardly focused, which is a problem lecturers can face. Selected brainstorming methods, however, can help you think about ideas in ways that move away from your own perspectives and take others, specifically student learners', into consideration. Used to generate ideas for lecture content, brainstorming about how others might see the content can help lecturers move beyond their usual thought patterns and think through content in new ways.

Key Idea

Using brainstorming strategies to develop lecture content can help you get unstuck, think outside the box, and come up with new ideas.

There are a number of useful brainstorming techniques, but the following are approaches we find particularly useful for generating lecture content:

Journalists' Questions Consider the six questions that journalists typically ask: who? what? when? where? why? and how? Write down each question and then work through them, responding in a way that fits your lecture topic of the day. Then examine your responses to determine whether you need to do additional work researching or expanding any sections to paint a complete picture.

Role Storm Imagine yourself as someone else who has to give a lecture. For example, that person might be an expert in the content area ("What would Albert Einstein say to students about relativity?"), a politician ("What would Cesar Chavez say about immigration?"), an inventor (what would Steve Jobs say to business students about entrepreneurship?), a historic figure in the field ("What would Ada Lovelace say about women in mathematics?"), and so forth. The idea is to take a break from yourself and think about the topic from a different perspective.

Attribute Change Consider how you would think about the topic differently if you had an attribute changed and then brainstorm through several additional changes. For example, how would you think about the topic if you were a different gender? age? race? weight? nationality? religion? With each attribute change, you consider a new spectrum of thinking that you might have been subconsciously closed off from previously. This is a good technique for considering how to match your message to a diverse student audience.

Thinking Outside the Disciplinary Box As experts in our disciplines, our thinking can sometimes be constrained by the customary perspectives of those disciplines. When you think outside of that disciplinary box, however, it can encourage you to consider things in a new way. If, for example, you consider the concept of culture from the perspective of anthropology, it means the study of humankind. If you think of it from the concept of biology, it means taking a sample and then multiplying microbial organisms so that they reproduce under laboratory conditions. If you are preparing an anthropology lecture, how might thinking of the biological definition provide you with new insights?

What If? Consider the premise of "what if?" as it relates to your topic area. For example, an art history professor might consider, "What if I used a critical theory approach instead of iconographical analysis in this lecture?" A philosophy professor might ask, "What if Socrates had never lived?" To use this technique, simply ask yourself some what-if questions and see where the answers lead you.

Cubing Cubes are six-sided, so cubing prompts you to consider the topic six different ways. To follow the cubing process, respond to these six commands (University of Virginia, n.d.):

- Describe it.
- Compare it.
- Associate it.
- Analyze it.
- Apply it.
- Argue for and against it.

After responding to the question set, review what you wrote. Consider whether your responses suggest anything new about your topic. Consider potential interactions between the sides you identified. For example, are there repeating patterns or themes emerging that could help you approach the topic? Does one side stand out as particularly interesting? This approach should offer you a broader awareness of the topic's complexities, if not a sharper focus on which direction you may take it.

Example

The professor of a statistics course had been teaching the same course for several years. He believed that current students were less interested in the topic and therefore decided to brainstorm some new ideas for his introductory lecture. He began with an attribute change strategy, considering how he would feel about statistics if he were twenty-two years old, the age of most of his students. He then moved on to gender, considering what female students might think of statistics and wondering if, at a young age, they had bought into the fallacy that math is a subject for boys. He continued with this line of reasoning and believed at the end he had a fuller understanding of the students' perspectives.

He next moved on to a what-if brainstorm. He asked himself the following question: "what if statistics instead of algebra were the standard requirement?" He found this a productive line of thought and decided to use this brainstorm stem in the first class session as an activity for students, who were asked to work in small groups to answer the question themselves. He followed up with a full-class discussion. He believed that as a result of this new approach, students better understood the importance of the content and that he had established a positive tone for the academic term.

Key References and Resources

Furnham, A., & Yazdanpanahi, T. (1995). Personality differences and group versus individual brainstorming. *Personality and Individual Differences, 19,* 73–80.

Henningsen, D. D., & Henningsen, M.L.M. (2013). Generating ideas about the uses of brainstorming: Reconsidering the losses and gains of brainstorming groups relative to nominal groups. *Southern Communication Journal, 78*(1), 42–55.

MindTools. (n.d.). *Brainstorming: Generating many radical, creative ideas.* Retrieved from www.mindtools.com/brainstm.html

Osborn, A. F. (1963). *Applied imagination: Principles and procedures of creative problem solving* (3rd ed.). New York, NY: Charles Scribner's Sons.

University of North Carolina, Chapel Hill. (2014). *Brainstorming.* The Writing Center. Retrieved from http://writingcenter.unc.edu/handouts/brainstorming/

University of Virginia. (n.d.). *Cubing and think dots.* Retrieved from curry.virginia.edu/uploads/resourcelibrary/magc_cubing_think_dots.pdf

ENGAGING LECTURE TIP 7

Logical Patterns

Communication is often most effective when it consists of a clearly organized set of ideas that follows a consistent and logical pattern. There are many different *Logical Patterns,* such as chronological order, cause-and-effect, spatial order, topical order, and so forth. Using a solid *Logical Pattern* to improve communication effectiveness is critical for lecturers and students. For lecturers, a solid structure provides a blueprint for the lecture, giving it focus and direction. For students, clear organization enhances the ease of understanding and remembering the information presented.

Lecture content should suggest a *Logical Pattern* that follows naturally. As Fink (2013) observes when talking about course organization more broadly: "The goal is to sequence the topics so that they build on one another in a way that allows students to integrate each new idea, topic, or theme with the preceding ones as the course proceeds" (p. 142). The same holds true for a given lecture; the *Logical Pattern* should enable lecture ideas to build on one another organically and move toward accomplishing an end goal.

Key Idea

Using a *Logical Pattern* can help you to structure and present information in a way that students will recognize, understand, appreciate, and remember.

There are no rules for choosing a pattern of organization. We describe some of the most commonly used patterns of organization in the following paragraphs.

Topical This pattern involves structuring content according to topic but in a nonlinear approach. You simply divide content into inherent chunks or clusters, similar to how we described in Tip 10: *Sticky Note Diagrams.* A lecture for teachers about types of children's games might be organized, for example, by different age groups:

- Preschoolers
- Elementary schoolchildren
- Secondary schoolchildren

Comparison and Contrast A comparison-and-contrast pattern involves organizing information according to how two or more things are similar to or different from each other. It is a useful pattern to adopt when describing how a topic in relation to another will improve student understanding. In particular, if students have knowledge of one topic, the teacher can compare or contrast it with a new topic to highlight similarities and differences. Following are two different approaches to organizing content by way of a comparison-and-contrast pattern.

Example of Approach One	Example of Approach Two
Point 1	**Points of Comparison**
Comparison	Point 1
Contrast	Point 2
Point 2	Point 3
Comparison	**Points of Contrast**
Contrast	Point 1
Point 3	Point 2
Comparison	Point 3
Contrast	

Order of Importance For this pattern, concepts and supporting ideas are organized according to a hierarchy of value. Information might be structured according to an ascending or descending order of importance as shown in Figure 4.2.

Chronological Order Information is organized by the time in which each event has occurred, as shown in Figure 4.3.

Sequential Order Content is presented as a series of steps or actions that provides hooks for learners to remember. This pattern is often used when doing demonstrations. For example, a

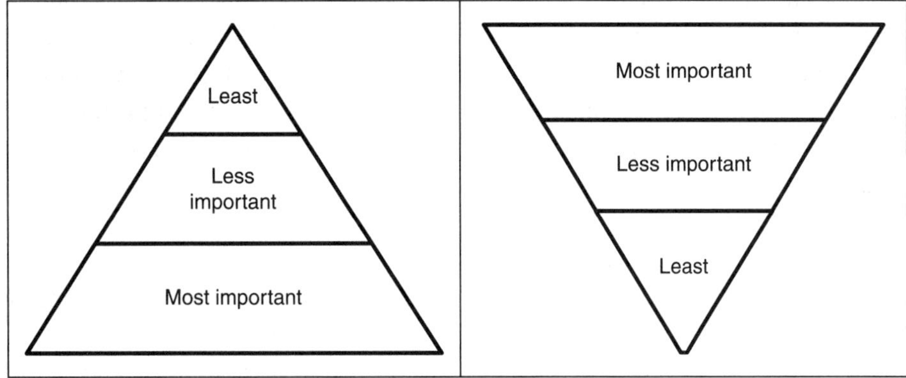

Figure 4.2 Order of Importance Example

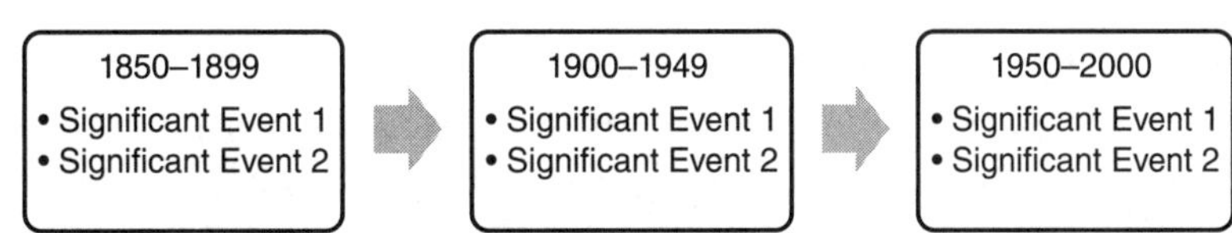

Figure 4.3 Chronological Order Example

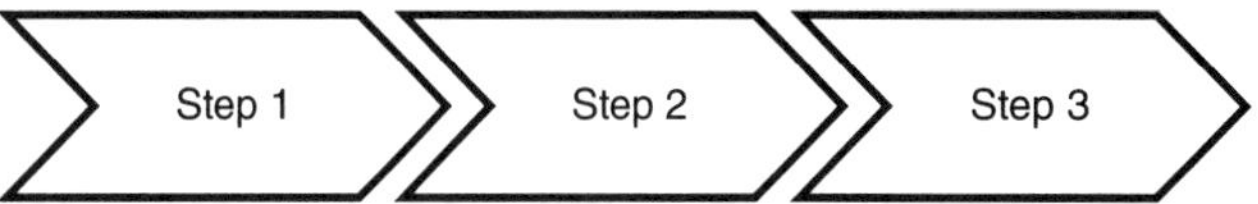

Figure 4.4 Sequential Order Example

professor doing a lecture demonstration on how to draw blood would likely choose a sequential order, as shown in Figure 4.4.

Cause and Effect When the content presents problems and solutions, a cause-and-effect structure can be a useful framework. This approach involves demonstrating important relations between variables and typically occurs in one of the two ways:

Example of Approach One	Example of Approach Two
Causes	**Cause 1**
Cause 1	Effect 1
Cause 2	Effect 2
Effects	**Cause 2**
Effect 1	Effect 1
Effect 2	Effect 2

Simple to Complex Instructional content might be organized from the simple to complex. The lecturer begins with information and ideas that are relatively easy for students to process and then gradually introduces more complex ideas or arguments. The ideas should build off of each other, and students have to listen their way through points A and B in order to understand point C. This strategy enables learners to build a knowledge base along with their confidence levels. It can also help to minimize learner frustration. For example, a professor offering a lecture on the human body might work through atoms, molecules, cells, tissues, organs, and organ systems as she leads up to the human organism.

Spatial Main points (especially places, scenes, or objects) are arranged by physical proximity or direction relative to each other. This might mean left to right, top to bottom, front to back, inside to outside, or clockwise. For example, a professor might describe a volcano from bottom to top, starting with magma, moving to bedrock, moving to the conduit, and so forth.

Problem and Solution The lecturer defines a problem and then offers information about a solution or solutions. When introducing problems, the lecturer provides different aspects and offers evidence of the problems. In the solution section, the lecturer not only presents potential solutions but also evidence to support the solutions. For example, a lecturer might introduce a problem on global warming, describing the various aspects of it and evidence to support that the problem exists. Then the lecturer might identify some potential solutions, such as boosting energy efficiency, promoting green energy, and managing forests.

Example

A professor giving an overview of the Cold War used chronological order to organize the introductory lecture. She used the time periods shown in Figure 4.5 to introduce broad ideas and big events. In subsequent lectures, she followed up on each period, using events within each time period to structure the content.

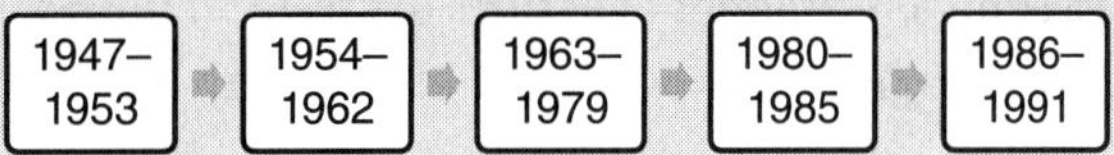

Figure 4.5 Chronological Order Example

Key References and Resources

Carnegie Mellon University, Eberly Center on Teaching Excellence and Educational Innovation. (n.d.a). *Design and teach a course.* Retrieved from www.cmu.edu/teaching/designteach/design/contentschedule.html

Fink, L. D. (2013). *Creating significant learning experiences: An integrated approach to designing college courses.* San Francisco, CA: Jossey-Bass.

ENGAGING LECTURE TIP 8

Rule of Three

The *Rule of Three* is a basic communication principle that suggests that during written or oral communication, presenting information in threes is the best approach. This is because a three-part structure combines the brevity that helps us stay within the confines of working memory while also offering a sufficient amount of entities to create an interesting, identifiable pattern. Thus using the *Rule of Three* can help us make our lecture content more engaging, enjoyable, and memorable.

Key Idea

People like things to be presented in threes and in particular like a beginning, middle, and end; thus, structuring your lecture using the *Rule of Three* can be a successful approach.

To implement the *Rule of Three* as you write your lecture, develop your content in three main sections: (1) a beginning, (2) a middle, and (3) an ending. In each of these sections, consider including three points.

Beginning

1. Introduce the topic in a way that catches the students' attention and helps them become interested in the topic, such as using one of the following options:
   - Quotation
   - Question
   - Visual
   - Statistic
   - Physical object
   - Startling statement
   - Anecdote
   - Story
   - Personal experience
   - Related and appropriate joke
   - Sound effect
   - Testimony or success story
   - Expert opinion
2. After you have caught the reader's attention, provide an overview of the topic that you will soon be explaining in more detail.
3. Tell students how you expect them to use the lecture material. For example, you might inform them that they will use it in a group activity or that they will need it for an upcoming quiz or exam. Or you might use this opportunity to define and explain any unfamiliar terms that you plan to use.

Middle

In this section, provide students with information about the topic in more detail. To do so, choose three main concepts, or content chunks, that you want to cover that represent the main educational content of the lecture. Chunking the information will enable students to relate smaller details to bigger ideas.

In addition to the larger chunks, you will also want to generate examples that demonstrate these key points to facilitate student retention of information. These may be passages from a text, historical examples, selected data from a report, and so forth. Choose examples that you can explain fully in a few minutes and that broaden or deepen students' understanding of the subject matter. You might even continue the *Rule of Three* by providing three details for each content chunk, as illustrated in Figure 4.6.

Ending

Bring the topic to a close, again using the *Rule of Three.* For example:

- Provide students with a summary of the three key points from the middle.
- Check understanding with a question and eliciting a quick show of hands, ask students to write a minute paper, or assign some other task that requires students to process the content you covered in the middle section of the lecture.
- Provide students with something that will keep them talking about the topic. For example, you might pose a question for students to consider further, assign a problem for further analysis, or offer a thesis or proof that explains the information you gave earlier. Such a conclusion will help students retain the other details you included in your lecture.

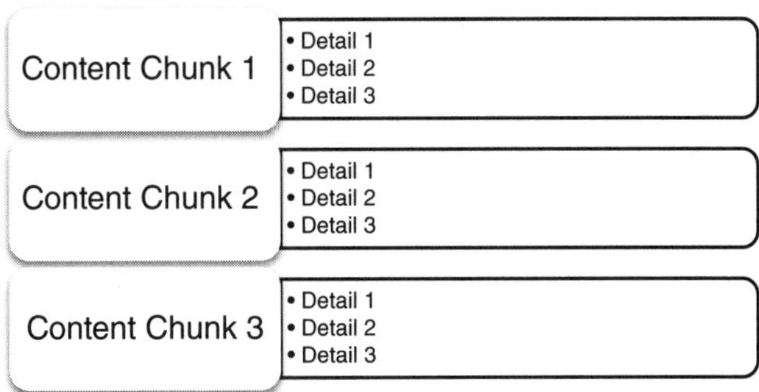

Figure 4.6 Rule of Three Content Chunks Example

Example

The instructor of an introduction to photography course decided to use the *Rule of Three* to organize her lecture on a visual design principle known as the rule of thirds. In chunk 1 of her lecture, she showed a photograph to introduce the concept, which states that images are more compelling if the subject is not placed dead center in the photo. Instead, the photographer visualizes lines dividing the frame horizontally and vertically into equal thirds and places the subject at one of the four intersections of the horizontal and vertical lines. In chunk 2 she showed photographs from three famous photographers to illustrate application of the principle. And in chunk 3 she displayed a series of photographs that she had created that violated the principle and asked the students to identify in which of the three sectors the image was out of balance.

Key References and Resources

Edutopia. (2016). Using the rule of three for learning [Web log post]. Retrieved August 22, 2016, from www.edutopia.org/blog/using-rule-three-learning-ben-johnson

London Deanery. (2012). *Improve your lecturing.* Retrieved from www.faculty.londondeanery.ac.uk/e-learning/improve-your-lecturing-1/structure

The Regents of the University of Minnesota. (2006). *Effective lecture preparation and delivery.* Reprinted by Washington State University Graduate School. Retrieved from https://gradschool.wsu.edu/effective-lecture-preparation-and-delivery/

CHAPTER 5

Structuring the Session

Interactive lecture sessions can vary widely by structure. Some professors might begin by adding just a few active learning methods to a single lecture session. They might, for example, start with a hook, use a note-taking technique to help student focus and retain content, and end with an assessment. Others may change activities frequently within a session, beginning and ending with active learning activities and alternating between short lecture segments and active learning activities throughout the session. The key is to be intentional about the structure of the session, choosing presentations and supporting activities with care. In this chapter, we provide Tips related to how to structure an interactive lecture session. The Tips are summarized in Exhibit 5.1.

Exhibit 5.1 Structuring the Session Tips

This Tip . . .	Provides guidance on how to . . .	It is particularly useful for . . .
Tip 9: *Linked Lecturettes*	Craft multiple short, self-contained lectures and link them together to form one longer talk	Addressing attention-span limits and building in flexibility as well as opportunities for students to do active learning activities
Tip 10: *Select-a-Structure*	Structure a lecture with intentionality so that it is best-suited for a particular learning goal	Thinking through the many different facets of the lecture, including formality, duration, interactivity, format, and medium
Tip 11: *Bookends, Interleaves, and Overlays*	Conceptualize the sequencing and interaction between instructor presentation and student learning activities	Planning what students can do in conjunction with your presentation so that they are actively learning throughout the class session
Tip 12: *Lecture Plan*	Map how you develop content, organize information and carry out the lecture within a specific time period	Providing you with a quick glimpse of what you will need to do to accomplish your goals as well as providing a mechanism for improving the lecture for next time
Tip 13: *Double Planning*	Chart out what students will be doing in addition to what you will be doing	Thinking through how to keep students learning actively and how to help them move to higher levels of mental activity as they work

ENGAGING LECTURE TIP 9

Linked Lecturettes

A lecturette is a short, self-contained presentation of approximately fifteen to twenty minutes in length. *Linked Lecturettes* consist of stitching two or three lecturettes together within a larger presentation.

Linked Lecturettes have several advantages for lecturers. A lecturette's length works within the constraints of the individual attention span, which research suggests decreases in lectures after approximately fifteen or twenty minutes. *Linked Lecturettes* provide you with some flexibility in the order in which you present different segments of content, which meets the needs of lecturers who like to be more spontaneous in their delivery. *Linked Lecturettes* also present obvious times to break for other kinds of learning activities such as writing or small-group discussion. Finally, by linking three together, you can capitalize on the *Rule of Three* (Tip 8) which, put simply, suggests that people generally prefer to receive information chunked into threes and can remember such chunked information better.

Key Idea

Crafting several lecturettes and linking them together in one larger talk addresses attention span limits and provides you with more flexibility so that you can be more spontaneous in your teaching.

To create *Linked Lecturettes*, consider the following processes:

Step 1: Decide what function you want each lecturette to serve. You should lecture only when it serves a purpose (see Tip 2: *SMART Lecture-Learning Goals* for additional information). Not only should the overall lecture serve a purpose but also you should have a specific purpose for each smaller unit of content, the lecturette. When you think about a specific lecturette, consider whether it will do one or more of the following:

- Preview upcoming information in the text
- Summarize and synthesize ideas
- Emphasize and elaborate on new ideas
- Demonstrate a specific section of the text, the way it applies in practice
- Introduce theories or perspectives not addressed directly but related to those in the text
- Introduce problems, case studies, or other individual or group application exercises

Step 2: Create the lecturettes. Recrafting longer lectures into shorter segments can be challenging initially. Choose subtopics from within longer lectures and plan to create a number of short, focused lecturettes that can help students reach specific learning outcomes. You can use Tip 5: *Sticky Note Diagrams* to help you determine the main chunks and the key ideas within each chunk.

Step 3: Prepare connectors or connecting activities to intersperse with the lecturettes. Because the lecturettes should be standalone content that you can pull out and use in different ways, you will need connectors to stitch the ideas together. You can do this with a few sentences or slides to signal transition of ideas. Alternately, consider some of the activities we present later in this book as connectors as well as activities from other books in the College Teaching

Techniques series: *Student Engagement Techniques* (Barkley, 2010), *Collaborative Learning Techniques* (Barkley, Major, & Cross, 2014), and *Learning Assessment Techniques* (Barkley & Major, 2016). For example, you might provide students with a single question regarding some aspect of the lecturette for a quick discussion, such as a think-pair-share. Or you might assess whether students have reached a learning goal by implementing a quick write or a quick quiz. Or you might use the lecturette to prepare students to work on a segment of a longer group assignment, such as a jigsaw or debate.

Step 4: Explain the process of Linked Lecturettes to students ahead of time. You will want to tell students from the beginning of the lecture what the overarching theme is, what central ideas appear in the different lecturettes, and the way in which you see the lecturettes connecting. Stress that you are linking ideas and, if appropriate, explain that you will also be integrating other activities. By providing your rationale for using lecturettes combined with activities, students likely will be more receptive and ultimately successful in understanding your organization and purpose. If you are particularly flexible and have several lecturettes from which you may choose, consider giving students the option to select which topics they would most like to have you lecture about. This approach will work best with advanced students who have some idea of the information that they need to know.

Example

A professor teaching a history of science and technology course was preparing a three-hour class session focused on the contributions of ancient China. She organized it in a series of four lecturettes, each focusing on a single invention celebrated as symbolic of ancient China's advanced science and technology: (1) the compass, (2) gunpowder, (3) papermaking, and (4) printing. Between each of the lecturettes, she had students work in small groups to build a section of a concept map, in which students organized the information they had learned in an ever-expanding graphic that identified the relationships between the inventions as well as their impact on the development of civilization in China and throughout the world.

Key References and Resources

Barkley, E. F. (2010). *Student engagement techniques: A handbook for college faculty.* San Francisco, CA: Jossey-Bass.

Barkley, E. F., & Major, C. H. (2016). *Learning assessment techniques: A handbook for college faculty.* San Francisco, CA: Jossey-Bass.

Barkley, E. F., Major, C. H., & Cross, K. P. (2014). *Collaborative learning techniques: A resource for college faculty* (2nd ed.). San Francisco, CA: Jossey-Bass.

Ford, N., McCullough, M., & Schutta, N. T. (2012). *Presentation patterns: Techniques for crafting better presentations.* Boston, MA: Addison Wesley.

Middendorf, J., & Kalish, A. (1996). The "change-up" in lectures. *National Teaching and Learning Forum, 5*(2), 1–5.

Santa Clara University, Office of the Provost. (n.d.). *Mini-lectures.* Retrieved from www.scu.edu/provost/teaching-and-learning/digital-resources-for-teaching-drt/teaching/mini-lectures/

Walker, J. D., Cotner, S. H., Baepler, P. M., & Decker, M. D. (2008). A delicate balance: Integrating active learning into a large lecture course. *CBE—Life Sciences Education, 7*(4), 361–367.

ENGAGING LECTURE TIP 10

Select-a-Structure

Many of us conceptualize the lecture as a single, monolithic entity. In truth, however, lectures come in many different shapes and sizes. In this Tip, we suggest thinking through the many different facets of the lecture and intentionally structuring the kind of lecturette that is best suited for a particular task. *Select-a-Structure* encourages faculty members to think through the formality, duration, interactivity, format, and medium of a lecture.

Key Idea

Lectures differ along several lines, and it is useful to think through each of these in order to craft the most effective lecture structure for a given lecturette or mini-lecture to be presented in an interactive lecture session.

The following aspects of the lecture are adapted from Major, Harris, and Zakrajsek (2015, pp. 3–5).

Formality

- **Formal lecture.** A well-organized, tightly constructed, and highly polished presentation
- **Semiformal lecture.** A presentation similar to the formal lecture, but less elaborate
- **Informal lecture.** A loosely planned or impromptu talk

Duration

- **Full-session lecture.** The full class period in continuous exposition of content
- **Lecturette.** Approximately fifteen to twenty minutes, often linked with other lecturettes
- **Mini-lecture.** A brief, focused content presentation that lasts about five to fifteen minutes
- **One-minute lecture.** Approximately one minute of focused content; termed *micro-lecture* when designed for online delivery

Interactivity

- **One-way**. Little interactivity with questions entertained at the conclusion of the lecture
- **Two-way, limited.** Occasional interactivity initiated by instructor
- **Two-way, negotiated.** Occasional interaction initiated by instructor or students
- **Participatory.** Students involved in varied exchanges initiated by instructor and students

Format

- **Socratic lecture.** A series of carefully sequenced questions, requiring logic and inference along with knowledge of a reading assignment to answer, directed at a single student at a time
- **Point-by-point lecture.** A presentation of a single idea, question, or issue, typically organized in outline format

- **Lecture-demonstration.** A presentation modeling a process or activity, typically offered in a chronological order
- **Storytelling lecture.** A narrative used to illustrate a concept, typically with character development and an exposition, rising action, climax, falling action, and resolution
- **Problem-solving lecture.** A demonstration of working through a problem to reach a solution, typically illustrating the sequence of steps necessary to reach the solution
- **Oral essay.** An argument with primary thesis or assertion, with supporting justification and details, often told in order of importance

Medium

- **Oral only.** A direct talk to students without technological intervention
- **Chalk-and-talk lecture.** A talk given while generating notes in real time using a medium that students can see, such as chalkboard or whiteboard
- **Multimedia lecture.** A talk given with an accompanying audiovisual presentation, which highlights key points
- **Video lecture.** A talk recorded and then edited to create a video that is often used with online learning and blended learning and flipped classrooms

These various elements can be combined in a great variety of ways. One instructor might choose to give a semiformal, point-by-point, multimedia lecturette, and another might offer an informal, mini-lecture demonstration, oral-only presentation.

Full lectures are not part of the interactive lecturing model because the research is generally clear that they are not the best approaches for optimal student learning. Instead, the interactive lecturing model involves instructors creating shorter presentation segments and combining these with activities that students do. Together, the combination makes the class more interactive, and the session will likely alternate between two-way, negotiated and participatory interactivity.

In setting the structure for a given lecture, you can view your options in a manner similar to the spin mechanism on a resettable combination padlock and then combine various aspects to create the most effective lecture for your purposes. See Table 5.1 for a quick list of the various elements.

In this Tip we have illustrated a few key aspects of lecture structure. As Broadwell (1980) points out, the lecture "is virtually limitless in application, either to situation, subject matter or student age and learning ability" (p. xii).

Table 5.1 *Select-a-Structure* for Interactive Lecturing

Formality	Duration	Interactivity	Format	Medium
• Formal • Semiformal • Informal	• Full-session Lecture • Lecturette • Mini-lecture • One-minute lecture	• One-way • Two-way limited • Two-way, negotiated • Participatory	• Socratic • Point-by-point • Demonstration • Storytelling • Problem-solving • Oral essay	• Oral only • Chalk and talk • Multimedia • Video

Example

The professor of an introduction to biology course was committed to creating a course that students would find engaging. She felt that one strategy to achieve this was to create variety in the way she structured her class sessions. She used *Select-a-Structure* to intentionally combine different lecture elements. By frequently changing the manner in which she structured her presentations, she found that students came to class with a more positive attitude because they were curious about how she would structure the session that day. The variety in presentation also made her class sessions fresh and interesting.

Key References and Resources

Broadwell, M. M. (1980). *The lecture method of instruction.* Englewood Cliffs, NJ: Educational Technology.

Major, C. H., Harris, M., & Zakrajsek, T. (2015). *Teaching for learning: 101 techniques to put students on the path to success.* New York, NY: Routledge.

Ronchetti, M. (2010). Using video lectures to make teaching more interactive. *International Journal of Emerging Technologies in Learning, 5*(2). doi: 10.3991/ijet.v5i2.1156

ENGAGING LECTURE TIP 11

Bookends, Interleaves, and Overlays

When we lecture, we typically deliver information to students by talking to them as they sit quietly and listen. But our conception of the interactive model lecture involves integrating this oral presentation with activities that involve students so that they are dynamic and active participants in the learning process before, during, and after the lecture. *Bookends, Interleaves, and Overlays* offer a way to structure your class session to accomplish this integrative structure.

Key Idea

Incorporating learning activities that function as *Bookends, Interleaves, and Overlays* to a lecture presentation can help students to be active participants throughout the class session.

Integrating engaging presentations and active learning techniques requires careful thought and planning. Interactive lecturers strive to ensure that students are prepared for direct instruction and that the presentation is carefully situated and combined with active learning methods. To accomplish, this we recommend situating active learning assignments in conjunction with lecture presentations by interspersing them as *Bookends, Interleaves, and Overlays.* Each of these devices serves a distinct instructional purpose.

Bookends *Bookends* are structures that are positioned on either side of the presentation to help support the lecture (Smith, 2000; Smith, Sheppard, Johnson, & Johnson, 2005). A *Bookend* might come before a presentation, (such as through a preparation guide or online module) or it might be used to start a presentation (such as a quick prediction exercise). A *Bookend* might also come at the end of a presentation, such as a summary or reflection exercise. Sometimes you can start a presentation with a *Bookend* and then revisit the same *Bookend* at the end of the presentation, for example, asking students to reflect on what they already know about a topic before presenting on it and then asking students to reflect on and identify key learning or questions they still have after the presentation. (*Note:* this device corresponds with the "prepare" and "assess" sections of the model we presented in Figure 2.3.)

Interleaves *Interleaves* involve alternating between lectures and active learning; *interleaves* thus occur in-between presentation segments to help break up the lecture so students have time to process. You might, for example, choose to interleave presentations with quick pair discussions. (*Note:* as with *Overlays, Interleaves* correspond to the "attend" section of our model in Figure 2.3.)

Overlays *Overlays* are learning activities used during the presentation so that students can focus their attention on the lecture content. *Overlays* may involve techniques that help promote active listening or note-taking activities. (*Note:* this device corresponds to the "attend" section of our model in Figure 2.3.)

Building any class session can be a challenge, but by structuring your session using *Bookends, Interleaves, and Overlays* you can ensure you are incorporating techniques to help students remain active and engaged during a lecture presentation. Thus *Bookends, Overlays, and Interleaves* provide a means to support and extend presentations in ways that focus on improving student learning.

Example

In the following example, we demonstrate how to use *Bookends, Overlays, and Interleaves* to structure a single fifty-minute class session. We illustrate the use of five active learning techniques, which we describe more fully in Part 3 of this book:

- **ALT 5:** ***Update Your Classmate.*** Students write a letter to a student, real or fictional, who missed class the day before to explain the missing information and its importance.
- **ALT 13:** ***Guided Notes.*** The instructor hands out a set of incomplete notes that students complete during the lecture.
- **ALT 24:** ***Real-World Applications.*** After hearing about an important principle, theory, or process, students develop real-world applications of what they have just learned.
- **ALT 26:** ***One-Sentence Summary.*** At the end of the lecture, students summarize it in a single sentence.
- **ALT 31:** ***Lecture Wrapper.*** At the end of the lecture, students write what they think the three most important ideas of the lecture were on an index card. After they hand those in, the instructor reveals the three most important ideas from the lecture.

Following is an example schedule:

<table>
<tr><th>Bookend</th><th>Overlay</th><th>Interleave</th><th>Overlay</th><th>Interleave</th><th>Overlay</th><th>Bookend</th></tr>
<tr><td>5 mins</td><td>15 mins</td><td>5 mins</td><td>15 mins</td><td>5 mins</td><td>15 mins</td><td>5 mins</td></tr>
<tr><td rowspan="2">Update Your Classmate</td><td>Guided Notes</td><td rowspan="2">One Sentence Summary</td><td>Guided Notes</td><td rowspan="2">Real-World Applications</td><td>Guided Notes</td><td rowspan="2">Lecture Wrapper</td></tr>
<tr><td>Lecture presentation</td><td>Lecture presentation</td><td>Lecture presentation</td></tr>
</table>

Key References and Resources

Smith, K. A. (2000). Going deeper: Formal small-group learning in large classes. In J. MacGregor, J. L. Cooper, K. A. Smith, & P. Robinson (Eds.), *New Directions for Teaching and Learning: Strategies for Energizing Large Classes; From Small Groups to Learning Communities, 81,* 25–46.

Smith, K. A., Sheppard, S. D., Johnson, D. W., & Johnson, R. T. (2005). Pedagogies of engagement: Classroom-based practices. *Journal of Engineering Education,* pp. 1–16.

ENGAGING LECTURE TIP 12

Lecture Plan

When creating a lecture, it can be exciting to think about the content and fun to create the slides and handouts. In an interactive session, it is also rewarding to think about the activities students can do. At this point it can be tempting to skip straight to the class session itself without spending the time to really think through how the class session will go from start to finish. Consider creating a *Lecture Plan* to help you think through the nuts and bolts of the session ahead of time.

There are two main types of *Lecture Plans.* One type is a list of the different lectures you will hold during a given academic term, which you may well share with students. The other, and what we mean here, is a plan for a single lecture that lays out your objectives for that lecture, specific time frames for giving the lecture and taking breaks, and areas for note-taking so that you can refer back to the plan the next time you will give the same lecture.

A *Lecture Plan* provides you with a map for developing content, organizing your information, and carrying out the lecture. It provides you with a quick glimpse of what you will need to do to accomplish your goals. A good *Lecture Plan* also prompts you to make notes about how you will improve going forward.

Key Idea

A *Lecture Plan* can act as a road map that helps you organize your ideas and materials.

Lecture Plans can have several key sections:

Purpose. State your purpose to make clear the general and specific reasons you are conducting a lecture. See Tip 1: *Big Why, Little Why* for additional guidance on how to describe your purposes. You will also want to make the purpose clear to students from the start, and having these articulated in advance can help you achieve this.

Goals. Set goals by stating specifically what you want to achieve in the lecture. Your goals are the broad, overarching intentions you have, such as giving students foundational knowledge, helping them to learn how to learn, and so forth. See Tip 2: *SMART Lecture-Learning Goals* for assistance on this process.

Objectives. Clearly express what students will know and be able to do by the end of the lecture. Objectives often start with the stem: "By the end of this lecture session, students will be able to . . ." Setting these expectations will enable you and students to better gauge whether you have achieved what you intended in your lecture.

Student-entry characteristics. Before you begin, it is helpful to understand what students already know or can do so that you can build on their existing knowledge and experiences. See Tip 3: *Student Characteristics Analysis* for guidance on what kinds of information you might include in this section.

Timing. This section includes your best estimate for how long things will take. Try to plan lecture segments of no longer than fifteen to twenty minutes before a brain break or a changeup activity.

Details of content and activities. Decide how to teach specific segments of the content. You may, for example, divide a one-hour lecture into three fifteen-minute segments, with different activities in between.

Learning materials. Indicate what materials you will need in order to achieve your learning goals, such as lecture slides and handouts.

Observations. Make notes of any observations and reflections about the lecture you might have. Consider how students responded to the teaching strategies you used. Looking back over and using these notes can help you consider the positive and negative aspects of your approach and plan wisely for future lectures.

Example

A professor of higher education used a *Lecture Plan* template adapted from the Health Education and Training Institute (2012) to organize her upcoming lecture on the topic of student engagement, as shown here:

Administrative Details	
Lecture title	Student Engagement
Time available	75 minutes
Student entry characteristics	At entry, students are familiar with theories of motivation and likely have some experience at college-level teaching.
Group size	25 to 30
Room configuration	Movable tables and chairs
Equipment and materials required	Laptop or computer, projector, whiteboard, markers, and eraser
Presession preparation	Visit course site and complete the readings and accompanying questions.
Teaching Details	
Lecture purpose: To provide students with information they will need in order to become successful teachers; to focus on "student engagement," a necessarily complex concept; and to provide explanation and details that will benefit students	
Learning goals: Students will gain foundational knowledge of student engagement.	
Learning objective: At the end of the session, students will be able to do the following: • Define *student engagement.* • Explain different types of engagement. • Identify strategies for engaging students.	

Session Plan		
Time (mins)	**Lecture Segment or Student Activity**	**Materials**
5	Gain attention and rapport. *Talk for a couple of minutes about the difficulty of engaging students.* Explain purpose and reason for learning about the topic. State goals. State objective. Link to entry characteristics. Tie to previous lecture on cognitive overload. Review participation expectations. *Brief the participants on whether they can ask questions intermittently or at the end.* Outline content and structure. *Briefly outline contents and structure of the presentation.*	Slide deck
5	Student activity	
15	Review the concept of intellectual engagement.	Slide deck, whiteboard, and markers
5	Student activity	
15	Review the concepts of emotional engagement.	Slide deck, whiteboard, and markers.
5	Student activity	
15	Review the concept of cognitive engagement.	Slide deck, whiteboard, and markers.
5	Student activity	
5	Conclusion Review, questions, and answers	Annotated bibliography
Follow-Up		
Observations/notes		

Key References and Resources

Health Education and Training Institute. (2012). *The learning guide: A handbook for allied health professionals facilitating learning in the workplace.* Sydney, Australia: HETI. Retrieved from www.heti.nsw.gov.au/Global/allied-health/Session_workshop_lecture-plan-template.docx+&cd=8&hl=en&ct=clnk&gl=us&client=safariStafford

Stafford, K., & Kelly, M. (1993). An introduction to lecturing (Workshop Series No. 10, pp. 5–6). City Polytechnic of Hong Kong, Professional Development Unit (now City University of Hong Kong, Centre for the Enhancement of Learning and Teaching). Retrieved from http://teaching.polyu.edu.hk/datafiles/r18a.doc

ENGAGING LECTURE TIP 13

Double Planning

In addition to planning for what you will be doing, consider planning for what *students* will be doing for the duration of your class session. Many of the techniques we describe in Part 3 of this text will help you identify activities that will keep students active and engaged during the lecture. Adapting a *Lecture Plan* to include what students will be doing is a relatively simple task, and so in this Tip we encourage *Double Planning*; that is, we recommend identifying learner activities in advance as you make your formal lecture plans.

Double Planning helps you ensure that students have the appropriate skills or take the actions to accomplish what you expect during a lecture. In addition, it may help you to encourage students to be good lecture participants, a skill they often lack. *Double Planning,* then, will help you keep students active and engaged during the lecture by helping you plan effective learning activities, including closing and reflection activities.

Key Idea

During *Double Planning,* you plan for what students will be doing in addition to planning what you will be doing, ensuring that students maintain active engagement throughout the lecture session.

Making a formal *Double Plan* typically involves creating a simple T-chart. In the following example, we've modified our *Lecture Plan* session segment to include the student activities as a sample of a *Double Planning* outline. For future lectures, it can be particularly important to record specifically which activities went well and which could be improved because this information can remind you in the future whether to keep the same activities or to try out new ones.

Example

A professor of higher education modified the *Lecture Plan* she had created to organize her upcoming lecture on the topic of student engagement to include what students would be doing as well. Her modified plan follows.

Double Planning: Interactive Lecture Session on Student Engagement
Prior to the session, students will have read Barkley's (2010) *Student Engagement Techniques: A Handbook for College Faculty* and will have posted a book review on the course site.

Time (mins)	You	Students	Materials
5	Gain attention and rapport. Explain purpose and reason for learning about the topic. State goals. State objective. Link to entry characteristics. Tie to previous lecture on cognitive overload. Review participation expectations. Outline content and structure.	Listening	Slide deck
5	Student activity	Engaging in a learning activity ALT 25: *Pre-Post Free Write*	
15	Review the concept of intellectual engagement.	Taking notes ALT 13: *Guided Notes*	Slide deck, whiteboard, and markers
5	Student activity	Summarizing and translating what they have learned ALT 26: *One-Sentence Summary*	Note cards
15	Review the concepts of emotional engagement.	Taking notes ALT 13: *Guided Notes*	Slide deck, whiteboard, and markers
5	Student activity	Responding to a quick two-question quiz to ensure they are following the content ALT 20: *Snap Shots*	Poll
15	Review the concept of cognitive engagement.	Taking notes ALT 13: *Guided Notes*	Slide deck, whiteboard, and markers
5	Student activity	Ensuring they have good notes from the session ALT 16: *Note-Taking Pairs*	
5	Conclusion Review, questions, and answers	ALT 31: *Lecture Wrapper*	Annotated bibliography
Notes and Observations			

Key References and Resources

Barkley, E. F. (2010). *Student engagement techniques: A handbook for college faculty.* San Francisco, CA: Jossey-Bass.

Health Education and Training Institute. (2012). *The learning guide: A handbook for allied health professionals facilitating learning in the workplace.* Sydney, Australia: HETI. Retrieved from www.heti.nsw.gov.au/

Lemov, D. (2010). *Teach like a champion: 49 strategies that put students on the path to success.* San Francisco, CA: Jossey-Bass.

CHAPTER 6

Leveraging the Language

Having researched and developed content in preparation for an interactive lecture, you have likely accumulated a great deal of information related to the topic. If you decide to inform students about the plan for the session, you will have even more to communicate. Students can find listening to all of this information challenging. They can get lost in what you are saying and not be able to see how it is connected to what they are, or should be, doing. Indeed, human capacity for listening attentively is one of the key drawbacks of the lecture.

Lecturers, however, can use language to good effect to help students keep track of the central focus and the format of a lecture. Certain language structures can aid student understanding and thus can help improve learning. These structures can show that the ideas follow a logical order and build on each other, creating presentation flow. If the presentation proceeds well from point to point, listeners will be able to follow the progression of ideas and have an easier time grasping the information and the connections between it and class activities. In this chapter, we provide Tips for using language to signal the structure of the content and of the session as shown in Exhibit 6.1.

Exhibit 6.1 Leveraging the Language Tips

This Tip . . .	Provides guidance on how to . . .	It is particularly useful for . . .
Tip 14: *Aristotelian Triptych*	Organize your content into a classic, easily recognizable, three-part format	Clearly communicating the content of your message
Tip 15: *Signposts*	Use verbal cues to indicate where you are in the overall lecture	Providing students with a sense of direction and helping them get and keep their bearings
Tip 16: *Internal Previews and Summaries*	Plant cues for upcoming material and provide an accounting of material that has been presented	Focusing students on key ideas and information so that they don't have to guess what is most important
Tip 17: *High-Impact Language*	Choose words and phrases carefully in order to make your points with precision	Delivering strong lectures that inform students in a powerful way

ENGAGING LECTURE TIP 14

Aristotelian Triptych

The *Aristotelian Triptych* is simply this: tell them what you are going to tell them, tell them, and then tell them what you told them. This classic three-part approach is useful whenever you need to make a lecture presentation because it provides a simple, straightforward framework that helps students understand and then remember what you have said. It is particularly useful for demonstrating your mastery of the ideas and building a case for the information you have shared.

Key Idea

The Aristotelian Triptych is a good way to provide support to a lecture. It enables you to reinforce the key message and most-important supporting idea.

When deciding to use *Aristotelian Triptych* for a given lecture, or lecture segment, there are three phases:

1. **Tell them what you are going to tell them.** In the opening segment, you describe why you are talking on this particular topic and why students will need it. You should consider two aspects: what you want to say and what the audience needs to hear. It is easy to focus on the first half and forget the second. Knowing what your students need to hear in order to engage with the message is critical to your message. You are there to provide them leadership, and, in this segment, you can.
2. **Tell them.** This section is where you share the argument and general content of your presentation and explain the details. As a teacher, it is the best time for you to make a strong case for your message. Students will need to understand why what you're saying is important and how they will use the ideas and information.
3. **Tell them what you just told them.** Here you reiterate the most salient points. This step basically involves providing a summary. For teachers, this is also an opportunity to give learners a reason to learn the materials. You can also invite students to tell you what you just told them. Consider some of our techniques in Part 3 of this book.

The *Aristotelian Triptych* is a formula for a presentation, and although some argue that it can make a presentation a boring one, it need not be formulaic if you use your content and engage your personality in the delivery.

Example

A business professor found that students were having difficult fully understanding and remembering the concept of market segmentation. He decided to use the *Aristotelian Triptych* to structure his lecture, introducing the topic, providing a detailed description of the process, and then summarizing the key elements.

Key References and Resources

Smith, K. A. (2000). Going deeper: Formal small-group learning in large classes. In J. MacGregor, J. L. Cooper, K. A. Smith, & P. Robinson (Eds.), *New Directions for Teaching and Learning: Strategies for Energizing Large Classes; From Small Groups to Learning Communities, 81,* 25–46.

Smith, K. A., Sheppard, S. D., Johnson, D. W., & Johnson, R. T. (2005). Pedagogies of engagement: Classroom-based practices. *Journal of Engineering Education,* pp. 1–16.

Tiscone, R. (2006). *Aristotle's tried and true recipe for argument casserole.* Retrieved from https://info.legalsolutions.thomsonreuters.com/pdf/perspec/2006-fall/2006-fall-9.pdf

ENGAGING LECTURE TIP 15

Signposts

The structure of a lecture is often tacit, but making it more explicit can be beneficial to the listeners who might not otherwise perceive it. Effective lecturers typically describe the overall structure of the lecture at the beginning of a talk, and then along the way they make reference to where they are in terms of the overall structure. These references are usually in the form of words, which may also appear as text or visuals on a presentation slide. This indication of the overall structure and subsequent references to it are what we mean by *Signposts.*

Signposts are important in lectures for several reasons. Using *Signposts* can provide students with the cues they need in order to follow the main points. They can provide students with a sense of direction and enable students to anticipate new information, an act that can deepen their learning. They can also help prevent students from losing track of the narrative flow, particularly if they are novice learners in the area, English is not their native language, or if the topic is particularly complex. *Signposts* are specifically intended to help students stay on track or find the track again if they lose their way. Moreover, they can help students maintain attention by providing them with a sense of how much longer the lecture will be.

Key Idea

Signposts are verbal clues indicating where you are in the overall lecture that can provide students with a sense of direction and help them get and keep their bearings.

There are several key ways to use *Signposts:* to signal the overarching structure of the presentation, to stress the purpose, to provide background knowledge, to indicate when you have reached key junctures (transitions and lists, points, sub-points, and alerts within each juncture), and to conclude your lecture.

Signal the Overarching Structure

When providing the overarching structure, the type of *Signposts* you offer are highly dependent on the logical pattern that you have chosen. Consider the examples in Exhibit 6.2.

Exhibit 6.2 Signposts Indicating Lecture Structure

Signpost	Structure Indicated
In today's lecture, I will focus on three main points.	Topical
In today's lecture, we will consider five main events associated with . . .	Chronological
In our time together, we will consider three potential solutions to the problem of *X.*	Problem and solution
In this lecture, we will consider three effects of *X* on *Y.*	Cause and effect

Stress the Purpose

You may want to provide a signal to help students understand the purpose of the lecture because it is not always readily apparent to them. See the *Signposts* in Exhibit 6.3.

Exhibit 6.3 Signposts Indicating Lecture Purpose

The purpose of this lecture is to . . .
The aim of this lecture is . . .
The goal I hope to accomplish in this lecture is . . .

Provide Background Knowledge

Before you offer new information, you may want to provide a brief summary of what students should know about the subject already. This information could relate to a previous lecture or to background reading students should have done, as shown in Exhibit 6.4.

Exhibit 6.4 Signposts Referring to Background Knowledge

As we know . . .
As we have seen . . .
As you've read since our last session . . .
We all understand . . .
You'll remember . . .

Indicate Key Junctures

Summarizing what students should already know alerts them to any gaps in their knowledge and also prepares them to receive new information.

Transitions and Lists

When providing signals about transitions or lists, choose *Signposts* that refer to the initial sign posting. So, for a chronological pattern, for example, you might say, "the next event."

Main Points

It is useful to choose words that help students distinguish between which information is most important and which is less important. Consider using some of the following signals to draw students' attention to important points as shown in Exhibit 6.5.

Exhibit 6.5 Signposts Indicating Main Points

Don't forget that . . .
I will highlight . . .
I want to stress . . .
I'd like to emphasize . . .
The important point here is . . .
The critical point is . . .
The most essential point is . . .
The fundamental point of this is . . .
We should bear in mind that . . .

Sub-points

In addition to describing the overall structure and providing directions or clues along the way, you can use *Signposts* to indicate direction within your key points. For example, you might consider using *Signposts* to introduce an explanation or definition, to introduce an example, or to introduce a digression in which you temporarily move away from the main topic to provide an interesting and relevant aside. Consider Exhibit 6.6.

Exhibit 6.6 Signposts Indicating Sub-points

Explanation	Definition	Example	Digression
What this means is . . .	This is called . . .	One of the most dramatic examples is . . .	By the way . . .
This term means . . .	This is known as . . .	A good illustration is . . .	You may be interested to know . . .
By way of explanation . . .	This may be defined as . . .	For instance . . .	Incidentally . . .

Alerts

In addition to the just described uses for *Signposts,* consider creating *Signposts* to alert students to information they will need to know for upcoming quizzes and exams. Some faculty members like to include these because they believe it enhances attention during note-taking. Others are concerned that if students learn to expect these alerts, they then only pay attention to these particular words. Whether or not to include the following items depends on the context and the students. If you include them, consider the examples in Exhibit 6.7.

Exhibit 6.7 Signposts Providing Alerts

This is important.
Know this.
Remember this.
This is a test question.
You will likely see this information again.

Conclude the Lecture

You may end the lecture with a summary of the main points. Consider the signposts in Exhibit 6.8.

Exhibit 6.8 Signposts for Conclusion

First we looked at . . . and we saw that . . . Then we looked . . . and I suggested that . . . Finally . . . .
In summary, . . .
In conclusion, I will emphasize that . . .

In this Tip, we have described *Signposts* language. If you are using a slide deck, you can include some of this language in your slides. Indeed, we recommend using a title slide or a section header so that these slides look different from your primary content slides.

Example

A professor in an economics course was preparing a cause-and-effect lecture on inflation and the economy. She chose to use a number of *Signposts* to make the overall structure of the lecture apparent to students. For example, she opened with, "Today we will consider the three main effects of inflation on the economy." In subsequent *Signposts*, she said, "The first effect we will consider is the cost of living," "The second effect . . .," and "The third and final effect we will consider is . . . ." Figure 6.1 provides an example of a slide she used to reinforce her spoken comments:

Figure 6.1 Presentation Slide Signpost Example

Key References and Resources

Gillet, A. (2015). *Using English for academic purposes: A guide for students in higher education.* Retrieved from www.uefap.com/listen/struct/liststru.htm#emphasis

University of Leicester. (n.d.). *Signposts.* Retrieved from www2.le.ac.uk/offices/eltu/presessional-course-information/downloads/sl-materials-week-2/signposts-doc

University of Southern California, Center for Excellence in Teaching. (n.d.). *Preparing and structuring lecture notes.* Retrieved from http://cet.usc.edu/resources/teaching_learning/docs/teaching_nuggets_docs/3.1_Preparing_and_Structuring_Lecture_Notes.pdf

ENGAGING LECTURE TIP 16

Internal Previews and Summaries

Internal Previews and Summaries are devices that can signal the structure of ideas within a lecture. *Internal Previews* mean planting clues in the lecture for a later reveal, and *Internal Summaries* are taking the time to give a brief accounting of what you have already covered. These strategies work by reviewing what you have addressed and by highlighting what is to come.

Internal Previews and Summaries help students focus on key ideas and information without having to guess which are the most important. Students are better able to tune into what points you have talked about and what point you are about to talk about, which can help students track where they are in the lecture. Giving them guidance on where they have been and where they are going helps students stay focused. Moreover, letting them know how much they have remaining can provide incentive for paying attention. Finally, this strategy reinforces relationships between ideas and examples in your lecture, which can improve retention of information. When you use *Internal Previews and Summaries* properly, lectures should flow more smoothly, and complex ideas should be more comprehensible.

Key Idea

Internal Previews and Summaries can help students track how the lecture is progressing and better understand the overall structure of the lecture.

Internal Previews

Internal Previews direct student attention to the ideas you will cover next. To use this device, simply describe what is to come next. You can also consider previewing as something that occurs in two parts. The first part is the *plant,* which is where you hint that something important will soon be revealed. Once you have made the plant, you have to ensure that you bring a *payoff* and reveal the important part that you alluded to earlier. Forgetting the payoff can leave students feeling confused and disoriented. *Internal Previews* can be accomplished through statements such as "I would like to make a couple of important points here," "we will look at the problem and the solution," or "in this section there are several items to note."

Internal Summaries

Internal Summaries remind the learners what sub-points you have already discussed. *Internal Summaries* are excellent ways to reinforce and clarify essential ideas. To use this device, simply paraphrase the key information you have just covered. *Internal Summaries* can be accomplished through statements such as "To summarize what I just explained . . .," and "To reinforce the most essential ideas I have just discussed . . . ."

To make best use of connectors, we recommend using a combination of *Signposts* to signal the overarching structure of a lecture and *Internal Previews* and *Summaries* to indicate relationships between ideas.

Example

A professor was giving a lecture that had four key ideas related to organizational behavior. She began by stating that there are four key themes she would address (*Signposts*) and that they all started with the letter *c*. She then began to address the first theme: change. After the first theme, she said, "OK, so the first theme was about change (*Internal Summary*), what do you think will be next? Remember, it starts with the letter *c* (*Internal Preview*). She took guesses from the class, some of which were correct: culture was the next theme. She continued providing *Internal Summaries* and *Internal Previews* when possible for the next two themes: communication and conflict.

Key References and Resources

Ford, N., McCullough, M., & Schutta, N. T. (2012). *Presentation patterns: Techniques for crafting better presentations.* Boston, MA: Addison Wesley.

McLean, S. (2012). Emphasis strategies. *Communications for business success.* Retrieved from https://2012books.lardbucket.org/pdfs/communication-for-business-success-canadian-edition.pdf

University of Hawaii. (n.d.b). *Using connectives.* Retrieved from www.hawaii.edu/mauispeech/pdf/connectives.pdf

University of Pittsburg. (2007). *Speaking in the disciplines: Transitions.* Retrieved from www.speaking.pitt.edu/student/public-speaking/transitions.html

ENGAGING LECTURE TIP 17

High-Impact Language

Effective lecturers choose their language carefully in order to make their points with precision. Maximizing the language effect is also known as using *High-Impact Language,* which consists of choosing words and phrases that enable you to inform students in a powerful way. Using *High-Impact Language* will help you deliver stronger lectures. Your use of words that are clear and concise and that carry a specific message will help students better understand and remember your general message.

Key Idea

Using *High-Impact Language* conveys a stronger message and can help students understand and remember the key takeaway points from the lecture.

Following are tips for achieving *High-Impact Language.*

Avoid Choosing Words That Sound Pompous

Select short words rather than long words, Saxon words instead of Latin words, and modern words rather than old-fashioned words. For example, don't say

- *Aliment* when you can say *food*
- *Desiderate* when you can say *desire*
- *Elucidate* when you can say *explain*

Keeping your language clear and direct enables you to communicate more effectively because it requires less effort on the part of the listener.

Avoid Jargon

Avoid jargon whenever possible. For example, don't say

- *At this juncture* when you can say *now*
- *Operationalize* when you can say *do*
- *Utilize* when you can say *use*

Using jargon can make you seem insincere, so avoiding it is generally best.

Avoid Dead wood and Filler Words

Some words serve virtually no purpose other than filler, and you should try to avoid these words when writing out your lecture. Deadwood words include *very, really, totally, and so forth.* When you speak, likewise you should limit filler words; we say *limit* because filler words are almost impossible to avoid entirely. A filler word is a meaningless utterance, whether a word or sound that often fills a speech pause or hesitation. These fillers include *um, ah, uh, er, so, like, okay, right,* and *you know.* Relaxing and slowing down the pace of your presentation can help reduce the incidence of fillers.

Use Active Voice

Using the active voice adds strength to your words.

Passive	Active
The bat was swung.	Jane swung the bat.
The ball was thrown.	John threw the ball.
The stick was fetched.	The dog fetched the stick.

Active sentences are clearer and more concise and hence carry more impact. If you are unsure whether your sentence is active, you can use the "zombie test." If you can insert the words *by zombies* after the verb and have it make sense, you probably have used passive voice (e.g., The bat was swung *by zombies.*).

Use Words That Speak to the Senses

To keep listeners attentive, engage their senses. Think about what they can see, hear, smell, or feel. Consider the following sentences:

Not Addressing the Senses	Addressing the Senses
Be enthusiastic when you teach.	Teach like your soul is on fire.
Your lecture should interest your students.	Your lectures should grab your students' attention.

When you use language that taps into sensory experiences, you help students to engage with the point you are trying to make.

This Tip applies in *most* instances. We acknowledge that there are times at which it is useful to choose more formal language, to select larger rather than smaller words, to use passive instead of active voice, and so forth. When you make such choices intentionally and sparingly, it will improve the emphasis of your point. Our Tip here is intended to suggest that, in general, the best plan is to choose the clearest and most concise language you can.

Example

A professor of music history wrote a draft of a formal guest lecture, paying attention only to the main points he wanted to make. The following sentence is an example:

> A few performers in the eighteenth century were very famous, had lots of fans, and the payment given to them for their performances was significant. Although we think that the idea of famous performers is something new to today, they were the world's first divas.

He then went back and revised it, attempting to create more direct language, as follows:

> Superstars are one of the hallmarks of the entertainment world. By definition, they are impossibly famous, enjoy a cult following, often adopt a pseudonym (such as Lady Gaga), are pursued by groupies, and make more money for a single performance than most of us earn in a lifetime. Although seemingly an outgrowth of contemporary popular culture, it was actually the eighteenth century that gave music its first superstars.

Key References and Resources

Gillet, A. (2015). *Using English for academic purposes: A guide for students in higher education.* Retrieved from www.uefap.com/listen/struct/liststru.htm#emphasis

Heller, R. (2002). *High-impact speeches: How to create and deliver words that move minds.* London, UK: Prentice Hall Business.

CHAPTER 7

Designing Effective Audiovisuals

Lecturing today practically implies use of audiovisuals, particularly in the form of presentation software and slide decks. But are audiovisuals always necessary? Are they always a good idea? Try to recall some of the best speeches of all time. Which ones come to mind? Martin Luther King's "I Have a Dream" speech? Abraham Lincoln's "Gettysburg Address"? Susan B. Anthony's "Women's Rights to Suffrage"? Of the speakers and speeches that came to your mind, consider this question: who had the best PowerPoint? Of course most of the speakers didn't have access to presentation packages, computers, or projectors, so perhaps the question is unfair. But consider this one instead: how many of these speeches would have been improved by the use of audiovisual supports? Our guess is not any.

Why use audiovisuals during lectures at all? Many of our most important communication acts occur without the use of slides. There is something powerful about the human voice on its own. There is something useful about speaking directly to another person or a group of people. Indeed, speaking without slides has several advantages. If you don't use slides, you don't have to worry about technology failure. If you don't use slides, students pay more attention to you. Moreover, slides can lock you in to what you will say, when you will say it, and how you will say it. If you are an expert on your topic, you may want more flexibility than preset audiovisuals will allow.

There are, however, many times that it is better to use audiovisuals. They can help students pay attention. If you have complicated ideas, audiovisuals can host graphs and illustrations that can help students better understand. Sometimes it is simply more appropriate and effective to convey information visually rather than orally (Mayer, 2017). Having effective audiovisuals can make you seem more prepared as a speaker. Moreover, audiovisuals can help you as a speaker by reminding you of points you want to make and ensure that you stay on track. In this chapter, we offer several Tips that focus on creating and using presentation slides and other audiovisuals effectively. We summarize these Tips in Exhibit 7.1.

Exhibit 7.1 Creating Content Tips

This Tip . . .	Provides guidance on how to . . .	It is particularly useful for . . .
Tip 18: *Template Temperance*	Use your own ideas rather than predetermined templates to create your presentation slides	Making your presentation unique
Tip 19: *Less Is More*	Keep slides minimalist in design	Creating more compelling presentations
Tip 20: *Context Keeper*	Designate an element that you repeat to unite a group of slides	Showing that a slide group is related to a single idea
Tip 21: *Invisible Slide*	Place a blank slide in your presentation at a strategic place	Refocusing student attention on you
Tip 22: *Slide Replacements*	Use physical objects instead of slides to convey lecture content	Varying the elements of your lecture presentation to keep it interesting

Key Reference and Resource

Mayer, R. E. (2017). *Principles for learning from multimedia with Richard Mayer.* Retrieved from https://hilt.harvard.edu/blog/principles-multimedia-learning-richard-e-mayer

ENGAGING LECTURE TIP 18

Template Temperance

Have you ever noticed how often presenters' presentations look alike? This is largely because presentation packages such as PowerPoint, Keynote, and Prezi come with built-in slide templates. These templates format slides so that when you choose a theme, it selects the font, the colors, picture placement, and so forth.

These software packages enable us to create audiovisuals for a lecture quickly and efficiently. They produce presentations that are attractive, typically incorporate fonts that are easier for the widest number of people to read, and automatically incorporate a header hierarchy that can help all students, particularly those with disabilities. However, these preset templates can also assert a certain cognitive style that can constrain ideas. Because of this, we can omit information, gloss over details, or treat all issues as if they are of equal weight, regardless of whether they actually are. Moreover, because we see presentations that look fairly similar to each other, we can tire of them. If, for example, Susie goes to Dr. Smith's class and Dr. Smith is using the Civic template, and then goes to Dr. Jones's class who is also using the Civic template, and then on to Dr. Walker's class, who is also using the Civic template, Susie will very likely tire of seeing the Civic template.

We can resist the pull toward sameness and use such templates more effectively. To engage in *Template Temperance,* we can use what is good about templates while actively striving to avoid overly homogenizing the lecture presentation.

Key Idea

Use presentation package templates sparingly. Don't allow the software package to structure your ideas—find the ideas first and then use what is good about presentation software to make your presentation unique.

If you have good technical and design skills, create your own template with a font and colors that you feel best represents you. If you don't have great technical or design skills, or if you are under time pressure when creating your lecture presentation, use a template and edit the master slides to achieve a unique look.

Create your own template:

- Consider the font. Be sure your font is accessible for individuals with disabilities. It's best to choose a sans serif font. You can edit the one from the template, staying within the same font family.
- Use a strong palette of solid colors. Consider whether you want bold, contrasting colors or softer, more pastel colors. Choose no more than five colors.

Edit an existing template:

- Modify existing templates to customize the look. The template will provide you with coordinated master slides for title slides, slides with images, slides with bulleted lists, and so forth, which you can alter.
- Avoid using font shadows. Shadows make text more difficult to read, so avoid it unless the shadow is somehow central to your point.
- Use animation sparingly. Templates provide opportunities for animation, but animation can be distracting to students and can interfere with their learning.
- Use sound effects sparingly, if at all, because they can be exceedingly distracting.
- Use high-quality images and incorporate your own pictures and illustrations. One of the best ways to make a template look uniquely yours is to incorporate pictures and illustrations. There are plenty of images available for free on the Internet (with Creative Commons licensing), or you can subscribe to a service such as Shutterstock. Using your own photos or illustrations is even better.
- Use standard, subtle transitions. Flashy transitions, such as sound effects and animation, can draw attention away from content.

In summary, we suggest temperance when using a presentation package template. Don't let the package choose what you will do. Decide what you want the presentation to look like, and then make the software work for you.

Example

Figure 7.1 is an example of one of Elizabeth's slides using Keynote, in which she modified the most basic white template by selecting her own font and incorporating an image she had purchased from Shutterstock.com.

Figure 7.1 *Template Temperance* Presentation Slide Example

Key References and Resources

Ford, N., McCullough, M., & Schutta, N. T. (2012). *Presentation patterns: Techniques for crafting better presentations*. Boston, MA: Addison Wesley.

Gabriel, Y. (2008). Against the tyranny of PowerPoint: Technology-in-use and technology abuse. *Organization Studies, 29*(2), 255–276.

ENGAGING LECTURE TIP 19

Less Is More

Most of us have heard of and likely experienced a PowerPoint presentation when a presenter displays too much text on a single slide, which he or she then proceeds to read. The audience is caught between the choice of whether to pay attention to the slide or the speech because we cannot do both simultaneously, and typically chooses to read the slide because most people read faster than the typical rate of human speech. Then we must wait as the speaker dutifully attends to each word on the slide, the same words we've long before finished reading. We are bored. Hmmm, perhaps a quick check for messages on the phone while waiting for the speaker to catch up . . .

Poorly designed slide presentations interfere with our main messages. There are better methods, however, and speakers who use presentation software effectively have much to offer us as we seek to find our own styles. These speakers tend to go with minimalist slide design, showing only a few words or a single carefully selected image to support their oral presentation. We call this Tip *Less Is More* to signify the minimalist approach to slide design.

Key Idea

Keep slides minimalist in design. *Less Is More* provides a design principle that can help you create more interesting and effective slide presentations.

To do more with less, consider the following suggestions:

- Use simple but visually powerful slides.
- Use keywords to support your ideas; words should be easy to understand even and especially if the ideas behind them are complex.
- Create powerful slides by using high-quality images, which can be more memorable than text.
- Don't read from the slides; information is only interesting once, so let the students read a keyword or two to have it anchor the message you are trying to convey.

The challenge of minimalist slide design is that the lecturer really has to know his or her content. Thus this challenge is also one of the benefits of this approach because it challenges lecturers to be prepared and to think through the lecture ahead of time.

There are several pioneers of minimalist slide design who can serve as models while you learn to craft your own *Less Is More* style. Some of the notable ones are as follows.

Takahashi The Takahashi method uses one or two oversized keywords as a visual for the slide. Presenters who use this method do not use charts, pictures, abstract designs, or bulleted lists. It is a quickly paced presentation approach that relies on many more slides than a typical presentation.

The oversized keyword(s) help the audience follow the presentation and understand the main emphasis of each idea. A Takahashi style slide might look like what is shown in Figure 7.2.

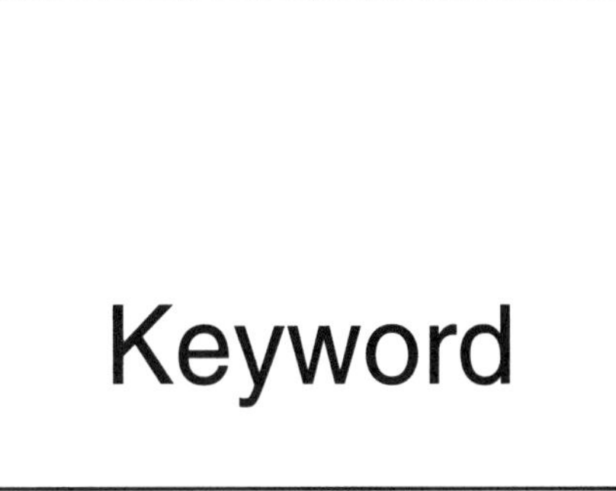

Figure 7.2 Takahashi Slide Design

Kawasaki The Kawasaki approach is also known as the 10–20–30 method. During the presentation, the speaker uses 10 slides, 20 minutes, and 30-point font or larger. This approach keeps the presentation clear and concise. It is direct and also tends to keep the audience's attention. A slide using the Kawasaki method might look like what is shown in Figure 7.3.

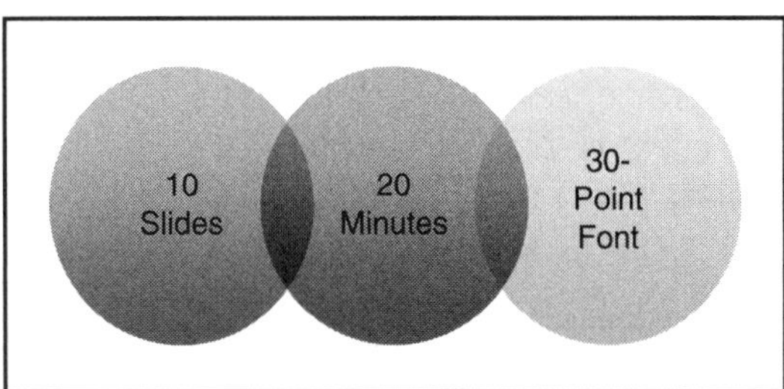

Figure 7.3 Kawasaki Slide Design

Lessig The Lessig method is another minimalist technique using slide decks. Using this method, one might spend fifteen to twenty seconds on a slide, using keywords on the slide or full-slide images to support the words of the speech. Slides look like what is shown in Figure 7.4.

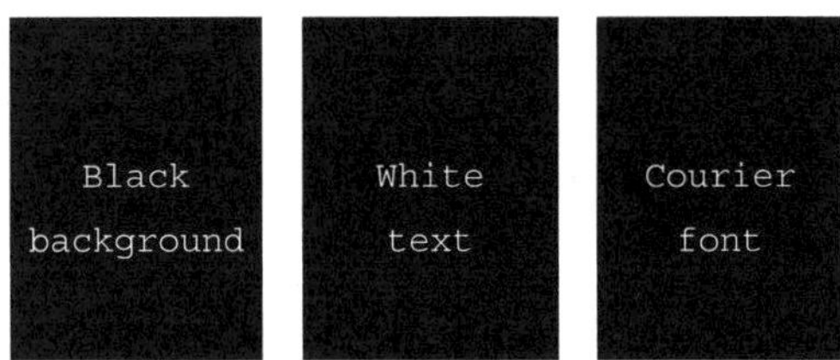

Figure 7.4 Lessig Slide Design

Godin Godin's method involves use of bold fonts, contrasting colors, and striking images to convey ideas in order to produce visually appealing presentations that create an emotional connection between the presenter and the listeners. Godin's rules are six words or fewer, no cheesy images, no transitions, limited sound used only for impact, and no printed handouts of the slides. Slides have elements similar to those shown in Figure 7.5.

Figure 7.5 Godin Slide Design

Example

Figures 7.6 and 7.7 show two of Claire's slides from a 1998 lecture about problem-based learning.

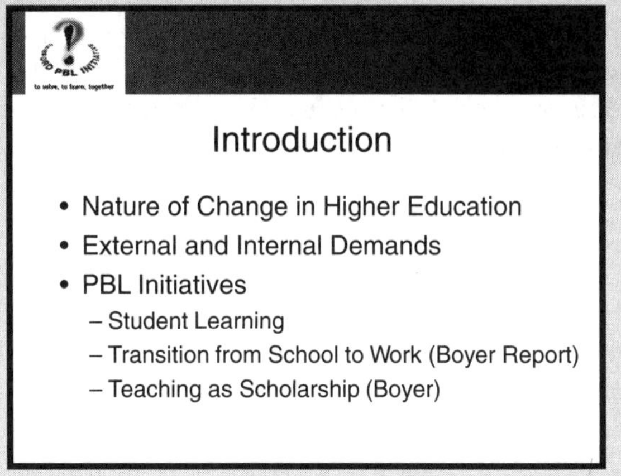

Introduction

- Nature of Change in Higher Education
- External and Internal Demands
- PBL Initiatives
  - Student Learning
  - Transition from School to Work (Boyer Report)
  - Teaching as Scholarship (Boyer)

Figure 7.6 Too Much Text Slide Example

Process

- Students confront a problem.
- In groups, they organize their previous knowledge and new ideas and attempt to define the nature of the problem.
- Students pose questions about what they do not understand.
- Students design a plan to solve the problem and identify resources they need.
- They begin to gather information as they seek to find viable solutions to the problem.

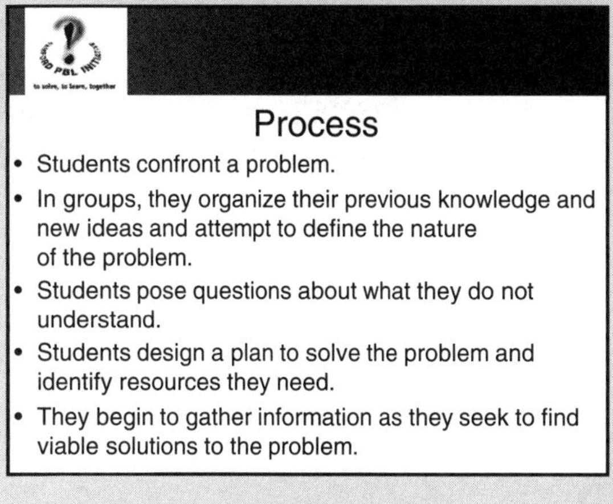

Figure 7.7 Too Much Text Slide Example

Figures 7.8 and 7.9 show two of our slides from a 2016 lecture about our book, *Learning Assessment Techniques: A Handbook for College Faculty.*

Figure 7.8 Minimal Text Slide Example

Figure 7.9 Minimal Text Slide Example

In the first set of slides, you can see the overreliance on and overabundance of text. The audience must choose whether to listen or read. In the second set, which we prefer, we combine minimal text with images. The speaker conveys the message orally and the slides exist to support the message, not replace it.

Key References and Resources

Barkley, E. F., & Major, C. H. (2016). *Learning assessment techniques: A handbook for college faculty*. San Francisco, CA: Jossey-Bass.

Godin, S. (2001). *Really bad PowerPoints*. Retrieved from www.sethgodin.com/freeprize/reallybad-1.pdf

Slide Comet. (n.d.). *Presentation design techniques*. Retrieved from http://journaux.cegep-ste-foy.qc.ca/educenligne/public/Fichiers_attaches/presentationdesigntechniques-130510022136-phpapp02.pdf

Slide Genius. (2016). *Five effective PowerPoint delivery methods for presentations*. Retrieved from www.slidegenius.com/blog/5-effective-powerpoint-delivery-methods-for-presentations/

ENGAGING LECTURE TIP 20

Context Keeper

Excellent lecturers tend to present just a few main points in any given talk (see Tip 8: *Rule of Three*). They also typically have good methods of illustrating their ideas in ways that help listeners follow the overall structure of the lecture. In Tip 15: *Signposts,* for example, lecturers use verbal signals to accomplish this.

A *Context Keeper* is another way, but rather than being a verbal sign, it is a visual way to reveal the structure in a presentation accompanied by slides. After the initial reveal, the *Context Keeper* appears in several subsequent slides to signal that the slides are related. The *Context Keeper* changes when the lecturer presents a new section of the lecture.

Lecturers can use *Context Keepers* when their lecture consists of discrete sections to help students follow the organization of a lecture. These indicators help students to see relationships between ideas presented on slides that might not otherwise be obvious. *Context Keepers* also can help to illustrate differences in seemingly similar content. Moreover, they can help students maintain attention as they have something specific to watch for: a change in sections illustrated by the *Context Keeper*. In addition to helping illustrate the overarching structure and relationship of ideas, *Context Keepers* also help to keep slides visually interesting, which also encourages student attention.

Key Idea

When creating your slide deck, designate an element (*Context Keeper*) that you will repeat in a group of slides that are related to a single idea.

There are many different approaches to *Context Keepers*. Consider the following options when developing your slide deck.

Background Color Use a different slide background color for each section of related ideas. Color is a powerful element, and changing the color can signal a shift in ideas. It also can signal a shift in mood or tone appropriate to the content. If you do use color as a context keeper, use soft colors or contrasting colors that don't decrease visibility. For example, you could alternate between a black background and white text and a white background with black text to signal changes in ideas—you would not want to try, for example, a bright orange background with bright green text—the slide would be difficult to read. Colored background and text can also make slides unreadable for students with colorblindness. Also beware of low-contrast background and text that can be difficult to read for students with visual impairments.

Visual Image Use the same image to unify slides in a given section of the lecture. You can move the image around on the slide for variety, but using the same image across all slides in a specific section will signal to students that the slides belong to a cluster of ideas. When you move to the next section, use a new image. Alternately, you can choose a visual element to return to after completing each section to drive home a central thesis.

Twitter Hashtags Use a hashtag, perhaps as a header or footer, on each section of slides. For example, if you are lecturing on the history of instructional technology, you might use #film for all of the slides that deal with instructional film, #radio for all of the slides that deal with instructional radio, #television for all of the slides that deal with televised education, and so on.

Slide Transition Although in previous Tips we have advocated for keeping slides as simple as possible and only using animation sparingly, one of the ways animation can be used to good effect is to serve as a *Context Keeper*. At the start or end of each section, you can use a fade-in or fade-out transition animation to signal the change of sections. The animation serves as a bridge to new information.

Example

The slides shown in Figure 7.10 provide an example of using different levels of background shading as a *Context Keeper*.

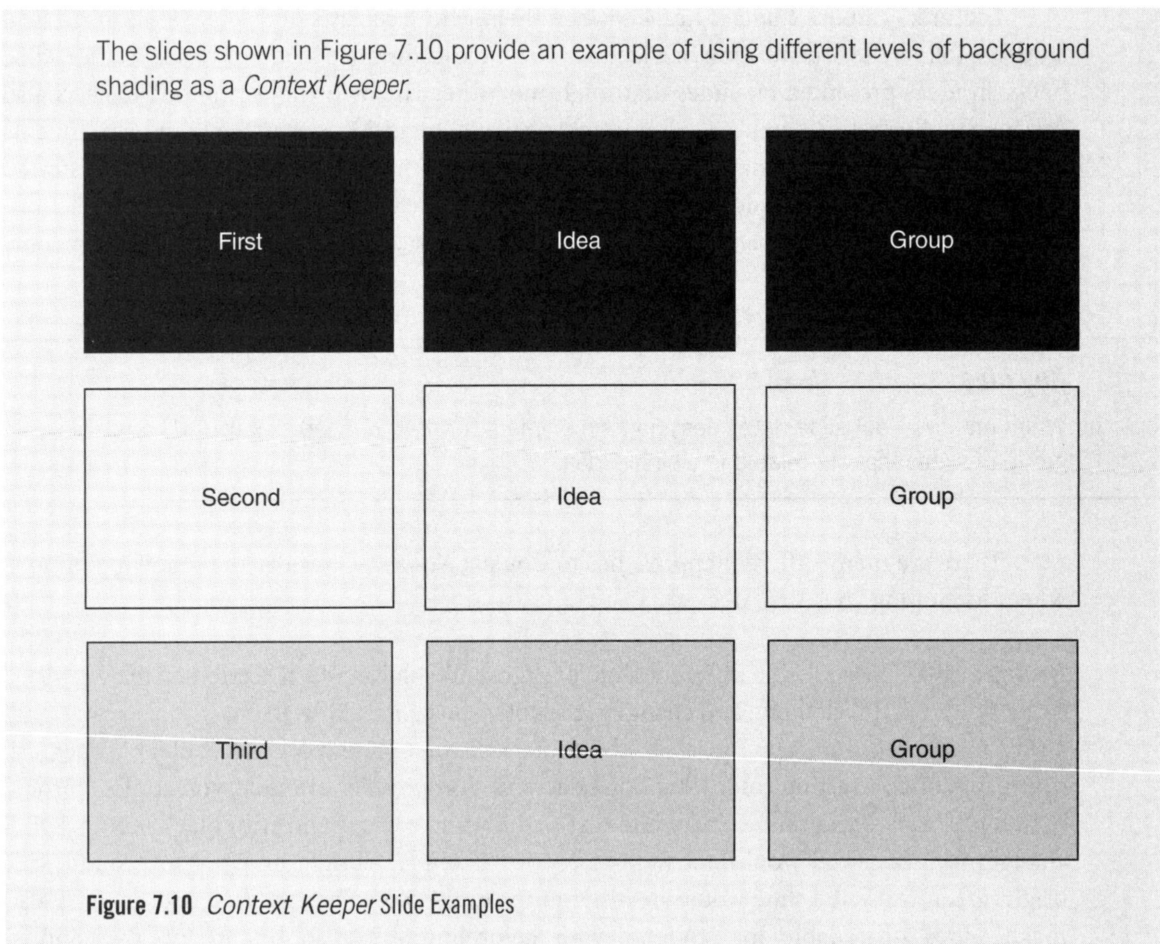

Figure 7.10 *Context Keeper* Slide Examples

Key References and Resources

Ford, N., McCullough, M., & Schutta, N. T. (2012). *Presentation patterns: Techniques for crafting better presentations*. Boston, MA: Addison Wesley.

Williams, R. (2010). *The non-designer's presentation book: Principles for effective presentation design*. Berkeley, CA: Peachpit Press.

ENGAGING LECTURE TIP 21

Invisible Slide

Slides done well can be very effective, but sometimes slides can be done so well that the audience stops paying attention to what the presenter is saying and starts focusing solely on the slide content. Or in another scenario, if the speaker has moved on but the slide has not advanced, the audience is viewing stale content. Moreover, slide after slide with no change can become repetitive and lack surprise and spontaneity. For these reasons, consider occasionally including an *Invisible Slide,* also known as a blank slide or a blacked-out slide, at strategic places in your lecture.

Using an *Invisible Slide* from time to time redirects students' focus from the slide back to you. You can use the visual pause to summarize what you have just said or to set the stage for the information that is to come, or both. It gives students a mental break from text after text or image after image, and it also adds an element of surprise. Thus the *Invisible Slide* can help you maintain student interest in and attention on what you have to say.

Key Idea

Using an *Invisible Slide* means placing a blank slide in your slide deck at a strategic point in the lecture to help refocus student attention on you.

There are several ways you might consider using an *Invisible Slide:*

- **Start your lecture presentation with an *Invisible Slide.*** With this approach, you connect with students first, before directing them to content and your slides. This approach can make you seem more real and more approachable.
- **Use an *Invisible Slide* at key points during your lecture presentation.** This approach enables you to connect with students at critical points, for example, to provide *Signposts* (Tip 15) or to direct student attention to the lecture structure through *High-Impact Language* (Tip 17). It will also draw their attention back to you and break up the monotony of the slide deck.
- **End with an *Invisible Slide.*** The conclusion is the last thing students will hear from your lecture. Ending with an *Invisible Slide* during your conclusion draws student focus and attention back to you. It also provides you with a chance to simply talk to students.

In addition, when ending a lecture with an *Invisible Slide,* you might also consider providing concluding remarks during a blank slide and then revealing one final slide to remind students of your e-mail address, office hours, or other ways to contact you should they have any additional questions. This will enable you to sum up by speaking with them face-to-face but then also provide relevant information about how they can connect with you after class.

Many software packages offer a feature that allows you to go to a blank screen at any point in the presentation. During a Power Point slide show, press the W key to go to a white slide or the B key to go to a black slide. To resume the presentation, you hit escape. Although this feature is useful, we also believe that you can strategically place some blank slides in the slide deck. These will help you to remember to move away from your deck and talk to students directly.

Another use of a blank slide is to include an element in the slide that is invisible initially but that displays when you are ready for it. For example, you can set the slide originally to appear as blank or to appear with minimal text and then have a hidden element, such as a background image, set to reveal with animation; for example, a speaker might use a fade-in approach to reveal slide elements. The image exists and is in place, but it won't be revealed until the animation happens. Although some speakers like to use this approach, and it can be effective when used sparingly, we recommend that you use this technique only infrequently—if you overdo it, students will get tired of it and can even be distracted by animation.

Example

Figure 7.11 provides an example of using an *Invisible Slide* at the end of a lecture.

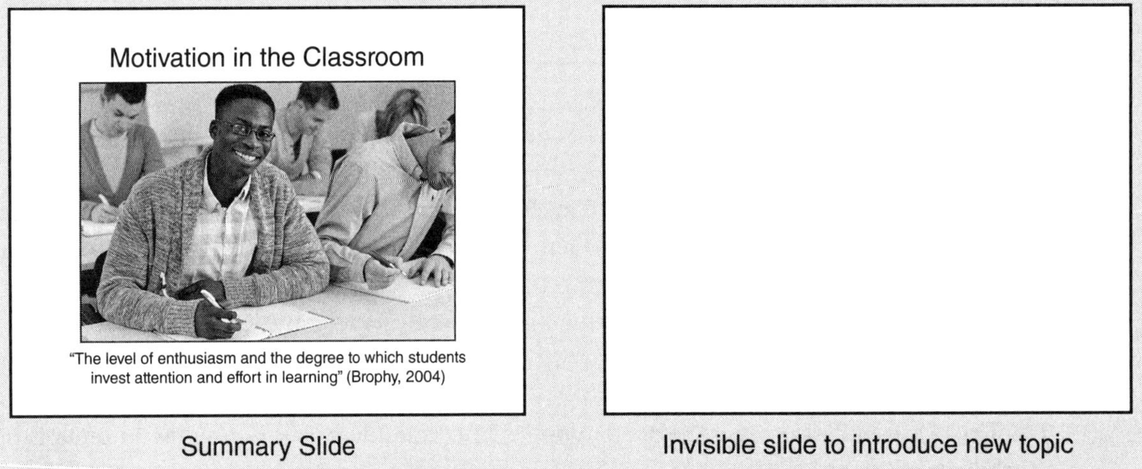

Motivation in the Classroom

"The level of enthusiasm and the degree to which students invest attention and effort in learning" (Brophy, 2004)

Summary Slide

Invisible slide to introduce new topic

Figure 7.11 End-of-Lecture Use of the *Invisible Slide*

Figure 7.12 shows an example of using an *Invisible Slide* in which an element that is initially invisible displays at a later time:

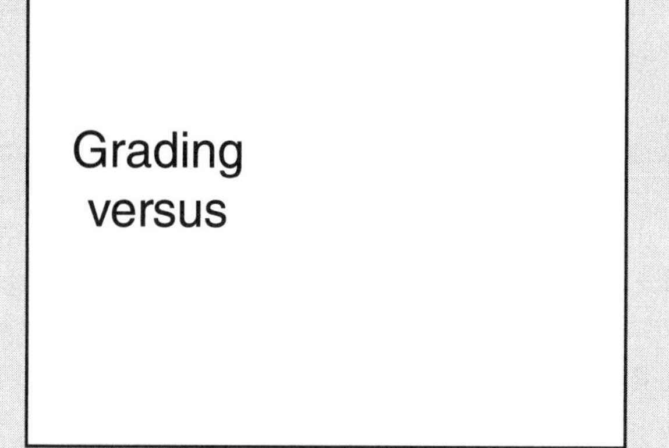

Slide with hidden element

Grading
versus

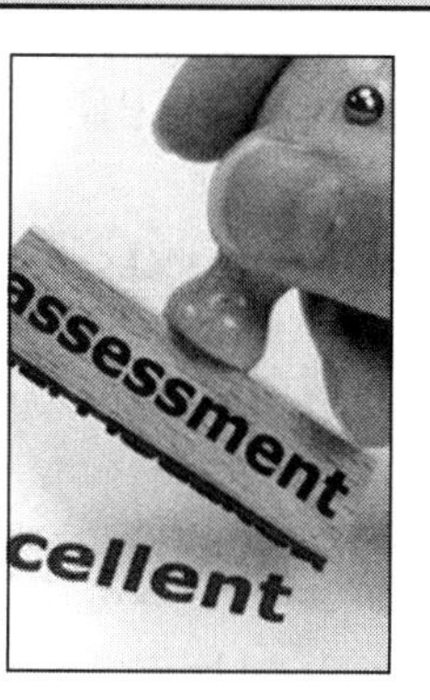

Slide with hidden element revealed

Figure 7.12 *Invisible Slide* Example

Key References and Resources

Ford, N., McCullough, M., & Schutta, N. T. (2012). *Presentation patterns: Techniques for crafting better presentations.* Boston, MA: Addison Wesley.

Presenter News. (2014). *Use a blank slide for a powerful presentation.* Retrieved from https://presenternews.wordpress.com/2014/06/16/use-a-blank-slide-for-a-powerful-presentation/

ENGAGING LECTURE TIP 22

Slide Replacements

Slide decks, whether created through PowerPoint, Keynote, Prezi, or other programs, seem to be the default mode for any kind of oral presentation, including lectures. Students seem to expect slide presentations as well. We know that visuals can enhance listeners' experience and understanding, and that knowledge coupled with student expectations can often prompt us to choose to create a slide deck, whether we really want to or not. The downside of this new default, however, is that many people have grown weary of slide decks, particularly if the slide-based talks aren't done extremely well.

There are alternatives to slide decks, however, that still allow for creating visually engaging lectures. Using *Slide Replacements* means choosing a different form of visual support for a lecture that takes the place of a slide deck. Using *Slide Replacements* in lectures has several advantages. It allows for a form of presentation that students will not expect, and the surprise can be refreshing for them. Students can have a tendency to tune out during slide presentations, so choosing a different format can be motivating for them. Using *Slide Replacements* gives you more flexibility in developing your own form because you won't have a default setting making decisions for you. Indeed, you can even go without slides, as our colleague Jose Bowen advocates (2012).

Key Idea

You don't have to use presentation slides to have a visually effective presentation. Use *Slide Replacements* as a unique approach to a visual lecture.

Consider using the following *Slide Replacements:*

Props Most of us spend considerable time in front of a screen, whether it is a smartphone, computer, or television. Props offer students something physical to look at. Whether you hold up a model of something, a book, an audiotape, or other, using props during a lecture can have some advantages. Props can break up monotony of an oral-only essay. Props can energize and entertain. They enable students to focus on a concrete rather than an abstract concept. You can even pass around some props, so students get to hold the object, which is appealing to yet another of their senses.

Video A good video has a vibrancy that static slides lack. It typically has movement and sound and perhaps music and dialog. Video can help you create the right emotional atmosphere to begin or end a lecture or alternately to illustrate a specific point. If you do choose to use video, make sure it is really compelling and try to keep it short, or students will feel like you are simply using it as a substitute for teaching and are thereby shirking your professional responsibilities.

Flip Chart The advantage to flip charts is that you create the visuals you need in the moment that you need them with the students right there with you. The act of creating something during the moment can help draw students into the activity and the talk in ways that a slide might not. Even if you prewrite the content, flip charts can give the feeling of a real and in-the-moment experience. Unlike slide decks, you can add to flip charts easily during a presentation.

Signs Instead of using slides, you could choose to hold up physical slides or signs with a word, phrase, or picture on it, and flip them in sync with your talk. Signs can hold students' attention by illustrating key points as you flip through along with your lecture. (Think of Bob Dylan in "Subterranean Homesick Blues.").

The Board Many college instructors make effective use of a chalkboard or whiteboard. You can write short words or phrases on the board to supplement your ideas, just as you would display in a slide. The challenge is that the board can be misused, a situation that can be avoided by taking several steps. For example, make sure all students have an unobstructed view of the board. Ensure that you do not keep your back turned to the students for long. Don't try to write out more than a word or very brief phrase—it will pull you away from students and to the board (see Tip 43: *Weatherperson*). Make sure that your handwriting is legible and that you are spelling the words correctly. You might also consider designating part of the board to information that will remain for the whole lecture and part that you can erase and change as you go along. Whiteboards and interactive screens can combine attributes of slides and the traditional blackboard.

Example

A professor was giving a lecture on upcycling. She chose not to use a slide deck because she felt she wanted to be more present and spontaneous with the students. Plus she planned that presentation would be a small percentage of the way in which she would use overall class time.

She used an old suitcase as a prop. To begin her presentation, she described upcycling and why it is important. She put her suitcase forward. She showed students all sides, including the inside. She then asked students to think about several ways to upcycle the suitcase. After a minute, she put them in pairs to discuss. After several pairs had shared their ideas, she held a full-class discussion on upcycling.

Key References and Resources

Berkun, S. (2013). How to present well without slides [Web log post]. Retrieved August 31, 2016, from http://scottberkun.com/2013/how-to-present-well-without-slides/

Bowen, J. A. (2012). *Teaching naked: How moving technology out of your college classroom will improve student learning*. San Francisco, CA: Jossey-Bass.

Mayer, R. E. (2017). *Principles for learning from multimedia with Richard Mayer*. Retrieved from https://hilt.harvard.edu/blog/principles-multimedia-learning-richard-e-mayer

Morgan, N. (2011). 10 things to do instead of PowerPoint. *Forbes*. Retrieved from www.forbes.com/sites/nickmorgan/2011/06/13/10-things-to-do-instead-of-power-point/#39f7ad182ca7

CHAPTER 8

Crafting Handouts and Supplements

If you have kept your slides to just a few words or images as we suggested in Tip 19: *Less Is More,* a copy of your slides won't mean much to students out of the context of the lecture session. It will also mean that you will likely have a large number of slides, and printing them is not only unhelpful to students but also inefficient, uneconomical, and bad for the environment.

Students will appreciate some kind of handout, however, that can assist them in understanding and recalling lecture content. This handout can be distributed, posted online, or sent as an e-mail attachment. In this chapter, we offer tips on how to craft useful materials to supplement and extend your presentation. We summarize the Tips in Exhibit 8.1.

Exhibit 8.1 Crafting Handouts and Supplements Tips

This Tip ...	Provides guidance on how to ...	It is particularly useful for ...
Tip 23: *Lecture Map*	Create a handout that succinctly reveals the intellectual infrastructure of a lecture	Helping students navigate their way as they listen to and later recall lecture content
Tip 24: *Content-Rich Handout*	Give students a comprehensive, data-intense resource that supports the lecture presentation	Providing students with detailed information so that they can focus attention on understanding rather than taking extensive verbatim notes
Tip 25: *Infodeck*	Use presentation software to create a document that combines text and visual information related to lecture content	Creating a more-effective follow-up reference than your slide deck
Tip 26: *Annotated Reference Page*	Create an abstract along with a list of sources related to the lecture topic	Providing students with references they can go to for further information

ENGAGING LECTURE TIP 23

Lecture Map

Despite your best efforts to craft a clear and logically coherent lecture, sometimes an audience needs additional guidance in order to follow your train of thought. This is particularly true when the audience is unfamiliar with your topic. A *Lecture Map* provides such guidance through a representation of the key areas or intellectual structure of the lecture content.

Using a *Lecture Map* can help students understand the lecture as a conceptual whole. It can help orient them to the content by conveying the central concepts you will cover and illustrate how the pieces fit together. A *Lecture Map* also helps students maintain focus and attention by encouraging them to actively seek to fill in the gaps between those key pieces. In addition, because the *Lecture Map* provides an itinerary of sorts for the lecture, it is helpful for students to know where they are at a given moment during the talk, which helps them to focus on what you are saying. A *Lecture Map* makes an excellent handout that can also help students structure their notes according to the key points.

Key Idea

A *Lecture Map* reveals the intellectual infrastructure of a lecture so students can better follow it.

A *Lecture Map* can range from a simple listing of topics to a complex graphic of the lecture content. To create a *Lecture Map,* complete the following steps:

1. Determine the scope of your map. For this, you should have already developed the lecture content (see Chapter 4 for Tips on how to generate the content) and now have a good idea of how to bound the content to illustrate it in the map.
2. Consider what you will include on your map. You may choose key concepts (see Tip 5: *Sticky Note Diagrams* for a process for identifying them) or organizational elements from other Tips, such as Tip 7: *Logical Patterns* and Tip 15: *Signposts.*
3. Determine how detailed your map will be. You will typically choose three to five key points, but if you are using Tip 9: *Linked Lecturettes,* you may choose to join more concepts together.
4. Consider how the ideas may be best visually represented. You may want to use a list or outline. You could choose a graphic organizer, such as a flow chart, a concept map, a Venn diagram, or a free-form, loose, spatial arrangement. Alternately, you may want to consider creating your own *Sketch Notes* (Technique 17) to serve as a lecture map.
5. Choose how you will create the map. You may choose a simple word processing program and use drawing features such as SmartArt, but there are also several mapping programs available online for free use (e.g., Popplet or Bubbl.us) that can help in creating more complex maps. Or you may want to do it by hand.
6. Create a handout so that students can keep the map visible at all times.

Although a *Lecture Map* makes an excellent handout, if you prefer, you can hang a *Lecture Map* somewhere in the classroom (or post it online). If you choose this route, you should ensure that students can see the map at all times during the lecture.

In addition to a map of a specific lecture, you can also consider creating a larger map of the full course content, mapping out where each lecture fits within the broader context of the course content.

Example

A professor teaching graduate students about the profession of teaching was preparing for a lecture on relative grading and created the following *Lecture Map* cast as Technique 13: *Guided Notes* that students could use to take notes during the lecture.

Education Lecture Notes: Relative Grading

What is relative grading?

____

____

____

Name three forms of relative grading:

1. ____________________________
2. ____________________________
3. ____________________________

When should instructors use relative grading?

____

____

____

When should instructors avoid relative grading?

____

____

____

Figures 8.1 to 8.3 provide additional styles of lecture maps.

Definitions
Structures
Mechanics
Measurements of pulmonary functions
Cellular respiration, pulmonary disorders
Blood gases, diffusion
Neural control of respiration
Hemoglobin (and disorders)
Transport of CO_2
Acid-base balance

Figure 8.1 Simple List Lecture Map: Physiology of Respiration
Source: Adapted from Sarma (2015).

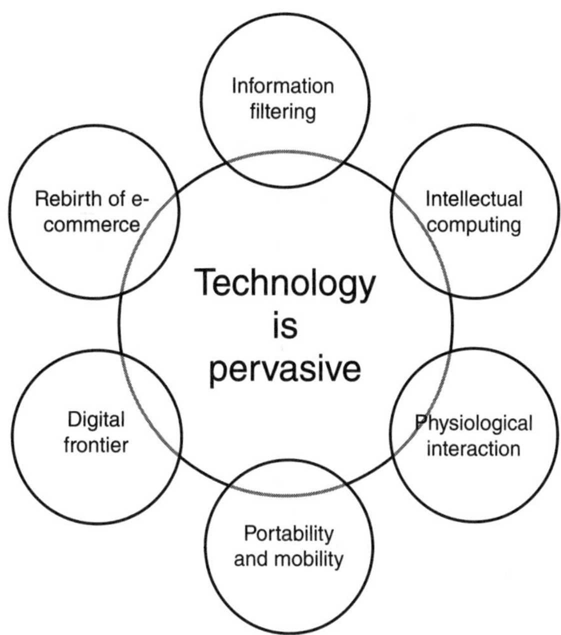

Figure 8.2 Graphic Organizer Lecture Map: Emerging Technologies
Source: Adapted from Walker (n.d.).

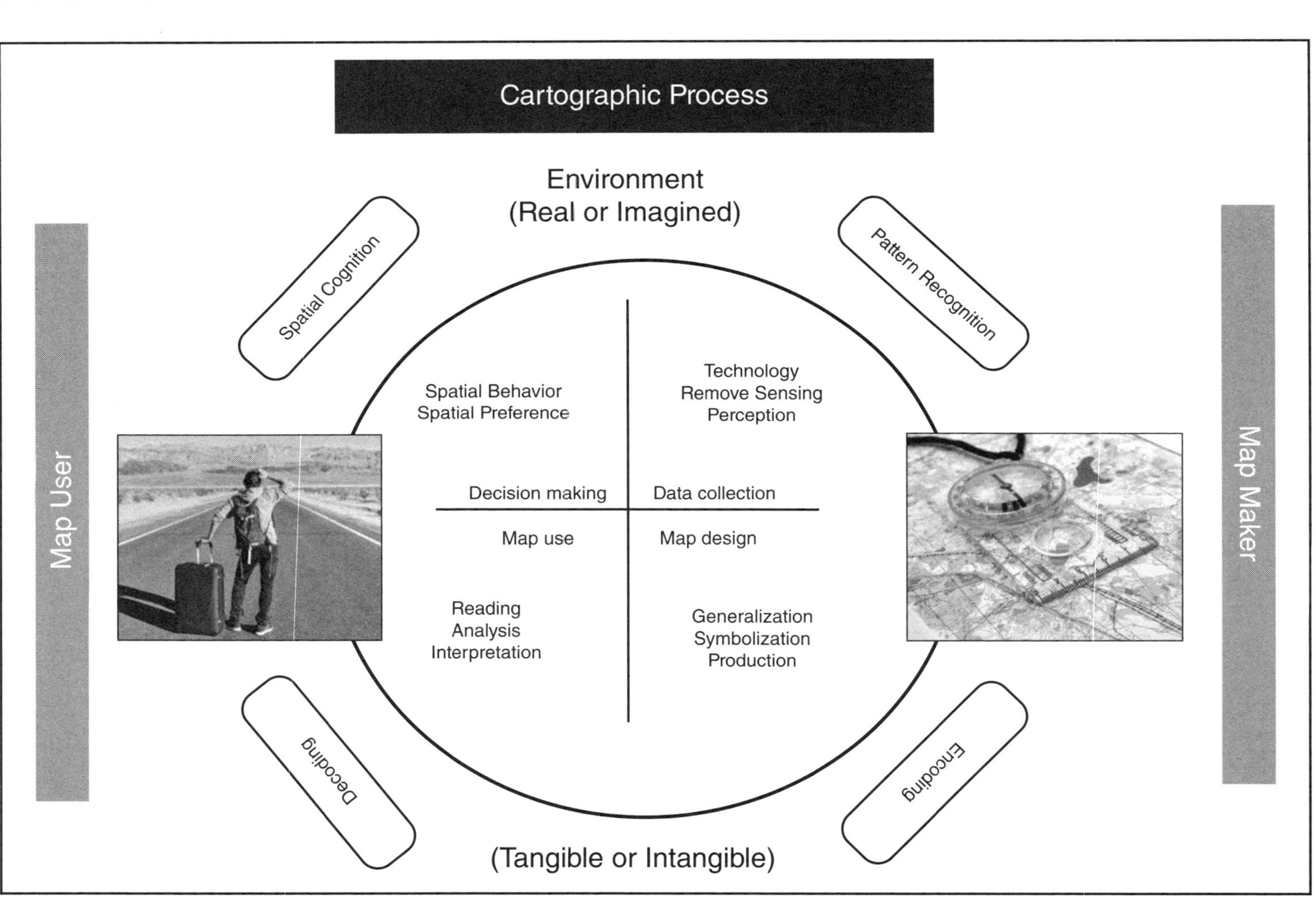

Figure 8.3 Visual Representation Lecture Map: Cartography

Source: Adapted from Tsou (2015).

Key References and Resources

Gooblar, D. (2013c). Lecture map. *Pedagogy Unbound.* Retrieved from www.pedagogyunbound.com/tips-index/2013/8/23/make-a-lecture-map-to-help-students-follow

Sarma, R. (2015). *Guest lecture to biomed department.* Retrieved from http://slideplayer.com/slide/4716954/

Staley, C. (2003). *Fifty ways to leave your lectern.* Belmont, CA: Wadsworth/Cengage Learning.

Tsou, T. (2015). *Geographic and spatial reasoning.* Retrieved from http://map.sdsu.edu/geog104/lecture/unit-2.htm

Walker, J. (n.d.). *Emerging trends and technologies.* Retrieved from http://slideplayer.com/slide/6321152/

ENGAGING LECTURE TIP 24

Content-Rich Handout

Students will often ask instructors for their presentation slides after a lecture. Slides do not make the best handouts, however, because they are designed for the purpose of being displayed rather than for reading and studying later. When done well, they will contain only minimal information, perhaps just a few words or an image. Thus students are not likely to benefit from these slides outside of the context for which they are intended: the lecture itself. Moreover, not only is reviewing minimalist slides ineffective for studying but also the idea of students printing the high number of slides seems wasteful and is not something that we want to encourage.

Many times, however, when students ask for slides, what they really want is a handout. They want something that they can take with them from the lecture to refer to later, for example, when studying for a test. Written documents are the best option for providing detailed information from the lecture. Thus, instead of simply handing out copies of your slides, consider creating *Content-Rich Handouts* to accompany your lecture. *Content-Rich Handouts* are intentionally designed documents that convey written information about the lecture topic. They may also contain images, figures, or diagrams to better illustrate the content.

The purpose of *Content-Rich Handouts* is to provide students with a useful artifact from your lecture that can take the place of slides handouts. They should supplement rather than replace the lecture. They should be documents that provide students with information that they can learn from on their own at a later time.

Key Idea

Slides and handouts are different things. Instead of printing, posting, or e-mailing slides from your lecture, create a *Content-Rich Handout* that will benefit students by providing them with a focused resource.

To create a *Content-Rich Handout,* follow these steps:

1. Review your lecture and identify the important points; write them out. Use these points as your main headers and subheaders, as appropriate.
2. Provide supporting details and explanations for each point. Write in complete sentences, not simply bullet points (of course if you want to add in a list with bullet points, that's fine—the goal is to write fully formed, useful content).
3. As you create the content, make sure it is important and useful. Avoid providing any unnecessary or distracting details.
4. Consider whether an illustration, graphic, or chart would make the content more comprehensible.

5. Think about the design and how to lay the information out. Many people simply use word processing and export to a PDF, and others use desktop publishing software to create a professional look.
6. Include a clear identification of the lecture, with your name, course information, the lecture name, and date.
7. Consider adding scholarly references that students could turn to for further reading or studying.
8. Decide when you will give the students the handout. Some faculty members prefer to provide the handout before the lecture so that students may glance at it, and others prefer to provide it at the end of the lecture so that students are not distracted. A good guiding principle is that if your material is particularly complex, providing it ahead of time and allowing students the opportunity to read through it will likely be effective. Otherwise, provide it at the end of the lecture or class session.

Example

Elizabeth, a music history professor was preparing a lecture on Native American music. During class time, she wanted students to be able to focus on her presentation without excessive anxiety that they capture every word in their notes. She told students at the beginning of class that she wanted them to be engaged and "present," and that she would provide a handout at the end of class that they could use for later reference. See Figure 8.4 for her lecture slides and Figure 8.5 for the corresponding handout she provided.

Commonalities in Traditional Native American Music

1. Functional
2. Strong spiritual associations
3. Primarily vocal, correlated with text and dance

Commonalities in Traditional Native American Music

4. Structural Characteristics
   a. Rhythm
   b. Melody
   c. Harmony
   d. Texture
   e. Instrumentation
   f. Form

Figure 8.4 Lecture Slides

Lecture Seven

Traditional Native American Music

Native American culture is preserved by the thousands of people with Indian ethnicity who participate in contemporary powwows.

Structural Characteristics

Music was functional

Native American music had a practical purpose, and consisted primarily of songs and dances that were related to various activities such hunting, healing, and preparing for or celebrating battles. Music was not created for its aesthetic beauty, but rather as an element within a larger context. Music to accompany sacred rituals or to serve as the sacred act itself was very important

Music had strong spiritual associations

Many Native Americans believed that music possessed spiritual power that was given to human beings through songs. The stories describing these gifts varied, with some groups believing that all songs were given at the beginning of time, while others believed that the music existed in the universe and was conveyed to humans as needed through dreams or visions. Because music was so powerfully connected to the spiritual world, music was judged by how effective it was in contributing to the function, such as healing or sustaining crops, rather than how it sounded. In a similar manner, musicians and composers were not valued for their musical knowledge, technical

competence, or creativity, but for their expertise in spiritual matters. Many songs were owned by individuals and valued for their personal power. Because of this, the individuals needed to protect the songs and perform them only under special ritualistic or ceremonial circumstances.

Music was strongly correlated with text and dance

Native American music was primarily vocal and because of this, there was a strong correlation with text. The musical phrase closely resembled the rhythm and contour of the way the words would be spoken. There were also many Native cultures that used verbal structures that are not part of regular spoken language. One example is "vocables," which are non-translatable syllables such as hey, ya, and ho that don't translate into any specific text but rather convey an emotional meaning or identified a particular song or kinds of songs. Dance was also an important part of rituals, and so the music for the dance was closely related to dance movement.

Music was primarily vocal with percussive accompaniment

Singing was the dominant way to create music. Many types of vocal embellishment (such as gutturals, "quivers" and slurs) were incorporated into a song as well as the imitation of the sounds of birds and animals. The sung melodies were often accompanied by drums or rattles.

Rhythm, Melody, and Harmony

European-based rhythmic organization is divisive, but in indigenous cultures the rhythmic organization was additive, with a steady, uniform beat serving as the foundation for the piece, often derived from the heartbeat. Most melodies were constructed in a small range, rarely over an octave. They were also frequently downward terraced or descending in contour, starting on a higher note and then moving downward. Often the melody ended at about an octave below where it started. The scales were organized into patterns that were different than the dominant major and minor system with which we are most familiar, and they consisted of microtonal pitches that were closer together than our current Western pitch system.

Textures, Form, and Instrumentation

Monophony and heterophony were the most typical textures. An interesting value was that music consisted of sound occupying space, so Native Americans often valued sound coming from multiple directions, such as singers moving around and engulfing their listeners with song. The organization of the form was dictated by the text or the dance movements, and the style of performance was typically direct or responsorial. The use of incomplete repetitions was also common, which means that the second version of a phrase did not include the beginning notes of the phrase's first iteration.

Figure 8.5 Handout

Key References and Resources

Ford, N., McCullough, M., & Schutta, N. T. (2012). *Presentation patterns: Techniques for crafting better presentations.* Boston, MA: Addison Wesley.

Johnson, A. (n.d.). *Good handout design: How to make sure your students are actually learning from your lecture notes.* Retrieved from www.pcc.edu/resources/tlc/cascade/documents/PCCHandouts_handout.pdf

Reynolds, G. (n.d.). *Presentation zen: How to design & deliver presentations like a pro.* Retrieved from www.garrreynolds.com/Presentation/pdf/presentation_tips.pdf

ENGAGING LECTURE TIP 25

Infodeck

The development of presentation packages such as PowerPoint, Keynote, and Prezi has shaped how people communicate and what we expect from communications. Presentation packages enable us to create and share documents with images, text, and even audio and video. Some people like the presentation format so much that they create and share content that is not ever meant to be presented but instead is meant to be used or consumed at the audience's leisure and at the individual's own pace. Documents created with presentation tools and meant to convey information on their own are called *Infodecks,* and they allow for multimodal distribution of information.

An *Infodeck* provides the means for distributing information without a live presenter. *Infodecks* permit lecturers to use a spatial layout that is congruent with the content to share information. These decks also allow for including diagrams and images as elements of communication. They encourage professors to highlight key points and minimize text in a way that will facilitate students' understanding of the information.

Sharing an *Infodeck* does not mean sharing slides from the presentation. Indeed, an *Infodeck* may be used in lieu of the slides. *Infodecks* can be particularly useful when accompanying an oral-only presentation because they provide students with information they want, and have even come to expect, outside of the class so that the lecturer can be more in-the-moment with the students. *Infodecks* can also be useful in online classes and with video lectures, with the lecturer talking directly to the students during the video lecture and supplementing this with an *Infodeck.*

Key Idea

Providing students with an *Infodeck* that combines text and visual information related to the lecture content can be a more-effective follow-up reference than your slide deck.

Creating an *Infodeck* is easy in theory but challenging in practice. *Infodecks* should be content-rich, multimodal documents from the outset.

- Decide that you will not use the document you are about to create for a presentation; begin your work with the intention to create a standalone document that possesses the unique positive qualities of an *Infodeck.*
- Choose the presentation software of your choice.
- Use the software to create slides that have text and images to share information related to an upcoming or just presented lecture. Limit text so that you don't create what Fowler (2012b) describes as a *slideument*—a document that uses presentation software but includes too much text.
- Add audio if you wish (many presentation packages now allow you to add in audio segments to accompany each slide).

- Determine how you will share the *Infodeck* with students. It can be distributed on a printout or alternately distributed electronically, such as online. (*Note:* distributing through attachment can be a challenge if students don't all have the same software; instead, choose an online platform that is compatible across software.)

Infodecks may also be used in addition to slides from a lecture. In Chapter 7, we suggested several presentation formats that rely on using many slides in a given lecture, often with a single word or image. Printing these slides is not desirable because they likely hold little meaning outside of the presentation and the excessive printing would be wasteful. *Infodecks* can cover the same content with fewer slides and more explanation. Thus they can stand in for lecture slides, which are meant to be viewed in the moment.

Example

Figure 8.6 is an example of a page from an *Infodeck* we created on learning assessment techniques.

What is a Learning Assessment Technique (LAT)?

A Learning Assessment Technique (LAT) is an integrated structure that helps teachers to do the following:

1. Identify significant learning goals
2. Implement effective learning activities
3. Analyze and report on learning outcomes

Each technique is embedded within a three-phase, six-step process designed to support teachers in their efforts to assess student learning efficiently and effectively.

Figure 8.6 Sample *Infodeck*

Key References and Resources

Ford, N., McCullough, M., & Schutta, N. T. (2012). *Presentation patterns: Techniques for crafting better presentations.* Boston, MA: Addison Wesley.

Fowler, M. (2012a). *The future is not just NoSQL, it's polyglot persistence.* Retrieved from https://dzone.com/articles/polyglot-persistence-future

Fowler, M. (2012b). *Infodeck.* Retrieved from http://martinfowler.com/bliki/Infodeck.html

Robinson, S. (2013). *Beware of the SLIDEUMENT!* Retrieved from www.slideshare.net/SheilaBRobinson/unconventional-wisdom-26429659/43-Beware_the_SLIDEUMENT_This_is

ENGAGING LECTURE TIP 26

Annotated Reference Page

Most of us who make presentations or give lectures in class draw information from several sources in preparation for any given session. It can be useful to provide students with information about the sources we used. An *Annotated Reference Page* is a handout that begins with an abstract and then provides a list of sources related to the lecture topic. Each citation is followed by a brief annotation or discussion of the source. Typically, an *Annotated Reference Page* is used as a supplementary resource in conjunction with other handouts.

An *Annotated Reference Page* provides students who want to learn more about a topic with a starting point. It can help them to see how complex a topic is as well as how much work goes into lecture presentation. Using an *Annotated Reference Page* also models good professional practice by citing sources and illustrating the kinds of sources that are appropriate to scholarly work.

Key Idea

Provide students with an *Annotated Reference Page* to supplement a lecture and other lecture handouts.

To create an *Annotated Reference Page*, complete the following steps:

1. Write an abstract that describes the lecture topic. This content should be relatively brief, typically ranging from one hundred to three hundred words.
2. Select the references that you will include in the handout. You don't have to include every source you reference. Instead, you may want to choose the top three to five sources.
3. Provide citation information for each source. The citation will include the relevant bibliographic information, formatted according to your particular academic field (e.g., MLA, APA, Chicago). Citations are typically organized alphabetically but also may be organized in order of importance or alternately in order of appearance in the lecture.
4. Provide a discussion (annotation) of each source in which you summarize the content of the source, assess its usefulness, and perhaps describe your reaction it.
5. Be sure to include pertinent course information on the handout, such as the name of the course, your name, the date, and the lecture topic.

Example

Abbreviated Annotated Bibliography on Note-taking

Abstract

The question of whether to provide students with handouts from a college-level lecture has been a challenging one for many professors to answer. On the one hand, some faculty members believe that students should shoulder the burden of learning outside of the classroom. They also believe that good note-taking reinforces learning. On the other hand, some faculty members believe that they are responsible for student learning, including some of the learning that happens outside of the classroom. They also believe that even if note-taking can reinforce learning, not everyone has the skill or ability to take good notes. A compromise between these two positions is the approach most supported by the literature. That is, instead of providing a full set of lecture notes, scaffold learning by providing one that encourages learning. In addition to this *Annotated Reference Page,* we also recommend creating a Tip 23: *Lecture Map,* Tip 24: *Content-Rich Handout,* or Tip 25: *Infodeck.*

Related Sources

Brazeau, G. (2006). Handouts in the classroom: Is note taking a lost skill? *American Journal of Pharmaceutical Education, (70)*2, 1–2.

This article considers note-taking to be a skill. The author also believes that professors should be responsible for helping students to develop this skill. The author advocates for less content in any slides a professor uses in class and few to no handouts in order to encourage student note-taking. This article provides a useful review of the literature on the topic area.

Fjortoft, N. (2005). Students' motivations for class attendance. *American Journal of Pharmaceutical Education, 69,* 107–112.

The researcher sought to uncover factors that contributed to class attendance. Findings indicated that providing partial handouts to fill in during class motivated students to attend. The author also found that providing full lecture notes was related to student absences.

Kobayashi, K. (2006). Combined effects of note-taking/-reviewing on learning and the enhancement through interventions: A meta-analytical review. *Educational Psychology, 26,* 459–477.

This study reported the results of a meta-analysis of thirty-three research studies investigating student note-taking. The researcher examined the constructs of note-taking and note-taking with and without handouts. The researcher found that note-taking with a handout presenting a general outline correlated with the largest positive effect on student performance.

Titsworth, B. (2004). Student note taking: The effects of teacher immediacy and clarity. *Communication Education, 53,* 305–320.

This author evaluated the quality of student notes taken in multiple situations. Study results indicated that students who are provided with cues about organization or who participate in classes that develop ideas more deeply instead of broader coverage of several topics prepared notes that appeared more thorough and accurate than did their counterparts. The author suggested that instructor approaches can effect changes in student note-taking patterns.

Key References and Resources

Mitkis, J. (2009). *The use of classroom handouts.* Retrieved from www.westpoint.edu/cfe/Literature/Mikits_09.pdf

University of Central Florida. (2011). *Annotated bibliography.* University Writing Center. Retrieved from https://uwc.cah.ucf.edu/wp-content/uploads/sites/9/2016/10/Annotated_Bibliography_MLA.pdf

CHAPTER 9

Demonstrating Readiness

As college teachers, most of us want students to come to class prepared, but sometimes we lose sight of the importance of being prepared ourselves. Effective lecturing requires extensive preparation. Demonstrating that you are prepared for the session and invested in student learning goes a long way toward promoting a positive learning environment. Research indicates that students are more motivated to learn when their professor demonstrates enthusiasm, professionalism, and caring, and being well prepared for each class conveys these qualities to them. In this chapter, we offer Tips that will help you to prepare for your presentation and thus ensure that the class session goes smoothly. We summarize the Tips in Exhibit 9.1.

Exhibit 9.1 Demonstrating Readiness Tips

This Tip ...	Provides guidance on how to ...	It is particularly useful for ...
Tip 27: *Out Loud*	Practice your lecture in real time	Smoothing out your delivery, uncovering potential problems, and fine-tuning your message
Tip 28: *Lecture Supply Kit*	Pack a bag of supplies that you can take with you to every lecture	Ensuring you have the tools required to present effectively
Tip 29: *Dress for Success*	Dress appropriately when delivering a lecture so that students see that you are a professional	Conveying to students that you take your role as a teacher seriously
Tip 30: *Book and Check*	Make sure the room and equipment are appropriate and functioning well	Uncovering potential problems so that you can solve them prior to the lecture

ENGAGING LECTURE TIP 27

Out Loud

Most lecturers who are considered great at their craft have earned their distinction by hard work and perseverance. They know that it takes time and energy to create a memorable lecture and then careful, concentrated practice to do it well. As a college instructor, you have many responsibilities, and you will not likely have the time and energy to invest this kind of effort in every lecture. However, for those lectures that are particularly important or challenging, we recommend that you practice it *Out Loud* and in real time.

Practicing enables you to polish and refine your work. Your ideas will likely sound different in your head than they do out loud, so practicing gives you a chance to revise and refine. *Out Loud* also enables you to be more confident, which usually results in a better delivery. Moreover, this Tip can help you gauge how much time the presentation you have planned will actually take, which can help you to ensure that you have the appropriate amount of material for the class session as well as improve the timing and pacing of the session.

Key Idea

When you practice a lecture, it not only smooths out your delivery but also enables you to fine-tune your message.

After you have planned your lecture, practice it aloud. If you have slides, work through the slide deck from start to finish. In your practice(s), aim for the following:

- Focus on the content to discover any problems with your language or flow, locate any missing transitions between ideas, and identify any information you need to add or remove.
- Consider your timing and pacing. Time the practice run to ensure that the lecture fills the time you have allocated for it (see Tip 12: *Lecture Plan*). Check your overall rate of speech and think about whether it feels too fast or too slow.
- Try audio or video recording this practice because doing so will make you more aware of any undesirable habits. For example, you may find that you need to eliminate waste words (*uh, um, like*). Alternately, you may find that you fidget or pace while talking and thus you can try to reduce these behaviors.

If you have the opportunity, do a trial run in the space in which you will give the lecture, particularly for the first lecture of a course. This step will help you to figure out details such as where you have to look to see slides, how you can move around the room comfortably, and where and how students will be seated.

Example

A new adjunct instructor who was scheduled to be evaluated by her dean was particularly anxious because the evaluation was high stakes: this evaluation would determine whether she would be offered an assignment the next term. She followed the advice in *Out Loud* and practiced her lecture several times, revising it after each delivery. Not only did this procedure help ease her anxiety but also it helped ensure that she gave her best possible lecture.

Key References and Resources

Ford, N., McCullough, M., & Schutta, N. T. (2012). *Presentation patterns: Techniques for crafting better presentations.* Boston, MA: Addison Wesley.

University of Waterloo. (n.d.). *Lecturing effectively.* Centre for Teaching Excellence. Retrieved from https://uwaterloo.ca/centre-for-teaching-excellence/teaching-resources/teaching-tips/lecturing-and-presenting/delivery/lecturing-effectively-university

ENGAGING LECTURE TIP 28

Lecture Supply Kit

As college instructors, we have plenty of things to do. Our teaching activities alone take considerable time and attention, and we are often prepping multiple sections at once. We spend so much time planning the content and the pacing that we can sometimes leave the details unattended. For example, if during a lecture we decide to write on the board and only then realize that there are no markers available, it is not only disruptive to our flow but also can leave us looking underprepared.

Dealing with details in advance can make us better at our jobs and our lectures go more smoothly. In this Tip, we recommend preparing a *Lecture Supply Kit* that you can take with you to each class session. This *Lecture Supply Kit* should be filled with the things that you think you will or could potentially need during the session.

Key Idea

Pack a bag of supplies that you can take with you to every lecture to ensure that you have the tools you need.

When assembling your kit, consider the following items:

High Tech

- **Laptop.** Even if your room has a computer and projector, unless you believe that it is guaranteed to work, you may want to bring along your own laptop as backup.
- **Wireless slide remote.** If you are using slides, bring along your own slide remote so that you can move around and still advance your slides.
- **Laser pointer.** If you need to point out details on a slide, particularly in a large class, you may want to bring along a laser pointer. Some slide remotes come equipped with those as well.
- **AC adapter, power brick, charger.** Even if you think your laptop has a full charge, you may be surprised how quickly it can run down. If you are using your own laptop, consider packing a backup means for accessing power.
- **Projector adapter.** If you are bringing a laptop and you use a Mac and your institution uses Windows (or vice versa) you may also need to include a projector adapter.
- **USB drives.** You may store your presentation on a USB drive, but you should also ensure that you have at least one backup: another USB drive, a portable hard drive, or a cloud storage system such as Dropbox or Box.

Low Tech

- **Writing space and writing implement.** Even if you plan to use a slide deck, you will likely occasionally need or want to write something somewhere that the students can see. You may have a whiteboard or a chalkboard fixed in the classroom, but if the board is under the projector screen and forces you into an either-or situation, you may find you want to regularly bring flip chart paper. Additionally, you will want spare chalk or dry erase markers.

- **Pencil, pen, and paper.** You may find that you would like to make a note of something to follow up on from the session. Be sure you have something to write with and to write on.

Basic Survival

- **Bottled water.** You will want to have something to drink in order to stay hydrated. Even talking for short periods of time can cause wear to your vocal cords, and you may find that you have a dry throat that you need to soothe.
- **Cough drops or mints.** Sometimes water is insufficient to soothe a dry throat. Consider bringing along cough drops or mints.
- **Tissues.** Be prepared for a sneeze, a cold, a spill, or other unexpected event that can cause you to need to have tissues or a handkerchief or even wet wipes to manage the problem.

Example

An adjunct professor who taught on several different campuses in a large, traffic-congested urban area wanted to be calm, collected, and professional despite the myriad stresses of her "freeway flyer" commute. She therefore purchased a portable office roller bag for books and course file folders and then also stocked it with things she anticipated she might need at one time or another. This included the various items already identified in this Tip, but also basic office supplies, food, and a laminated quick reference card that included the phone numbers for roadside assistance as well as the classified staff members at the different institutions she could call should she encounter an unavoidable delay or experience an emergency.

Key References and Resources

Ford, N., McCullough, M., & Schutta, N. T. (2012). *Presentation patterns: Techniques for crafting better presentations.* Boston, MA: Addison Wesley.

University of Waterloo, Center for Teaching Excellence. (n.d.). *Lecturing effectively.* Retrieved from https://uwaterloo.ca/centre-for-teaching-excellence/teaching-resources/teaching-tips/lecturing-and-presenting/delivery/lecturing-effectively-university

ENGAGING LECTURE TIP 29

Dress for Success

One thing that many of us find appealing about the professoriate is the lack of a formal dress code. Indeed, when we are being socialized into the profession as graduate students, the typical attire can be jeans and sweatshirts. It would be nice to think that what we wear as professors doesn't matter, that students want to learn from us despite our appearances. However, there is evidence to suggest that what we wear *does* matter to students. They have indicated that they pay attention to our attire in plenty of student evaluations (and likewise in students' discussions of their professors on Twitter) in which they focus on what the teacher has worn rather than the teacher's teaching effectiveness. We suspect that our attire matters to many of our colleagues as well. Although most of us clearly have the general idea that we need to dress professionally, there are a few special considerations for those of us dressing specifically for our teaching roles.

Key Idea

Dress for Success when delivering a lecture so that students see that you take your role as a teacher seriously.

A few suggestions for dressing for success:

- **Dress in something that makes you feel like you look good.** It helps to feel like a million dollars when you are giving a lecture. Ensuring that you do will increase your confidence level, and students will be able to sense that.
- **Dress in something that allows you to move.** Don't wear clothes that restrict your movement. Most of us don't stay fixed in the exact same position throughout a lecture, and our clothing needs to go along with us. Don't wear anything painful—like an overly tight waistband or shoes that hurt your feet. Students will be able to sense your discomfort, even if they can't identify the source of it.
- **Dress consistently with the persona you are trying to convey.** As college instructors, we craft our own teaching personas, whether we do so intentionally or unintentionally. Our clothing contributes to that. We may adopt the traditional dress of the professors (the tweed coat and button-down), or we may choose to intentionally subvert it and dress more casually.
- **Dress to signal your professional affiliation.** We may decide to go formal with a suit and a tie or heels if those are the norms of our disciplinary fields (e.g., if we teach in law or business). We may go with upscale casual, for instance, if we teach in teacher education. Or we wear clothing that is field or discipline specific, for example, lab coat if we teach a science lab, dance attire if we teach dance, exercise clothes if we teach physical education, or a smock if we teach art. What we wear signals our professional affiliation.
- **Dress like a grown-up.** Whatever you decide to wear to convey your persona, it is probably a mistake to try to look hip, trendy, or like a student because doing so can make professors look foolish.

Example

A newly hired professor who had just graduated herself wanted to dress in a manner that clearly distinguished her from the students she was now teaching. Her current wardrobe consisted of the informal clothing she had worn as a graduate student. She therefore decided to make an appointment with a personal stylist at a department store in the city to which she had moved after accepting her new position. The personal stylist worked with her to identify a style that not only supported a professional persona but also was appropriate for the cultural norms and weather patterns of the new locale. She could not afford to immediately purchase a new wardrobe, but she began with some foundational pieces and added to her wardrobe as she could afford it. When the academic term started, being *Dressed for Success* helped the professor to feel more confident.

Key References and Resources

Jensen, E. (2008). A call for professional attire. *Inside Higher Ed.* Retrieved from www.insidehighered.com/views/2008/02/08/call-professional-attire

Lang, J. M. (2005). Looking like a professor. *Chronicle of Higher Education, 51*(47). Retrieved from http://old.biz.colostate.edu/mti/tips/pages/LookingLikeaProfessor.aspx

Morgan, N. (2013). How to avoid disaster: Six rules for what to wear when giving a speech. *Forbes.* Retrieved from www.forbes.com/sites/nickmorgan/2013/12/05/how-to-avoid-disaster-six-rules-for-what-to-wear-when-giving-a-speech/#2c5dd6022dce

ENGAGING LECTURE TIP 30

Book and Check

How many times have you been at a scheduled presentation where the lecturer arrives a few minutes late looking a bit lost and frazzled? Or at a presentation in which the lecturer comes in on time but then has to fumble with the technology for several minutes of the session before getting it to work? Or perhaps the lecturer has embedded a video in his or her slide deck that won't play, or alternately that can't be heard because the audio is not turned on? College and university students experience situations such as these too often. *Do not be this professor!* Instead, *Book and Check* your space and your technology well ahead of the lecture.

Using the *Book and Check* Tip can prepare you to go to your lecture session with confidence. Being assured that you are ready will help you appear and be more calm and collected during the lecture itself. It will also help students have a positive impression of you. Instead of looking incompetent, you will look professional and self-assured. When you appear to treat students with respect—the respect that comes with adequate preparation and being considerate of their time—they will return the sentiment.

Key Idea

Make sure the room and equipment are appropriate and functioning in advance of the lecture.

Before Your First Lecture

- **If it is not preassigned, book your room.** If you plan well ahead, you may be able to request a room that is most appropriate for your needs.
- **Check the technology that comes with the room.** If necessary, reserve the additional technology you will need for the session or term.
- **Visit your lecture space before the first class meeting.** Consider the layout of the desks and where the front of the classroom is. Decide where you will stand to lecture and how you will move. Doing so will help you mentally prepare for the session.

Before Every Lecture

- **Plan to arrive early, earlier than you think is strictly necessary.** You may find that you need the time to get ready, and if you don't, you can greet the students as they arrive.
- **Ensure the technology is in working order.** In particular, if you are using slides, make sure that the computer will turn on and that the projector is in working order.
- **Make sure that the technology is turned on before your lecture begins.** If you are using a video, make sure that it will play and that the sound is working.

- **Have a backup plan, particularly for technology.** Even if you have checked ahead, and even if you arrive early enough, there will likely be glitches. Have a plan B in case of technical failure. For example, consider *Slide Replacements* (Tip 22) as a backup plan. With a backup plan, you will be prepared for unforeseen glitches and be able to respond in a manner that students will respect and appreciate.

Example

An instructor who was chronically late and unprepared for class justified his behavior by saying that he simply had too many things to do. But when his tardiness became an increasingly frequent complaint in student evaluations, the dean suggested he enroll in a time management class being offered through the university's community short-course program. As a student in the course, the instructor was surprised to learn how many negative explanations there were for chronic tardiness (the late person needed the extra attention, was selfish and inconsiderate, disrespectful of the people he kept waiting, and so forth), and being on time had many positive associations (the punctual person was in control of his or her life, respectful of other people's time, valued the activity sufficiently to prepare appropriately, and so forth). The course also gave him strategies for planning his time better. He and students were happier with his new efforts to be punctual and prepared for class.

Key References and Resources

Stanford Teaching Commons. (n.d.). *Lecture guidelines.* Retrieved from https://teachingcommons.stanford.edu/resources/teaching-resources/teaching-strategies/checklist-effective-lecturing/lecturing-guidelines

University of Waterloo, Center for Teaching Excellence. (n.d.). *Lecturing effectively.* Retrieved from https://uwaterloo.ca/centre-for-teaching-excellence/teaching-resources/teaching-tips/lecturing-and-presenting/delivery/lecturing-effectively-university

CHAPTER 10

Generating Enthusiasm and Interest

Those of us who have been teaching for some time know that motivation is critical to students' ability to learn. Students who are highly motivated to learn from our lectures are willing to focus their attention and invest the effort required to understand and remember the information we present. Research on lecturing and learning supports the importance of motivation for learning, particularly highlighting declines in learning due to low motivation (see, for example, Bolkan, Goodboy, & Kelsey, 2016; Komarraju & Karau, 2008). We *want* students to be motivated to learn from our lectures, but getting them to engage with a presentation can be difficult, especially if they don't have much interest in the topic. How can we help students be motivated to put in the effort to learn from our lectures?

Although there are many definitions of and theories about motivation, researchers who specialize in motivation in the classroom (e.g., Wentzel & Brophy, 2014) rely on the *expectancy* × *value* model as an explanation. This model suggests that the amount of effort that people are

Exhibit 10.1 Generating Enthusiasm and Interest Tips

This Tip . . .	Provides guidance on how to . . .	It is particularly useful for . . .
Tip 31: *Lecture Preview*	Pique student interest in the upcoming lecture	Preparing students to come to the lecture already interested and ready to focus their attention on your presentation
Tip 32: *Meet and Greet*	Make students feel welcome before the start of each lecture	Signaling to students that you care
Tip 33: *Icebreakers*	Use fun and low-threat activities to help students get to know each other	Building class community
Tip 34: *Keep the Lights On*	Maintain a vibrant learning environment	Keeping students alert and encouraging visual contact between you and students
Tip 35: *The Hook*	Grab attention at the very beginning of the lecture	Seeding engagement from the start of your presentation
Tip 36: *Value Display*	Communicate the value of the lecture information	Demonstrating to students that the topic is worthy of their attention

willing to expend on a task is in proportion to the degree to which they expect to be able to successfully perform the task (*expectancy*) and the degree to which they value the rewards as well as the processes of the task itself (*value*). The techniques in Part 3 of this book are especially useful for promoting the high-expectancy component of motivation because they are designed to help students be successful in their efforts to learn from your lecture presentation. The Tips in Part 2 of this book are generally helpful in addressing both components of the motivation model, but the Tips in this chapter are especially useful for setting up conditions that encourage students to find value in your lecture presentation. We summarize the Tips in Exhibit 10.1.

References

Bolkan, S., Goodboy, A. K., & Kelsey, D. M. (2016). Instructor clarity and student motivation: Academic performance as a product of students' ability and motivation to process instructional material. *Communication Education, 65*(2), 129–148.

Komarraju, M., & Karau, S. J. (2008). Relationships between the perceived value of instructional techniques and academic motivation. *Journal of Instructional Psychology, 35*(1), 70–82.

Wentzel, K. R., & Brophy, J. (2014). *Motivating students to learn* (4th ed.). New York, NY: Routledge.

ENGAGING LECTURE TIP 31

Lecture Preview

Many of us provide a list of lecture topics in our syllabus, but students may not have viewed that document recently enough for it to stimulate their interest in the upcoming presentation. Consider doing a *Lecture Preview* about a forthcoming lecture. In a *Lecture Preview,* you share information about the topic and the lecture's main points in order to help students better prepare for the lecture. The preview can be sent electronically through the course site, e-mail, or social media.

A *Lecture Preview* lets students know that you are excited about the topic and are looking forward to it. If students think you are excited about it, they will likely be more excited, too. Advance preparation and enthusiasm for the topic will have a positive effect on the reception of the lecture and also has the potential to improve attendance and participation.

Key Idea

Pique student interest about the topic ahead of time with a *Lecture Preview.*

Following is the kind of information you might share:

- **The title.** Give your lecture a formal title and share the title with students. Choosing a title can often help you decide what the central message is, and it can help students understand it as well.
- **A short description.** Sharing a short description conveys information essential for students to think about prior to the lecture itself. If done well, it can also stimulate student interest in the lecture.
- **A rationale for why the topic is important**. In your preview, you can share information about where the lecture fits within the overall scheme of the course topics, within a given major, or even to potential future employment or functioning as a good citizen in society. This information can help students understand why they need this information.
- **A guiding question.** Offering a question to guide thinking before the lecture itself can encourage students to think ahead, and thus they will be more prepared for new information.

How you could share follows:

- **Class announcement.** This is one of the most common approaches to the *Lecture Preview.* At the end of class, simply announce the lecture topic for the next class session. The advantage to this approach is that you have a captive audience. The disadvantage is that absent students will not hear it.
- **Social media.** In a tweet with the course hashtag or a Facebook post on a dedicated course site, you can announce the topic of the lecture and any thoughts you have about it.

The advantage is that you use a communication form with which many students are comfortable. The disadvantage is that some students may not have access.

- **E-mail blast.** Sending an e-mail to the class enables you to share more information than you might otherwise be able to communicate at the end of a class or that you could fit into a tweet. Not all students check e-mail regularly, however.
- **Course site or blog.** If you have a course site or blog, you can share fuller information about the lecture, including visuals or audio to supplement the text. Some students, however, may not check the site regularly prior to class. A weekly "here's what we're doing in class this week" blog post or learning management system (LMS) announcement, either first thing Monday morning or last thing Friday afternoon, also helps a professor's organization.

Although you need not use all of the sharing forms of *Lecture Preview,* using multiple approaches helps you to reach the most students.

Example

An instructor of an English literature course wanted to generate enthusiasm and increase student preparation for her upcoming lecture on "The Lady of the Lake." Following are examples of the ways she implemented a *Lecture Preview.*

Class Announcement

Next session we will focus on "The Lady of the Lake," an influential poem that is fascinating for its cultural influence. Look forward to seeing you here.

Twitter Blast

Looking forward to #ENG534 this week. "Come one, come all" to learn more about "The Lady of the Lake." So pleased to be talking about such an important poem!

E-mail

Greetings ENG 534! Monday we focus on "The Lady of the Lake." The lady has played a pivotal role in countless stories, and I think you will find Scott's take on her to be truly individual. I will offer a brief lecture on the poem that I have titled "The influence of Scott's The Lady of the Lake: What Franz Shubert and Fredrick Douglass have in common." I will describe the six cantos as well as what I believe are the poem's key cultural influences. We will have an extended discussion about the poem, its meaning, and its significance. Be sure to complete the readings and think through the issues you can identify in the poem. Look forward to seeing you there!

Course Site

Lecture title. "The influence of Scott's 'The Lady of the Lake': What Franz Shubert and Fredrick Douglass Have in Common"

Lecture description. The lady has played a pivotal role in countless stories, and Scott's take on her is truly individual. I will describe some past depictions of the lady and compare and contrast them with Scott's. I will also share some ways in which Scott's work was influential in culture.

Guiding questions. What is different about this "Lady of the Lake" compared to earlier portrayals? What is so compelling about the story? What were its identifiable influences on culture? Why was it so influential?

Preparation. Be sure to complete the readings and think through the key questions. Look forward to seeing you there!

Key Reference and Resource

Ford, N., McCullough, M., & Schutta, N. T. (2012). *Presentation patterns: Techniques for crafting better presentations.* Boston, MA: Addison Wesley.

ENGAGING LECTURE TIP 32

Meet and Greet

Have you ever gone to a lecture where the speaker is at the front of the room looking very busy and certainly aloof? Or, have you gone to a lecture in which the speaker met you at the door or walked around the room talking with members of the audience? If so, which approach do you prefer? Most students probably prefer the second. A *Meet and Greet,* in which you briefly speak with students before the formal class session begins, can be a very good way to begin each lecture session.

Meet and Greet is important because it sets the tone for the class. Greeting the students signals that you care about them and are interested in getting to know them, which tends to improve student perception of not only you but also your teaching. By meeting students before the lecture begins, you may learn about the students and thus can target information to the particular group, or you may get information from them that can somehow help you during the lecture.

Key Idea

Greeting students before the start of each lecture session signals to them that you care. You can also use the interaction to glean helpful information.

Some ideas for the *Meet and Greet* are as follows:

- **The handshake.** If your class size allows it, meeting students at the door and shaking hands can make a strong connection with them.
- **The "name, please."** If you are trying to match names and faces, ask students to say their names as they enter the classroom.
- **The "hey, I know you."** If you want students to know that you have been paying attention, make a comment when they enter the room that shows that you know who they are. For example, "got your e-mail and sent you a response" or "hope the game went well last night" or "nice! A new laptop!" Some signal that you are making connections can help students to feel recognized and valued.
- **The small talk.** If you want to seem like a real person to students, you can simply engage them in some small talk. You might chat about the weather, an upcoming movie or sporting event, or a topic in the news.
- **The entry ticket.** If you want to check student understanding or completion of reading assignments, assign a question before class and ask students to bring their responses with them to class on an index card, being sure to include their names and the date. This is also a quick way to check roll. (See "Entry and Exit Tickets" in Barkley and Major, 2016, pp. 91–95, for additional guidance on using this technique to promote and assess learning.)

- **The handout.** As students enter the room, provide them with a handout for the session. (See Tips in Chapter 8 for ideas for good handouts.) This signals that you have important content and that you intend to get down to business immediately and not waste any class time.

Example

A professor received comments on her evaluation that she seemed aloof and unapproachable. In truth, she was simply shy, but she recognized that it was important for her to find a way to connect better with students. She therefore planned her time so that she could be at the door to greet students when they arrived. Concerned that she would be too uncomfortable engaging in informal conversations, she decided to combine her greetings with collecting entry tickets that gathered information about student understanding of key concepts and ideas. In this way, she was able to communicate to students not only that she cared about them as people but also that she was committed to helping them learn.

Key References and Resources

Barkley, E. F., & Major, C. H. (2016). *Learning assessment techniques: A handbook for college faculty.* San Francisco, CA: Jossey-Bass.

Ford, N., McCullough, M., & Schutta, N. T. (2012). *Presentation patterns: Techniques for crafting better presentations.* Boston, MA: Addison Wesley.

Lemov, D. (2010). *Teach like a champion: 49 strategies that put students on the path to success.* San Francisco, CA: Jossey-Bass.

ENGAGING LECTURE TIP 34

Keep the Lights On

Picture this: you've just begun your lecture and a student asks, "Can you turn off the lights so we can see the slides better?" You've got great slides. You worked hard on them. You *want* students to see them. And you may even think you want them to focus on the slides rather than focusing on you. Moreover, you may worry about eyestrain from having a bright room light and a bright slide screen. You consider turning the lights off to accommodate the student's request.

Our advice, however, is that you resist the temptation and *Keep the Lights On.* In the earlier days of slide projectors, many presenters did need to turn off the lights, but not so today. Most projectors today are bright enough to display slide content without dimming the lights. Moreover, *Keep the Lights On* allows for a more engaging lecture in which students actively listen and participate.

Key Idea

Keep the Lights On during a lecture to improve your communication with students.

Key points to support our suggestion to *Keep the Lights On* are as follows:

- **Your lecture will be more engaging.** Students will likely not be as engaged in a dark room, particularly if they don't see you or can avoid eye contact with you. If they wanted a simple narration of slides, a screencast or webinar would do just about as well. Being able to see each other can increase engagement between you and the students.
- **Students will understand you better if they can see you.** Facial expressions and body language help to convey meaning. The students are interpreting meaning based on your words (verbal), your voice (tone), and your nonverbal language (visual). Visual cues help people predict auditory cues that follow. The more students can see and hear you, the better they will understand your message.
- **Students won't be as likely to nap.** A dimly lit lecture hall is an invitation to nap, particularly if the lecture is immediately after lunch or early in the morning. Leaving the lights on can help tired students stay awake.
- **It will be easier for students to take notes.** If you want students to take notes during the lecture, they should be able to see what they are doing. Remember that you may have students with vision problems. Leaving the lights on can help them see what they are doing while they take notes from the lecture.

If you must make a compromise, try dimming some of the lights. In more modern rooms, it is likely possible to turn off the lights on the screen while keeping them on the lecturer.

Example

A professor who taught a class right after lunch struggled to keep students awake and engaged. It was particularly challenging because she relied on presentation slides and turned the lights off in order to display the slides more vividly. When she realized that a new projector had been installed in the classroom and that she no longer needed to dim lights to preserve slide display quality, she decided to *Keep the Lights On.* This, in combination with other strategies, such as Tip 9: *Linked Lecturettes,* helped her offset students' low energy so that they were more alert and participatory.

Key References and Resources

Beyond Bullets. (2012). *Seeing the speaker's face improves communication.* Retrieved from www.beyondbullets.com/2005/01/face.html

Reynolds, G. (2005, February 3). Keep the lights on [Web log post]. Retrieved August 31, 2016, from www.presentationzen.com/presentationzen/2005/02/keep_the_lights.html

Reynolds, G. (2016). *Top ten delivery tips.* Retrieved from www.garrreynolds.com/preso-tips/deliver/

University of California, Davis. (n.d.). *Effective presentation and visuals for PowerPoint.* Faculty Support for Technology in Teaching and Research. Retrieved from http://facultysupport.ucdavis.edu/techtip/powerpoint/Effective%20presentation/index.html

ENGAGING LECTURE TIP 35

The Hook

Many lecturers launch immediately into their talks without much in the way of introduction. There is a better approach. We recommend that you begin lectures with *The Hook,* which is an attention-getting device that you use to help students engage in the lecture from the outset.

The Hook should be compelling enough to encourage students to set aside thinking about other things to focus on the lecture. If you seed engagement at the beginning, students are likely to try to stay with you throughout the session. *The Hook* also sends a signal to the students about your lecture style so that they are better able to follow you, and it also provides them with a glimpse of the central message of the talk, which in turn can help their comprehension.

Key Idea

Use *The Hook* to grab students' attention at the very beginning of the lecture.

There are many different approaches to *The Hook,* including the following:

- **Quotation.** A quotation from someone famous in your field or perhaps from popular culture can set the theme of a given lecture, be thought-provoking because it also borrows authority, and help students to see the importance of the topic. Using the same quote to start and end the session can bookend the lecture and reinforce the lecture's theme.
- **Intriguing question.** A good question can help focus students' attention on the most important issue you are to discuss. Bringing the question back at the end of the session can help students understand the value of the lecture, particularly if you have, at least in part, answered the question. Alternately, consider introducing a new intriguing question that relates to the initial question and that may pique interest in the upcoming lecture.
- **Statistic.** Provide an interesting or impressive statistic to start and end a lecture. This can draw in student learners and help them to understand the importance of a topic.
- **An alternate universe scenario.** You can capture student attention by providing a provocative what-if scenario.
- **Open-ended rhetorical question or series of rhetorical questions.** You can start a lecture by asking students to consider an answer to a rhetorical question. Avoid asking a question that can be answered with a simple yes or no. If the question is not thought-provoking, students may shut down and quit listening.
- **Contrarian statement.** You can begin a lecture by taking the opposite viewpoint on something that may be conventional wisdom.
- **Unusual detail.** Consider starting a lecture with an unusual detail or little-known fact.
- **A story.** Stories can be one of the most effective ways to start a lecture. People make sense of the world through stories, and moreover, we simply enjoy them.

The key to *The Hook* is to know your audience so that you can gauge how best to capture their attention. When you plan *The Hook,* try to imagine how students will react to it. Only use a relevant hook; if you try to use one just to be clever, students will know.

Example

A professor in a course on leadership wanted to seed engagement at the very beginning of each lecture. She therefore developed a repertoire of *Hooks,* including the following.

Quotations

- "A genuine leader is not a searcher for consensus but a molder of consensus."—Martin Luther King Jr.
- "Management is doing things right; leadership is doing the right things."—Peter Drucker
- "The first rule of leadership: everything is your fault."—Hopper, *A Bug's Life*

Statistic or fact. "According to the Grant Thornton International (2015), the percentage of women in senior business roles globally is 24; the percentage of firms with no women in senior management is 33."

An alternate universe scenario. "What if Steve Jobs had not been born?"

Open-ended rhetorical question. "How do leaders become leaders?" or "What characteristics are essential to be a leader?"

Contrarian statement. "Good leaders work smarter, not harder. That's what people say. I don't believe that. I believe that great leaders are exceptionally hard workers."

Unusual detail. "Leaders have been around since humans began to live together in clans and tribes. Leadership research, however, is a relatively new field, with the first analyses of leadership starting only in the early twentieth century."

A story. The following story is attributed to Gandhi and recounted by Andersen (2012) in her book on leadership to illustrate leading by example:

> A young mother came to Gandhi leading her little boy by the hand and said, "Mahatma Ji, my son eats far too many sweets, and I'm concerned for his heath. If you tell him to stop, he will do it out of respect for you." Gandhi nodded, looked thoughtful, and then asked the mother to return in two weeks. Puzzled, the young woman did as he asked.
>
> Two weeks later, she returned and waited again to have the chance to speak to the master. When she came to the front of the line, she bowed respectfully to Gandhi and said, "Mahatma Ji, I came to you before and asked you to help my son understand he must not eat so many sweets. You asked me to return in two weeks, and so here we are." Gandhi smiled and said, "Ah yes, I remember." He turned to the little boy and said gravely, "Son, your health is very precious, and eating too much sugar could hurt your body and your teeth. You must stop eating so many sweets. Will you do that?" The little boy ducked his head, awed, and replied, "Yes, Gandhi Ji."
>
> The mother thanked Gandhi and then said, "Forgive me Mahatma Ji, but why did you make us wait? I don't understand why you couldn't have said that same thing two weeks ago." Gandhi replied, "Two weeks ago, I was eating too much sugar myself."

Key References and Resources

Andersen, E. (2012). *Leading so people will follow.* San Francisco, CA: Jossey-Bass.

Grant Thornton International. (2015). *Women in business: The value of diversity.* Retrieved from www.grantthornton.global/globalassets/wib_value_of_diversity.pdf

Linkedin Slide Share. (2014). *TED Talk takeaways: 8 ways to hook your audience.* Retrieved from https://blog.slideshare.net/2014/07/30/set-your-hook-to-capture-your-audience

ENGAGING LECTURE TIP 36

Value Display

By virtue of our roles as faculty members, students tend to confer high status on us and expect us to live up to it. We should honor their beliefs in us by striving to live up to their expectations. We can do this by working diligently to craft a lecture that adds value to student learning and then communicating the importance of the message through verbal and nonverbal methods.

Value Display communicates the lecture's importance to students and thus may help to improve students' interest and motivation. If you can communicate the reasons students should care about the topic, student motivation to put in the energy and effort required to learn will most likely improve.

Key Idea

As lecturers, we should communicate the value of the lecture information, whether we do so verbally or nonverbally.

The *Value Display* begins with your understanding of the importance of the topic yourself *and* your role in communicating that information to students. There are a few specific techniques that can help you.

Value Pitch Not all students will immediately recognize the importance of the lecture topic. A value pitch involves expressly stating the value of the lecture material and describing how students may be able to use the information in the future. For example, you might point out how it is foundational to understanding new content or is required understanding for students in that academic major.

Without Apology Sometimes lecturers apologize for what students have to learn. This most often happens when they are required to teach specific content that they do not particularly care for. A lecturer in such a situation might say something like, "OK, this is the boring part, but you have to know it, so . . ." or "We'll get through this technical part and move on to more interesting things soon." Don't apologize for the lecture content. Don't acknowledge that it's boring. It is what it is. Own it, be enthusiastic, and figure out how to teach it.

Strong Voice Sometimes students break off into conversations. They can be taken with a point you have just made or they can simply be off topic. Don't talk over student conversations. Instead, as Lemov (2010) suggests, stand up and stand still. Use the power of quiet, and wait until students stop talking. Move closer to them if you have to. And if they simply don't stop, interrupt them and either ask them to share or ask them to stop. In this way, you signal that the lecture is important and that they need to hear it.

No Hijacking From time to time, multiple student questions or extended comments can have the effect of hijacking a lecture. Take questions, but don't let them completely sidetrack the lecture; if the content is important enough to share, you owe it to the students to finish. Answer questions concisely. If students continue to ask questions, tell them to hold their questions until the end of the lecture segment. Alternately if the questions seem to be coming from one student, ask the student to see you after class or during office hours; this will prevent other students from becoming irritated with the one student as well.

Example

A new professor wanted to promote a climate of relaxed informality in her classroom. Part of her strategy for implementing this was to encourage students to ask questions whenever they had them. She discovered, however, that there were a few students who asked questions excessively, disrupting the flow of her lecture and using up valuable time for explanations that would be coming soon or that most students neither needed nor wanted. She therefore shifted to a policy in which she asked students to wait until designated points in her presentation to ask questions. In this way, she was able to maintain the focus and momentum of her talk—thus reinforcing its value—while also reassuring students that there would be a time when she would answer any questions they had.

Key References and Resources

Ford, N., McCullough, M., & Schutta, N. T. (2012). *Presentation patterns: Techniques for crafting better presentations.* Boston, MA: Addison Wesley.

Lemov, D. (2010). *Teach like a champion: 49 strategies that put students on the path to success.* San Francisco, CA: Jossey-Bass.

CHAPTER 11

Managing the Session

Being an effective teacher requires more than the mastery and delivery of disciplinary-based material. It requires knowledge and skills related to pedagogy, an area in which most higher education faculty members are not trained. Pedagogy is the method and practice of teaching. Knowledge of what constitutes good pedagogy helps teachers take academic content and make the kinds of choices that enable students to learn it. Together, disciplinary knowledge and pedagogical knowledge create a powerful combination that enables teachers to be more effective in sharing knowledge so that learners can comprehend and retain it. Although this book is fundamentally about good pedagogy, the Tips in this chapter address an important aspect of pedagogical practice: strategies for managing a particular class session. We summarize these Tips in Exhibit 11.1.

Exhibit 11.1 Managing the Session Tips

This Tip . . .	Provides guidance on how to . . .	It is particularly useful for . . .
Tip 37: *Terms of Engagement*	Set standards for student engagement before the lecture begins	Thinking about and communicating what engagement means to students in terms that they'll understand
Tip 38: *Classroom Technology Policy*	Create a policy for managing students' use of technology while you are presenting	Providing students with guidance up-front on what is and is not appropriate regarding technology use during lectures
Tip 39: *Silent Signals*	Use nonverbal signals to facilitate two-way communication in the lecture classroom	Checking in with students in ways that minimally disrupt the flow of your presentation
Tip 40: *Every Minute Matters*	Take advantage of the full time you have with students in class	Maximizing classroom time to make a difference in student learning
Tip 41: *Extensions*	Use activities to fill time gaps that result in meaningful learning	Providing you with a repertoire of pedagogically sound activities from which you can draw as needed

ENGAGING LECTURE TIP 37

Terms of Engagement

Student engagement is a powerful influence on lecture presentation success. If students do their jobs and are attentive during the lecture, and if you have done yours and are well prepared, you will most likely deliver a successful lecture. If students are uninvolved and passive, your lecture will not be a success even if your delivery has been outstanding.

It can be tempting to blame students for any lack of engagement, particularly when you have done your job in preparation and delivery. However, students—particularly ones new to higher education—may not know how to engage in a lecture. They may not know how to read ahead of the session or to prepare, take notes, and think critically for the purpose of formulating questions. They may not know how to focus their attention. They may not know how to reflect on what they have learned.

Many of our techniques in Part 3 of this book can help scaffold those activities so that students *do* learn how to be good lecture participants. But in addition to those, you can help students understand their roles in lectures by setting *Terms of Engagement,* which are a listing of the expectations for student participation in a lecture.

Key Idea

Set the standards for student engagement before the lecture by documenting the *Terms of Engagement* so that students understand that they are expected to be active participants.

To develop a useful set of *Terms of Engagement* tailored to your unique situation, consider the following suggestions:

- Decide what students should do before a lecture to prepare for it. Should they think through what they already know about a topic? Read from a textbook? Develop a list of questions?
- Clarify your expectations for how students should act during the lecture. Should they take notes? Think of appropriate questions?
- Consider what students should do after a lecture. Should they fill in any gaps in their notes? Write and reflect on what they have learned?
- Develop a set of terms based on these expectations.
- Share the terms with the students early in the course; consider including them in the syllabus or alternately creating a separate handout, which you may or may not want to have them sign to signal their agreement to the terms.

Example

An instructor of a freshman course prepared a handout that she distributed along with the syllabus the first day of the semester. She explained that teaching and learning is a two-way process and that she would do everything she could to prepare engaging class sessions but that students would need to put in effort as well.

Terms of Engagement

Preparation

- **Read ahead of time.** Preliminary reading can make it easier for you to understand the lecture because it encourages you to think about the topic, become familiar with basic vocabulary, and prompt you to consider what you know already and what you need to learn. Even if no reading has been assigned, it can be helpful to browse through the relevant textbook chapters to familiarize yourself with the topic.
- **Take care of yourself.** Get plenty of sleep. Eat well; don't come hungry, but don't carb out ahead of time either because that can make you sleepy. Exercising before a lecture class can help you increase your ability to pay attention.

During the Session

- **Concentrate.** Take a deep breath, and then turn your mind to the lecture topic. If you notice yourself start to daydream, pull yourself back.
- **Listen actively.** Don't simply wait for the ideas to infuse themselves into your brain. Ask yourself questions about the topic. Think about how the ideas relate to what you already know. Think about what you understand and don't. Think about what you agree with and don't.
- **Acknowledge the lecturer.** Make eye contact and occasionally nod if you understand or agree with something. This will signal that you are paying attention while also helping you to do so.
- **Take notes.** Note-taking helps you remember information. It also helps you stay focused. It gives you a study guide for later. But don't try to take down every word. Instead, record key ideas. Doing so makes you think about the key ideas rather than details that are less important. Also, if you try to record everything, you will definitely miss hearing some important information.
- **Stay awake.** Heuston (2013), a former truck driver–turned–college lecturer, has some tips for paying attention. If you feel yourself begin to fall asleep, lift your foot three inches off the ground, or an arm three inches off the desk, and hold the pose. As long as your muscles are tensed or active, you won't fall asleep.
- **Ask questions.** If you have questions about the lecture content, raise your hand or alternately see me after class or send me a message through our course's online site.
- **Don't pack up before class is over.** You may miss important information if you begin to pack your bags before the class is over. Plus you distract your fellow students. Wait for the formal announcement.

After the Session

- **Review your notes.** If you review your notes soon after class, the information will be fresh, and you can fill in areas you may have missed or clarify anything that might be confusing on a later review.
- **Review the handouts.** An immediate review can help you retain the information. A review right before a quiz or exam can also help you remember key information.
- **Self-assess.** Ask yourself questions about how much you understood about the content.

As a variation, consider having students write the *Terms of Engagement* themselves. This approach will have the benefit of student buy in. You may wish to provide them with a sample, however, so that they know where and how to begin.

Key References and Resources

Gooblar, D. (2013b, September 13). Help your students stay awake in class [Web log post]. Retrieved August 31, 2016, from www.pedagogyunbound.com/tips-index/2013/9/12/help-your-students-stay-awake-in-class?rq=truck

Heuston, S. (2013). Trucker tips: Helping students stay awake in class. *College Teaching, 61*(3), 108.

ENGAGING LECTURE TIP 38

Classroom Technology Policy

A common issue that faculty members face is whether students should be allowed to use personal technology in the classroom. Many faculty members worry about the distraction technology potentially brings. Furthermore, it can be discouraging to see students apparently disengaged while we are trying to teach them something critical. For this reason, many professors ban the use of laptops, tablets, and smartphones in class.

However, some professors believe that students are adults and should be allowed to make their own decisions about their behavior in class, whether those behaviors are good or bad. They also correctly note that such a ban may discriminate against students with disabilities. Even if they allow students who register with disability services to use technology in class, many students choose not to register. Moreover, allowing students who do register "outs" them to the class, which should be avoided for a number of reasons. Additionally, some faculty members choose to harness technology for pedagogical purposes, for example, having students respond to questions through online polling systems that students access through their phones.

One way to address these issues is to create a *Classroom Technology Policy.* Determine what the role of technology is in your classroom and set boundaries for appropriate use. Deciding what your policy will be ahead of time will provide guidelines for civil behavior in class. It will help students to understand what is and what is not allowable. And it will help you accomplish your pedagogical goals.

Key Idea

Choose a *Classroom Technology Policy* that fits with your pedagogical beliefs and that provides students with guidance on expectations.

Developing Your Policies

When you develop your policy, consider the following elements:

- **Purpose.** Why are you implementing the policy? What do you hope it will accomplish?
- **Tools to be covered.** Will your policy encompass laptops, cell phones, tablets, other?
- **Use.** How will the policy be employed? Will students be allowed to use certain tools for specific tasks (e.g., laptops for note-taking) but not for others (browsing the Internet)?
- **Expectations.** What do you expect students to do specifically? Leave the technology at home? Keep it in their backpacks or purses? Keep laptops closed? Other?
- **Consequences.** What consequences will students face if they do not follow the policy? Grade reductions? Extra points for adhering to it?

Innovative Practices

Some professors have been creative devising their technology policies. We offer the following examples:

- **Ask students to create an acceptable-use policy for technology in the classroom.** A few professors have given students control of the policy, having students use Google Docs to allow outside-of-class collaboration (see the following example).
- **Have a course discussion and explain the implications on learning.** A few professors have held full-class discussions about the role of technology during class, such as cell phone distractions and implications for learning.
- **Implement tech breaks.** Some professors stop class at specified intervals for a tech break, encouraging students who do not want or need the break to catch up on note-taking or get some fresh air.

Example

Following is a slightly modified student-developed policy from a University of British Columbia (n.d.) physics class.

Physics 101—Section 102: In-Class Electronics Policy

The following usage policy of all electronic devices during lecture time is defined in this document. It is based upon the foundational value that attending students are mature, adult, college-level learners who are committed to learning and attending due to personal choice.

Mobile phones: All mobile phones must be off or on silent/vibrate during the lectures and should in no way disturb others around you. The use of mobiles phones as class aids (calculators, dictionary, note-taking, and so forth) is allowed.

Phone calls: No phone calls should be answered during class, except in the case of exceptional circumstances. These could be, for example, health of close family, child-care, or hearing back from a potential future employer. In such exceptional circumstances, the student is expected to leave the auditorium as quietly and quickly as possible so as not to disturb fellow students. Under no circumstances should voice conversations occur inside or within hearing distance of the lecture theatre.

Other uses of phones: Use of phones for texting, e-mail, games, social networking, and so forth is not allowed. If you feel you simply cannot restrain yourself, then you should not access your technology during class.

Tablets: Tablets can be used anywhere in the auditorium for classroom-related activities (connecting to the Internet for class-related information, taking lecture notes, completing in-class worksheets, and so forth). Discretion is expected for all activities. If your neighbors are distracted by your activities, it is your responsibility to stop and minimize the distraction.

Laptops: Laptops are to be used exclusively for course-related material and as long as you keep the distractions to your fellow students to a minimum.

All other uses: If you cannot restrain yourself from looking at your laptop for non-course-related material, don't use it.

Music: It is recommended that you get used to working without music as music devices will not be tolerated in midterms or finals.

Following is an example of a teacher-developed classroom technology policy adapted from University of Northern Colorado (2015).
In this course, students should refrain from the following activities:

- Using any electronic handheld device or wearable technology not directly related to the learning of class material
- Using a cell phone or tablet for verbal, text, audio, video or still picture communication. (Cell phones, pagers, or notification devices should be placed in the "off" or "silent only" mode and should not ring during class time.)
- Using iPods or other audio devices for audio such as a smartphone (except for hearing assistance devices)

A laptop should not be used for purposes other than note-taking or researching current class session material (i.e., no e-mail, texting, general Internet browsing, instant messaging, social media, and so forth).

Key References and Resources

Bates, S., & Lister, A. (2013, September 23). Acceptable technology in the classroom. Let the students decide [Web log post]. Retrieved from www.pedagogyunbound.com/tips-index/2013/9/23/acceptable-technology-in-the-classroom-let-students-decide

Gooblar, D. (2014). *Smartphones in the classroom? Let students decide.* Retrieved from https://chroniclevitae.com/news/289-smartphones-in-the-classroom-let-students-decide

Kamanetz, A. (2015). How to get students to stop using their cellphones in class. *National Public Radio.* Retrieved from www.npr.org/sections/ed/2015/11/10/453986816/how-to-get-students-to-stop-using-their-cellphones-in-class

McDaniel, R. (n.d.). *Wireless in the classroom.* Retrieved from https://cft.vanderbilt.edu/guides-sub-pages/wireless/

University of Northern Colorado. (2015). *Monfort College of Business classroom technology guidelines.* Retrieved from http://studylib.net/doc/13960385/monfort-college-of-business-classroom-technology-guidelines

ENGAGING LECTURE TIP 39

Silent Signals

A transmission-model lecture consists of one-way communication from a professor to a group of students. By contrast, an interactive lecture encourages the teacher and the students to engage in communication. One form of two-way communication that we may not often think of is intentional nonverbal communication. Thoughtful use of *Silent Signals,* or nonverbal exchanges between students and teachers, can positively affect the classroom climate and facilitate learning.

Key Idea

Nonverbal *Silent Signals* can facilitate communication in the lecture classroom.

There are many different *Silent Signals* that teachers and students can use to improve the college classroom climate. They are most effective if you establish the signals before you need them. Also, although use of *Silent Signals* can be used with good effect, if you use too many of them they will quickly wear thin. Choose wisely and only use the one(s) that will best facilitate your particular learning session.

Example

Following are some examples of common lecture classroom situations and some attending *Silent Signals* that could help to facilitate communication:

Concluding an activity. You may want to pause the lecture and ask students to complete a short writing assignment, participate in a short interactive discussion, or apply lecture concepts in a group activity. Students need to be mindful of the time they have to complete the work. Tell them ahead of time how you will signal when they should return their attention to your presentation. Consider the following:

- Set an online timer so that it runs and is displayed on a screen.
- Have a physical timer visible at all times.
- Post a card to show how much time students have to continue working, such as five-minute, three-minute, and one-minute warnings.
- Raise your hand at the front of the room so that students can see you would like their attention.
- Flash the light.
- Clap and ask the students to start clapping with you when they hear you.
- Ring a bell. (Although the last two signals are not silent, they are nonverbal.)

Checking for understanding. If the lecture topic is complex and you want to know whether students are following you or whether you need to provide additional explanations or elaboration of points, consider using *Silent Signals* for a less-disruptive approach to having students communicate their level of understanding to you. Possible *Silent Signals* you could implement are as follows:

- Thumbs up: Yes, I understand.
- Thumbs at half-mast: I am not sure.
- Thumbs down: No, I don't understand.

Checking for appropriate pacing. You may want to know whether students are keeping pace with your presentation or whether they need a minute to catch up. Consider offering them a pause button. You may want to set limits in advance; for example, tell students if you see *x* number of signals, you will pause for one minute before resuming your lecture. Here are some standard nonverbal signals:

- T-shaped, or time-out sign, hand signal
- Raised index finger

Checking if students have questions or comment. You may want to know whether students have comments or questions during the lecture, and one or the other is perhaps more important in a given point in time in the lecture. Consider the following:

- Raise your hand if you have a question.
- Form the letter *c* with your hand for comments.

Key References and Resources

Gooblar, D. (2013a, August 13). Give your students a pause button [Web log post]. Retrieved August 31, 2016, from www.pedagogyunbound.com/tips-index/?category=Effective+Lecturing

Magnan, R. (1990). *147 practical tips for teaching professors.* Madison, WI: Atwood.

ENGAGING LECTURE TIP 40

Every Minute Matters

Like it not, in higher education, we still measure courses in terms of time. We teach courses that are worth a certain number of credit hours each academic term. We teach courses that meet for one or more sessions each week. We teach for a certain number of minutes or hours each class session. Even for those of us who teach online, there is often an expectation that the course should take the equivalent amount of time that it would take if it were being held face-to-face. In *Every Minute Matters,* we propose that professors use the full amount of class time to the best possible end. Whether it's starting a session, transitioning between lecture and a hands-on activity, or ending a session, you can always be teaching, and students can always be learning.

Key Idea

When we teach, consider using every minute of time that we have at our disposal to make a difference in student learning.

When you think of "every minute," it is important to recognize the range of activities that go on at the beginning, middle, and end of a class session. Consider the following.

Starting Class

Informal chats with students about topics unrelated to the learning goals for a particular session are an important part of creating a positive class climate and of getting to know students. They will make students feel more comfortable and welcomed. We suggest showing up to class a few minutes early to have those conversations. When you and students chat *before* class, it frees you to begin class on time and to use every minute at your disposal for ensuring that students meet their learning goals.

Lecturing and Facilitating Learning

Lecturing for a full-class session is not efficient time use because students cannot maintain attention for that long. Instead, consider developing a solid class plan that combines lectures and student activities so that you have engaged students for the maximum amount of time. Working within the limits of human attention and providing opportunities to reset attention is the best way to make *Every Minute Matters.*

Ending Class

It is sometimes tempting to end a class session a few minutes early. When we come to a natural breaking point in the content with just a few minutes left on the clock, it can feel almost natural to say, "Well, we're almost out of time" or "We don't have enough time to start something new" or simply "Let's call it good for today." Although a single occurrence of this may amount only to four or five minutes, this time becomes significant if it becomes a regular pattern, and we end up shortchanging learning. In the following table, you can see what happens if you end class five minutes early each session.

Class Length	Sessions per Week	Lost Time over a Sixteen-Week Semester	Hours of Lost Class Sessions
50 minutes	3 times	240 minutes/4 hours	4.8
75 minutes	2 times	160 minutes/2.7 hours	2.1

When you are clear on your goals and have done careful planning, you can ensure that you maximize learning by taking advantage of the important time you have with students. For ideas of what to do with an additional five minutes, see Tip 41: *Extensions.*

Example

An instructor typically waited a few moments for stragglers to arrive and get settled before starting his lecture because he wanted the class to be able to focus on his presentation and not get distracted by latecomers. But when he noticed that more students started arriving late, he reevaluated how he spent the class hour. He chose instead to start on time, informing students that if they arrived after he had checked attendance, they were responsible for entering quietly and sitting in the back of the room and then seeing him after class to get partial credit for being present. Soon, most students arrived on time and he felt relieved to be using the scheduled class time in ways that were evident to students that he valued their learning sufficiently to use their time together for maximum effectiveness.

Key Reference and Resource

Lemov, D. (2010). *Teach like a champion: 49 strategies that put students on the path to success.* San Francisco, CA: Jossey-Bass.

ENGAGING LECTURE TIP 41

Extensions

Even with the best-laid plans, you cannot anticipate perfectly how every single minute of a class session will play out. Sometimes things will run long, other times short. The question is what to do when you have a few spare minutes and do not have time to launch into new material. Planning ahead by creating a short activity that may last between one and five minutes can help you fill potential gaps with a meaningful learning activity. Such an activity is called an *Extension* because you can use it to add on to your planned material to extend the teaching and learning time.

Extensions activities help you to prepare fully and to ensure that students do not find themselves with nothing to do. When done well, *Extensions* provide students with an opportunity to apply, practice, or deepen new knowledge or alternately to enable you to assess their learning. *Extensions* should not simply fill time but rather should achieve the goal of extending and enhancing the learning of the class session.

Key Idea

Prepare *Extensions* to use when you have a gap during class time that you want to fill with meaningful learning activities.

Consider the following activities as potential extensions of your interactive lecture sessions to have ready when you need them. We compiled these activities from several sources, including our other books in the College Teaching Techniques series, Karen Smith Center (n.d.), Edutopia (2016), and Middendorf and Kalish (1996).

- **Brainstorming on the board.** Pose a question or other prompt and ask students to call out related concepts and terms; write the concepts on the board as students call them out. If possible, group them into categories as you record the responses.
- **Total physical response.** Ask students a selection of true-false questions. Students either stand or sit to indicate their answers (e.g., if they think the answer is false, they stand; if they think it is true, they sit). Getting students moving can be beneficial to improving attention, so this activity can be useful prior to a lecturette.
- **Pass the pointer.** Place a relevant image on a screen or post on a flip chart; share a laser pointer with a volunteer, and ask the student to identify key features or to ask questions about any unclear attributes of the image.
- **Pass the chalk.** Hand a student a piece of chalk, a pencil or pen, or a soft toy. Whoever has the item must answer your next question. The student then gets to choose another student and pass the item along. Continue for several questions.
- **Students as teachers.** Tell students that collectively they are to assume the role of teacher. Role-play as the student, and ask the teachers questions about the content. The teachers answer your questions. This activity also works well as a review.

- **Five words.** Give students a topic. Ask them to list five words they would use to describe the topic. Tell them to be prepared to explain and justify their choices, and then take responses from the class.
- **Picture prompt.** Show students a relevant image without explanation. Ask students to write about the image using terms from the lecture or alternately to name or describe the processes and concepts illustrated.
- **Simile.** Ask students to complete the following prompt: "What we learned today is similar to ____________________."
- **Quote minus one.** Share a quote that is relevant to your topic, but leave out an important word. Ask students to guess the missing word. For example: "______________ is what remains after one has forgotten what one has learned in school." This extender can precede a class discussion.
- **Twitter post.** Ask students to define a term or describe a concept in under 140 characters.
- **Truth statements.** Ask small groups to list three things they know to be true about the topic or issue from the lecture.
- **Top-ten list.** Ask students to develop a list of the most important takeaways from the class session, starting with ten and working up to one. Give them the option to use humor.
- **Flash-talk mini-lecture.** Ask students to create a flash talk to extend a concept or idea you just discussed. A flash talk is a brief one- to five-minute lecture. Individuals or small groups may develop the content, but individuals should present. Call on as many volunteers as time will allow. (You can also create several flash talks to intersperse in a class session as needed.)
- **Buzz groups.** Form groups of students to discuss content-related questions informally, generating lots of ideas quickly to prepare for and improve whole-class discussions. (For a fuller description of this technique, see Barkley, Major, & Cross, 2014, CoLT 3.)
- **Quick write.** Ask students to write for one minute to summarize a point, write a list of the new things they have learned during the session, or say what from a lecture they found to be unclear (the muddiest point). (See Barkley & Major, 2016, LAT 6, for detailed information about Quick writes.)
- **True or false?** Write different statements related to your topic on index cards. Half of the cards should contain statements that are true, half false. Pass out the cards, and ask students to determine which theirs is. They can work individually or in small groups, depending on the size of the class and the number of statements you can develop.
- **Concept mapping.** Ask students to write keywords onto sticky notes and then organize them into a visual map, using lines to connect the concepts.
- **Bumper stickers.** Ask students to craft the language for a bumper sticker to illustrate a particular concept or the most important point from lecture.
- **Tabloid titles.** Ask students to write a tabloid-style headline that illustrates the topic of the session.
- **Drawing for understanding.** Ask students to illustrate an abstract concept or idea. Ask students to share their drawings with each other.
- **Bonus discussion questions.** Create a list of extra questions for discussion. If you originally planned five or six discussion questions, for example, add an extra two to three. If you are not planning to hold a class discussion, craft a few discussion questions anyway that you could use for an extension. If you ask for opinions rather than a recall of facts (which are often perceived as quizzes in disguise), it will open up opportunities for participation.

- **Classroom opinion polls.** Choose a poll question related to a concept or idea you have just shared and take an informal poll with students signaling their responses by hand raising. This is a useful approach for starting a discussion.
- **Student pollsters.** Select a few students to serve as pollsters. Give each an index card with a single question on it. Ask the pollsters to travel through the room, polling their peers on a topic relevant to the course. Next ask them to report the results to the full class.
- **Exit tickets.** Ask students to reflect on a reading assignment, video, lecture, or something similar and then write a brief response to a question on an index card that is designed to gather information about their understanding of core facts, terms, concepts, and ideas. Ask students to hand in their cards at the end of a session (Barkley & Major, 2016, LAT 3).

The most important consideration in creating a good *Extension* is making sure that it is directly related to the learning goals and the topic of the class session and is not simply busy work or filler. Students will know which it is and respond accordingly.

Example

An experienced professor was aware that the combination of students who enrolled in her course each academic term was unique and that, consequently, her collaborative learning activities would take varying amounts of time depending on the students who were enrolled that term. She therefore developed a repertoire of high-quality extension activities and created presentation slides that included explanation, purpose, and instructions that she could draw from whenever students finished the scheduled activity earlier than anticipated. Students shared that they appreciated her planning for these occasions because it indicated to them her deep commitment to ensuring that their time in her class was worth their investment on multiple levels.

Key References and Resources

Barkley, E. F. (2010). *Student engagement techniques: A handbook for college faculty.* San Francisco, CA: Jossey-Bass.

Barkley, E. F., & Major, C. H. (2016). *Learning assessment techniques: A handbook for college faculty.* San Francisco, CA: Jossey-Bass.

Barkley, E. F., Major, C. H., & Cross, K. P. (2014). *Collaborative learning techniques: A resource for college faculty* (2nd ed.). San Francisco, CA: Jossey-Bass.

Edutopia. (2016). Using the rule of three for learning [Web log post]. Retrieved August 22, 2016, from www.edutopia.org/blog/using-rule-three-learning-ben-johnson

Karen L. Smith Faculty Center for Teaching and Learning. (n.d.). *Interactive techniques.* Retrieved from www.fctl.ucf.edu/teachingandlearningresources/coursedesign/assessment/content/101_tips.pdf

Middendorf, J., & Kalish, A. (1996). The "change-up" in lectures. *National Teaching and Learning Forum, 5*(2), 1–5.

Millis, B. J., & Cottell, P. G. (1998). *Cooperative learning for higher education faculty.* American Council on Education. Phoenix, AZ: Oryx Press.

CHAPTER 12

Presenting Like a Professional

Most professors are not trained professional speakers. Nevertheless, if we choose to do lecture presentations, we will be judged on how well we make them. More important, however, is that the quality of our lecture presentations influences how well students will learn, and we should therefore strive to do the best we can. There are several guidelines for public speakers that, if followed, can help you be more confident, more engaging, and more professional in your lecture presentations. In this chapter we offer four Tips for professional speaking that we find particularly appropriate for classroom lecture presentations. We summarize these Tips in Exhibit 12.1.

Exhibit 12.1 Presenting Like a Professional Tips

This Tip . . .	Provides guidance on how to . . .	It is particularly useful for . . .
Tip 42: *To Script, or Not to Script*	Choose between reading or not reading from a script	Drawing on notes or scripts in ways that will still make your talk feel natural and direct
Tip 43: *Weatherperson*	Assume the stance of a weatherperson when lecturing	Providing ways to talk more directly and engagingly to students
Tip 44: *Pedagogical Moves*	Use gestures and body positioning to facilitate communication in the lecture classroom	Reinforcing your message nonverbally
Tip 45: *Voice Modulation*	Use volume, pitch, and inflection effectively	Learning how to modify your voice so that you draw students in and help them stay alert and focused

ENGAGING LECTURE TIP 42

To Script, or Not to Script?

In higher education, we sometimes hear tales of the professor pulling out worn, yellowed notes and reading from them to the students. We also occasionally hear about a professor reading directly from a textbook. Although thankfully this doesn't happen often, it does still happen occasionally, which we can say with some certainty because we have witnessed it directly. And from this experience, we can say categorically that you should not read the textbook to students. Short of this, reading from a script is one of the best ways we can think of to do a bad job of lecturing. So much can go wrong: lack of inflection, eye contact, body language, connecting with one's audience. For this reason, we generally do not recommend reading from a script. However, we do suggest that you may find it quite useful to initially write a script or at least to make some scripted notes. Writing out your notes in advance will help you to ensure that you have thought through the presentation from start to finish. It will help you to fine-tune ideas, arguments, examples, and language. It produces a more polished product.

If you do fully script the lecture, however, we suggest that you then toss out the script. The result will be a well-planned lecture, but one that is simultaneously spontaneous and flexible. It enables you to create a refined talk that flows and is polished. If you have written notes, you may choose to keep those. Many presentation packages enable you to display your notes in presenter view along with the slide. The caveat here, however, is that you should likely only view them in outline form; otherwise, you might be tempted to read from them.

That said, we recognize that there are times when it may be desirable to use a script during the lecture presentation itself. If you have new research that you want to share but you have not yet had time to develop a formal presentation on, you might want to read from a script. If you have extreme anxiety about speaking in public, you might want to use a script to help support you through it. If your native language is different than the one you will be lecturing in and you feel the need to be sure that every word is accurate and deliberate, using a script could be a benefit. And although we don't recommend reading from a script unless unusual circumstances call you to do so, if you do choose to read, you should plan to read with style. This means plenty of practice so that it feels like you are talking directly to the students.

Key Idea

In an interactive lecture session, reading from a script is generally not the best option. If you do decide to use a script during the lecture, read it with style.

The best approach is to script or develop extensive notes on your presentation and then toss the notes and do the talk from memory. This approach becomes easier with experience and practice, however, and we recognize that many teachers will feel more comfortable using notes or alternately a full script.

Lecture Notes

Although the idea of the yellowed pages of full-size tablet paper comes to mind when one thinks of a professor's notes, using this is not the best approach. Presentation slide notes are the most effective if you are using a slide deck because they will display without being seen by students. Do not use your slides as notes because you will end up reading them, and students will be bored. If you are not using presentation software, then index cards can be a good approach. Following are some suggestions for lecture notes to use during the presentation:

- Avoid writing in full sentences. Instead, jot down key ideas or phrases in a bulleted list. The idea is to simply jog your memory.
- Make sure your notes are easy to read. That will mean writing legibly or using sufficiently large font and leaving white space.
- Practice with the notes so that you use them with style. Avoid shuffling, switching from hand to hand, or gesturing with them. Practice glancing at them long enough to see the point and then continue the talk.

A Lecture Script

Again, you should only use a lecture script if there are special circumstances that call you to do so. Here are a few suggestions for writing a lecture script:

- Think back through your purpose, goals, and objectives that we discussed in Chapter 3.
- Consider the guidance in Chapters 4 to 6 to make any decisions regarding structure and content.
- Create a basic outline.
- Using your outline, write a rough draft.
- Revise, revise, revise.
- Check what you've written; try reading it out loud.

So how do you make it feel like you are speaking without a script when reading directly from one? We have a few suggestions as well as a couple of examples for you to consider.

- Watch your pacing. Plan to read at a pace of about 120, with formal speeches between 150–160 words per minute. Speed up to show excitement, and slow down for emphasis and to address particularly complicated ideas.
- Resist making excessive physical gestures.
- Vary your vocal inflection, raising your voice to add emphasis as needed.
- Build in some pauses. When we speak without notes, we have natural pauses. When we read, such pauses are often lacking. It is beneficial to be intentional about including pauses.
- Consider using slides along with your reading because they can give you something else to focus on. Make notes to yourself about when to change slides.
- Practice until you could almost recite the script from memory.

If your issue is anxiety, consider using scripted and outline notes. Make a two-column table, have your presentation fully scripted in the left column, and include briefer notes on the right side.

Sample Scripted and Outlined Notes

Full Script	Notes
On the left-hand side of this T-chart, write out the full version of your lecture. Feel free to write out what you plan to say word-for-word in this column.	Notes go here.
Try to use notes only when you begin because it will feel more natural to the students if you speak to them rather than read to them.	Use only notes if you can.
Having a full script here in the left column can provide you with a greater sense of security because you can revert to it if a note is insufficient prompting.	Refer to the script if you must.

Using this approach, you can feel confident speaking from the notes, knowing that if you panic, you have the written text to fall back on.

Example

A newly hired assistant professor was scheduled to teach his first class. It was a large lecture, and he was feeling nervous about being in front of such a big group. He decided he would script out his lecture in full because he wanted to be sure he had the arguments sufficiently refined and captured. But he decided to use a combination of lecture and outline notes when he gave the actual lecture. That way, he could plan to use the outline, but if he had to revert to the script, he could. His first lecture went well, and he did not use the script. He determined to use only notes from then on.

Key References and Resources

Reynolds, G. (2009, May 12). Making presentations in the TED style [Web log post]. Retrieved August 31, 2016, from www.presentationzen.com/presentationzen/2009/05/making-presentations-in-the-ted-style.html

Williams, J.B.W. (2006). *How to give a sensational scientific talk.* Retrieved from http://chem.virginia.edu/wp-content/uploads/2009/05/talk_in_pdf

ENGAGING LECTURE TIP 43

Weatherperson

Sometimes lecturers seem to forget that they have a group of students listening to them and watching them. So taken are they with the ideas they are presenting that they actually turn away from the students and lecture directly to the whiteboard or screen. A piece of advice that we can offer with confidence is this: students absolutely will not engage with the back of your head. We suggest that instead you should assume the stance of a *Weatherperson* and always speak directly to the students.

When you make eye contact with individual students, you catch their attention. When you look at the audience, you engage with them. When they see your face, they are more likely to accurately read your level of enthusiasm and will be more physically able to understand your words. Attentive and engaged students who know you are passionate about the topic and who can hear you clearly are more likely to listen and learn.

Key Idea

Assuming the *Weatherperson* stance enables you to interact more directly with students, which will improve their engagement and learning.

Following are suggestions for implementing the *Weatherperson* Tip:

- **You've got to love the weather.** One thing that most weather people demonstrate is passion for the weather. Their enthusiasm borders on contagious as they walk us through various fronts and wind patterns. Passion pays off, so one bit of advice we can adopt from a *Weatherperson* is to love our content (see also Tip 36: *Value Display*).
- **The students are more important than the slides.** Weather people make an effort to look at the audience rather than the screen. It is tempting and even easy to get caught up with looking at our slides or our writing on the board, but students are more important. If you actually look at students, it signals to the students that you care about them and their learning.
- **If you can get a heads up, do.** Most weather people can see what is coming next before the audience does. Many of today's presentation packages have presenter view so that you can see what slide is coming next in addition to the one that is displayed behind you. This can be exceedingly helpful for your flow.
- **The visual will most likely be there, whether you are looking directly at it or not.** Weather people trust that the image that they see on the computer screen in front of them will be visible to the audience. If you are using slides, you should have a display in front of you so that you do not have to turn around to look at the slide. Once you get it set up, when you see it on the screen, you should trust that it is projected behind you. Students will tell you if they are not seeing anything or are not seeing the correct thing. If a fixed classroom setup doesn't allow for a display in front of you, print an outline of the presentation to have with you at the front of the class.

- **You can move around a bit.** Weather people tend to move around the map displayed behind them. They tend to gesture from north to south and from east to west. Most of us do not have to remain fixed to the podium (the exception would be if audio equipment necessary for a large class is fixed to the podium). It is possible to move around a bit while talking, and indeed for many of us it feels more natural. However, avoid pacing because this can be distracting.

Example

An instructor relied on presentation slides to help cue him regarding content, but he found that his lecture was often clunky because he would advance to the new slide, look at the screen, and then start talking about what the slide projected. He then found out how to set his presentation package's preferences in a manner that enabled him to preview the next slide while the current slide was projected. With this, he was able to maintain a better flow to his talk and also keep his focus on the students in the class.

Key References and Resources

Feeney-Hart, A. (2014). *Top 10 tips for being a weather presenter.* Retrieved from www.bbc.com/news/entertainment-arts-30180596

Ford, N., McCullough, M., & Schutta, N. T. (2012). *Presentation patterns: Techniques for crafting better presentations.* Boston, MA: Addison Wesley.

ENGAGING LECTURE TIP 44

Pedagogical Moves

Most professors who lecture do more than just talk in order to communicate. Rather, they draw from a range of nonverbal communication devices through physical movement and changes. These *Pedagogical Moves* can involve shifts in facial expressions, hand gestures, or body positioning. *Pedagogical Moves* can serve several functions:

- They can stress a message the lecturer has made verbally; for example, a single backhand applause, a fist pound on the lectern or table, or a simple physical move to the front of a lectern can provide emphasis to a point.
- They can contradict a message the speaker has said, perhaps with irony. If a professor uses sarcasm as a device, for example, he or she can eye roll to signify that a statement is sarcastic, make a "stink face," or give a thumbs-down hand gesture. (*Note:* be careful with sarcasm in the classroom because some students may be slow to pick up on it.)
- They can replace a message. For example, if a professor is describing a car crash, he or she could clap hands together to substitute for the word *impact*; if the professor is indicating a "stomp" he or she can simply make the physical move of a stomp to replace the word.

Pedagogical Moves don't have to be fancy or elaborate; indeed, they should feel natural and flow naturally while you talk.

Key Idea

Use *Pedagogical Moves* as a way to communicate nonverbally with students.

Suggestions for Full-Body Movement

- Relax before you get started. Don't plod to the lectern or rush out immediately after completing your lecture; you will appear nervous or disinterested. Instead, approach your talking area with an even stride or pace.
- If you stand to present, stand with your feet about shoulder width apart. If you do not stand, determine how you will feel most comfortable when presenting.
- Ask yourself whether you are comfortable in your positioning—if the answer is no, adjust your stance.
- Use full-body movement judiciously. Don't pace back-and-forth, sway, or lean over the lectern or table.

Suggestions for Your Hands

- If you will use your hands to gesture, keep them at a ready position, which involves keeping your arms bent at the waist and your hands relaxed. Avoid clasping your hands together, hugging your body, putting your hands in your pockets, or locking your hands behind your back, which can make gesturing difficult and clumsy.
- Pay attention to the position of your elbows. To allow for free movement of your hands and forearms, ensure there's space between your elbows and your body. If your arms hang with your elbows positioned stiffly at your sides, your gestures will look short and artificial.
- Remember that the meaning of gestures can differ across cultures and regions, so it's important to be careful to avoid using gestures that some cultures might find offensive. For example, the OK gesture in the United States means money in Japan and zero in France. George W. Bush's famous "hook 'em horns" gesture means your wife is cheating on you and is an offensive gesture in many countries. If you have a gesture of habit, you should look it up to make sure it is appropriate for the students in your courses.
- Remember also that some hand gestures can come off as pretentious, so make sure you need the gesture and that it supports the point.

Suggestions for Eye Contact

- Keep your eyes on people, rather than your notes, as much as possible.
- Make eye contact with individuals. Although some speech coaches advise looking just above the heads of the students, it will be obvious to them that you are gazing in the air.
- Shift your gaze to different individuals around the room. Choose a person who is giving you positive feedback and make eye contact. Next shift your attention to a person in another part of the room and engage that person's gaze. By the end of the lecture, the goal is to have distributed your gaze evenly around the room.
- Check whether your gestures are effective by gauging where your students are looking. If they appear focused on your arms or hands instead of your face, your gestures may be distracting rather than helping them.

Suggestions for Facial Expressions

- Try to assume your normal resting face position as frequently as possible. Too little or too much facial expression can be distracting.
- Use facial expressions that are consistent with the ideas and how you feel about them. If you are describing a chilling event in US history, Pearl Harbor, for example, don't try to smile about it; if you are describing a wedding at the end of a comedy in a literature class, don't look dour.

Gestures can add a subtle touch to your delivery, and they can carry pedagogical meaning. However, they can become the most-distracting element of the lecture if ill-used or overdone.

Example

After a lecture presentation and during a break, a student asked the professor if she was nervous. She didn't feel like she had been particularly nervous during her talk and asked what had given that impression. The student told her that she had been wringing her hands while she was talking. She was unaware of it until then, but she realized that what she was doing was simply fidgeting, and the students thought she seemed stressed out of nervousness. She decided to be more intentional about her hands while she talked. She kept her elbows slightly away from her torso and her hands just in front of her and she used them to signal but otherwise tried to keep them still and unwrung.

Key References and Resources

Cotton, G. (2013). *Gestures to avoid in cross-cultural business: In other words, keep your fingers to yourself!* Retrieved from www.huffingtonpost.com/gayle-cotton/cross-cultural-gestures_b_3437653.html

Segal, J., Smith, M., & Boose, G. (2017). *Nonverbal communication: Improving your nonverbal skills and reading body language.* Retrieved from www.helpguide.org/articles/relationships/nonverbal-communication.htm

University of Pittsburg. (2008a). *Nonverbal delivery.* Retrieved from www.speaking.pitt.edu/student/public-speaking/suggestions-verbal.html

ENGAGING LECTURE TIP 45

Voice Modulation

There is an unfortunate but common image of the lecturing professor droning on and on in a dull, monotone voice. However, professors need not be monotone; rather, they can raise or lower their voices, increase or decrease their rates of speech, and stress particular words and phrases to make their lectures more engaging. In this Tip we recommend that professors practice voice modulation to engage and inspire students. Modulating your voice enables you to draw students in, help them stay alert, and refocus their attention.

Key Idea

Modulate your voice to help keep students active and engaged during a lecture.

You may modulate your voice in several key ways.

Volume Volume is how loud your voice sounds to students. Gauge what the volume of your voice should be in your classroom when it is full. You can do this by practicing while it is empty and then adjusting as needed when it is full; you can simply ask students at the back of the class if they can hear you to be sure. If your voice is too soft, students will not be able to hear you or will stop listening to you. If you are too loud, they may think you are shouting and tune you out. Moreover, after finding the normal volume, you can draw attention to your lecture by varying it. Speaking softly can be used as an attention getter, and speaking loudly can also help you illustrate key points.

Pitch Pitch refers to how high or low your voice is. Generally you will want to lower your voice to the lowest level in your comfort range. Lower voices tend to be easier to understand, whereas higher-pitched voices can sound shrill and be aggravating, particularly over a microphone. However, lecturers can also intentionally vary the pitch of their voices. Lowering the voice pitch on a select word or phrase gives it authority and emphasis. Going up in pitch can add interest to a sentence and encourages engagement.

Rate Rate is the speed in which you speak. A typical conversational speech rate is about 120 words per minute, but formal speeches tend to be a bit faster paced, ranging from 150 to 160 words per minute (Dlugan, 2012). That said, one of the biggest mistakes lecturers can make is to speak too quickly. Slowing down helps get your point across to students. However, speeding up occasionally for emphasis can add excitement and energy.

Pauses Pauses are breaks in speaking. They signal to listeners that you are moving on to a new idea. They can also add expression to a lecture. They are best used deliberately in order to achieve a desired effect. For example, you can pause to introduce a new idea to give students time to absorb what you are saying. Or you can pause to display a slide or other visual aid, which provides students time to process the visual without missing your next thought. You can also use pauses, however, simply to catch your breath. When you do pause, however, avoid vocalized pauses such as *ummm* or *ah* or *er* because these can be distracting and annoying and ultimately detract from your message.

Example

A professor who lectured periodically during his interactive lecture course found that students often asked him to repeat what he had just said. One student finally in frustration said, "You are going too fast." The professor realized that he was overly excited about the topic and was speeding through the ideas faster than the students could hear and simultaneously take notes. He decided to modulate his speed. Students appreciated the effort, and he even noticed that he received a higher rating on his communication effectiveness at the end-of-term student evaluations of teaching.

Key References and Resources

Dlugan, A. (2012). *What is the average speaking rate?* Retrieved from http://sixminutes.dlugan.com/speaking-rate/

University of Pittsburg. (2008b). *Verbal delivery tips.* Retrieved from www.speaking.pitt.edu/student/public-speaking/suggestions-verbal.html

CHAPTER 13

Asking and Answering Questions

Asking good questions is an important lecturer responsibility, yet it is often done ineffectively, and few students respond. Some general suggestions for asking questions follow.

- Ask some questions that are pitched at a level that most students could answer so that more than just the highest-achieving students have a chance to participate.
- Try a mix of close-ended and open-ended questions. Asking closed questions, ones with a correct answer or a limited number of correct responses, enables you to make a quick assessment of student understanding of the information they have just heard. In addition, some students will simply be more comfortable answering a question for which they are sure they know the answer. Asking open-ended questions, when there is not necessarily a right or wrong answer, enables you to stimulate discussion and interaction, allow for speculation, and allow students some opportunities to share ideas, information, and opinions. And some students will be more enthusiastic about responding if they have a chance to share their ideas and opinions.
- Ask specific questions. Asking a question such as "Are there any more questions?" almost guarantees that students will not participate, particularly if class is nearly over and they see an opportunity to leave soon if they don't respond.

Responding to students' answers to your questions can also be challenging. Some general suggestions follow.

- Address the question's quality. If it's a good question, say so, and then answer it. If it's tangential, acknowledge that as well by saying something along the lines of, "That's really interesting but a little off of our point, so I'll be happy to talk to you after class."
- Try to stay on point. If you go off on a tangent, students can have difficulty determining what the answer to the question was.
- Address the whole class when you respond to the answer, rather than the one student. You are addressing the class, not having a conversation with a single student.

In addition to these general suggestions, in this chapter, we offer Tips related to asking and answering student questions. We summarize these Tips in Exhibit 13.1.

Exhibit 13.1 Asking and Answering Questions Tips

This Tip . . .	Provides guidance on how to . . .	It is particularly useful for . . .
Tip 46: *Write a Question*	Integrate a post-presentation writing assignment so that students can formulate good questions	Helping students learn to think critically about lecture presentations
Tip 47: *Echo Chamber*	Repeat students' answers	Ensuring that you understand the question correctly and that the whole class hears it
Tip 48: *Wait Time*	Wait after you have asked a question	Generating more and better responses
Tip 49: *Right Means Right*	Correct incorrect answers tactfully	Making sure misinformation is corrected while still promoting participation

ENGAGING LECTURE TIP 46

Write a Question

"Any questions?" the teacher asks. Predictably there's silence. Part of the issue is that students have simply been thinking about what the lecturer has been saying and trying to understand it at a basic level. They have not been thinking about whether they have any questions about the material. The switch from active listening to questioning is abrupt, and they simply haven't had time to process.

There's a relatively easy fix for this challenge: *Write a Question*. Simply ask students to spend a minute or two crafting a question about the content before you ask them if they have any questions. If you provide students with some time to compose their thoughts first, they will have a better chance not only of coming up with a question but also of coming up with a good one.

Key Idea

Provide students with time to compose a question before you ask them whether they have any in order to give them time to process.

Because students may not be good question writers, you may need to provide them with some scaffolding. Consider the following approaches to having students write questions:

- **Provide a model question before asking students to write their own.** Sometimes students simply don't know how to begin, and providing a sample can help model the thinking process and give them a basis for starting.
- **Provide question stems.** Sometimes students need a helping hand, particularly when they have not frequently been challenged to think of their own questions. You can provide this help by suggesting a list of question stems appropriate to the lecture content. Consider some of the following as a starting point:

How would you define . . .?
How would you identify . . .?
How would you recognize . . .?
Why did the . . .?
What was the . . .?
Which facts showed . . .?
What was the main idea of . . .?
Will you restate . . .?
Could you elaborate on . . .?
How would you generalize . . .?
What would result if . . .?
What do you think of . . .?
How does this relate to . . .?
What was the problem with . . .?
What are the pros and cons of . . .?
How would you solve . . .?
How could you verify . . .?
Would it be better if . . .?
What is your opinion of . . .?
How would you improve . . .?

- **Give several answers and ask students to write a question for each answer.** Another way to implement the *Write a Question* activity is to provide several answers and ask students to create a question that matches each answer. You can then ask them for the questions and see if you can come up with the appropriate answer, which not only provides you with insight into their levels of understanding but also can be fun for students.
- **Ask students to partner with a student next to them to write questions.** Students may feel anxious if they can't come up with a question on their own. Allowing them to work with a partner takes off some of the performance pressure. It also enables you to cold call for responses from teams rather than the individual, which can be less intimidating for students.
- **Use a topic grouping.** Display a list of the topics you covered and ask students to write the topics from the lecture they were most interested in on an index card. Have them mill around the room to find others with the same topic and work together to create two to three good questions. Again, strength in numbers helps to alleviate some anxiety.

Most of these activities take just a minute or two (the topic-grouping activity being the exception) and so can provide a good return on the investment of time.

Example

A professor who taught a large lecture class often asked students if they had questions. He then felt awkward when no one raised their hand and the whole class just stared at him in silence. He knew that students probably did have questions but that they were anxious about appearing stupid or inappropriate in front of their peers. He therefore organized students into small group teams at the beginning of the term so that he could move back-and-forth quickly between lecture and collaborative work and then used these same base groups to implement *Write a Question.* Instead of asking students in general if they had questions, he now instructed students to talk together in their teams to formulate questions.

Key References and Resources

Anderson, L. W., & Krathwohl, D. R. (2001). *A taxonomy for learning, teaching and assessing: A revision of Bloom's taxonomy of educational outcomes* (Complete edition). New York, NY: Longman.

Illinois State University, College of Education. (n.d.). *Revised Bloom's taxonomy question starters.* Retrieved from https://education.illinoisstate.edu/downloads/casei/5-02-Revised%20Blooms.pdf

ENGAGING LECTURE TIP 47

Echo Chamber

Echo Chamber means that when you take a question, you repeat or rephrase it out loud, which then can serve many purposes. First, it ensures that the other students in class know what question was asked. Especially in large classrooms, not everyone can hear the question, and without the question for context, the teacher's response probably doesn't mean much. Second, it avoids duplicate questions from students. When all students can hear the question, they are less likely to repeat each other. Third, the teacher gets to check his or her own understanding of the students' question before responding. Fourth, repeating the question ensures that the teacher clarifies its meaning for the rest of the class. This is especially useful if the question was long and rambling; rephrasing it can enable you to summarize it and share the general meaning. Fifth, repeating the question gives the teacher a moment to formulate a better response. Finally, repeating the question offers you the chance to alter it slightly, if necessary. In particular, if the question is not on point, you can gently redirect it so that it is appropriate and so that it contributes something positive to the class. (*Note:* if the question is not worthy of repeating, don't.)

Key Idea

When a student asks a question in class, repeat it to ensure that you understand it correctly and that the whole class hears it.

After you have repeated the question, consider the following:

- **Direct your answer to everyone.** Although one student has asked the question, you are answering it for the whole class you are teaching. In addition, avoid the urge to walk closer to the student asking the question when you answer it because this can exclude the rest of the class. Instead face the full class when you offer a response.
- **Get confirmation from the questioner.** After responding, get feedback from the questioner as to whether your answer has adequately addressed the question. You can opt for a nonverbal signal, such as looking at the questioner and raising your eyebrows or shrugging your shoulders. You can also simply ask, "Does this address your question?" The response will likely be a nod or alternately a confused look. Respond accordingly.
- **Promote a discussion.** Sometimes when a question is open-ended, the best strategy is to get students involved in a discussion to encourage a variety of opinions.
- **Admit if you don't know the answer.** Simply tell students you will research the answer to the question and let them know what you learn, or alternately, ask for a volunteer to look it up.
- **Take another question or conclude.** At this point, you can either ask for additional questions, or if you are running out of time for the activity, restate your main point and conclude the session.

As Ford, McCullough, and Schutta (2012) suggest, paraphrasing a question is a skill in itself, and thinking about a response while you paraphrase one is an even greater skill. You get better with practice, however.

Example

A professor teaching in a large lecture hall wanted to ensure that the Q&A portion of the class session was effective. He used several different strategies to accomplish this, including repeating or paraphrasing each question to ensure that all students heard and understood the question, and therefore he had context for his responses.

Key References and Resources

Ford, N., McCullough, M., & Schutta, N. T. (2012). *Presentation patterns: Techniques for crafting better presentations.* Boston, MA: Addison Wesley.

Zaremba, A. J. (2011). *Speaking professionally: Influence, power and responsibility at the podium.* New York, NY: Routledge.

ENGAGING LECTURE TIP 48

Wait Time

Research demonstrates that when a teacher poses a question in a typical college class session, he or she typically waits for less than one second before calling on someone. There are significant challenges to this practice. In particular, any responses you get cannot be very well thought out. In addition, you are likely to get the same students responding over and over—those who think fast or those who are extroverted enough to be comfortable with thinking on the fly. Moreover, this practice can promote inequities in the classroom because male students—particularly white male students—tend to speak in response more than female or minority students (Mintz, n.d.).

Increasing the *Wait Time,* a concept created by Rowe in the 1970s, improves responses. *Wait Time* is the time between a question and an answer. The idea is to wait at least three to seven seconds to get a lengthier response, a more technically correct response, a better-quality response, and a wider variety of responses. You will also likely get more volunteers and fewer students who respond with "I don't know." Allowing sufficient *Wait Time* is particularly important when the questions are substantive and high level, requiring thoughtful responses.

Key Idea

Wait three to seven seconds after you have asked a question to allow sufficient time for better responses.

Stahl (1994) recommends several different types of think time or *Wait Time,* some of which we have adapted as follows:

- **Post-teacher question *Wait Time.*** The professor pauses for a few seconds before taking responses. This *Wait Time* provides students with sufficient uninterrupted time to first consider and then respond to the question. Lemov (2010) suggests that you may wish to provide some guidance during this time (e.g., "I'd like to see a few more hands before taking responses." "I'd like to see a few hands from people who haven't had a chance to participate yet today." "I see some people jotting down ideas. This is a great idea. I'll wait a few more seconds so that people can finish.")
- **Post-student response *Wait Time.*** The class waits for a few seconds of uninterrupted silence after a student has responded and considers offering their reactions, comments, or answers in response to the first student. This *Wait Time* provides other students with sufficient time to think and decide whether they want to say something of their own.
- **Post-student question *Wait Time.*** Teacher pause time is characterized by the teacher taking a few seconds of uninterrupted silence to deliberately consider how to respond to a student question or comment. Teachers need time to think, too.
- **Post-teacher response *Wait Time.*** The class waits for a few seconds of uninterrupted silence after the professor has responded to a student question. Students consider

volunteering their reactions, comments, or answers in response. This *Wait Time* provides students with an opportunity to think and decide whether they want to contribute something of their own.

The silence of the wait period will likely feel uncomfortable. There is also a trick on finding exactly how long to wait because too long will cause discomfort and too short will not yield the desired results. Practiced well, however, *Wait Time* can greatly improve responses.

Example

An instructor liked to follow her presentations of material with a whole-class discussion, and she worked hard to craft interesting, thoughtful questions to pose to the class. Yet, she felt very awkward when either no one or the same few students raised their hands to respond to her questions. Her anxiety would increase as she wondered if students really didn't have any thoughts to share or if they simply didn't understand or hear her question. To ameliorate her discomfort, she often just answered the question herself. Recognizing that this was not fostering the kind of discussion she had hoped to have, she informed students that she was going to start implementing *Wait Time* to give them the time they needed to formulate their response.

Key References and Resources

Lemov, D. (2010). *Teach like a champion: 49 strategies that put students on the path to success.* San Francisco, CA: Jossey-Bass.

Mintz, S. (n.d.). *Gender issues in the college classroom.* Retrieved from www.columbia.edu/cu/tat/pdfs/gender.pdf

Rowe, M. B. (1987). Wait time: Slowing down may be a way of speeding up. *American Educator, 11*(1), 38–43.

Stahl, R. (1994). Using "think-time" and "wait-time" skillfully in the classroom. *ERIC Digest.* Retrieved from http://files.eric.ed.gov/fulltext/ED370885.pdf

ENGAGING LECTURE TIP 49

Right Means Right

We have been in classroom situations in which we have asked a question, a student responds, and the answer the student gives is simply wrong. We have also observed this in other teachers' classrooms. We all struggle with how to handle it. Our responses run the gamut from "Well that's an interesting point. Does anyone else have a thought about this?" to "Right. Um. Okay. Well, thank you." Most of us want to reinforce participation and not shut the student down. Indeed, the classroom needs to be a safe place for participation.

There are consequences, however, to not acknowledging that an answer is simply wrong. First, you can reinforce the student's misunderstanding if you don't correct the error. Second, you can affirm incorrect information to the rest of the class. Third, you can lose the students who do know the right answer. For these reasons, we suggest that you adopt a *Right Means Right* stance.

Key Idea

When a student answers a question incorrectly in class, it is important to correct it.

Having a few responses available that you can use as needed can help you to uphold the standards of *Right Means Right.* Following are some common ways answers are incorrect, or at least not fully correct, with some sample responses.

Vague or Incomplete Answer

Probe for more information by using questions such as the following:

- Could you give me an example of what you mean?
- Could you elaborate on that point?
- Could you explain how you got to that answer?
- That's good so far. Can you finish the last part?
- Okay, but there's more to the answer than that.

These questions also work well for correct answers.

Partially Correct Answer

Highlight the part that is correct and clarify where the answer is wrong. Consider the following sample responses:

- You are correct about *x*, and that's great; but you're wrong about *y*. So we need to correct *y* so we have a fully accurate answer, and here's how we can do that.
- I'm with you on *x*, but you lost me on *y*. Let's figure this out.
- Right, except you forgot *x*. So when we consider *x*, we get a fully correct answer.

Wrong Answer

State that it's wrong and offer a correction. Consider the following sample answers:

- Thanks for giving it a try. That's a really common misconception or mistake. Let's consider why that is . . .
- I'm glad you made that mistake. Many students make the same one, and here's the reason for that . . .
- Actually, I think you forgot to consider a few facts that might change your answer. What about *x, y,* and *z*? What do you think now?
- Okay, that's an example. I asked for the definition. Can you provide that?
- Oh, that's very close, but it's not quite right. Who can tell me the correct name?
- That would be correct if *x* were true, but this situation is different because of *y*.
- I see why you might think that because these two concepts are easy to confuse. However, we're talking about *x* specifically and not *y*.
- No, but thank you for trying.

Sometimes a wrong answer says something about the way you have phrased the question. You may want to rephrase it before you move to another student contributor, and you will most certainly want to rethink it before asking the question the same way in future sessions.

Many times when a student provides a wrong answer you gain some insight into how students may be thinking about the question. You can use this opportunity to move students toward a better understanding.

The trick to following *Right Means Right* is knowing the students and understanding which type of response will work the best in the given situation.

Example

An instructor was committed to creating a classroom environment in which students felt safe to express their thoughts and feelings without censure. Yet she also recognized that by not correcting a student's misunderstanding, she was unintentionally reinforcing the misunderstanding not only for the individual student but also for the whole class. She therefore decided to implement *Right Means Right* and practiced a variety of ways to correct a student's comments gently but clearly.

Key References and Resources

Hunter, M. (1982). *Mastery teaching: Increasing instructional effectiveness in secondary schools, colleges, and universities.* El Segundo, CA: TIP Publications.

Lemov, D. (2010). *Teach like a champion: 49 strategies that put students on the path to success.* San Francisco, CA: Jossey-Bass.

University of Michigan, Center for Research on Teaching and Learning. (n.d.b). *Classroom challenge: Handling wrong answers.* Retrieved from www.crlt.umich.edu/node/712

Weimer, M. (2008). Ways of responding to wrong or not very good answers. *Faculty Focus.* Retrieved from www.facultyfocus.com/articles/teaching-and-learning/ways-of-responding-to-a-wrong-or-not-very-good-answers/

CHAPTER 14

Signaling the Takeaways

Providing closure means wrapping up your lecture presentation in ways that help students feel as though it has come to a satisfying finish. Thoughtful endings promote the perception that the lecture is a complete, balanced unit. When abrupt endings can feel brusque and disquieting, more intentional endings can feel fulfilling and encourage students to want to come back to the next class session. A sense of closure can be achieved by the lecturer summing up the key information, correcting misunderstandings, or simply wishing students a gracious farewell. In this chapter, we provide four Tips for what you can do to provide students with closure at the end of a lecture presentation. We summarize the Tips in Exhibit 14.1.

Exhibit 14.1 Signaling the Takeaways Tips

This Tip . . .	Provides guidance on how to . . .	It is particularly useful for . . .
Tip 50: *The Synthesis*	Summarize the central and supporting ideas of the lecture	Reinforcing core concepts in ways that deepen understanding and strengthen retention
Tip 51: *The Connector*	Connect the current lecture to past and future content	Helping students integrate lecture information into a cohesive whole
Tip 52: *The Power Close*	End the lecture on a high note	Emphasizing the importance of the talk and encouraging students to look forward to returning to class
Tip 53: *The Graceful Goodbye*	Send students on their way from class with style	Maintaining and fostering enthusiasm for the class

ENGAGING LECTURE TIP 50

The Synthesis

Have you ever been to a lecture or presentation when you got to the end and wondered what it was all about and what the key points were? We have. And we would bet that students have, too. In a lecture presentation, particularly a complex one, we think it is critical to circle back around and provide students with a reminder of the key points and overarching message. We suggest you accomplish this through *The Synthesis* of the lecture, in which you combine the central ideas into a whole.

The Synthesis reinforces the message you have shared with students. It also helps students to assess whether what they thought they got from a lecture was what you were hoping they would get, which in turn enables them to informally assess their learning. Moreover, *The Synthesis* provides guidance on where they may need to continue to work if they see the gaps between what they should have learned and what they believe they learned.

Key Idea

At the end of the lecture, provide a brief *Synthesis* of the central and supporting ideas.

A *Synthesis* can be as simple as "The three most important points I want you to remember from this lecture are . . ." or you might consider an approach such as any of the following:

Graphic Organizer Use a graphic such as an adaptation of the Frayer model shown in Figure 14.1 to display the core components of your synthesis.

Synthesis Frame Provide students with a template of sentence stems that provide the shape of a lecture-synthesizing essay but not the content and then have individual students or

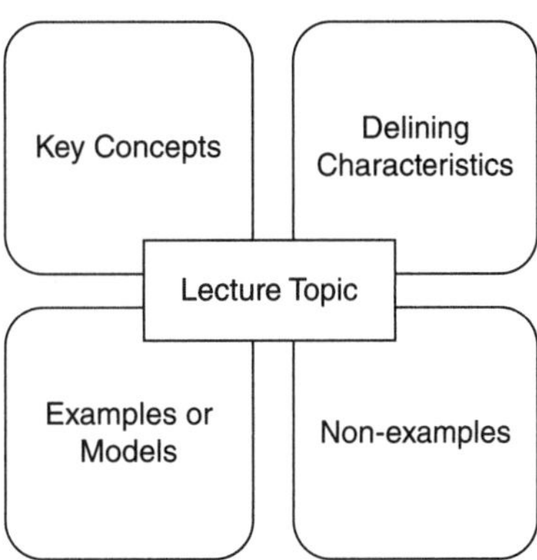

Figure 14.1 Synthesis Graphic

Source: Adapted from Vanderbilt University (2016).

teams complete the sentences, expressing their thoughts in their own words but within a clear, organized framework.

Cloze Activity Provide students with a list of terms from the lecture along with a paragraph that synthesizes the lecture but with blanks in which students fill in from the given list of terms.

Example

To provide a synthesis for a lecturette on organizational change, a professor chose a cloze activity to ensure students understood the central ideas. She crafted several sentences that summarized the main concepts and then took out keywords and left blanks for students to fill in from the list of options. Following is an example:

alteration | institutions | reorganization | restructuring | units

Organizational change occurs when ____________________ or ________________ undergo some kind of____________________. Organizational change is sometimes referred to as __________________________ or ________________________.

She instructed students to fill in the blanks. She walked around the room to ensure students were completing the worksheet.

Key References and Resources

Lewis, A., & Thompson, A. (2010). *Quick summarizing strategies for use in the classroom.* Retrieved from www.gcasd.org/Downloads/Summarizing_Strategies.pdf

Vanderbilt University. (2016). *Building vocabulary and conceptual knowledge using the Frayer model. IRIS Center.* Retrieved from https://iris.peabody.vanderbilt.edu/module/sec-rdng/cresource/q2/p07/#content

ENGAGING LECTURE TIP 51

The Connector

Learning is about making connections. We know from neuroscience that when the brain first encounters something new, it immediately searches for past learning that is similar to, or associated with, the new learning. If the brain can locate these existing understandings, the corresponding neuronal networks are activated. This reinforces the already-stored information and assists in interpreting and assigning meaning to the new information. Thus learners literally build their own minds by constantly making and changing connections between what is new and what is already known. In our lectures, we can assist learners in this process by taking on the role of *The Connector.* In this Tip, we suggest you help students by using the end of your lecture presentation to make explicit the connections between the lecture you have just given and past and future content.

Key Idea

The Connector makes explicit connections among past, present, and future content in ways that help learners integrate new information into existing understandings.

To implement this Tip, end each lecture with a brief description of how the content builds on what students learned in the previous session and also lays the foundation that prepares them for the upcoming session. Consider creating a graphic such as Figure 14.2 to support your verbal comments.

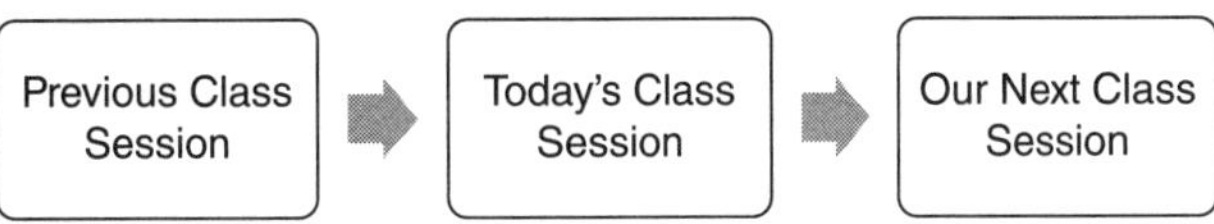

Figure 14.2 *Connector* Graphic

Example

In a course on the development of American music, the professor created a *Connector* slide that she used at the end of each lecture to help students understand how that day's lecture fit into the sequence of lectures for the academic term. An example of this type of slide is provided as Figure 14.3. It was easy to update the slide with appropriate topics, and by elaborating on the slide with just a few comments, she believed she helped students quickly see the connections underlying the lecture content throughout the academic term.

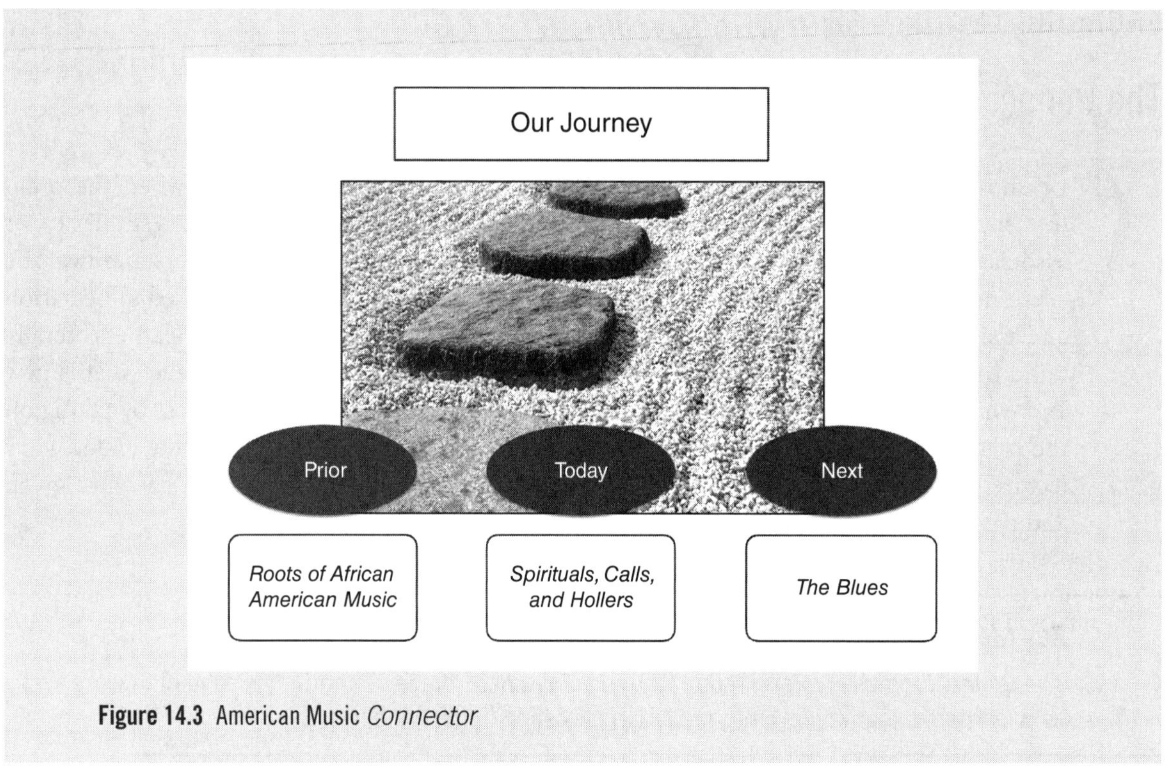

Figure 14.3 American Music *Connector*

Key Reference and Resource

Barkley, E. F., Major, C. H., & Cross, K. P. (2014). *Collaborative learning techniques: A resource for college faculty* (2nd ed.). San Francisco, CA: Jossey-Bass.

ENGAGING LECTURE TIP 52

The Power Close

Sometimes the end of a lecture can feel like a car running out of gas. The lecturer slows down, shows what appears to be the last slide, says "thank you," and then the class just stops. The students begin shuffling paper, pack up, and leave. This is not the best way to use class time. We suggest instead that you use *The Power Close.*

The Power Close involves ending your lecture presentation on a high note that hammers home the importance of the talk. It can keep students thinking about the subject as well as encourage them to come back to the next lecture. *The Power Close* also brings the talk full circle, so that the beginning and the ending of the lecture are related, which reinforces the perception that the lecture is a complete, balanced unit.

Key Idea

The Power Close is a way to create a strong ending to your lecture that also reinforces the central message.

Here are several ways to close a presentation:

- **Back to the beginning.** If you started with a quotation or story or other hook (see Tip 35: *The Hook*), invoke that hook at the end of the lecture. Recalling it brings it back to students' minds, and it provides them with a sense of closing the loop.
- **A provocative question.** One way to end a lecture is by asking students a question that is an extension of the lecture. A question tends to draw students in, to make them stop and think. It can also be a segue to the next lecture session.
- **An image.** If you are using slides, you can share a single powerful image or even a cartoon. The idea is to appeal to students' visual senses in a way that helps them solidify learning from the lecture.
- **A call to action.** Many great lectures end with a call to action. Consider whether there is something that students should do as a result of having participated in your lecture. It may be something to improve society (e.g., "Contact your senator if you want change.") or it could be calling students together to work (e.g., "I'd encourage you to meet for coffee or a Google Hangout to discuss this lecture in preparation for the upcoming quiz.").
- **One more thing.** Steve Jobs is known for his famous use of "one more thing" to add to the end of a presentation. This can be an effective tool in a lecture as well. After it seems that you have finished, simply say "one more thing." The thing should be relevant, however, and an extension of what you have just talked about.
- **Feedback.** Consider using a classroom assessment technique to end the lecture. Use a muddiest point exercise in which you ask students to write for one minute on the thing they found the most confusing in class. Or use a minute paper in which you ask students to

describe one of the key concepts in the lecture so that you can gauge understanding. Alternately, create a survey with three to five questions to ask them whatever you want to know about the lecture (e.g., how useful did they find it, how well do they think they know the content, how well do they feel they would do on a test?).

Example

In "Introduction to Mass Culture," the instructor concluded an introductory lecture on media and culture by posting the slide shown in Figure 14.4 and informing students that in the next class session, they would hear and discuss the fascinating, real-life story of "The Lost Cell Phone."

Figure 14.4 "The Lost Cell Phone"

Key Reference and Resource

BBC Active. (2010). *Ten ways to make lectures more dynamic.* Retrieved from www.bbcactive.com/BBCActiveIdeasandResources/Tenwaystomakelecturesmoredynamic.aspx

ENGAGING LECTURE TIP 53

The Graceful Goodbye

Just as you greeted students on the way into the interactive lecture session, we suggest that you bid them a *Graceful Goodbye* at the end. Indeed, you should give your goodbye as much attention as your greeting. *The Graceful Goodbye* involves acknowledging that students chose to come to class, chose to listen, and chose to stay to the end. Be courteous in return. It demonstrates respect for students and it also helps put a punctuation mark at the end of a class session, making a clear and distinct ending. Rather than being confused, students will know what to do at the end of a class session, which will improve their overall experience.

Key Idea

Take time to send students on their way from class with style using *The Graceful Goodbye.*

For the *Graceful Goodbye*, create an end-of-class checklist that you use in each class session that helps you to attend to details and wish students farewell. Consider some combination of the following options:

- **The pause.** Signal for students' attention and as soon as you have it, pause for about thirty seconds. Let them take a quiet moment to finish any note-taking, gather their thoughts, and prepare for the transition. This pause should mark for your students the start of the final routine.
- **Handouts.** Provide any handouts that you have created for the class (such as Tip 25: *Infodeck*). Alternately, if you have posted the information online, make sure everyone knows how to access it and remind them to do so.
- **Homework or assignment review.** Even if it is clearly posted on the syllabus, and even though students are adults and responsible for their lives, it can be exceedingly helpful to them if you take a few minutes to make sure students know what is due next and that they understand what they are to do. You can summarize and also open the floor to any questions.
- **Exit ticket.** If you assigned a minute paper or muddiest point, you may want to ask students to turn it in as they leave the room. This can provide you with a way to acknowledge students and thank them individually while you also gather information that you can use and revisit in the next class session.
- **Sneak peek.** Provide a sneak peek of the interactive lecture session to come. Doing so will help build enthusiasm for the topic and may help to improve lecture attendance at the next session. (See Tip 31: *Lecture Preview* for more ideas.)
- **Final thoughts.** After everything is done, you can end the session with a final thought. It may be a simple: "And I wish you all a great day." Or "I look forward to seeing you again next week, same bat time, same bat channel." Or "Thank you for your attention and I've really enjoyed talking with you today." In short, offer a positive message before you leave.

- **Time to pack and go announcement.** When students feel that the class is ending, they might begin packing up. This can be distracting for other students as well as for you. If you make it a point to regularly make an announcement for when it is time to pack up, students will learn to wait for the invitation. You may need to put it in your *Terms of Engagement* (Tip 37) that students must wait and even spell out the consequences. For example: "students who pack up early have to take out everything they put away and be the last ones to leave the class."

Keep your *Graceful Goodbye* simple and specific and do it the same way every day. Before long it will be routine and an efficient way to end the class session.

Example

The instructor of a course titled "China: Traditions and Transformations" concluded each interactive lecture session by taking a few moments to offer a *Graceful Goodbye.* Figure 14.5 is an example of a slide he used as he shared his sneak peek, which also included the upcoming homework assignment.

Figure 14.5 *Graceful Goodbye* Example

Key Reference and Resource

Reynolds, G. (2016). *Top ten delivery tips.* Retrieved from www.garrreynolds.com/preso-tips/deliver/

PART THREE

ACTIVE LEARNING TECHNIQUES

Introduction

Teaching and learning is a two-way process. Despite our best efforts to teach students through engaging presentations, it is ultimately the responsibility of each student to put in the effort to actually learn from it. Thus, although the Tips in Part 2 of this book offered guidance on how to maximize the effectiveness of your lecture, we now turn our attention to what you can assign *students* to do to support their learning from your presentation. We do so by providing you with thirty-two active learning techniques (ALTs). These techniques are structures that support active learning during an interactive lecture session. That is, they are intentionally designed activities that help students with what they can do to engage before, during, and after the lecture. These techniques are based in research that shows what kinds of activities support learning in lectures so that you can be confident that you are doing your best to provide the kind of learning environment that will prepare students to excel in today's increasingly complex world.

Organization of the Active Learning Techniques

We present techniques in four key areas—prepare, attend, use, and assess—which are further subdivided into chapters, as illustrated in Figure P3.1.

Prepare. This section of the book is based on research suggesting that preparing students to receive presented material can improve student learning in lectures. We can help students do this by providing them with assignments to work ahead, access prior knowledge, or use that knowledge to anticipate lecture content.

Chapter 15. Actively Preparing. In this chapter, we present techniques that ensure that students have completed out-of-class assignments prior to attending interactive lecture sessions.

Chapter 16. Anticipating and Predicting New Information. Here, we present techniques that ask students to consider what they already know about a topic by making predictions about what is to come. This helps to foster motivation and engagement for lecture presentations.

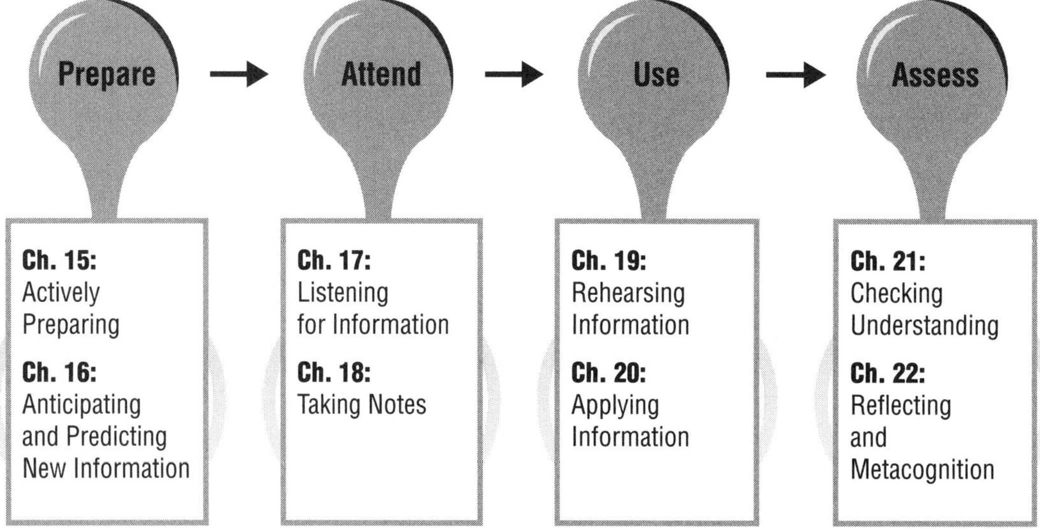

Figure P3.1 Organization of Active Learning Phases and Techniques

Attend. This section derives from research that says if students pay attention, they will learn more. These chapters are intended to provide techniques that encourage students to focus their attention and listen actively to the lecture or to create a meaningful record of information they learn in the lecture.

Chapter 17. Listening for Information. In this chapter, we describe techniques to encourage student attention by asking students to listen for specific information that will be presented in the lecture.

Chapter 18. Taking Notes. Because students often lack note-taking skills and because these skills are important to student learning, in this chapter, we describe techniques for effective note-taking during and after a lecture.

Use. This section is based on research that suggests that in order to remember and understand new learnings, students should use content, ideas, and information in ways that give it significance, such as through rehearsal or application.

Chapter 19. Rehearsing Information. In this chapter, we describe techniques that help students recall basic facts and information as well as summarize and synthesize the information.

Chapter 20. Applying Information. Because using information ensures that students have sufficient grasp of information to be able to apply it in new situations, in this chapter, we offer techniques for application.

Assess. In this section, we address the important role of self-assessment and metacognition to student learning by offering chapters that focus on student reflection on their learning processes and products.

Chapter 21. Checking Understanding. In this chapter, we provide techniques that encourage students to produce artifacts that enable them to check their understanding.

Chapter 22. Reflecting and Metacognition. In this chapter, we offer techniques that encourage students to reflect on their learning in lectures.

Basic Elements of Active Learning Techniques

Each technique has the same format, with the same elements, as follows.

- **Description and purpose.** In this section, we provide a brief description of the technique and explain what educational goals it can best help accomplish.
- **Preparation.** In this section, we offer faculty members information about what they will need to do prior to class to successfully implement the technique. In some instances, preparation is as simple as developing a prompt; in others, it is much more involved and requires creating complex documents to share with students, so ahead-of-time preparation is essential.
- **Procedures.** In this section, we provide basic step-by-step instructions that faculty members can use as a springboard for implementing the technique in class.
- **Examples.** In examples, we share ways faculty members have used the techniques in practice. We provide three different examples in each technique: one from a lecture class, one from a large lecture class, and one from a video lecture.

- **Variations and extensions.** In variations and extensions, we describe ways to change the basic structure, often involving collaborative learning or extending the activity by adding in an assessment.
- **Observations and advice.** In observations and advice, we provide cautions and caveats for implementing these techniques to help ensure your success.

Active Learning Techniques and Different Instructional Contexts

Today's college teachers work in a variety of educational activities and environments, and what constitutes a lecture presentation looks different in each of these. In addition, each form presents a unique set of challenges to lecture success. Although we provide a basic description of how to implement a given technique in the "Procedures" section, we recognize that offering an interactive lecture in a seminar is very different from offering one in a large lecture or an online or flipped class. Thus in our "Examples" sections, we give attention to different types of lecture courses to illustrate how the procedures work in the different environments.

Lecture. When we provide an example from a *lecture,* we mean a course with anywhere from five to fifty students. Our examples that appear under the leader *lecture* come from the following:

- **Seminar talks.** These courses involve teachers and five to twenty-five students, typically fifteen to twenty, sharing ideas and information with each other. Although seminars can be largely discussion and activity-based, there often are "times for telling." It can be difficult, however, to shift naturally from discussion to a presentation. Thus we include some lecture examples in Part 3 that describe how these play out in practice.
- **Medium-sized lecture courses.** These courses often are listed as *lecture* in course guides. They are usually offered in standard classrooms, and students may even have the ability to move tables and chairs together. These courses typically have twenty-five to one hundred students, most often about fifty. In these classes, students can get comfortable listening, making it more difficult to change to active learning activities. Thus some of our lecture examples focus on this type of class.

Large lecture. When we use the term *large lecture,* we mean a course with more than one hundred students. The examples we use in these come from two types of courses:

- **Large lectures.** These courses have more than one hundred students. They are most often offered in large lecture halls. They are useful for conveying information and for expressing enthusiasm about a subject to a large group of students (Davis, 2009). They also present unique challenges to learning, however, including student anonymity; tenuous student motivation, engagement, participation in class discussions and activities, and attendance (including absences, late arrivals, and early departures); difficult paperwork management (such as taking attendance, handing out materials, collecting and recording tests, providing makeup work); teaching to students with widely varying abilities and preparation; and difficulty in offering timely feedback on instruction. For these reasons, in our techniques, we offer examples of *large lectures.*
- **Very large lectures.** These courses often have three hundred–plus students and have exacerbated challenges of those common to the *large lecture.* In our *large lecture* examples, we occasionally feature *very large lectures.*

Video lecture. Many lectures today are not done on-site but rather are offered as video presentations that students can watch on their own time. This format presents new challenges, and for this reason, we offer an example of how each technique has been implemented as a video lecture. These examples come from three types of courses:

- **Online courses.** These are courses in which 80 to 100 percent of the course is carried out in an Internet-based instructional environment. Students in these courses can feel isolated from the teacher and from each other. Some of our video lectures in Part 3 are about online courses.
- **Blended or hybrid courses.** These are courses in which 30 to 80 percent of the course is offered in an Internet-based instructional environment. Although these courses offer a combination of on-site and online instruction, the on-site meetings can feel distant and infrequent. Some of the video lecture examples are focused on blended courses.
- **Flipped courses.** Flipped courses are an instructional model in which students meet for the allocated amount of class time, but the order of elements common in some courses is reversed. Rather than reading and completing activities outside of class and then coming to class to hear a content-intensive lecture, students in flipped classes typically watch short video lectures or complete other content-rich preparatory work and then, during the on-site class session, participate in discussions, exercises, or projects. Some of the video lecture examples are focused on flipped courses.

Thus the techniques in Part 3 of this book are intended to offer guidance on active learning techniques that you can use to maximize student engagement during interactive lecture sections. For additional advice about how to build a class session by weaving together engaging presentations and active learning techniques, see Chapter 5, "Structuring the Session" in Part 2 of this book.

Key Reference and Resource

Davis, B. G. (2009). *Tools for teaching* (2nd ed.). San Francisco, CA: Jossey Bass.

CHAPTER 15

Actively Preparing

Students who come to class having done the assigned reading will most likely learn more than those who don't, but getting students to prepare appropriately is one of the perennial problems in college teaching. Research reports indicate that on any given day, only 20 to 30 percent of students who show up to class have completed their preparatory reading (Weimer, 2015a). This can make teaching quite challenging because professors have to then determine whether to proceed with their original plans or make adjustments to accommodate the majority of students who have not done the advance work.

How can teachers convince students to do the out-of-class readings and assignments? A study conducted by Hattenberg and Steffy (2013) offers us insight on what approaches produce the best results. The researchers surveyed 423 students in eight sections of an introductory sociology course that served students with diverse backgrounds. Students were provided with a list of required and optional activities that ranged from quizzes to being called on randomly in class to answer questions. Students were then asked to rate on a scale of one to ten how effective the activity was in getting them to do the preparatory reading. The researchers found that students clearly considered required activities to be more effective than optional ones.

Most faculty members would not be surprised that external motivators are the best way to guarantee that students are doing the readings or completing other out-of-class activities. Although as college professors we should continue to strive to foster students' intrinsic motivation to learn, implementing approaches that require students to come to class prepared appear to be most effective in ensuring that they do so. For these reasons, we have aimed in this chapter to include techniques that students will find interesting and helpful (thereby bolstering students' intrinsic motivation) and that also produce a learning artifact that you can assess and grade (attending to students' extrinsic motivation). The techniques are summarized in Exhibit 15.1.

Exhibit 15.1 Techniques for Actively Preparing

This technique . . .	Helps students learn actively by having them . . .
ALT 1: *Active Reading Documents*	Follow a detailed process for comprehending and applying information from a reading by answering the questions in a teacher-created document
ALT 2: *Know-Wondered-Learned*	Complete a handout that asks them to list what they know about a topic, wonder about a topic, and have learned about the topic
ALT 3: *Two-Minute Question-Development Talks*	Pair up for two-minute talks where they discuss the out-of-class assignments and develop questions for the lecture
ALT 4: *Individual Readiness Assurance Tests*	Complete a series of questions on previously assigned reading material at the start of a class session

Key References and Resources

Hattenberg, S. J., & Steffy, K. (2013). Increasing reading compliance of undergraduates: An evaluation of compliance methods. *Teaching Sociology, 41*(4), 346–352.

Weimer, M. (2015a). Getting students to do the reading. *Faculty Focus.* Retrieved from www.facultyfocus.com/articles/effective-teaching-strategies/getting-students-to-do-the-reading/

ACTIVE LEARNING TECHNIQUE 1

Active Reading Documents

Complexity involved in	
Planning	MODERATE
Developing Materials	HIGH
Implementing in Class	LOW

Description and Purpose

Getting students to do the assigned reading prior to class—and to do it well—is a persistent problem for many college teachers. Research indicates that most students simply don't read at all, particularly when there are no immediate consequences for not doing so. Even students who have done the reading may just have skimmed it, not read deeply enough to engage with the content in a way that would help them understand and process information for an upcoming class session. The result is that it is difficult for the teacher to know how best to target their lecture presentation because students will then attend class with widely varying levels of preparedness.

Active Reading Documents (*ARDs*) are carefully prepared forms that guide students through the process of critical and careful reading. In particular, *ARD*s walk students through knowledge retrieval and comprehension because students must access and make sense of the new information to complete the document. *ARD*s can scaffold reading assignments so that students read at more-sophisticated levels of comprehension and analysis. They not only help students prepare for a given session but also help them develop careful reading skills that can be used in other contexts. *ARD*s also provide teachers with an artifact that can be evaluated and count toward the course grade, which can motivate students to do the preparatory work out of class and at an appropriate level.

Preparation

- Choose a reading assignment.
- Create a handout with corresponding tasks for the reading assignment (see following).
- Decide how you will assess the information.

Name: **Date:**			
Please complete the tasks identified in the "Description" column in the "Your Response" column,			
Task	**Objective Level**	**Description**	**Your Response**
1	Foundational knowledge	State the main idea of the reading.	
2	Foundational knowledge	State the key supporting points or arguments.	
3	Application	Demonstrate the organizational structure of the reading assignment, whether through an outline, a flow chart, a hierarchy, a matrix, or other.	
4	Application	Write three questions you would ask students if you were the professor teaching this reading assignment.	
5	Integration	Describe three original connections you see across idea or concepts *within the reading.*	
6	Integration	Describe three original connections you see across ideas or concepts *between* this reading and other readings, chapters, or lectures from this class.	

Procedures

1. Distribute the *Active Reading Document.*
2. Assign the reading. Ask students to bring their *ARD*s to the next class session.
3. Collect the document.
4. Assess the document.

Video Lecture	Large Lecture
If you are teaching online, distribute the *ARDs* to students after you have assigned a reading. Have them submit responses as an assignment prior to watching your video lecture. Most learning management systems (LMSs) will allow you to require a submission as a prerequisite for viewing the video lecture.	If you are teaching a large lecture course, choose only a couple of components (e.g., the main idea and the organizational structure) and ask students to complete the assignment with one prompt on each side of the card and use a simple plus-check-minus grading system.

Examples

Calculus (Lecture)

In this course, the professor assigns homework for each learning module that students must complete prior to a class meeting. The homework asks students to read about the processes to solve the problems that are the focus of the upcoming module. While reading, students complete an *ARD*, which asks them to translate the processes they have read about into their own words. Students submit their *ARD* responses through a course management system, and the professor does a quick plus-check-minus assessment. The professor also selects a sample of completed assignments for closer examination to determine how best to target her lecture to address any issues she sees during her *ARD* review. Students bring their *ARD*s to class in hard copy so that they can ask the questions they have about the steps in the process.

Introduction to Philosophy (Large Lecture)

In this survey, students examine several key writings, principles, and concerns of philosophy. The professor requires reading and critical examination of the writings of classical, modern, and contemporary thinkers to introduce students to important philosophers and to provide students with information about knowledge, perception, freedom, and determinism. The course is also meant to help students improve critical thinking and writing skills, especially so that they can learn to write more organized and effective argumentative essays. However, the professor was worried that students were not reading deeply enough to be able to develop good arguments about the primary sources. The professor decided to use *ARDs* to guide students to do their reading at a deeper level and then come to the lecture better prepared to grapple with the concepts and ideas she presented.

Medical Terminology (Video Lecture)

In this flipped course, students learn the principles of word building to improve their medical vocabulary. Most students who take the course intend to enter the health care industry. They learn about root words, prefixes, and suffixes, and they work on pronunciation and spelling as well. It is often dry reading, however, and the professor wanted to be sure that students were getting the main points. He created *ARDs* that ask for basic information about the word structure, a sentence using the word in context, and making connections between words based on their roots, prefixes, or suffixes.

Prior to the first unit, he posted an introduction to the lesson. In this introduction, he notified students that they would need to complete *ARDs* on each learning module's assigned readings prior to accessing the video lectures or attending the in-class active learning sessions. He noticed that quiz scores improved dramatically, and he anticipated that the exams would also show an improvement in student grades.

Variations and Extensions

- Have students form pairs to review the documents, and ask students to revise their *ARDs* based on their discussions. Consider assessing only the revision.
- Consider offering feedback and allowing students to revise their original *ARDs* before assigning grades. This may be time-consuming for large classes, but you can consider grading drafts on a simple plus-check-minus basis.

Observations and Advice

This technique is particularly helpful in introductory classes and for novice learners. It is also especially effective early in the semester, and once students have the basic idea of how to read critically, you may want to discontinue.

Students may find this assignment to be challenging the first few times, and it may be particularly stressful to them if you will grade the assignment. Yet you will likely want to do so to ensure that students take the assignment seriously.

Having students bring their *ARD* drafts to class can strengthen class discussions and helps students to further clarify their understanding of the material and to revise their *ARDs* accordingly.

Key Reference and Resource

Dubas, J. M., & Toledo, S. A. (2015). Active reading documents (ARDs): A tool to facilitate meaningful learning through reading. *College Teaching, 63*(1), 27–33.

ACTIVE LEARNING TECHNIQUE 2

Know-Wonder-Learned

Complexity involved in	
Planning	LOW
Developing Materials	LOW
Implementing in Class	LOW

Description and Purpose

Know-Wonder-Learned (*K-W-L*) involves creating a chart to help students think about out-of-class reading or other assignments prior to coming to a class. Before starting an assignment, students complete the *Know* portion of the chart, indicating what they already know about the topic. They also record what they still *Wonder* or want to know about the topic. After completing the reading, in the *Learned* portion of the chart, students indicate what they have just learned about the topic through the assignment, trying when possible to address the *Wonder* column; if they cannot answer the *Wonder,* they can ask you those questions during class discussion.

The *K-W-L* chart is fundamentally a graphic organizer, a structure that enables students to organize new knowledge. Such a structure prompts students to arrange thoughts, ideas, facts, terms, or other critical course content into a graphic format. *K-W-L* requires students to access their prior knowledge of the topic. It establishes a purpose for reading, it requires them to formulate questions about a topic, and it provides a built-in way for students to monitor their comprehension. *K-W-L* can also be used to establish goals and objectives, engage students in a new topic, and illustrate the learning that has occurred.

Preparation

- Identify a reading, video, or other out-of-class assignment.
- Determine how students will record their responses, whether on index cards, a template that you provide, a sheet of their own paper, online, or using an LMS. Consider a template like the following:

Know-Wonder-Learn Template

Know	Wonder	Learned

Alternately, you may ask students to create three columns on a blank sheet of paper, with the appropriate headers as follows:

- **Column 1 (*Know*)**: What do you already *Know* about the topic before you complete the assignment?
- **Column 2 (*Wonder*)**: What do you *Wonder* or *Want* to know? What knowledge do you want to gain from the assignment?
- **Column 3 (*Learned*)**: What did you *Learn* about the topic by completing the assignment?

- Next determine what students will do during each phase. For example, they might include bullet points for the *Know* portion, questions for the *Wonder* portion, and statements for the *Learned* portion of the activity.

Procedures

1. Assign the reading or other out-of-class assignment and distribute the *K-W-L* chart or tell students how to create one.
2. Ask students to complete the *Know* and *Wonder* sections prior to doing the work of the assignment.
3. Collect student responses. Consider gathering up the questions before the lecture, reviewing them quickly before you begin your talk and offering an impromptu discussion.

Video Lecture	Large Lecture
Post a discussion thread with prompts for the *Know* and *Wonder* portions of the chart and ask students to respond to the prompts. This strategy helps you to assess students' background knowledge and discover what students would like to learn. Assign the reading and then ask students to post about what they *Learned* and to identify any remaining questions they have. Alternately simply create an "assignment" that students submit.	Assign the chart and ask students to keep their responses to a single sentence. Ask them to hold on to their charts during class to see how many of the *Wonder* portions of their chart you answer during lecture. Open the floor for discussion of the remaining questions at the end of your lecture. Take up forms at the end-of-class and assess them as plus-check-minus for completion.

Examples

Introduction to Physics (Lecture)

A physics professor was preparing a lecture on gravity. She believed all students would have some prior knowledge of the topic, but she thought there would be a wide range among students as to the level of prior knowledge. She assigned an article to help bridge the gap but wanted to be sure that students read the work thoughtfully. She decided to use *K-W-L* charts. She asked students to complete the charts as follows: *Know* before the reading, *Wonder* during the reading, *Learned* after the reading. She was able to group students into two categories: (1) lower levels of understanding and (2) higher levels of understanding. Following are some examples responses from each of the groups.

Know	Example response group 1	That it weighs people and objects down so that they don't float into space; Isaac Newton's theory
	Example response group 2	Every object that has mass attracts every other object that has mass.
Wonder	Example response group 1	How did Newton discover gravity?
	Example response group 2	What determines how fast an object falls to the ground?
Learned	Example response group 1	The amount of gravity is dependent on the amount of mass.
	Example response group 2	Air resistance influences how fast something falls.

She decided to put students into pairs for a *Note-Taking Pairs* (ALT 16) assignment and put a student from group 1 and group 2 into each pair.

Sports Management (Large Lecture)

In this large lecture course, the professor knew that having students actively prepare for class would not only help them better understand her lecturettes but also would help them be better participants in the group activity. The professor used an introductory textbook. When she assigned a new chapter, for example, "Sport for Persons with Disabilities," she asked students to complete a *K-W-L* chart. She posted a template to the course site similar to the following and asked students to keep the responses to a few phrases.

Name: **Date:**	
Before you read the assignment, answer the following prompt by listing two to three phrases.	
Know: What do you already know about sports for persons with disabilities?	
Wonder: What do you want to know about sports for persons with disabilities?	
Read Chapter 3, *then* answer the following prompt:	
Learned: What new things about sports for persons with disabilities did you learn from reading the chapter?	

She assessed with a simple plus-minus for completion and then drew a sample that she looked at more thoroughly. The professor started class by addressing any unanswered *Wonders*.

History of the United States from 1914 to Present (Video Lecture)

A professor teaching an online history class was beginning a unit on World War II, focusing on the Holocaust. The teacher asked the students to post to a discussion board what they already know about the topic, providing them with the following prompts:

Prompt 1: What do you already *Know* about World War II?

- What images and words do you associate with World War II?
- What names come to mind when you consider the war?
- Does WWII make you think of a specific geographical location?
- How have you seen the war portrayed in books, arts, and the media?

Prompt 2: What do you *Wonder* about World War II? Phrase your response in the form of a question, for example:

- What events precipitated the war?
- How did ordinary people influence key events related to the war?
- How did the cultural environment influence the war?
- How did geography influence the war?
- What has been the legacy of World War II?

She reviewed student questions and created a series of video responses in which she addressed misconceptions from the *Know* prompt and in which she responded to common questions in the *Wonder* prompt. She then released a video lecture on WWII along with her video responses. She concluded the series by asking students to write a one-page statement describing what they learned from the lectures.

She believed students had learned much about WWII from the lectures, which she could tell by comparing their *Know* and *Learned* responses. And students were particularly complimentary of her videos in which she directly responded to their questions.

Variations and Extensions

- You may extend this activity by adding other columns to this chart such as *W* ("Why is this information important?" "Who are the main characters?" "Where did I find this new information?"); *H* ("How did it happen?" or "How can you learn more?") or *S* ("Something I hope to remember").
- To vary this activity, use prompts to structure the *Wonder* portion of this activity, such as the six questions of journalism: who? what? where? when? why? how? (Angelo & Cross, 1993).
- Another variation on *K-W-L* is to ask students to work in groups to respond to the prompts.
- Consider using this activity in combination with entry and exit tickets (Barkley & Major, 2016, LAT 3).

Observations and Advice

If students lack sufficient prior knowledge, they may feel uncomfortable completing the *Know* phase of the activity. They are also likely to have misconceptions, so be prepared to directly refute those; *K-W-L* can be a good tool for diagnosing misunderstandings, but responding to them directly is critical to the success of the activity.

The point at which students will turn in the work influences the activity. For example, they may turn in index cards at each phase or the completed template at the end of the activity. The former may provide you with information about student misconceptions so that you can address them during the lecture. The latter may provide them with an opportunity to self-correct their own misconceptions, which is an important skill for students to develop.

Key References and Resources

Angelo, T. A., & Cross, K. P. (1993). *Classroom assessment techniques: A handbook for college teachers* (2nd ed.). San Francisco, CA: Jossey-Bass.

Barkley, E. F., & Major, C. H. (2016). *Learning assessment techniques: A handbook for college faculty*. San Francisco, CA: Jossey-Bass. Adapted with permission of publisher.

Fengjuan, Z. (2010). The integration of the know-want-learn (KWL) strategy into English language teaching for non-English majors. *Chinese Journal of Applied Linguistics, 33*(4), 77–127. Retrieved from http://218.4.189.15:8090/download/9b1c7bc7-e2b2–40ea-b8b6–42be6b38f911.pdf

Huffman, L. E. (1998). Combine focus questions (5 W and 1 H) with K-W-L. *Journal of Adolescent & Adult Literacy, 41*(6), 470–472.

Ogle, D. M. (1986). K-W-L: A teaching model that develops active reading of expository text. *Reading Teacher, 39*(6), 564–570.

ACTIVE LEARNING TECHNIQUE 3

Two-Minute Question-Development Talks

Complexity involved in	
Planning	LOW
Developing Materials	LOW
Implementing in Class	MODERATE

Description and Purpose

During *Two-Minute Question-Development Talks (TQDTs),* student pairs share ideas and information about out-of-class assignments. Their exchange involves two questions: "What was the main thing you learned from the assignment?" "What questions about the assignments do you have?" The pair then develops a single question about the upcoming talk. The exchange requires students to recall prior learning from the assignments, to think more deeply about it by creating questions, and to focus their attention on the topic about to be addressed.

Preparation

- Give an assignment prior to class to help students prepare. The assignment could be a reading, a video, a podcast, or something else.
- Consider whether you want to set up time limits for the talks (e.g., the first student talks for thirty seconds, then they switch roles and the second student talks for thirty seconds, and then they repeat the process). If so, figure out how you will prompt a change in the role of speaker and listener (e.g., ring a bell, flash the lights in the room). Alternately, decide if you would rather allow the conversation to flow more naturally because some students will simply have more to say about certain topics than others.
- Determine whether and when you will ask students to report out to the full group about their pair discussions. Engaging a few volunteers each time can be useful.
- Determine how you will collect the questions that each pair develops. Index cards can be a quick way to gather the information.

Procedures

1. Ask students to form pairs.
2. Ask members of each pair to take turns talking during a two-minute time period, sharing what they learned about the topic from the assignment and then together crafting a single question about the assignment.
3. Respond to questions, but tell students to ask original questions only as the Q&A proceeds.

Video Lecture	Large Lecture
For an online variation of *TQDTs,* provide a discussion prompt asking students to post a summary of the reading and a question. Because this is a many-to-many discussion rather than a one-to-one discussion, this approach has the advantage of having many different voices asking questions. Consider asking students to respond to the questions to which they know the answers.	This technique will work well in a large lecture class. It is a quick pair activity that enables students to exchange knowledge, assuming they have done the readings (consider pairing with ALT 4: *Individual Readiness Assurance Tests*). You may have to limit the time on the Q&A portion and ask students who have remaining unanswered questions after the lecture to e-mail you their questions, letting them know how you will respond (e.g., to the full-group e-mail list or discussion board).

Examples

Introduction to Cultural Anthropology (Lecture)

The professor of this course uses *TQDTs* regularly throughout the term. For example, to start the class session following assigned readings introducing the concept of culture, the instructor asked students to turn to their neighbors. He told them to talk for approximately two minutes, quickly summarizing what they knew about the topic of "culture" from the readings. He also asked them to work together to develop a question about the reading assignments and to write this question on an index card he provided. When the conversations seemed to be trailing off, he asked for a few volunteers to share their ideas and to ask their questions, to which he responded. He then asked both members of the pair to sign their names on the card that contained their question, collected these, and proceeded with his lecture.

Business Computer Systems (Large Lecture)

In this large lecture, students focus on computer hardware and software concepts. The course meets for one hour of large lecture per week and three hours of lecture-lab (lecture-lab sections have about twenty-five students per section). The professor uses a textbook and assigns a chapter prior to each course session. At the start of class, he assigns *TQDTs.* He asks students to pair up, take about a minute to exchange ideas about the main point of the reading, and then develop one question together. He asks students to write their questions on an index card and turn them in with both students' names. He sometimes does a quick sorting of questions and addresses the main ones during the lecture.

College Algebra (Video Lecture)

An algebra instructor decided to use *TQDTs* in her blended course, which mostly enrolled first-year students. She planned each learning module to last one week of the academic term. During the week on rectangles, she asked students to visit the course site and complete the preclass activities there including the readings. In class, student pairs worked to describe the main thing they had learned about rectangular coordinates from the reading and to develop a single question. She spent class time responding to questions. After class, students watched a video lecture on the rectangular coordinate system, and the instructor felt students were well prepared to understand the presentation information.

Variations and Extensions

- Consider making a list of questions to help students study for quizzes. To make this more efficient, ask students to submit their responses electronically, for example, through an LMS discussion prompt.
- If you do not announce the activity ahead of time, consider giving students a minute or two to think or write prior to forming pairs. This variation is similar to ALT 19: *Think-Pair-Share.*

Observations and Advice

If students know they will have to talk with their peers and thus reveal whether they have done the out-of-class assignments, the peer pressure may encourage them to do the work. Letting students pair with friends, however, can undermine this, particularly if the friends are close enough to be forgiving. Mix up the pairs so that students don't always work with friends and they don't have the same partners each time.

When students have not prepared, they may feel anxious about the discussions, and their partners may feel annoyed with having to carry the weight of the discussions. Perhaps pair this technique with ALT 4: *Individual Readiness Assurance Tests.* Use the reporting-out phase to quickly clarify misunderstandings or gaps in understanding so that you can fill them prior to moving forward with new information.

Key Reference and Resource

Barkley, E., Major, C. H., & Cross, K. P. (2014). CoLT 1: Think-pair-share. *Collaborative learning techniques* (pp. 153–158). San Francisco, CA: Jossey-Bass.

ACTIVE LEARNING TECHNIQUE 4

Individual Readiness Assurance Tests

Complexity involved in	
Planning	MODERATE
Developing Materials	MODERATE
Implementing in Class	LOW

Description and Purpose

Individual Readiness Assurance Tests (iRATs) are closed-book quizzes that students complete after an out-of-class reading, video, or other homework assignment. Quizzes typically have five to twenty multiple-choice quiz questions and usually are administered at the start of a class session. Results from the quizzes demonstrate whether students have mastered basic vocabulary and other foundational concepts they need in order to understand the lecture content. *iRATs* are a concept developed by team-based learning advocates (Michaelsen, Davidson, & Major, 2014) but have application in almost any course in which instructors want to encourage and assess student preparation for class.

iRATs can serve as cues about the most important course concepts and thus help students focus their attention to the topic of the presentation. The quizzes can ensure that students are directly accountable for their own preparation for learning in lectures. When used regularly, they can also provide students with feedback on how well they are doing in learning material on their own.

Preparation

- Choose a reading assignment, video, or other activity that helps students gain knowledge that they will complete out of class.
- Write five to twenty multiple-choice questions related to the content that will demonstrate whether students have completed the work.
- Determine how you will administer the *iRAT.* A handout with or without a Scantron can be useful. Team-based learning advocates often use scratch-off sheets for *iRAT;* the advantage of the scratch-off sheets is that they provide students with immediate feedback on their results. Another option is to have students complete the quiz prior to coming to class through electronic administration.

Procedures

1. Ask students to complete an out-of-class, content-rich assignment.
2. When class begins, announce the activity, pass out the *iRAT* you have developed, and tell students how long they have to complete it.

3. Ask students to take the test and then collect them.
4. Grade the results and provide students with feedback.

Video Lecture	Large Lecture
If you are teaching an online course, you may want to use an LMS test or quiz function. It is a good idea to do this as a timed quiz so that students will not have sufficient time to look up the answers but rather will have to answer questions on their own.	If you are teaching a large lecture section, consider using an individual response system (clickers) or assigning the test out of class so that it is automatically graded.

Examples

Chemistry (Lecture)

A chemistry professor starting a new term was concerned about students not completing their out-of-class reading assignments, and he was also concerned about the number of students from the past term who did not attend class meetings. He decided to use graded *iRATs* at the start of each class session throughout the semester. He thought that the quizzes would give students incentives not only to study but also to show up for class.

For example, while introducing a unit on nuclear magnetic resonance analysis, the professor assigned an overview article for students to read and study prior to coming to class. At the start of the first class session of the unit, students took an *iRAT.* The quiz consisted of ten questions, with one spectra per question, and students had to select the correct chemical structures for each. At the completion of the quiz, the professor collected the exams and proceeded with a lecture on measuring coupling constants and annotating splitting patterns.

The professor noticed a rise in attendance over the semester as students began to understand that he would administer *iRATs* at the start of each class session. He also noticed that although average student scores on the *iRATs* started out lower than he would have hoped, the class average gradually increased over the semester. Students also told him that the *iRATs* helped them understand what was important so that they could better study for major examinations.

History (Large Lecture)

The professor of this American history course decided he wanted to use interactive lecturing. The professor chose to combine short lectures on critical concepts in history along with more specific content (e.g., he discussed historical empathy prior to a unit on slave resistance in the American South). With such a large class, however, he wanted some assurance that students had completed the reading so that he could target his lecturettes, confident that students had the appropriate background knowledge. He decided to use *iRATs.* Each time he assigned a reading, students had to complete a timed online quiz related to the reading prior to coming to class.

Philosophy of Mind (Video Lecture)

In an online philosophy course, the professor felt that students were not completing the readings but rather were relying solely on her video lectures to learn content. The readings, however, had essential foundational information that provided necessary background for fully understanding the lectures. For example, during the Cartesian dualism unit, the professor had the students read Rene Descartes's Meditations 1 and 2 prior to watching her video lecture for the unit. In her lecture, she synthesized information from multiple sources, including Bloom's "Therefore I Am" and Churchland's "Matter and Consciousness." Clearly students could not really process the synthesis without having read the source material.

The professor decided to use *iRATs* to encourage students to read the assigned source material prior to watching the video lectures and to assess whether they had done so. To start, she created a test bank of forty questions. The professor had students complete an *iRAT,* which she presented as a timed test, to assess student readiness for the lecture. The test drew ten questions from the test bank. Students had to earn at least a 70 percent on the test before proceeding to the video. If they did not pass with at least a 70 percent, they had to retake the test with new questions until they did; students were allowed to retest twice. Any students who did not pass the *iRAT* by the third attempt were required to contact the professor by e-mail to request another chance and to identify a strategy about what they would do differently to do better on their fourth attempt.

The professor found that the *iRATs* did help with student comprehension because students made better grades on essays and exams after she implemented them. She also found that most students were able to pass the exam by the third attempt. The one student who did not e-mail her acknowledged skim reading the assignment in an attempt to pass the test; she asked the student to submit an outline of the material prior to the student's fourth, and successful, *iRAT* attempt.

Variations and Extensions

- Consider asking students to rate their confidence in their answers. This variation will help students think through whether they really do know something, which could be influential on their future preparation strategies.
- After students take the *iRAT* as an individual, put them into groups and have them complete the same tests. This group readiness assurance test (gRAT) approach is similar to test-taking teams (Barkley, Major, & Cross 2014, CoLT 12) and team tests (Barkley & Major, 2016, LAT 9). After the groups take the gRAT, allow students to appeal any questions they feel had an incorrect answer (Michaelsen et al., 2014).

Observations and Advice

Writing good questions can be a challenge. Avoid creating questions that ask about picky details and write ones that instead focus on the most important concepts from the assignment. This approach will help students to understand the *iRAT* as an important part of learning, rather than to see it as unnecessary busy work.

In addition, avoid making the questions too hard or too easy. If the questions are too hard, students will become discouraged. If they are too easy, students will not take the *iRATs* seriously.

Key References and Resources

Barkley, E. F., & Major, C. H. (2016). *Learning assessment techniques: A handbook for college faculty.* San Francisco, CA: Jossey-Bass.

Barkley, E. F., Major, C. H., & Cross, K. P. (2014). *Collaborative learning techniques: A resource for college faculty* (2nd ed.). San Francisco, CA: Jossey-Bass.

Hrynchak, P., & Batty, H. (2012). The educational theory basis of team-based learning. *Medical Teacher, 34,* 796–801.

Michaelsen, L. K., Davidson, N., & Major, C. H. (2014). Team-based learning practices and principles in comparison with cooperative learning and problem-based learning. *Journal on Excellence in College Teaching, 25*(3/4), 57–84.

CHAPTER 16

Anticipating and Predicting New Information

Making predictions is a strategy in which learners use information they have gleaned from other assignments and their own personal experiences to anticipate what they are about to hear in a lecture. Learners make their predictions based on a pattern of evidence. Predicting is not only about figuring out what is next but also forming hypotheses, asking questions, recalling facts, inferring, and drawing conclusions. This strategy helps students make connections between their prior learning and the information being communicated by the lecturer.

Learners involved in making predictions focus on the lecture and are strategically thinking ahead and also refining and verifying their predictions. Instructors can help students develop proficiency in this skill by providing them with practice. In this chapter, we present four techniques that have students make predictions about information to come in a lecture session. We summarize the Techniques in Exhibit 16.1.

Exhibit 16.1 Techniques for Actively Preparing

This technique . . .	Helps students learn actively by having them . . .
ALT 5: *Update Your Classmate*	Write a memo to a student, real or fictional, who missed class the day before to describe the missing information and explain why it might be important to the upcoming lecture
ALT 6: *Sentence Stem Predictions*	Receive a sentence stem to complete that prompts them to predict information to come in the lecture
ALT 7: *Guess and Confirm*	Write down facts they expect to learn from lecture, then check off the list during lecture, and at end discuss what they expected to hear but didn't and ask questions about it
ALT 8: *Preview Guide*	Receive a set of statements about the topic and indicate whether they agree or disagree with the statement; at the end of the lecture, they indicate whether they changed their mind

ACTIVE LEARNING TECHNIQUE 5

Update Your Classmate

Complexity involved in	
Planning	LOW
Developing Materials	LOW
Implementing in Class	LOW

Description and Purpose

At the beginning of a class session, students write a memo to a real or fictional student who missed the previous session. In one version of the memo, students explain how an idea from the prior session's lecture that either the teacher or they select is particularly central to understanding. In an alternate version, students write a summary of the entire prior lecture. Students in either version explain why the missed information was central to understanding the current day's session.

Update Your Classmate requires students to recall prior knowledge before learning new material. This helps them activate their schemata on the topic as well as rehearse information, which they can then build on with the information from the current day's lecture. The last step of having students describe why the information will be important asks them to make predictions and create connections between concepts in their schemata.

When students know they will have to connect prior information to the new information, it provides them with a task that can help them focus their attention. *Update Your Classmate* is a useful way to structure that activity and it can be done throughout the semester. Conveying the information in a memo also gives the recall task an authentic feel to the information, which students may find more interesting.

Preparation

- First, decide what you will do with the information before you implement this technique because this will influence how you carry it out. If your intent is a quick check to assess understanding, you may have students fill out the information on notecards. If you want a fuller account of their knowledge, you may wish to design a template such as the one included in the "Example" section.
- Next, determine how often students will complete this activity, whether at each class session or only at critical times (e.g., prior to a quiz or exam).

Procedures

1. Announce the activity, the time that students will have for writing, and the parameters of the assignment.
2. Provide the template for the assignment if you have created one.
3. Ask students to begin work on the memo and call time when the activity is ending (typically five to seven minutes).
4. Collect and assess the memos and consider reporting key themes back to students.
5. Present the lecture.

Video Lecture	Large Lecture
Alter the assignment structure, for example, by using the scenario that some students were not able to download and view the course videos for the scheduled assignments. Ask students to post summaries of the content to help their fellow classmates who were having technical difficulties.	Although writing assignments can be a challenge in large lectures, quick ones can be manageable and support student learning. What this requires is developing a simple, swift assessment process and then reviewing a sample of responses in more depth. This can help you to adapt your presentation to the needs of the specific group of students.

Examples

Introduction to Engineering (Lecture)

A professor began the semester of an introduction to engineering course that met on Tuesdays and Thursdays of each week with a lecture on the topic of "What is engineering?" At the next class session, she informed students that a new student had added the course late and was starting that day. She asked the students to help her bring the new student up to speed. She asked the students to *Update Your Classmate* by filling out the memo template. She then proceeded to give a lecture on the topic of "What is design?" She collected the memos at the end of the class session and used them to check attendance and understanding.

Memo to a Classmate Template

To: My classmate who missed the lecture on Tuesday **From:** A concerned fellow student: ______________________ (name here) **Subject:** The course content you missed from class yesterday **Date:** January 16, 2018
Help your classmate who missed the first class session by outlining the three most important points from Tuesday's lecture. ______________________ ______________________ ______________________ ______________________ Stress why you believe the points from Tuesday will be critical to understanding today's lecture. ______________________ ______________________ ______________________

Introduction to Anthropology (Large Lecture)

The professor of this large lecture course believed that students were not making connections between the concepts in each week's assignments and instead perceived them as separate, stand-alone entities. The professor decided to use *Update Your Classmate.*

At the beginning of a session that was an introduction to evolution and adaptation and that followed one focused on culture, he asked students to complete a memo to a fictional classmate "Taylor" who missed the previous session. Students were to explain the key concepts related to culture and identify example groups who share it. They were then to tell Taylor why that particular information would be useful to understanding evolution and adaptation.

After giving students time to write, the professor asked two students to read their responses aloud and allowed others to contribute suggestions. He then collected all responses and later read a random sample. He developed an oral response, which he worked into the lecture the next day. He repeated the assignment periodically, particularly before exams, asking students to develop a synthesis of each of the lecture modules for students who might have missed a given week.

Nurse Educator Roles and Responsibilities (Video Lecture)

In this online course for graduate nursing students, the goal is to help nurses who will ultimately teach undergraduates about their roles and responsibilities as nurse educators. It is also intended to enable students to improve skills in curriculum development, classroom and clinical teaching, and evaluation methods. The course is for nurses who will work in a clinical setting and those who will work in institutions of higher education as faculty members. Students take the course in an entirely online environment, which is offered through a learning management system (LMS). The professor has video lectures, reading assignments, and activity assignments in each unit. In her unit on evaluation, the professor introduced the concept of formative assessment. To ensure the students had watched and understood the video lecture, she asked the students to post an assignment in the form of a memo to a student who could not access the video due to Internet connectivity issues. She asked students to explain in the memo why formative assessment was essential to understanding the next topic: summative assessment.

Variations and Extensions

- Instead of a letter-writing activity, *Update Your Classmate* may be done as a journaling activity. This approach has the advantage of having students keep track of their own responses, which may be collected and assessed periodically rather than daily.
- Use the activities as entrance and exit tickets (see Barkley & Major, 2016, LAT 3, for more information).
- Consider posting the responses for students who actually did miss the lecture. This approach will add to the authenticity of the assignment.

Observations and Advice

This technique is brief by design, and as such, it may be done frequently and as a regular part of the course. Thus, it is a flexible activity that has wide applicability in a range of disciplines and fields as well as class sizes. If done regularly, students can see progress in their ability to pay attention and to connect ideas.

You can use it to gauge attendance and attention as well as to assess student understanding. You may choose to do a quick tally and return the memos to the authors, or you may wish to use them to take roll and to keep them.

Key References and Resources

Barkley, E. F., & Major, C. H. (2016). LAT 3: Entry and exit tickets. *Learning assessment techniques: A handbook for college faculty* (pp. 91–95). San Francisco, CA: Jossey-Bass.

Fisher, D., & Frey, N. (2011). *Improving adolescent literacy: Strategies at work* (3rd ed.). Upper Saddle River, NJ: Pearson.

TEAL. (2011). *Just Write! guide.* Retrieved from https://lincs.ed.gov/sites/default/files/TEAL_Just WriteGuide.pdf

ACTIVE LEARNING TECHNIQUE 6

Sentence Stem Predictions

Complexity involved in	
Planning	MODERATE
Developing Materials	MODERATE
Implementing in Class	LOW

Description and Purpose

In this technique, the professor presents a partial sentence that is structured to prompt students to predict select aspects of the upcoming lecture. The professor may use several stems throughout the lecture to guide student prediction making. To make logical predictions prior to receiving new information, students must use information from previous lectures and their prior knowledge. Although students often enjoy what they see as a guessing activity, predicting requires moving beyond guessing and instead involves previewing the lecture content to anticipate what may happen in it.

Prediction helps students set a purpose for listening. As students make predictions, they are more likely to be invested in the content. Because *Sentence Stem Predictions* provide scaffolding for student learning, this technique should also improve student understanding. *Sentence Stem Predictions* provide professors with insight into student understanding about a topic. This technique can also reveal when and where students have misconceptions. When professors review student predictions, they can address in the moment any misconceptions or gaps in understanding.

Preparation

- Review your lecture plans and identify two to three potential places where it is possible for students to predict outcomes related to specific content.
- Prepare a list of sentence stems with phrases that will encourage students to make predictions at the different points during the lecture you have identified. The stems should be tailored to the lecture content. Here are some generic examples that can be adapted for a number of purposes:
    - I think I will learn . . . because . . .
    - I'll bet . . . because . . .
    - I predict . . . because. . .
    - I think . . . will happen because . . .
    - *X* will happen if . . .
    - I wonder if . . . because . . .

    - I suppose . . . because . . .
    - I imagine . . . because . . .
- Make sure you can respond to the prompts yourself.
- Decide how you will integrate the *Sentence Stem Predictions* into the lecture presentation. If you have a slide deck, creating a slide with the stems that students record on their own paper is a useful approach. You could also consider Poll Everywhere slides. Alternately consider providing a handout that students fill in as you announce the stems, as shown in the following example.

Stem 1:
I predict

____

____

____

because

____

____

____

Stem 2:
I predict

____

____

____

because

____

____

____

Stem 3:
I predict

____

____

____

because

____

____

____

Procedures

1. Announce the activity and tell students when they will make predictions (e.g., before the lecture and once or twice during the lecture).
2. Present the *Sentence Stem Predictions* and ask students to record their responses. Ask a few volunteers to share their answers.

3. Proceed with the lecture.
4. Continue the pattern of prediction followed by short lecture until you have completed your prompts.

Video Lecture	Large Lecture
Provide students with a *Sentence Stem Predictions* worksheet that they complete while you go through the lecture. When preparing your video lecture, include times where you ask students to pause the video to complete the relevant section of the worksheet. Ask students to submit their completed worksheet as an assignment. Alternately intersperse a video lecture with quiz questions that ask students to make predictions. Finally, consider setting up as a short quiz in an LMS that opens in a new window.	Use individual classroom response systems (clickers) for students to submit their predictions or a live polling site such as Poll Everywhere.

Examples

Constitutional Law (Lecture)

This on-site course involves the study of legal cases to understand essential principles of constitutional law. The professor uses case law to provide insight into how constitutional controversies are resolved and can influence subsequent case resolution. Because the case law helps judges, lawyers, and students predict the outcome of future cases, the professor decided to use *Sentence Stem Predictions* to have students make predictions as well.

In one lecture section on the subject of governmental intervention in cases of private property ownership, the professor introduced the case of *Kelo v. City of New London.* In this case, the government condemned private homes as part of redevelopment to sell to other investors. The professor provided a prompt so that students would consider the outcome of the case before she announced it:

I predict

____

____

____

because

____

____

____

The professor collected the responses and noted that many students predicted that the outcome would be that the court would say no, that the government could not condemn the property. The professor announced that the court said yes because it is acceptable when the government is doing so for economic development. She provided the rationale for the students.

The professor then gave the students a hypothetical case involving governmental action to take private property and asked the students to predict the outcome by completing the following sentence stem:

I predict

____

____

____

because

____

____

____

She used the technique several times throughout the lecture and noted that students' answers improved and that more students were answering the prompts correctly by the end of class than at the beginning. She believed that the *Sentence Stem Predictions* helped them to improve their understanding of the issue.

Introductory Physics (Large Lecture)

The professors of this large lecture course often asked students to predict what would happen during lecture demonstrations. They then asked students to record what had happened during the demonstration. They were not surprised that some of the students predicted incorrectly, but they were surprised that students observed the demonstration and then recorded it incorrectly. The professors were concerned that student prior knowledge, specifically misconceptions and lack of depth of understanding, were interfering with some of the students' learning.

The professors decided to use ALT 7: *Guess and Confirm* to test their hypothesis that inaccurate or insufficient prior knowledge was the problem. The professors measured student prior knowledge of a unit on introductory mechanics. They then asked students to predict the outcome of a lecture demonstration ("I believe *x* will happen because . . . ."). Then they asked students to record what they saw ("What actually happened was . . . ."). They scored the responses with a plus (correct) and a minus (incorrect). They found that students who understood the concepts prior to the demonstration were more likely to predict correctly and to remember the demonstration correctly afterward. They also found that students who observed the demonstration incorrectly were not likely to remedy the problem before a major test. That is, learning was contingent on a correct observation.

The professors determined that they needed to ensure that students had a good understanding of the concepts prior to participating in the interactive lecture demonstration. They decided to provide additional background readings coupled with ALT 4: *Individual Readiness Assurance Tests* in order to make sure students were sufficiently prepared to participate in the class activities.

Statistics (Video Lecture)

In this blended online statistics course, the professor was teaching a unit on making predictions. The professor created three short video lectures that were six to seven minutes each. Before releasing the first video, the professor asked students to complete a quiz with the following stem:

I believe I will learn about ________________________________ in this lecture series.

Students submitted responses to the *Sentence Stem Prediction,* which he reviewed. He noticed that most had accurately guessed that they would learn how to predict events, but they did not link it to the specific number of times a certain action would happen.

He released the first video with an introductory note that responded to their first prompt and specified that the lecture was about the number of times an event would happen. At the end of the second video, he described a scenario in which Chelley had to take a multiple-choice test in a class she had not attended all semester. The test had forty questions and she would have to guess at each answer from four possible answers per question. He posted a *Sentence Stem Prediction* as follows:

I believe that Chelley will answer x questions correctly.

He noticed several of the students missed the question, but in an on-site class meeting, he focused on telling students how to solve the problem. At the end of the next video lecture, he posed a problem about a mother who was bringing two boxes of cookies and two boxes of cupcakes to a class party. Students would randomly select a box from which to get a treat. He posted a quiz with the following prompt:

I believe that x number of students will get a cookie.

Students seemed to engage with the videos, and he believed that they did so in part because of the *Sentence Stem Prediction* quizzes.

Variation and Extension

- Use graphic organizers to help students make predictions and possibly to adjust or confirm them.

What I expected to happen	What actually happened

Observations and Advice

Some students may be tempted to coast and answer with surface-level thoughts or even to say, "I don't know." Inviting them to clarify why they think by asking "How do you know you're correct?" can help discourage the easy out.

Students should be as specific as possible about their predictions. Because this technique is more open-ended than prediction activities that have close-ended choices, this can be more challenging to accomplish. When you write your prompts for your specific lecture, try to tie them to something concrete, for example, by asking students to predict specific outcomes or tying the responses to a set of percentages.

Be sure that you integrate the "because" into the questions. You want students to think through their predictions and provide a rationale for them.

Key References and Resources

Finley, T. (2014). *Dipsticks: Efficient ways to check for understanding.* Retrieved from www.edutopia.org/blog/dipsticks-to-check-for-understanding-todd-finley

Marzano, R., Pickering, D., & Pollock, J. (2001). *Classroom instruction that works: Research-based strategies for increasing student achievement.* Alexandria, VA: Association for Supervision and Curriculum Development.

Wentzel, K. R., & Brophy, J. (2014). *Motivating students to learn* (4th ed.). New York, NY: Routledge.

ACTIVE LEARNING TECHNIQUE 7

Guess and Confirm

Complexity involved in	
Planning	LOW
Developing Materials	LOW
Implementing in Class	LOW

Description and Purpose

For *Guess and Confirm,* students anticipate and write down information and key ideas that they expect the professor to cover in a forthcoming lecture. During the lecture, students weigh their expectations against the information the professor actually delivers. Students keep track by marking the information they have correctly identified, recognizing what they expected to hear but didn't, and noting new information that they didn't anticipate.

By taking a guess, students activate prior knowledge, which in turn prepares them for what they are about to learn. In this way, students are matching their prior knowledge to new information. Guessing the information ahead of time also legitimizes the information they expect. Next, because students have to keep track of what they did anticipate and what they didn't, *Guess and Confirm* requires students to be active listeners. Moreover, tracking what they anticipated hearing but didn't in fact hear helps students begin to understand that some information is more important than other. Finally, over time, this activity can help to improve student ability at self-monitoring and self-regulation.

Instructors can also use this activity as an assessment technique because they can review students' initial lists and the new notes for accuracy. In this way, *Guess and Confirm* provides instructors with information about how well students studied ahead. It also provides teachers with information about how well students are listening during a lecture as well as identifying the most essential information.

Preparation

- Examine your lecture content and do a quick count of how many concepts or facts you will cover. Try to determine how many concepts or facts students will record prior to the lecture. Between five and seven often is a sufficient number, but the number should not exceed the total number of facts or concepts you identified in the content.
- Determine how students will record their responses. You may suggest a format or create a handout that asks students to record the following information in columns: their best guesses about what is to come, space for checking when that information is mentioned, and a space for recording information they didn't anticipate.

Sample Handout for *Guess and Confirm*

Lecture Content Best Guesses	Check When Mentioned
What did you hear that you did not anticipate? ________________________ ________________________ ________________________	

- After determining how students will record their guesses, set aside time at the beginning of class for them to work. Also plan time for taking up responses at the end of the class session.
- Determine how you will assess student responses. You may want to do it with a simple plus-minus for completion or alternately assign a check for each correct guess and for each unanticipated additional point that they picked up during the lecture.

Procedures

1. At the start of class, provide students with instructions such as the following:
   a. Write down approximately (x) number of topics or facts you believe will be addressed in the lecture.
   b. Check or circle the topic or fact that you have written down when you hear it mentioned.
   c. Record any new topics or facts that you did not anticipate.
2. Proceed with the lecture.
3. At the end of the lecture, collect the *Guess and Confirm* sheets.
4. Review the information and talk about the results at the next class session.

Video Lecture	Large Lecture
When using this *Guess and Confirm* with an online video lecture, provide students with instructions prior to beginning the lecture and ask them to submit their responses at the end of the lecture through a course quiz or assignment in an LMS.	Index cards are a great place for students in large lecture classes to write a bulleted list of the concepts they expect will be covered in class. They can line through what they do hear and add asterisk points to show what they heard but did not expect. These cards can serve as exit tickets (Barkley & Major, 2016, LAT 3).

Examples

Introduction to Social Dance (Lecture)

In this introduction to social dance, students participate in a range of activities, from listening to lectures, to small-group discussions and activities, to hands-on experience with the dance forms. The professor noticed over time that students were less engaged in lecture and more engaged in the activities. Although he understood why this was the case, he also felt there were some concepts that he needed to convey in lecture in order to make the dance activities more meaningful.

He decided *Guess and Confirm* would be a good way to engage students in the lecture material. Prior to a lecture on nightclub dancing as social dance, he asked students to list the nightclub dance forms that they thought he would cover and explain why. He then instructed students to listen to his lecture and put a check mark beside any dance that they guessed correctly. He also asked them to list dances that he covered that they did not anticipate and explain why they had not expected it. A typical response follows.

List the types of dances you anticipate I will talk about in this introductory lecture on nightclub dancing and explain why you expect it:
• Disco: This format is older, but I think clubs still mix in a disco song every now and then for a retro vibe. • Techno: This is fun to dance to. • Rave: I think of this as an event where DJs mix a lot of loud dance songs together. • Hip-hop: There are clubs that specialize in this form of music.
List the types of dances I mentioned in the lecture that you did not anticipate and explain why you did not expect it:
• Country: I don't think of country as a night club music genre. • Swing: I kind of think of swing as "old people" music.

After the lecture, the professor discussed students' responses. He felt that students were better at active listening during the lecture, and they seemed to enjoy discussing what they had not anticipated and why. He felt the activity was a nice transition into the next activity, which involved modeling some specific dances in each genre, paired with student practice with the dance forms.

Chemistry (Large Lecture)

In this large lecture chemistry course, the professor was holding an interactive lecture session on thermodynamics and chemical dynamics. The professor was concerned that students were being passive and only barely paying attention during the lecture, and she was also worried that students were not reading the preparatory material and thus were not really ready for class.

To try to address these problems, she decided to use *Guess and Confirm*. She assigned an out-of-class reading on the topic, telling the students that they would need the information in the next class session. When students arrived at class, she distributed index cards and then asked students to write a list of what they expected to hear about in her lecture based on the readings.

After students had worked for a couple of minutes, she informed students that she would now start lecturing, and she asked students to cross out what they heard as she lectured. She took up the cards at the end. Most students noted energy and entropy but they did not note more advanced concepts, such as chemical equilibrium or chemical kinetics. She felt they were not reading deeply enough and decided to assign ALT 1: *Active Reading Documents* going forward. She also told students that in the future, she would take up the cards before the lecture and assess them before giving them back and that they could confirm what they heard on the next quiz. She felt that students' reading picked up, as did student focus and attention during the lecture.

Introduction to Criminal Court Systems (Video Lecture)

In this online course, the instructor was concerned that students were too passive when watching the online video lectures and were not fully invested or paying attention to them. She decided to use *Guess and Confirm* to help students think about the content before the lecture and to focus on the information during the lecture.

In a learning module on the individuals one could expect to find in a criminal courtroom and their various roles and responsibilities, she created an assignment for students to use while watching the video lecture. The assignment asked students to identify individuals they anticipated learning about, those they expected to hear about but didn't, and whom they have heard about but hadn't anticipated. She also asked them to think through the "why" of their responses. She posted the assignment as an open-ended quiz in her LMS prior to posting the video.

At the end of the video, she asked students to record their responses. She then asked students to post their assignments. Following is a typical response:

Whom did you expect to hear about in the lecture and why do you expect to hear about them?
Lawyers: They are the main players in courtrooms. Jurors: They are the deciders. Judge: The judge runs the show. Defendant: The person who does the harming should be mentioned. Victim: The person who is hurt should be mentioned.
Whom did you expect to hear about but didn't?
Audience: There are always people watching a case, so I don't know why we didn't talk about them.
Whom did you hear about that you did not anticipate?
Defense attorney: I did not know what this person was called. Prosecutor: I did not think of this person. Bailiff: I forgot about the bailiff. Court reporter: I didn't even consider the court reporter.

She believed that the exercise helped students to focus their attention. She also believed that it gave her insight into what they knew and did not know already when beginning the module. For example, students anticipated lawyers but didn't make distinctions between the defense attorney and the prosecutor, which was an area in which she believed she could provide additional instruction.

Variations and Extensions

- Have students work in pairs to take notes. They can compare their answers prior to and at the end of the lecture. This approach helps to ensure students have made accurate notes.
- Students may also work in larger groups. Simply provide some discussion time at the start and end of the lecture and ask groups to submit a composite response. This approach has the advantage of solidifying information through the process of group discussion.

Observations and Advice

Guess and Confirm is particularly useful when used multiple times over the semester. Students will become better at anticipating the most important content. They will also become better listeners over time.

Key References and Resources

Barkley, E. F., & Major, C. H. (2016). LAT 3: Entry and exit tickets. *Learning assessment techniques: A handbook for college faculty* (pp. 148–152). San Francisco, CA: Jossey-Bass.

Bowman, S. (2001). *Preventing death by lecture! Terrific tips for turning listeners into learners.* Glenbrook, NV: Bowperson.

ACTIVE LEARNING TECHNIQUE 8

Preview Guide

Complexity involved in	
Planning	HIGH
Developing Materials	LOW
Implementing in Class	LOW

Description and Purpose

In this variation of a prediction guide (Barkley & Major, 2016, LAT 11), students state their beliefs about whether statements related to the lecture topic are true or false. At the end of the lecture, they reevaluate the statements and reconsider their assessments.

A *Preview Guide* helps students activate prior knowledge and schema. It also sets a purpose for the lecture, which can help students focus their attention and remain alert; students simply will want to know if their responses were correct. A *Preview Guide* can also increase student interest in a topic to come, which can in turn improve their motivation for listening to the lecture. Finally, a *Preview Guide* helps to point students to the most important concepts of the lecture.

Preparation

- Prepare a set of statements about the topic that students can rate as true or false. If the statements are complex, aim for about five to seven. If they are fairly direct statements, aim for ten to twelve.
- Create a handout of the statements in which you leave space for students to mark true or false before and after the lecture (see the following example).
- Think through how long it will take students to respond to the questions. You will typically want to provide just a few minutes for them to work through the handout at the start and end of a lecture.

Preview Guide Template

Directions: Read each statement in the following table. Write whether you believe the statement to be true (T) or false (F) in the "Before" column. You will revisit your responses at the end of the lecture and record new responses in the "After" column.

Statement	Before	After
1.		
2.		
3.		
4.		
5.		

Procedures

1. Announce the activity and provide students with the handout.
2. Ask them to read the statements and record whether they think each answer is true or false in the "Before" column.
3. Proceed with the lecture.
4. At the end of the lecture, provide students with time to complete the handout.
5. Collect the responses so that you can gauge students' prior knowledge and whether they understood the information in the lecture.

Video Lecture	Large Lecture
Provide students with a questionnaire as a quiz prior to releasing the video lecture or offering the lecture through VoIP. After students have completed the lecture, readminister the quiz. Consider the difference between the first and second quiz administration. Alternately, provide students with a handout as a Word document and ask them to record their responses prior to the lecture. Ask them to record the time that you answer the question in a video lecture (e.g., at 5.35 minutes into the lecture). Ask students to record their answers at the end of the lecture and then submit the Word documents to you for review.	You can use this activity in a large class by using clickers or software such as Socrative. Administer the guide as a true-false questionnaire before and again after the lecture.

Examples

Introduction to American Government (Lecture)

In an introductory course that satisfies one of the college's general education requirements, a course goal is for students to learn about foundations and bases of American government and democracy, including the Bill of Rights. The professor had been surprised over time to realize how little college students actually know about American government and how little they seemed to want to know about the topic. She was concerned that students were not paying attention to her lectures because of an apparent lack of interest. She decided to use a *Preview Guide* as a way to stimulate student interest in the topic and to help them focus during her lectures.

At the beginning of class, she handed out the *Preview Guide.* She told students that she would not grade the "Before" answers, but she would grade the "After" answers. She provided students with several minutes to complete the "Before" section of the guide; following is a sample of her questions.

Preview Guide

Directions: Prior to the lecture, record whether you believe the answer to each prompt is true or false by marking T or F in the "Before" column. At the end of the lecture, you will put T or F in the "After" column. You are welcome to work on this sheet during the lecture. At the end of the lecture, I will give you a few minutes to complete your "After" section, and then I will collect the guide; your grade will be counted in your weekly participation grade for the course.

Before	Statement	After
	According to the Supreme Court, some rights are more important than others.	
	Antifederalists believed that the Bill of Rights was unnecessary.	
	Jefferson supported the idea of a Bill of Rights.	
	The entire Bill of Rights applies to both state and federal government.	
	The Bill of Rights does not give a person the right to criticize a government official.	

She proceeded to lecture, and she noticed that students were following along with her on the *Preview Guide* and that they were recording their answers in the "After" column. She felt that the activity increased student attention and interest during her lecture.

Global Communications (Large Lecture)

In a large global communications lecture, the professor believed that in past sections of the course, many students were not engaging well with the lecture presentations. She decided to start using the classroom's clicker system in a variety of ways to help students focus on her presentation. For example, she decided to use the system to implement an adaptation of the *Preview Guide.* In a unit on multiculturalism, she posted a series of true-false questions prior to the lecture presentation and asked students to indicate their responses based on their pre-lecture understanding. She informed students that she wouldn't be grading their responses but that she would use their responses as a way of taking attendance.

She then informed students that they would be hearing the correct answers to the questions as the lecture proceeded and that at the end of the lecture, they would be asked the questions again, and this time their responses would be graded. She felt that this new approach helped students to pay more attention and also helped her monitor attendance and gather additional pre- and post-assessment information. Following is a sample of the kinds of questions she posed.

Sample Clicker Questions

Statement	Before Lecture	After Lecture
People in high-context cultures place a high value on productivity and direct communication.		
English is the primary language used in conducting multinational business, so businesses should use English to shape their marketing strategies.		

Multiculturalism in Student Affairs (Video Lecture)

A goal in this blended course was that students should gain an awareness of the knowledge, skills, and dispositions needed to be a multiculturally competent student affairs practitioner. One learning module in the course addressed the issue of privilege and how it affects students' chances of success in higher education. The professor decided to use a *Preview Guide* to build student interest in the topic. She posted a survey quiz and asked students to rate their agreement on a five-to-one scale with statements such as the following:

- You can tell a lot about someone by the way the person dresses.
- Most people who want to go to college can, as long as they get good enough grades in high school.
- Diversity and social justice are the same.
- College and universities are fairly well integrated due to affirmative action policies.

The professor then asked students to do the reading as well as watch her video lecture about privilege, in which she focused on college students specifically and considered issues such as race, class, and gender. She followed this with a discussion on the various topics and invited students to share their own relevant experiences. To conclude the module, the professor asked students to retake the quiz and then go to the class discussion board and post about whether their responses changed, where they think their responses changed the most, and what made them change or not change.

Variations and Extensions

- Have students pair to discuss their responses. Ask student pairs to come to a consensus.
- Consider using this as a full-class activity. If you have access to clickers, students can register a vote prior to the lecture and again after. If you don't have access to clickers, simply ask students to raise their hands to indicate whether they believe the statement to be true or not.
- Instead of having the "Before" and "After" in a single handout, do the activity in two steps. Students complete a handout prior to the lecture. Students also complete a separate handout after the lecture.
- Have students create their own statements that they believe to be true. Have them reevaluate their own statements at the end of the lecture.

Observations and Advice

It is important to write clear and concise statements so that students focus on the content or concept. If the sentences are overly complex or convoluted, they will spend too much time decoding them rather than trying to make a prediction.

Students may be concerned that they will be penalized if they answer the "Before" section incorrectly. This can be demotivating for them, and it can cause them to try to change their answers so that it appears that they knew the correct answer all along. Consider emphasizing that they will not be graded on the "Before" section but that you are trying to help them—and you—assess the value of the lectures in terms of improving their learning.

Particularly controversial topics can cause student discomfort when responding to the statements, especially if they believe their views will be unpopular. For such topics, you should consider whether the discomfort is desirable, and you should consider how to best allow a safe space for responding so that students have the freedom to change their minds, rather than feeling like they have to defend their views. Instant polling slides may be helpful in that they enable students to answer anonymously.

Key References and Resources

Barkley, E. F., & Major, C. H. (2016). LAT 11: Prediction guide. *Learning assessment techniques: A handbook for college faculty* (pp. 148–152). San Francisco, CA: Jossey-Bass.

Duffelmeyer, F. (1994). Effective anticipation guide statements for learning from expository prose. *Journal of Reading, 37,* 452–455.

Frederick, P. (1981). The dreaded discussion: Ten ways to start. *College Teaching, 29,* 109–114.

CHAPTER 17

Listening for Information

Some educators dismiss listening to a lecture as a passive learning activity, and they have some basis for this perception. Many students do not know how to listen to a lecture actively. They let their minds wander. They may get caught up in what the professor looks like or is wearing. If they are listening to what the professor is saying, they may be focusing on facts but not know which facts are the most essential, and consequently they get dragged down by the details.

But students can learn to be active listeners. Students can strive to understand foundational concepts and the underlying organization of the information. They can try to distinguish between main and supporting evidence. They can anticipate what is coming next. They can summarize to themselves what they are hearing and formulate questions about that which they do not understand. They can listen for what they do and do not agree with and try to not turn off when they hear the latter.

When you help students to develop active listening skills, you not only enable them to learn more from your lecture but also provide them with important success skills that will benefit them throughout their education, future employment, and life in general. In this chapter, we describe four techniques designed to help students listen actively for information. We summarize these Techniques in Exhibit 17.1.

Exhibit 17.1 Techniques for Actively Preparing

This technique . . .	Helps students learn actively by having them . . .
ALT 9: *Advance Organizers*	Refer to an organizational template to help them understand the structure of information to come in the lecture and then complete the organizational framework during the lecture
ALT 10: *Lecture Bingo*	Mark on bingo cards when they hear an answer to a question
ALT 11: *Listening Teams*	Work in teams, each of which has a specific assignment and discussion prompt for the day's lecture, after which each team reports out
ALT 12: *Live-Tweet Lecture*	Tweet the lecture to share important information they are learning using a hashtag provided by the instructor

ACTIVE LEARNING TECHNIQUE 9

Advance Organizers

Complexity involved in	
Planning	MODERATE
Developing Materials	MODERATE
Implementing in Class	LOW

Description and Purpose

An *Advance Organizer* is a tool that can help professors introduce a topic and provide students with a structure for viewing information they are about to learn. When using an *Advance Organizer,* the professor presents students with an organizational structure before formal instruction. Students fill in the structure while learning new information.

Advance Organizers help professors introduce a new topic. Moreover, they serve as a conceptual bridge between old and new information. They also help to establish a task and orient the learner to it by providing organizational clues that guide learners as they complete a visual map or diagram, highlighting relationships between ideas. Using *Advance Organizers* is a scaffolding technique that provides visual support to learners and helps them to categorize, infer, summarize, compare and contrast, and evaluate. *Advance Organizers* provide a structure for student thinking by previewing important connections among facts, concepts, or ideas. *Advance Organizers* also draw student attention to the most important information.

Preparation

- Choose an *Advance Organizer* that is compatible with the content you intend to convey.
    - *Expository organizers* describe the content that is to come, for example, through a rubric or definition.
    - *Narrative organizers* lead into the information through an article, story, or work of art.
    - *Graphic organizers* provide a structure for the information, such as through a table or chart. Graphic organizers are the most commonly used *Advance Organizer* and can visually depict expository and narrative information.
- Determine how you will present the organizer to the student, whether through a handout or an online format.

Because they are the most frequently used *Advance Organizers,* example graphic organizers are shown in Figures 17.1 to 17.8.

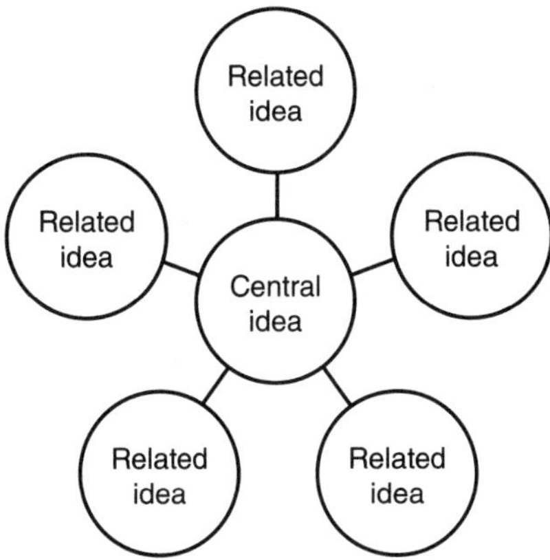

Figure 17.1 Semantic Map

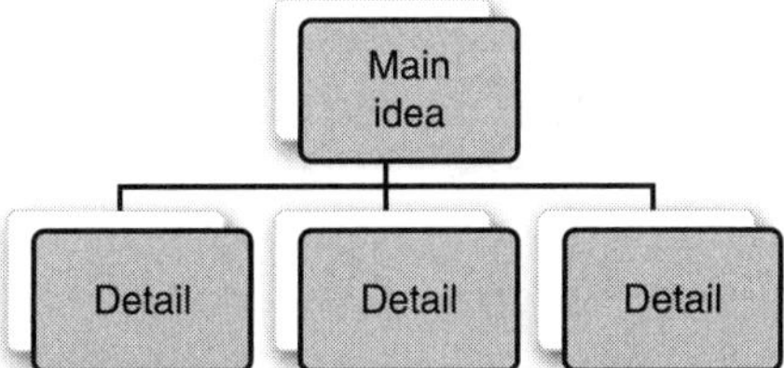

Figure 17.2 Main Idea and Detail Chart

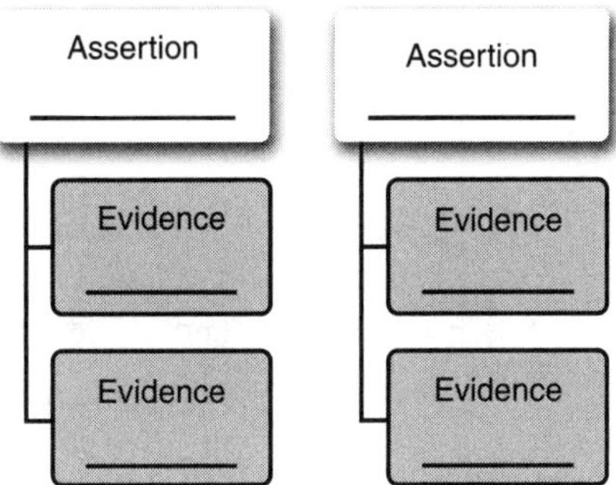

Figure 17.3 Assertion and Evidence Organizer

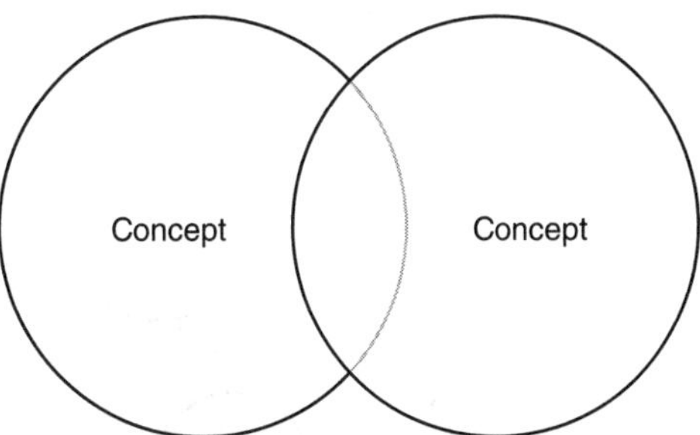

Figure 17.4 Venn Diagram

Figure 17.5 Sequence Chain

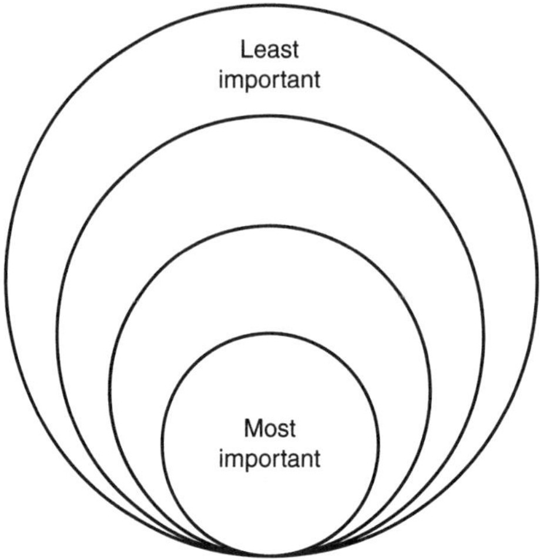

Figure 17.6 Zone of Relevance

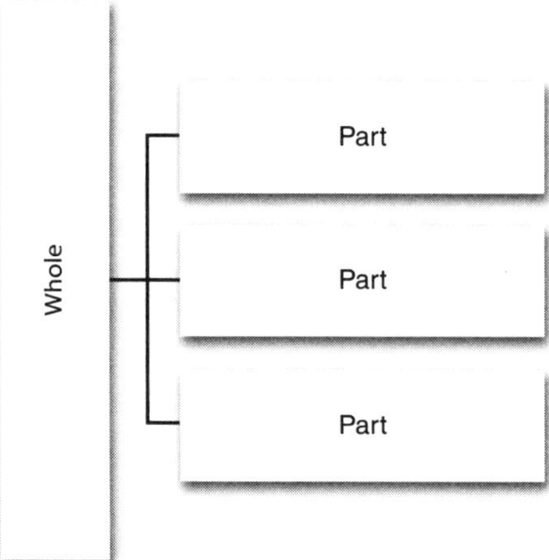

Figure 17.7 Brace Map

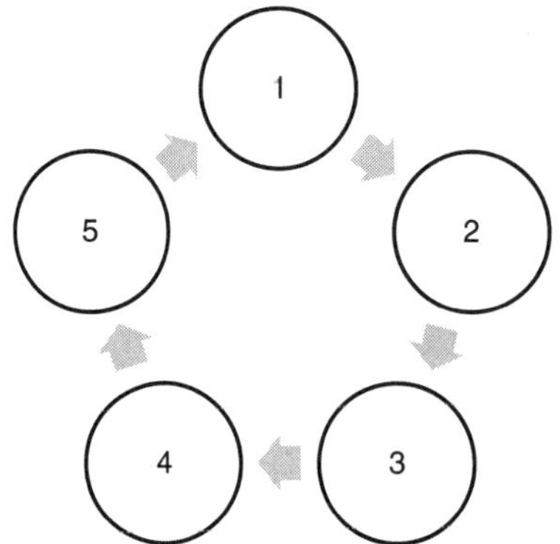

Figure 17.8 Cycle of Events

Procedures

1. Explain the purpose of the *Advance Organizer.*
2. Share the template you have selected with students.
3. Ask students to fill in missing content during your lecture.
4. Ask students to submit the organizer to you for review.

Video Lecture	Large Lecture
Determine whether students will be able to fill in the organizer online or will have to print, handwrite, and upload their results. Post your organizer and ask students to submit it as an assignment or a quiz, as appropriate.	If you have a very large class, printing the organizers can become time-consuming and costly. You can distribute them electronically prior to class and ask students to bring their own.

Examples

Freshman Composition (Lecture)

In this introductory writing course, the professor wanted students to know the basic structure of the five-paragraph essay. Later in the semester, the class would experiment with the writing form, but the professor believed that every student should understand that a well-developed essay often has several paragraphs and that each paragraph has support sentences as well as details and examples. He developed an *Advance Organizer* that he gave to students at the start of the class session. Then he walked students through a five-paragraph essay on the topic of the use of social media for college student learning.

Once he felt that students had a good understanding of the basic structure, he gave students a blank template and asked them to jot in ideas for their own essays as a prewriting activity (see Figure 17.9).

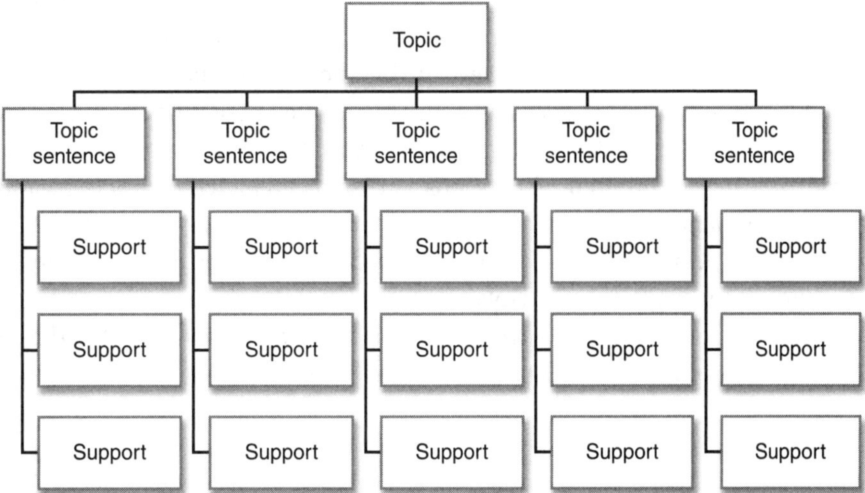

Figure 17.9 Blank Template for Prewriting Activity

After they had developed drafts of their essays, he asked them to compare the template to their papers to ensure that they had topic sentences and support sentences for each paragraph. By using the organizer template, he believed that students had more well-developed essays than they might otherwise have written.

Biology (Large Lecture)

In this large lecture section, the professor decided to move from full-class transmission lectures to interactive lecturing. He used a range of strategies, but he found one in particular to be effective in promoting student learning and metacognition: *Advance Organizers.*

Prior to each lecture presentation, he provided students with a graphic organizer. He used several existing structures, for example, a semantic map for characterizing organelles and a Venn diagram for illustrating the overlap between plant and animal cells. He found that he could not always easily adapt existing graphic organizers to his content, so he had to create new ones. For example, he created the following grid:

	DNA	**mRNA**	**tRNA**
Abbreviation			
Makeup			
Job			

Planet, Stars, Galaxies, and the Universe (Video Lecture)

As part of this blended astronomy course, the professor was teaching an introductory unit on the foundational physics of astronomy. The next module in the unit was about the phases of the moon, which would be followed by a module on eclipses. He knew that students often had difficulty remembering the different phases of the moon, and that many could not articulate what the moon looks like to the naked eye during the various phases.

He decided to use an *Advance Organizer.* He felt that depicting the phases of the moon as a cycle would help them understand his lecture about the phases more than having them simply memorize what the different phases look like, so he uploaded the cycle organizer as a word processing document (see Figure 17.10).

In his video lecture, the professor described the different phases of the moon, using a different slide for each phase and displaying Figure 17.11 at the end.

In class, he put students into groups and asked them to shade in the different circles to show the different phases as he lectured through the content.

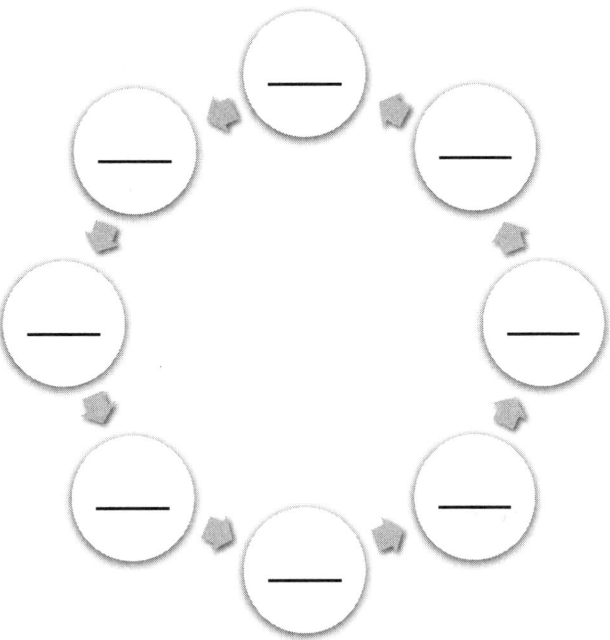

Figure 17.10 Cycle Organizer Example

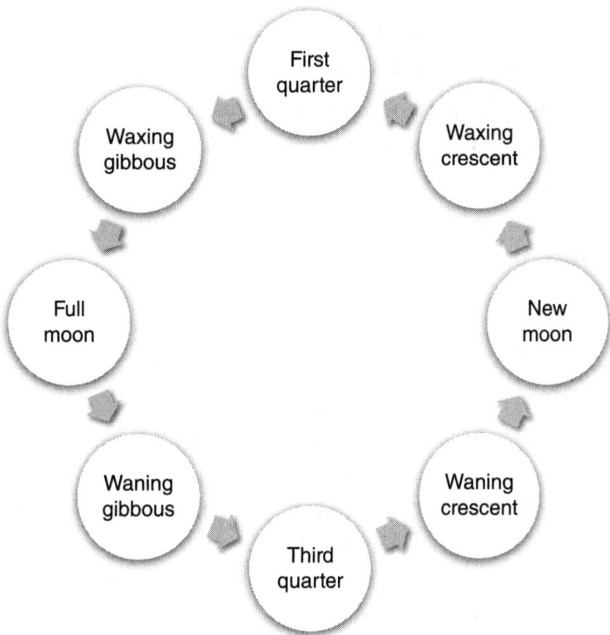

Figure 17.11 Cycle Organizer Example Filled In

Variations and Extensions

- Ask students to complete their organizers pre- and post-instruction.
- Use an *Advance Organizer* as a form for ALT 13: *Guided Notes.*
- Ask students to complete their work in pairs or small groups.
- If students have completed work such as reading prior to the session in a way that would sufficiently inform their thinking, consider asking them to create their own *Advance Organizers.*
- Use *Advance Organizers* as a technique to assess students' prior knowledge, knowledge gaps, and misconceptions prior to a lecture. Simply ask students to complete the organizers and review them ahead of the lecture session so that you can refute misconceptions or supply missing information as needed.

Observations and Advice

Advance Organizers help students understand the subject of study because they assist thinking. Students take an active role in learning through processing and reorganizing information. Filling in missing information on an organized structure provides students with an opportunity to learn from their own mistakes.

Advance Organizers can be particularly effective when combined with collaborative learning instructional strategies because they can provide students, who often lack a framework, with support. They can also provide the group a specific task to complete.

If a student can connect prior knowledge with what was learned and identify relationships between those ideas, they are actively learning. If students are novices in the field or discipline or likely to be unfamiliar with the graphic organizer, consider modeling its use and providing students with opportunities for guided practice. Using a digital medium to distribute the organizers can save time and resources that printing and paper require, and it can allow for easy revising and updating.

Key References and Resources

Ausubel, D. P. (1963). *The psychology of meaningful verbal learning.* New York, NY: Grune & Stratton.

Barkley, E. F., Major, C. H., & Cross, K. P. (2014). *Collaborative learning techniques: A resource for college faculty* (2nd ed.). San Francisco, CA: Jossey-Bass.

Chen, B., Hirumi, A., & Zhang, N. J. (2007). Investigating the use of advance organizers as an instructional strategy for web-based distance education. *Quarterly Review of Distance Education, 8*(3), 223–231.

Major, C. H., Harris, M., & Zakrajsek, T. (2015). *Teaching for learning: 101 techniques to put students on the path to success.* New York, NY: Routledge.

ACTIVE LEARNING TECHNIQUE 10

Lecture Bingo

Complexity involved in	
Planning	MODERATE
Developing Materials	MODERATE
Implementing in Class	HIGH

Description and Purpose

Lecture Bingo is an academic game in which the professor creates cards that contain key concepts—terms, facts, or themes—that are presented in squares that form a grid. Each student receives a card that has the concepts displayed on the card in a different order from every other student's card. Students listen to the lecture and mark the appropriate box when the professor addresses the concept. When the student has five squares in a row marked, he or she declares "bingo!"

Lecture Bingo helps students understand which are the most important points in a lecture by helping focus their attention on them. This technique requires students to engage in active listening, which helps them remain attentive to the lecture content. It is also fun for students, which helps to improve their motivation and engagement.

Preparation

- Prepare a lecture and identify twenty-five important terms, facts, or concepts.
- Create bingo cards by making a grid. Grids that are 5 × 5, as in the following example, are fairly common for the activity, but the next most common is a 3 × 3 grid.

Blank Lecture Bingo Card

- You will need one card per student in the course.
- Fill the blank cards' squares with the concepts you have developed. You will display one concept in each of the twenty-five squares. You should also randomize the order of concepts in each card so that each card is distinct. There are several online bingo card generators that will randomize multiple cards, which you can locate through an online search. Alternately, you can randomize the cards yourself in a word processing document.
- Determine how students will mark their cards. The easiest way is to ask them to hash or *x* through the block when they have heard the item. Alternately, you might pass out stickers for them to place in the box when they hear the concept mentioned.
- Determine how students will indicate that they have marked five squares in a row. You may allow them to yell "bingo!" out loud in class, or if you feel that would be disruptive to the class or uncomfortable for some of the students, you may ask students to raise their hands when they have bingo.
- Consider whether you will offer a prize or some kind of reward to motivate participation. For example, you might want to offer a small number of extra credit points, pencils, pens, or sticky notepads to the first five winners.

Procedures

1. Announce the *Lecture Bingo* activity and distribute the cards.
2. Ask students to mark their card for key terms, facts, or concepts as they hear you mention them in the lecture. Tell the students that they will get bingo when they have marked five successive spots in a horizontal, vertical, or diagonal row. Tell them how they should indicate when they have bingo.
3. Proceed with your lecture.
4. Watch or listen for the early winners and acknowledge them. Complete the lecture and allow as many students to obtain bingo as possible.

Video Lecture	Large Lecture
This activity is easy to use in a synchronous session. If you are using VoIP to lecture, distribute the cards ahead via e-mail and proceed with the lecture. Ask students to "raise their hands" in the session to indicate when they have bingo. The activity is more challenging to accomplish in an asynchronous session, but it is possible to send cards to students and ask them to use them as they watch a video lecture; they can submit their marked cards along with the video time stamp (such as 3:07) for each square as an assignment.	Consider posting the bingo cards as a PDF online and having students print up their own prior to coming to class. You will probably want to reward some of the winning students with a few points. For example, you might give the first five *x* number of points and the next five *y* number of points. Have the winning students submit their hard copies when they make bingo.

Examples

Geology (Lecture)

In this course, the learning goals indicated that students should be able to identify mineral and rock terms and techniques, such as igneous, sedimentary, and metamorphic rocks and mineral luster, fracture, cleavage, crystal, and chemistry. The professor decided to use *Lecture Bingo* to help students achieve these goals.

The instructor designed the game to correspond to a rock and mineral kit given to all students in the course. The kits included several samples and also a magnifying glass, a streak plate, and a tempered steel nail.

The bingo card squares contained twenty-five numbers. Each number corresponded to a set of descriptions on a card. A caller pulled the cards out of a hat, and a copy of the card was displayed on a projected slide for all students to see. The players chose the sample from their collection that best fit the called-out description. Some samples fit more than one answer, so students were required to make the best choice. The first person to win shared her board and samples with the class for closer examination.

Introduction to Clinical Pharmacy Skills (Large Lecture)

This course is required during the first year and consists of two fifty-minute class periods in a large lecture hall setting and one fifty-minute small-group lab per week. The professor believed that many students were waiting to study for the course until right before an exam, which she felt had a negative effect on student learning. She had also heard from fellow professors that students who had completed her course were not retaining information in subsequent courses. The professor decided to use *Lecture Bingo* to increase student interaction with materials in a timely fashion.

Instead of tying it to specific content from a single lecture, however, the professor decided to tie the bingo squares to the kinds of deep-learning activities she hoped to encourage across the semester. Students could earn one square each week for creative activities, all of which would be shared with the full class through a discussion board on the learning management system (LMS), such as the following:

- Written responses to the three lecture objectives
- Full set of lecture notes posted
- Practice quiz from the lecture posted
- Crossword with concepts of the lecture
- Poster to illustrate the central concept from the lecture
- Video illustration of the central concept of the lecture
- Identification of textbook errors related to lecture content

She also assigned squares for self-assessment of learning, which she scored through an online quiz.

The professor assigned 5 percent bonus for the final grade to students who had completed the activities to earn bingo during the semester. The professor found that all students completed at least one bingo activity and that most of the students did a sufficient number of activities to earn bingo. In an online survey, the majority of students reported that the bingo had increased their attendance and had improved their learning. The majority also said that the bingo game should be continued in future semesters.

Introduction to Accounting (Video Lecture)

In a flipped accounting course, students were to learn the components of a balance sheet, measures for analyzing profitability, measures for analyzing liquidity, and approaches to financial reporting. The professor decided to use *Lecture Bingo* to accompany his video lectures in an effort to help students focus attention.

He prepared a slide presentation with numbered slides to accompany his lecture, and he recorded himself presenting the lecture as a screencast. He also prepared bingo cards for students to complete during the lecture with key terms such as *assets, long-term investments, short-term investment, cash, accounts receivable, short-term notes receivable, inventories, supplies inventories, prepaid items,* and so forth. Under each term, he included a blank space.

As students watched the video lectures and heard the terms, they had to record the slide numbers in the box in the space provided under each term. The professor had students submit their bingo cards as assignments.

Variations and Extensions

- Instead of randomizing the cards, give all students the same card. In this way, you will know when students should have reached bingo. Moreover, you will be able to assess quickly who has the best grasp of the content and who needs additional assistance.
- Have additional cards for students who achieve bingo quickly and allow them to obtain bingo as many times as they can.
- To extend this activity and make it more complex, create cards that display a question that they will have to listen to the lecture to be able to answer, and ask students to fill in the answers as the lecture proceeds.
- Allow students to work in groups to complete the *Lecture Bingo* card, particularly when the material is complex and multiple opinions would be beneficial to the game.

Observations and Advice

Lecture Bingo is a useful way to keep students focused on new content, and it is particularly effective as a review strategy. If you are going to give bonus points to winners, keep a class roster handy so that you can easily mark who is to receive the extra points.

Key References and Resources

Silberman, M. (1996). *Active learning: 101 strategies to teach any subject.* Upper Saddle River, NJ: Pearson.

Weisskirch, R. S. (2009). Playing bingo to review fundamental concepts in advanced courses. *International Journal for the Scholarship of Teaching and Learning, 3*(1). Retrieved from http://digitalcommons.georgiasouthern.edu/cgi/viewcontent.cgi?article=1142&context=ij-sotl

ACTIVE LEARNING TECHNIQUE 11

Listening Teams

Complexity involved in	
Planning	LOW
Developing Materials	LOW
Implementing in Class	MODERATE

Description and Purpose

In this variation of the analytic teams technique (Barkley, 2010, SET 13; Barkley & Major, 2014, CoLT 17), students assume predetermined roles while listening to a lecture. Roles prescribe corresponding tasks, such as a proponent whose job is to find points of agreement or a critic whose job is to find points of disagreement. Students then pool knowledge they gained while carrying out their different listening roles and responsibilities.

This technique is useful for helping students stay engaged and focused on a lecture because it provides them with active listening responsibilities. These structured roles can also help students develop and expand their repertoire of analytic thought patterns. When they know they have a responsibility to share the knowledge they gained from owning a specific role with their peers, students have increased motivation to stay attentive and to complete their tasks appropriately. When they join with other students to pool their knowledge, they are engaged with each other in the action of sharing information.

Preparation

- Choose this technique only when your lecture topic is complex. Then, break the analytic processes required to understand the complexity into parts and assign corresponding roles. Although there are a variety of roles from which to choose depending on the specific analytic process and learning goals, the following examples can be applied to several kinds of assignments:
  - **Summarizers.** Prepare a summary of the most important points and explain why they are the most central.
  - **Example givers.** Give examples of key concepts presented and explain their relevance.
  - **Proponents.** List the points you agreed with and state why.
  - **Critics.** List the points you disagreed with or found unhelpful and state why.
  - **Questioners.** Prepare a list of substantive questions about the material.
- To ensure that the assignment is appropriate for analysis, take the time in advance to determine whether you could perform each of the assigned roles and that each role has a sufficiently challenging task.

Procedures

1. Form student groups of four or five and assign each team a specific role (e.g., summarizers, example givers, proponents, critics, questioners).
2. Present the lecture.
3. At the end of the lecture, give teams class time for individual members to pool their information and to develop a summary of it. Tell them that they will present a set amount of information to the full class, for example:
   a. **Summarizers.** Present the five key points of the lecture.
   b. **Example givers.** Present key relevant examples.
   c. **Proponents.** Present two points on which the team agrees and state why.
   d. **Critics.** Present two key points with which the team disagrees and state why.
   e. **Questioners.** Ask three questions about the lecture.
4. Consider a closure strategy that emphasizes roles and corresponding tasks. Having students stand up and share would be particularly appropriate for a fairly short lecture segment, whereas a panel or poster session would be fitting for a more-complex lecture series spanning several class sessions; in the latter, students need sufficient time for pooling and displaying their analyses.

Video Lecture	Large Lecture
To use *Listening Teams* in an online course, try a discussion forum. Form student groups, create a separate forum for each group with the posted prompt, and have students respond to the prompt for their teams. Consider having groups write a team analysis that presents their findings to be posted in a whole-class threaded discussion or create a page for group viewing. Students can view other teams' threads or analyses in an online version of a gallery walk, reading, and perhaps taking a follow-up quiz on what has been posted. Alternately, have students interact synchronously in an IM session to discuss their specific roles and responsibilities or use a microblog such as Twitter or Tumblr, where students take on different roles to comment on a topic or issue.	Consider assigning teams by geography—in short, a given quadrant of the room will have a specific role—then have students pair up with other students in their quadrants to pool their ideas. Limit the amount of time for reporting out by choosing a couple of pairs from each quadrant to speak.

Examples

Consumer Behavior (Lecture)

The professor of a marketing class was planning a lecture on the role of selective perception in consumer behavior. He knew that in the past students had had difficulty in being able to think through all of the different aspects of selective perception and how it influences customer interpretations of reality and their resulting actions. He decided to use *Listening Teams* to improve their understanding.

The professor split the room into quadrants. He assigned students in each quadrant a role as business consultants. Each quadrant had a different analytic focus, as follows:

- **Quadrant 1.** Selective exposure: Consumers seek out positive messages and avoid negative ones.
- **Quadrant 2.** Selective attention: Consumers notice messages that meet their needs and interest and have minimal awareness of ads that do not.
- **Quadrant 3.** Selective defense or blocking: Consumers subconsciously screen out stimuli they find threatening.
- **Quadrant 4.** Selective retention: Consumers remember messages that they deem important.

The professor then lectured to provide details about selective perception and more information on each of the roles along with the influence they have on perception. The professor then began the case-based portion of the lecture, in which he presented different case studies. Each case had a business owner who was seeking to market a product in a specific venue and wanted to know whether it would be a good use of advertising funds. For example, one business owner wanted to market a health club on the side of a bus. Another wanted to market cigarettes in a celebrity magazine. Another wanted to market a local farmer's market in a college student newspaper. A final business owner wanted to market her new hot sauce through a social media forum.

At the end of the lecture, the professor gave each team time to confer. He then asked them to report on their analyses of the business owner proposals from their perspective. The reports were excellent, and the professor believed that students had a much better understanding of the concept than in the previous semester.

Introduction to Biblical Studies (Large Lecture)

The purpose of this course was to introduce students to the critical study of the prophetic books of the Hebrew Bible, including the Christian Old Testament. The professor felt that the students were not engaging in the critical goals of the course, however, and rather simply accepted what they read or he said as fact. Because of this, class discussions were superficial and brief.

The professor decided to use *Listening Teams* to engage students in thinking about the course at a deeper level. He divided the room into quadrants, giving each quadrant a specific role:

Following the lecture, you will form a group and do the following:

- **Questioners.** Ask several critical questions regarding the material presented.
- **Affirmers.** Name several points or ideas you believe to be especially important and why.
- **Arguers.** Identify what point(s) you found unhelpful, or disagreed with, and why.
- **Examples givers.** Either provide examples that illustrate the points or discuss implications of the points.

He then proceeded with the lecture presentation after which he asked different quadrants for their contributions. The professor felt that the discussion was much more robust and interactive.

Media Studies (Video Lecture)

In this online course, the professor had a learning module on video game violence. The professor used *Listening Teams* to help students stay focused during the video lectures. In the lecture, he considered the question of whether violent video games should be banned. He assigned students to teams with a specific role that students were to assume while watching the lectures (summarizers, example givers, proponents, critics, questioners).

He then posted a discussion board prompt for each role. Students in the team populated the thread with responses, writing from the perspective of their roles. They then viewed the other teams' responses. At the end of the module, the students wrote a briefing paper, a one- to two-page analysis on the issue of video game violence designed to inform a policy maker of their perspective (Barkley & Major, 2016, LAT 43).

Variations and Extensions

- Assign the different roles to individuals instead of teams.
- Extend this activity for more than one class session. For example, teams can rotate roles, such as summarizer, character analyst, and question developer, across several lectures so that students have practice assuming all of the different roles.
- One of the significant challenges of *Listening Teams* is following up on the group discussion in a way that helps students meaningfully synthesize the various information and opinions they have heard. A useful way to extend the technique to require synthesis is to add in a briefing paper, as we described in our media studies example.

Observations and Advice

- The most-challenging aspect in preparing for this technique is ensuring a lecture topic is complex enough to yield a useful analysis when divided into component tasks. If the lecture is not sufficiently complex, one or more of the teams will be bored or unable to participate fully.
- Students typically prefer some roles to others. They may even resist being assigned certain roles and request that they be assigned roles with which they have already developed comfort and skill. Yet it is important that students develop their abilities in multiple roles.

Key References and Resources

Barkley, E. F. (2010). SET 13: Analytic teams. *Student engagement techniques: A handbook for college faculty.* San Francisco, CA: Jossey-Bass. Adapted with permission of the publisher.

Barkley, E. F., & Major, C. H. (2016). *Learning assessment techniques: A handbook for college faculty.* San Francisco, CA: Jossey-Bass. Adapted with permission of the publisher.

Barkley, E. F., Major, C. H., & Cross, K. P. (2014). CoLT 17: Analytic teams (pp. 249–254). *Collaborative learning techniques: A handbook for college faculty.* San Francisco, CA: Jossey-Bass.

Johnson, D. W., Johnson, R., & Smith, K. (1998). *Active learning: Cooperation in the college classroom.* Edina, MN: Interaction Book Company.

Silberman, M. (1995). *101 ways to make training active.* Johannesburg, South Africa: Pfeiffer.

ACTIVE LEARNING TECHNIQUE 12

Live-Tweet Lecture

Complexity involved in	
Planning	LOW
Developing Materials	LOW
Implementing in Class	LOW

Description and Purpose

In a *Live-Tweet Lecture*, the professor asks students to use Twitter, a microblogging platform that restricts posts to 140 characters, to share important ideas about the content of a lecture while it is in progress. The *Live-Tweet Lecture* enables professors to use social media to foster student engagement. It provides students with a specific task to complete during the lecture that requires them to actively engage with the content. The posts also enable back-channel discussion that can add insight and value to the lecture itself.

In addition to posting, students can also mark some tweets as "favorites" and return to them later, or alternately, they can retweet posts in order to extend the discussion to their followers. The technique can provide students with a collaborative set of class notes from the lecture. *Live-Tweet Lecture* makes intentional use of student cell phones, which means students have fewer opportunities to use them for personal purposes during class; this approach can help students view the phone as a tool that can assist their learning. Moreover, *Live-Tweet Lectures* also provide useful data by which instructors can gauge student understanding.

Preparation

- If you have not already done so, set up an account on Twitter (twitter.com).
- Ask students to sign up for Twitter. You may want to require sign-up for all students, or you may want to make it optional for those who wish to participate. You may also want to ask students to send their Twitter handles to you so that you can determine which of your students have tweeted.
- Decide what you will ask students to live-tweet. You may ask them to simply summarize the key points from the lecture. You might ask them to post their personal experiences related to a given topic. You might ask them to post questions as they occur to them.
- Create a hashtag, which is a word or phrase that is preceded by a hash (#) and used to identify messages focused on a specific topic (e.g. #AHE603LTL). The hashtag enables students to connect with each other and search for other students' posts, which in turn allows for a public, real-time conversation about the lecture among students.

Procedures

1. Announce the activity and invite students present at the lecture to actively tweet during the lecture itself. If you have a specific tweeting task for students (e.g., post questions you have about the content), be sure to announce it as well.
2. Begin the lecture.
3. At the end of the lecture, hold a discussion on the questions and ideas raised on the Twitter back channel.

Video Lecture	Large Lecture
If your online course has synchronous sessions during which you lecture, approach *Live-Tweet Lecture* in the same way you would in an on-site class. In an asynchronous course, "live" in the *Live-Tweet Lecture* happens differently than in an on-site course. Although students may still tweet "live" as they watch the lecture individually, the back-channel conversation that Twitter provides will be asynchronous. That is, students will watch the lectures at different times, so their tweets will show up in different places in the Twitter feed. However, the hashtag will enable students to search for each other's posts, and thus this technique still has the benefits of recording in-the-moment thoughts and of creating a collaborative set of class notes.	This approach to active listening works well for large and small classes alike. If you are concerned about students tweeting too much information, appoint selected students to summarize the hashtag after each session. Consider offering extra credit for student volunteers. You can also archive each week's tweets. Moreover, some LMSs allow for embedding tweets into the course management page.

Examples

College Teaching (Lecture)

In this graduate-level education course focused on teaching in colleges and universities, the professor required out-of-class engagement through Twitter as a part of course participation. Most students "followed" the instructor on Twitter as well as their classmates. She also decided to encourage students to live-tweet the lectures.

Prior to one class session, students read articles about technology in higher education. In class, the professor announced that she had a lecture on the topic of online learning as a form of instructional change. She told students that they could live-tweet the lecture and invited them to do so. As she proceeded to lecture, some students tweeted more than others, but many of the other students favorited and retweeted the students who tweeted. A portion of the exchange can be found in Figure 17.12.

The students reported that live-tweeting helped them stay focused on the lecture content, whether they were summarizing, favoriting, or retweeting. The professor noted that the tweeting activity was good for student attention, and she believed that students captured important points in their exchanges.

The History of the American University (Large Lecture)

In this course, the professor decided to use *Live-Tweet Lecture* and provided students with a hashtag before the lecture each week. Students in one section generated more than two thousand tweets (more than one hundred tweets per lecture), and more than half the class tweeted at some point or another.

Figure 17.12 Sample Tweet

Source: Reprinted with permission of the participants.

The professor was pleased with the technique. He felt it encouraged active engagement in lectures and prompted students to use their phones to good end during class. The professor also found that it created a repository of supplemental course material, disseminated content widely, and helped students who missed class catch up quickly. Moreover, the professor felt that it provided him with instant feedback on the lecture; he could quickly see what points had resonated with students and which had been unclear or boring—information he did not feel he would have received from students otherwise.

Communication Technology, Culture, and Society (Video Lecture)

In this communications course, students examine the ways that culture, technology, and society have influenced each other over time. They read various articles and apply the ideas from the readings to critical analyses of particular cases. The students who take the course are generally majoring in communication and information science. The professor created fifteen- to twenty-minute video lectures on various topics such as the telegraph, the advent of the Internet, the development of the information society, digital culture, and so forth. The professor felt that the students were not attending to the video lectures, so he decided to use *Live-Tweet Lectures.*

As students watched the lectures, they had to submit at least one tweet per fifteen-minute mini-lecture. The tweet could be an observation, a reflection, a question, or anything else that students deemed on topic. Students submitted tweets from their own course-specific Twitter accounts set up for the purpose of engaging in the activity, which also preserved student privacy and did not interfere with a student's personal tweeting. To collect student tweets, the professor created a separate Twitter account to compile tweets in one public feed using GroupTweet, which is an application that enables retweeting all tweets sent to a class account and making them visible to all students in a class.

Variations and Extensions

- Make the tweeting anonymous by using a computer lab for class. Prior to the students' arrival to class, log each computer into a Twitter account.
- Use tweeting as a pre-lecture activity. Ask students to tweet questions prior to each lecture related to the specific topic. Make sure your lecture addresses them, and ask students to post answers while you lecture.
- Ask students to create an aggregate of the tweets from the class as a final project. They could use a service such as Storify, which can combine posts to a hashtag into a single, chronological narrative and also allows the addition of comments. Alternately ask students to simply copy tweets into a word processing document.

Observations and Advice

Students may be nervous initially about having classwork viewed in the open, but they will likely overcome initial reticence and enjoy the activity after they have participated in this technique a few times. If you require students to sign up for Twitter, however, allow or suggest use of pseudonyms so that they do not need to provide personal information on the open web.

Be sure that you don't post any responses that could be construed as grading so that you do not violate students' rights to privacy. You may want to provide students with specific guidance about using Twitter. See the following information adapted from New York University (n.d.).

About Twitter

1. **How to get started.** When you first register at twitter.com, you will be prompted to choose a username. This username is your "Twitter handle."
2. **Your "tweets."** The messages used in Twitter are called *tweets* and they are limited to 140 characters, which challenges you to be concise with your message.
3. **Interacting.** If you want to communicate with another user, you simply use the @ symbol followed by the Twitter handle of the user as a reference. For example, @marcwai. In this way you "tweet at" another user.
4. **Whom to follow?** The power of Twitter is that it allows for viral dissemination of information. Hence, it is not only a useful tool to connect with your friends and keep abreast of their daily activities but also you can follow news organizations such as *Chronicle of Higher Ed* (@chronicle) or *NCAA News* (@ncaa), celebrities (movie stars and industry and thought leaders), and other organizations.
5. **Organizing your feed.** You might initially feel overwhelmed with the sheer number of posts, especially when you start to follow users who update a lot throughout the day. To manage the tweets, consider organizing the people you follow into lists and focus just on one group of users at a time. You can also use Tweetdeck, which is an application that enables you to group your feed into different columns (e.g., friends, news, work, or whatever category you choose to create).
6. **Hashtags.** If you have a favorite topic about which you tweet a lot, you can create a hashtag (which is the # sign) and then track all posts with that hashtag. For example, #nyudining would be an appropriate hashtag for tweets about NYU dining. This encourages other users to tweet using your hashtag and also makes it easy to track the conversation.

Source: Adapted from New York University (n.d.).

Key References and Resources

Aebel, I., & Lund, B. (2013). *Teaching with Twitter.* Retrieved from www.tamuk.edu/cehp/hkn/docs/Twitter.pdf

Birnholtz, J., Hancock, J., & Retelny, D. (2013). *Tweeting for class: Co-construction as a means for engaging students in lectures.* Retrieved from http://socialmedia.northwestern.edu/files/2012/09/twitternote_revision_CHI13_130123_camready_a2.pdf

Evans, C. (2013). Twitter for teaching: Can social media be used to enhance the process of learning? *British Journal of Educational Technology, 45,* 902–915.

New York University. (n.d.). *Twitter explained.* Retrieved from www.nyu.edu/content/dam/nyu/studentAffairs/images/Explained/twitter/pdf

Parry, D. (2008, January 23). Twitter for academia [Blog post]. Retrieved from http://academhack.outsidethetext.com/home/2008/twitter-for-academia/

Pate, A. G. (2015). *Tweeting during lectures/tutorials: Engaging learners-not clipping their wings.* Retrieved from www.gla.ac.uk/media/media_309215_en.pdf

CHAPTER 18

Taking Notes

Researchers have been examining the relationship between note-taking during lectures and student learning for nearly one hundred years. In 1925, Crawford sought to verify his observation that taking notes appeared to improve college students' quiz grades and found that taking notes was better than not, reviewing notes was critical to success, and organizing notes contributed to improved test performance. Over subsequent decades, researchers have verified these early findings in myriad ways, most often designing studies that fall along two different tracks related to the functions of notes. The first type of studies looks at the encoding function of notes: in what ways does having students translate and synthesize information help them to learn? The second type of studies looks at the external storage function of notes: to what extent does note-taking help students because it produces something they can refer to and study later? The results from both types of research suggest that students who know how to take and use good notes are well served by the activity during lecture and those who do not are at a disadvantage.

Using laptops for note-taking during lecture is another issue that researchers have examined. Hembrooke and Gay (2003) investigated the test results of students who used laptops for taking notes compared to those who did not and found that laptop users performed worse on recognition and recall of lecture content. These general findings were corroborated by Aguilar-Roca, Williams, and O'Dowd (2012), who studied more than eight hundred students in sections of a large introductory biology course and found that students who took notes by hand scored significantly higher than those who used a laptop for note-taking.

A widely discussed study by Mueller and Oppenheimer (2014) assessed the content of handwritten notes versus those taken on a laptop, and results were consistent: students who used laptops were more likely to use verbatim transcription of the lecture material than students who took notes by hand. Additionally, although longhand and laptop note-takers performed well on the factual recall questions immediately after the lecture, students who took notes by hand did better on conceptual understanding of the questions. A week later, the advantage of note-taking by hand was even stronger, with those students who took notes longhand doing better on factual recall and on responding to conceptual understanding questions.

Researchers have also shown that laptop note-takers often engage in activities that involve switching between tasks that are related to the lecture material and unrelated tasks, which naturally leads to poor student performance in lecture learning. Kraushaar and Novak (2010), for example, sought self-reports and used spyware to determine the amount and kind of multitasking and found that the average student engaged in task switching regularly and frequently and generated more than sixty-five new active windows per lecture, with roughly 62 percent of those windows unrelated to course content. Researchers found that students had unrelated applications open and in use about 42 percent of the time. Thus, in general, taking notes by hand is better than taking notes on a computer. These findings do not apply, however, to all students, particularly those with disabilities that make handwriting more difficult. Thus requiring handwritten notes or forbidding laptops in the classroom is often not a good approach.

What we can say from the research findings is that note-taking is an important learning activity for students. Taking notes may help students stay focused and attentive. They also may ease the cognitive load on the working memory, thereby helping students better understand what they are hearing and learning. These assets of note-taking can help resolve problems in student learning from lectures (Bui & Myerson, 2014; Cohn, Cohn, & Bradley, 1995). Because students are not always good note-takers, instructors can help students take better notes, whether by hand or by computer. In this chapter, we provide you with five techniques related to helping students improve their note-taking during interactive lectures. We summarize the Techniques in Exhibit 18.1.

Exhibit 18.1 Techniques for Taking Notes

This technique . . .	Helps students learn actively by having them . . .
ALT 13: *Guided Notes*	Complete during the lecture a framework of incomplete notes provided by the instructor
ALT 14: *Cued Notes*	Listen for cues from the professor and then record lecture notes related to the cue
ALT 15: *Coded Notes*	Use a system of codes (such as * = important point) to interact with their notes
ALT 16: *Note-Taking Pairs*	Work with a partner at the end of the lecture to compare notes and build a better set of notes
ALT 17: *Sketch Notes*	Recast lecture notes into a set of visual notes that use single words or phrases combined with simple images

References

Aguilar-Roca, N. M., Williams, A. E., & O'Dowd, D. K. (2012). The impact of laptop-free zones on student performance and attitudes in large lectures. *Computers & Education, 59*(4), 1300–1308.

Bui, D. C., & Myerson, J. (2014). The role of working memory abilities in lecture note-taking. *Learning and Individual Differences, 33,* 12–22.

Cohn, E., Cohn, S., & Bradley, J. J. (1995). Note-taking, working memory, and learning in principles of economics. *Research in Economic Education, 26*(4), 291–307.

Crawford, C. C. (1925). The correlation between college lecture notes and quiz papers. *Journal of Educational Research, 12*(4), 282–291.

Hembrooke, H., & Gay, G. (2003). The laptop and the lecture: The effects of multitasking in learning environments. *Journal of Computing in Higher Education, 15,* 1–19.

Kraushaar, J. M., & Novak, D. C. (2010). Examining the affects of student multitasking with laptops during the lecture. *Journal of Information Systems Education, 21*(2), 241–251.

Mueller, P. A., & Oppenheimer, D. M. (2014). The pen is mightier than the keyboard: Advantages of longhand over laptop note taking. *Psychological Science, 25*(6), 1159.

ACTIVE LEARNING TECHNIQUE 13

Guided Notes

Complexity involved in	
Planning	HIGH
Developing Materials	MODERATE
Implementing in Class	LOW

Description and Purpose

Guided Notes provide students with an organizational structure for taking notes during a lecture. In particular, the notes present students with specific questions to answer or blanks to fill in as the lecture progresses. The questions or blanks typically prompt students to identify and write in key facts, concepts, or relationships (Heward, 2001).

This technique helps students focus their attention on the lecture because they must engage cognitively in order to be able to complete the notes successfully. *Guided Notes* provide students with an additional advantage: they help students learn how to organize information by providing a skeletal structure for the purpose. In short, from the notes, students gain an understanding of which are the more important concepts and which are the less important ones as well as an insider view of how an expert in the subject area—the teacher—would organize the information.

Also, because the instructor supplies only the missing information during a lecture, the technique can also improve class attendance. The lecture, then, provides something of value, and students need to attend the lecture to access that value. This technique provides scaffolding that can help students learn to take better notes on their own as they gain more experience with them. Thus, because many students lack note-taking skills when they enter college, helping them develop these skills will enable students to reap benefits beyond a single course.

Preparation

- Develop a set of notes that provide a summary of the information in your lecture.
- Next, cut out key words, phrases, or concepts, leaving blanks in their place. Alternately, create a set of questions that students can answer sequentially while listening to the lecture.
- Finally, try filling in the notes yourself, or have a colleague or teaching assistant do it, to ensure that the framework provides sufficient structure without being confusing.

Procedures

1. Provide students with the *Guided Notes.* Tell them they will fill in the notes from information contained in the lecture.
2. Present the lecture.

3. Ensure that students are completing the notes by observing them while they are working or collecting the notes when they are complete.
4. Collect the notes at the end of the lecture or at regular intervals throughout the academic term.

Video Lecture	Large Lecture
This technique can help students stay focused during video lectures as well as on-site ones. Post the *Guided Notes* as an assignment and ask students to complete it while watching the video lectures.	To use *Guided Notes* in a large lecture, find a way to distribute the template ahead of time and electronically. You can post to a learning management system (LMS) or course website or alternately e-mail the template to the class. Decide whether to collect notes randomly or at regular intervals.

Examples

Physical Geography (Lecture)

A geography professor decided to use *Guided Notes* when teaching an introductory geography course with students who were primarily at the sophomore level. He tried the notes first in a lesson on internal processes, in which he discussed plate tectonics, volcanism, volcano distribution, and types of volcanoes. He used notes that contained important figures or graphs from the required textbook along with blanks for students to fill in key terms and definitions from the lectures. For example, he showed a plate tectonics map with the following questions:

What evidence supports plate tectonics?

___
___
___

What is the driving mechanism of plate tectonics?

___
___
___

The notes followed the lecture material and did not exceed two pages. Although the instructor did not notice any obvious differences on quiz scores, results from a survey of students suggested that a majority of them found the notes helped them pay attention to the lecture, prepare for exams, and retain information. More than 90 percent of the students believed that the *Guided Notes* they filled in were better than their own notes, and a similar percentage also wanted to continue the use of *Guided Notes* in future class sessions.

Hispanic Culture (Large Lecture)

This large lecture section was taught by a team of professors and had the unusual circumstance of being taught in Spanish. The professors knew that although students had placed into the course, they were operating at different levels of Spanish listening, speaking, and writing abilities and thus would be able to understand the lectures and take notes at varying degrees of success.

The professors decided to use *Guided Notes* to provide all students with the ability to take good notes. They offered their lectures with presentation slides and created *Guided Notes* as handouts that coordinated with the slide decks. The handouts consisted of sentence stems that students could fill out as the lectures proceeded. Students were able to download and print the handout before coming to class. The professors saw that nearly every student came to class with the notes each time and then decided to pair this activity with ALT 16: *Note-Taking Pairs.*

Introduction to Psychology (Video Lecture)

The professor of this online introductory psychology course decided to use *Guided Notes* in conjunction with video lectures. She knew that previous research had shown that providing notes in an outline ahead of lectures improves learning. She believed that the same would hold true for her online course lectures.

She prepared a video lecture on the limits of memory. Because she had scripted the lecture, she was able to use the script as the base for the notes and simply remove key terms from the transcript. Here is a sample of the notes:

> Some scholars have suggested that humans can only remember approximately ____________________ [insert a number] things, and only that many when we group them into meaningful ____________________.
> This recall limit is useful because it measures what is termed ____________________.
> Some scholars have shown that this limit can also predict ____________________.

She posted the twenty-minute lecture video on the course site. She instructed students to fill in the missing terms as they watched the video and to submit the notes as an assignment in the LMS after they completed the lecture. She was pleased with the results and believed that *Guided Notes* helped students to focus attention on the lecture.

Variations and Extensions

- Use a graphic organizer to organize the notes, such as a main idea and details chart as shown in Figure 18.1.

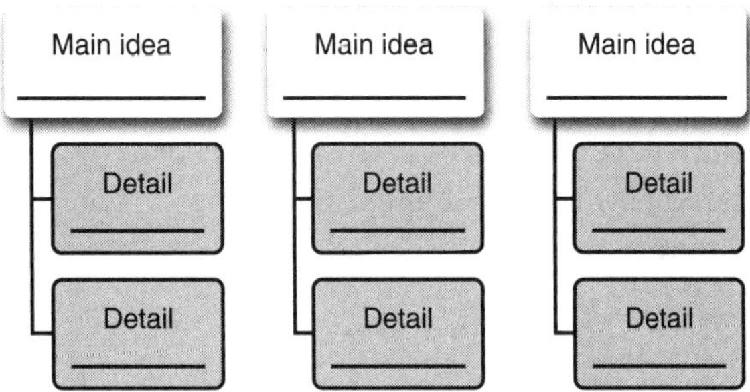

Figure 18.1 Sample Graphic Organizer

- Combine this activity with ALT 16: Note-Taking Pairs. Pause periodically and ask students to check with a peer sitting nearby to compare and correct their notes.

Observations and Advice

Students may ask you to supply the information for them. If you give it to them, you undermine the activity because the idea is to provide students only with the organizing structure. If they have real difficulty with completing the notes, ask them to work in small groups to compare answers—usually someone in the group will be able to supply the answer. If they are unable to get it as a group, check to ensure you are providing the required information in your lecture and also consider repeating part of the lecture in the next class session.

Guided Notes should be just that: guided. Fuller notes give students the answers and will mean less cognitive engagement on their part. However, overly unstructured notes leave students, particularly unprepared students, frustrated as they may have trouble deciphering what information to include.

You will want to ensure that students are completing the notes. You can do this visually if you are able to move around the room, or you could periodically collect notes and review them for accuracy.

You may want to fade the use of *Guided Notes* as the semester progresses. You may do so by requiring that students write an increasing share of the notes on their own until they are ultimately taking good notes completely independently.

Key References and Resources

Barnett, J. E. (2003). Do instructor-provided online notes facilitate student learning? *The Journal of Interactive Online Learning, 2*(2), 1–7. Retrieved from www.ncolr.org/jiol/issues/pdf/2.2.4.pdf

Heward, W. L. (2001). *Guided notes: Improving the effectiveness of your lectures.* Columbus, OH: The Ohio State University Partnership Grant for Improving the Quality of Education for Students with Disabilities. Retrieved from http://ada.osu.edu/resources/fastfacts/

Morrow, J. (2012). *Do guided notes improve student performance?* Retrieved from www.westpoint.edu/cfe/Literature/Morrow_12.pdf

Sidman, C. L., & Jones, D. (2007). Addressing students' learning styles through skeletal PowerPoint slides: A case study. *Journal of Online Learning and Teaching, 3*(4). Retrieved from http://jolt.merlot.org/vol3no4/sidman.htm

ACTIVE LEARNING TECHNIQUE 14

Cued Notes

Complexity involved in	
Planning	MODERATE
Developing Materials	MODERATE
Implementing in Class	MODERATE

Description and Purpose

In *Cued Notes,* students use a note-taking template, and the professor provides a cue prior to presenting a segment of information tied to the cue. The cue could be a single key word (e.g., *axons* or *dendrites*) or a simple question (e.g., "What is the nervous system?"). The professor shares the cue with students and encourages them to link the forthcoming information to the cue in their notes. The activity closes as students tie together the information by providing an overarching summary of the lecture.

Note-taking helps students concentrate during a lecture. Students also learn during the production of the notes, and they gain a deeper understanding than they would have if they had just been listening. Good notes also provide a tool for students to use when reviewing material prior to an examination. Thus, good note-taking can lead to better study practices and better learning outcomes. Students are often poor note-takers, however, and have difficulty distinguishing between main ideas and ancillary details. *Cued Notes* is a scaffold approach to support students during note-taking.

Preparation

- Review your lecture content and identify logical chunks of information. For each chunk, develop a simple cue. The cue can be a symbol, keyword, or question.
- Create an illustration of the *Cued Notes* to share with students or make a handout. Consider the Cornell Notes style, available as a free download through an Internet search, or construct your own using the *Cued Notes* template as a guide.

Cued Notes Template	
Course:__________ **Student's Name:**__________ **Lecture Date and Topic:**__________	
Cue	Notes
Summary	

Procedures

1. Begin your lecture. After the introduction, provide a cue and ask students to record it in the left-hand column of their notes.
2. Suggest that students record their main ideas in the right-hand column of the notes and present the segment of your lecture that corresponds to the cue.
3. Proceed with the lecture, alternating cues and lecture content.
4. At the end of the lecture, ask students to provide a summary of the full lecture at the bottom; you may choose to have them complete this step as homework.

Video Lecture	Large Lecture
Provide students with a template. Ask them to use the template while watching online lectures. You may wish to have them submit their notes as an assignment so that you can assess progress.	Provide students with the template as a downloadable PDF at the beginning of the term so that they can print and use it throughout the course. If you choose to assess and grade completed notes, determine how often you will collect them (such as twice per term) and how you will evaluate them (e.g., plus, check, minus).

Examples

Developmental English: Reading (Lecture)

The professor of a developmental English course planned a lecture on basic elements of fiction. She knew that most of her students were not proficient note-takers. She decided to implement *Cued Notes* to help them develop better notes and also to help them learn the material better.

She began by showing students how to format their notebook paper to take *Cued Notes.* Her lecture was organized on the seven elements of fiction. At the start of each segment, she wrote the cue on the board and asked students to write the cue in the left-hand column. She advised students to take fuller notes in the right-hand column, making sure to match the cue to the appropriate notes. She then proceeded to describe the element attached to the cue in detail, giving examples from the short story they had read the night before. At the end of the lecture, she asked students to write a summary of the lecture.

She collected the notes to check for accuracy. Following is an example.

Topic	**Student name**
Elements of Fiction	Steve Brown
Cue	**Notes**
Character	The person in a work of fiction or the characteristics of that person; you have to make inferences, for example, about what the character says
Theme	The underlying message the story is conveying; it is a central idea or meaning; it provides a unifying point for the story
Plot	The causal sequence of events; there is a Freytag pyramid that shows exposition, rising action, climax, falling action, and resolution
Point of view	The narrator's perspective; it refers to who tells the story and how it is told; there are several different points of view: third-person omniscient, third-person limited omniscient, objective, and first person
Setting	The location of a story's actions; it is the time and place in which the story occurs
Conflict	The incompatibility of goals or objectives of the main character
Tone	The attitude toward the story or toward the audience that is conveyed In a story
Summary	
There are several elements in a story, and each tells you something about the story's meaning.	

Nutrition in Health and Well-Being (Large Lecture)

This course is designed to teach the scientific principles of human nutrition using nutritional concepts to promote personal health and well-being. It is a popular course, and students meet twice per week for the lecture portion of the course and once per week for labs.

The professor wants to encourage active learning, but she also knows that it is easy for students to become passive, particularly during lecture presentations. She was also worried that in past semesters, some students did not seem to take many notes. They used their laptops, but she was not convinced that they were using them for note-taking, whereas other students were writing furiously the entire time. She felt that quiz and exam scores were suffering because some students were writing notes verbatim and thus not really processing, and other students were not taking notes at all. She therefore decided to use *Cued Notes.*

She posted the *Cued Notes* template at the beginning of the term in the course LMS so that students could access it at any time during the term. Each week, she presented carefully selected key word cues in her slide presentations and then used minimalist slide design (see Tip 19: *Less Is More*) to present the concepts that attended the notes. For example, for a session on food safety, she chose key words and phrases including *bacteria, cross-contamination, disinfectant, food contact surfaces, parasites, viruses,* and so forth. After displaying a single key word or phrase on a slide, she asked students to record the word(s) in their notes and to associate the information that followed with the specific cue. At the end of each month, she asked students to submit a folder with their cued notes so that she could assess them. This practice enabled her to target review sessions more effectively.

Psychology 101 (Video Lecture)

In this blended course, the professor has students complete *Cued Notes* with each video lecture. She supplies the students with a sample word document (following is a sample), which they fill in while watching the videos. She has students submit their notes as an online journaling assignment, which she checks periodically to ensure that students are keeping up with the videos and their notes.

Cue	Notes
What is intelligence?	It is intellectual functioning. It involves mental capacities including abilities such as reasoning, planning, problem-solving, thinking abstractly, and so forth.
What is the psychometric approach?	It is the field that focuses on the theory and practice of psychological measurement, including measurement of knowledge, abilities, and attitudes. The field focuses on the study of differences between individuals.
What is an intelligence quotient?	This is another name for one's score on IQ tests. The test compares your performance with other people your age who have taken the same test.
What is the common element on the IQ test?	General intelligence is the common element.
Summary	
This lecture was about intelligence testing and the IQ test as a measure of intelligence.	

Variations and Extensions

- Students can create their own cues along with the note-taking. They may not be proficient at this task initially, so it can be beneficial to provide the cues at first and then transition into having them produce their own.
- Students may pair with another student at the end of a segment or at the end of class to compare notes and ensure their accuracy. This is a variation of ALT 16: *Note-Taking Pairs.*

Observations and Advice

Students may need additional support in note-taking. Consider supplementing this technique with the five Rs of note-taking suggestions from University of Maine, Fort Kent (n.d.):

- **Record.** During the lecture, record in the main column as many meaningful facts and ideas as you can. Write legibly.
- **Reduce.** As soon after as possible, summarize these facts and ideas concisely in the Cue column. Summarizing clarifies meanings and relationships, reinforces continuity, and strengthens memory.
- **Recite.** Cover the note-taking area with a blank sheet of paper so that you can only see your jottings in the Cue column. Recount the facts and ideas of the lecture as fully as you can, not mechanically, but in your own words. Then, verify what you have said.
- **Reflect.** Draw out opinions from your notes and use them as a starting point for your own reflections on the course and how it relates to your other courses. Reflection will help prevent ideas from being inert and soon forgotten.
- **Review.** Spend ten minutes every week in quick review of your notes, and you will retain most of what you have learned.

Key References and Resources

Friedman, M. C. (n.d.). *Notes on note-taking: Review of research and insights for students and instructors.* Retrieved from http://hilt.harvard.edu/files/hilt/files/notetaking_0.pdf

Missouri State University. (2014). *Cornell note-taking* [brochure]. Retrieved from www.missouristate.edu/assets/busadv2014/p.22–23.pdf

Pauk, W. (2001). *How to study in college* (7th ed.). Boston, MA: Houghton Mifflin.

University of Maine, Fort Kent. (n.d.). *Cornell note-taking method.* Retrieved from www.umfk.edu/learning-center/studying-tips/notes/

ACTIVE LEARNING TECHNIQUE 15

Coded Notes

Complexity involved in	
Planning	MODERATE
Developing Materials	MODERATE
Implementing in Class	LOW

Description and Purpose

In *Coded Notes*, students use a coding system to record their thoughts about the content of the notes they take during a lecture. When the instructor pauses, students use a set of symbols to mark in the margins their reactions to information they have recorded in their notes. The *Coded Notes* symbols encourage students to constantly make decisions about their agreement or disagreement with ideas and concepts and to identify questions they have. *Coded Notes* also encourage students to identify new and important information that they have gained during the lecture.

Students tend to be ineffective note-takers, but taking good notes is critical to student success in higher education. One of the main problems with student note-taking is that students often try to transcribe verbatim what the instructor says, without processing the information. Applying a code, however, requires students to think about the information and concepts they have just written down. Students also self-assess when they use the codes because they indicate what they do and do not fully understand. Going through this process enables them to ask for clarification in the moment. This system of note-taking requires metacognition from students because students are monitoring their own comprehension as they use the codes.

Preparation

- Create a system of codes that reinforce the lecture content and purpose. The following are some sample codes that have broad applicability:
  ✓ I agree.
  X I disagree.
  ? I have a question about this.
  ?? I don't understand this.
  + This is new information.
  * This is an important point.
  ! Wow! This is really interesting.
- Create a handout or poster of the symbols and their meanings as a quick reference guide.
- Create a sample set of marked-up notes. Consider demonstrating the note-taking strategy to the whole class. If you do so, model the thinking process aloud while showing students how to code their notes.

Procedures

1. Announce the activity, and tell students that as they take notes, you want them to think about the information they are writing down. Explain that the purpose of the activity is to help them focus on understanding and using their notes effectively, recognizing what is the most important information in their notes, and identifying what they do or do not understand. Explain that you will pause the lecture from time to time so that they can code their notes.
2. Provide students with the codes and their meanings, and if you have a marked-up sample set of notes, provide those as well.
3. Begin your lecture.
4. Pause every fifteen minutes or so to give students time to code their notes.
5. At the end of the session, take time to ask students to report out some of their codes. Begin by responding to questions from students who recorded "?" or "??" in their notes. Then move to "!" codes to learn what intrigued them. When they note the most important ideas, compare their understanding with your own and be prepared to help correct any misconceptions.

Video Lecture	Large Lecture
You may wish to stress the importance of student note-taking in online courses because it simply may not occur to some students that they should take notes of video or VoIP lectures. Yet students who take notes tend to remember more content than students who do not. In an online course, students can take handwritten notes during a video lecture. Initially, it may be a good idea to suggest that they do so if they can because shifting back-and-forth between a video lecture and note-taking can be challenging. If they prefer or need to take notes electronically, students can use a simple word processor to do so. You can send them a template such as the video lecture *Coded Notes* template (see following) and ask them to take notes, record the minute or time stamp in the video in which they hear something to code and then record the code. If you want to review student notes, either have them scan their handwritten notes and send them to you electronically or alternately e-mail the Word document to you.	Post the codes where everyone can see them throughout the class session or alternately post a quick reference document online that students can print and bring to the session. Limit the number of individuals who respond in the reporting-out phase by randomly calling on students or asking for onc to two volunteers for each code.

Video Lecture *Coded Notes* Template	
Name: **Date:** **Assignment:**	**Code Key:** +—New information C—Connection ?—Question ??—Don't understand !—I agree X—I disagree
Notes:	**Codes**
	Min___ Min___ Min___ Min___ Min___

Examples

Law, Policy, and Ethics in Journalism (Lecture)

In this journalism course, the professor believes that students typically try to capture everything she says in her lectures verbatim in their notes. She does not believe that they process the information sufficiently, and she is concerned that they lose important information this way. She decided to use *Coded Notes* to help students think about and process what they write down.

In a planned lecture on copyright law in journalism, she explained the *Coded Notes* activity to the students, and she handed out a code sheet with the following symbols:

✓ I agree
X I disagree
? I have a question about this
?? I don't understand
+ This is new information
* This is an important point
! Wow!

The students took notes, and she paused every fifteen to twenty minutes to suggest that students code their notes using the guide. Following is a sample:

Copyright protects property.	✓
The purpose of copyright is to encourage progress by advancing arts and sciences.	+
Copyright may protect photos, stories, cartoons, and advertisements.	✓
Copyright does not protect ideas.	?
An infringement of a copyright means using someone else's work without getting the owner's permission.	✓
The copyright notice is optional. If the notice is not included, it does not affect the validity of a copyright.	?

At the end of the activity, she asked students to volunteer to report out on their codes. Many more students had questions than students in previous semesters. Some students also discussed new things they learned as well as ideas that intrigued them. She determined that she would use the activity again in future lecture sessions.

Introduction to Popular Culture (Large Lecture)

This large lecture course provides an overview, history, and critical analysis of popular culture as a window for understanding American society. The professor is always looking for ways to deepen student engagement. He decided to use *Coded Notes* in conjunction with his lecturette on censorship to challenge students to think more deeply about the topic as well as to prepare them to participate meaningfully in a small-group follow-up discussion. After the lecturette, the professor paused and shared a simple system of coding that involved only four codes: a checkmark for "I agree," an *x* for "I disagree," a plus sign for "this is something I didn't know," and an exclamation mark for "I find this really interesting." He asked students to use the system to code the notes they had just taken. After a few minutes, he asked students to share in their base groups how and why they had coded the information as they did. He found that by providing students with a framework, as well as a few moments to reflect on what they had heard in his presentation, they were able to organize their thoughts and were generally more willing and ready to participate in the small-group discussions.

Qualitative Research Methods (Video Lecture)

This graduate-level flipped course uses Internet-based learning for lectures in conjunction with a wide range of other activities. The instructor encourages students to take notes during the video lectures. She also occasionally has guest speakers present in synchronous sessions, for which she also encourages students to take notes. She has noticed, however, that when it is time for questions from the students, there is always a hesitation, and very few students volunteer with any substantive questions. She is worried that they are passive in the lectures and are not really processing the information.

She decided to use *Coded Notes* for a session in which she had invited a well-known qualitative researcher to attend her online course as a guest speaker through the LMS's VoIP function. The speaker was to share her research with the students, and the instructor wanted students to engage with her and to really learn from her.

Prior to the session, she announced the activity and asked students to take notes on the talk and to use a coding system to interact with their notes. She provided them with the following codes:

FA = fact
O = opinion
M = methodology
Me = method
FI = finding
C = conclusion

As the guest lecturer talked, students were to write down the key ideas. At the end of the guest lecture, they were to take five minutes to code their notes. The speaker then took questions from the students. This time, the students had a strong set of questions about the content, the assumptions, and the methods, and the professor was pleased with the results.

Variations and Extensions

- Follow up the coding activity with pairs or small-group discussion of the codes prior to opening up discussion to the full class. Doing so will give students an opportunity to rehearse their questions and provide insights so they may feel more comfortable talking in front of a full group.
- Once students become more comfortable with the coding process, ask them to generate additional codes specific to the course content.

Observations and Advice

It can be helpful to introduce only two or three symbols at a time until students become proficient in using them: * = important point, ? = "I have a question," and ?? = "I don't understand" are good places to start.

Key References and Resources

Historical Scene Investigation. (n.d.). *Interactive notation system for effective reading and thinking.* Retrieved from www.hsionline.org/cases/anthony/InsertReadngActivity%20.pdf

Vaughan, J. L., & Estes, T. H. (1986). *Reading and reasoning beyond the primary grades.* Boston, MA: Allyn and Bacon.

ACTIVE LEARNING TECHNIQUE 16

Note-Taking Pairs

Complexity involved in	
Planning	LOW
Developing Materials	LOW
Implementing in Class	MODERATE

Description and Purpose

In *Note-Taking Pairs,* the lecturing professor provides class time for student pairs to work together to improve their individual notes. During this activity, students revisit and cross-check notes with another source. Partners also attempt to help each other add missing information and correct inaccuracies so that their combined effort is superior to their individual notes.

Being able to take good notes is an important learning skill, yet many students are poor note-takers; their notes often are incomplete and inaccurate. The purpose of *Note-Taking Pairs* is to provide students with a structured activity so that they may pool information, fill in gaps, check for and correct mistakes, and help each other learn to be better note-takers. When used throughout the semester, this technique is also useful for helping students better understand complex concepts because they have time to rehearse and retrieve information while it is still fresh in their minds.

Preparation

- Before using *Note-Taking Pairs,* consider providing students with guidance about how to take good notes through a mini-lecture on note-taking, a handout, or with examples of effective notes.
- Plan your lecture so that you present material in ways that encourage students to take detailed notes. For example, speak slowly, provide handouts of complicated graphs and figures so that students can keep up, and use the whiteboard or presentation slide to show overall structure by using titles and headings (Davis, 1993).
- Consider when you will ask students to compare notes. You may wish to pause occasionally during the lecture, or you may simply provide a few minutes at the end of class.

Procedures

1. Ask students to individually take notes of the major points from a body of content, such as a lecture or a text chapter.
2. Have students form pairs, either at your direction or by choosing partners.

3. Invite partner A to begin by summarizing the main points from a section of the notes to partner B, who offers corrections and any additional information.
4. Then invite partner B to summarize the next section, and partner A to offer corrections and additional information.
5. Have the partners continue to alternate sharing summaries, corrections, and additional information until they have completed checking their notes.

Video Lecture	Large Lecture
Students who receive content in new ways in online courses, such as through videotaped lectures, often do not know the best way to organize and synthesize the information. Using *Note-Taking Pairs* can help students clarify their notes and can help them to develop effective note-taking strategies for online courses. Using this technique asynchronously also enables students to have more time to process and reflect on the notes. The challenge in an online environment is to have students who are separated by distance compare a physical set of notes, particularly when there may be additional challenges of persistence and regular attendance. To implement *Note-Taking Pairs* online, an effective approach would be to use documents or a wiki. Ask students to develop a set of notes using Google Docs or a wiki, which have capabilities for showing who contributed what. You can then review the documents to see how strong the notes are and how complete each student's contribution is. Alternately, you can ask students to use e-mail or your LMS's internal communication tools to compare and improve their notes. Divide students into pairs and ask them to share their notes as attachments. If you wish students to consolidate notes into a single-partner version, different font styles or colors can distinguish individual contributions.	This technique provides students in a large lecture course with an opportunity for collaborative learning, which can be challenging in auditorium classrooms. In very large classes, the noise level will be high, so you will want to establish a *Silent Signal* (Tip 39).

Examples

General Physics (On-Site)

A professor teaching this introductory course knew that he would lecture frequently and suspected that most students would not have good note-taking skills. He therefore decided to use *Note-Taking Pairs.* Rather than pairs, however, he divided the students into base groups and assigned roles for each base group team member (extensive note-taker, summary note-taker, question generator, and compiler—the last of whom was responsible for organizing, proofing, and posting notes on the course LMS for all students to see). Roles rotated each week. The professor felt that the technique improved student access to effective notes and that it created a useful repository of information. He also could assess the notes to determine any issues and target class lectures and review sessions accordingly.

Computer Science for Nonmajors (Large Lecture)

In this large lecture course, the professors were concerned about student note-taking abilities and decided to use *Note-Taking Pairs.* At the beginning of the semester, they assigned students into pairs and told students that the pairs would work together for ten minutes at the end of each major lecture to ensure that all students would have as complete and accurate a set of notes as possible. The professor reassigned pairs after each of the four major course examinations to give students the benefit of working with a number of their peers.

History of Western Civilization (Online)

The professor of an online course had been posting text lectures, and students were required to complete worksheets covering the information in the lectures as one of their weekly assignments. She discovered that a significant percentage of students were simply electronically copying segments of the lectures and pasting them in their assignments as the answers to the worksheet questions. For the next semester, she removed the posted lectures and published her lectures as a separate document that was sold along with the textbook in the college bookstore. This prevented students from simply copying and pasting the material. She also modified and expanded her worksheets to include questions requiring more critical interaction with the information as well as questions asking for simple summaries of various portions of the readings. She organized students into pairs and asked them to work first individually and then to e-mail each other to compare notes and to complete each worksheet. Students were given an initial deadline for their individual assignments and a second deadline for a collaborative version of their assignment.

Variations and Extensions

- Ask student pairs to sit together during the lecture. At various times throughout the lecture, stop and ask partners to participate in *Note-Taking Pairs.* You can offer specific prompts, such as, "Ask each other what the major point was so far and make sure that that point is clear in your notes." This technique keeps students' attention focused on the lecture and enables students to rehearse the information and to correct any misinformation or perceptions.
- Give students overnight to revisit their notes to make revisions and corrections and to add information before sharing the notes with a peer. This additional time will enable students to clarify their own thoughts and to make their writing more legible before sharing their notes with another.
- Consider making your lecture notes available to student pairs after using *Note-Taking Pairs* for students to recheck and thus revisit their notes a third time.
- Use *Note-Taking Pairs* for students to review homework assignments, check answers to homework problems at the beginning of class, or review for a test.

Observations and Advice

This technique can help reinforce course concepts, but it can also reinforce inaccuracy if both students in a pair have faulty information. Repeat and emphasize the main concepts frequently and review and assess the notes periodically to make sure that students are learning the correct information.

It is important that each student take something from the other student's notes to improve his or her own notes. If only one student is taking good notes, that student will probably resent helping the student who is taking poor notes. Structured prompts such as "What was the most important point?" can provide students with guidance about what they may contribute beyond a summary.

To assess learning, use the minute-paper method (Angelo & Cross, 1993, CAT 6, pp. 148–153) asking students to respond in writing to two questions: "What is the most important suggestion you got from your peer?" "What do you think is the most helpful suggestion you gave to your peer?" If the major purpose of the exercise is to improve written note-taking skills, occasionally collect notes before the peer conversation and again after. Or to simplify your review, ask students to highlight or indicate what changes they made as a result of discussion with a peer. If you are more interested in assessing the quality of the peer suggestions, ask students to hand in one set of their notes with suggestions by their peer made in a different-color pen or pencil.

Key References and Resources

Angelo, T. A., & Cross, K. P. (1993). *Classroom assessment techniques: A handbook for college teachers* (2nd ed.). San Francisco, CA: Jossey-Bass.

Barkley, E. F., Major, C. H., & Cross, K. P. (2014). CoLT 7: Note-taking pairs. *Collaborative learning techniques: A handbook for college faculty* (2nd ed., pp. 189–194). San Francisco, CA: Jossey-Bass.

Davis, B. G. (1993). *Tools for teaching.* San Francisco, CA: Jossey-Bass.

Johnson, D. W., Johnson, R., & Smith, K. (1998). *Active learning: Cooperation in the college classroom.* Edina, MN: Interaction Book Company.

Millis, B. J., & Cottell, P. G. (1998). *Cooperative learning for higher education faculty.* American Council on Education. Phoenix, AZ: Oryx Press.

University of Maine, Fort Kent. (n.d.). *Cornell note-taking method.* Retrieved from www.umfk.edu/learning-center/studying-tips/notes/

ACTIVE LEARNING TECHNIQUE 17

Sketch Notes

Complexity involved in	
Planning	LOW
Developing Materials	LOW
Implementing in Class	MODERATE

Description and Purpose

For *Sketch Notes,* students strive to illustrate the main concepts from a lecture as well as their interrelations. As the author of the *Sketch Note Handbook,* explains (Rohde, n.d.), *Sketch Notes* are notes created from a mix of handwriting, drawings, shapes, and visual elements such as boxes, lines, and arrows. The idea behind *Sketch Notes* is to boil down a large amount of information into a visual representation of words and simple symbols.

Sketch Notes requires students to reconceptualize their notes in a less-linear, more-visual fashion. The process of creating the *Sketch Notes* helps students think through information in a new way. These notes require students to process the information from the lecture, and this additional processing will improve their learning. Students have to show relations between concepts, and organizing the information in this way can help to cement it in their memories. This technique also helps to provide a visual representation of how students conceptualize the information; thus, it can be a useful assessment technique.

Preparation

- Prepare a handout that illustrates what a *Sketch Note* looks like. Create your own notes or use existing examples online, which you can find through a Google search. A good place to start is the Sketch Note Army's showcase of *Sketch Notes* (http://sketchnotearmy.com).
- Prepare some simple instructions for students. You don't want to be overly directive, but students will appreciate some basic tips. Consider the following suggestions from Berman (2011):

Text. Recording the verbal is quick, direct, and clear and is usually your primary sketch-noting tool. Capture the meaningful quotes and key points, and avoid trying to summarize everything.
Containers. Simply enclosing words in shapes brings emphasis and structure to an otherwise wild page. Some of the more common containers include (but are not limited to) quote bubbles, boxes, circles, and thought clouds.
Connectors. Connect ideas and pieces of stories with arrows and lines. A basic chain of thoughts can scintillate around the page and still be clear if they are linked with a simple set of connectors.
Frameworks. Some presenters will have a very obvious structure to their presentation, but oftentimes the insights may benefit from your own synthesis into an understandable underlying structure or model. Common frameworks include 2 × 2s, Venn diagrams, and continuums.

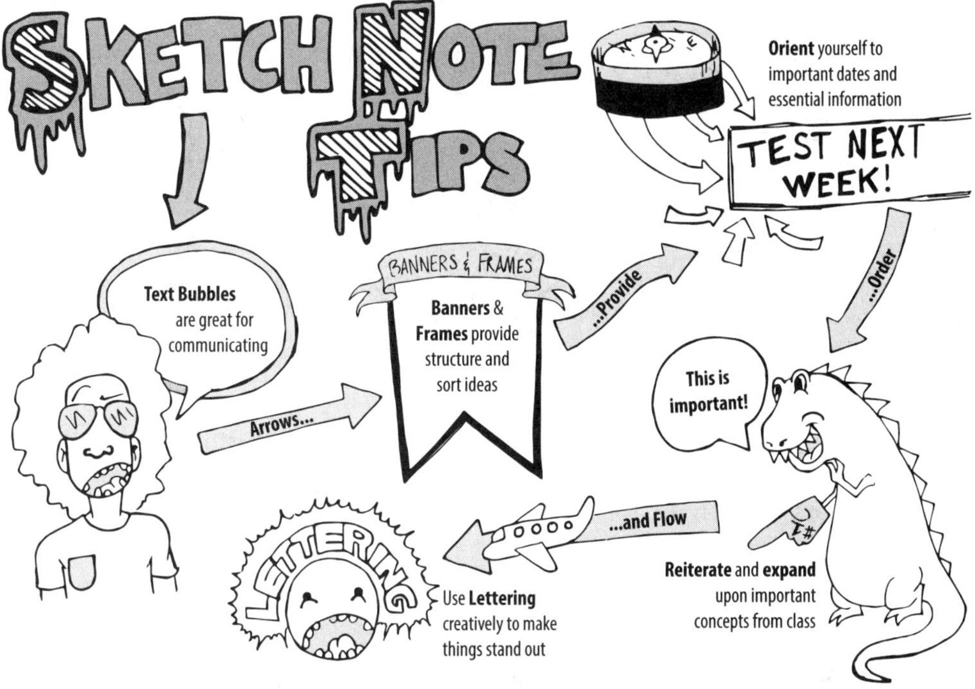

Figure 18.2 *Sketch Note* Tips

Source: Used with permission of Josh Wever.

- Consider the tips in Figure 18.2.
- Consider also giving students a few symbols to start. You can do an Internet search for some symbols (try the search term *sketch note symbols* for ones that are particularly relevant to your discipline or field.
- Also provide students with some ideas about what makes a good *Sketch Note* (e.g., Figure 18.3).

Procedures

1. Announce the activity and share a *Sketch Note* sample with students.
2. Proceed with the lecture.
3. Provide students with time after the lecture to transform their linear notes and the information they retain in their memories into *Sketch Notes.* Because of the complexity of creating notes, it can help students to work on them as a homework assignment.
4. Collect the notes and review them for relevance and to determine whether you need to follow up in your next lecture with additional information or insights. Consider also having students display their notes so that they may learn from each other.

Examples

College and University Teaching (Lecture)

This course engages students in intensive study of the issues, policies, and principles associated with teaching in higher education. Topics addressed in the course include history and philosophy of college teaching, internal and external influences on instruction, faculty and students, instructional models and methods, documenting and assessing teaching, and instructional improvement.

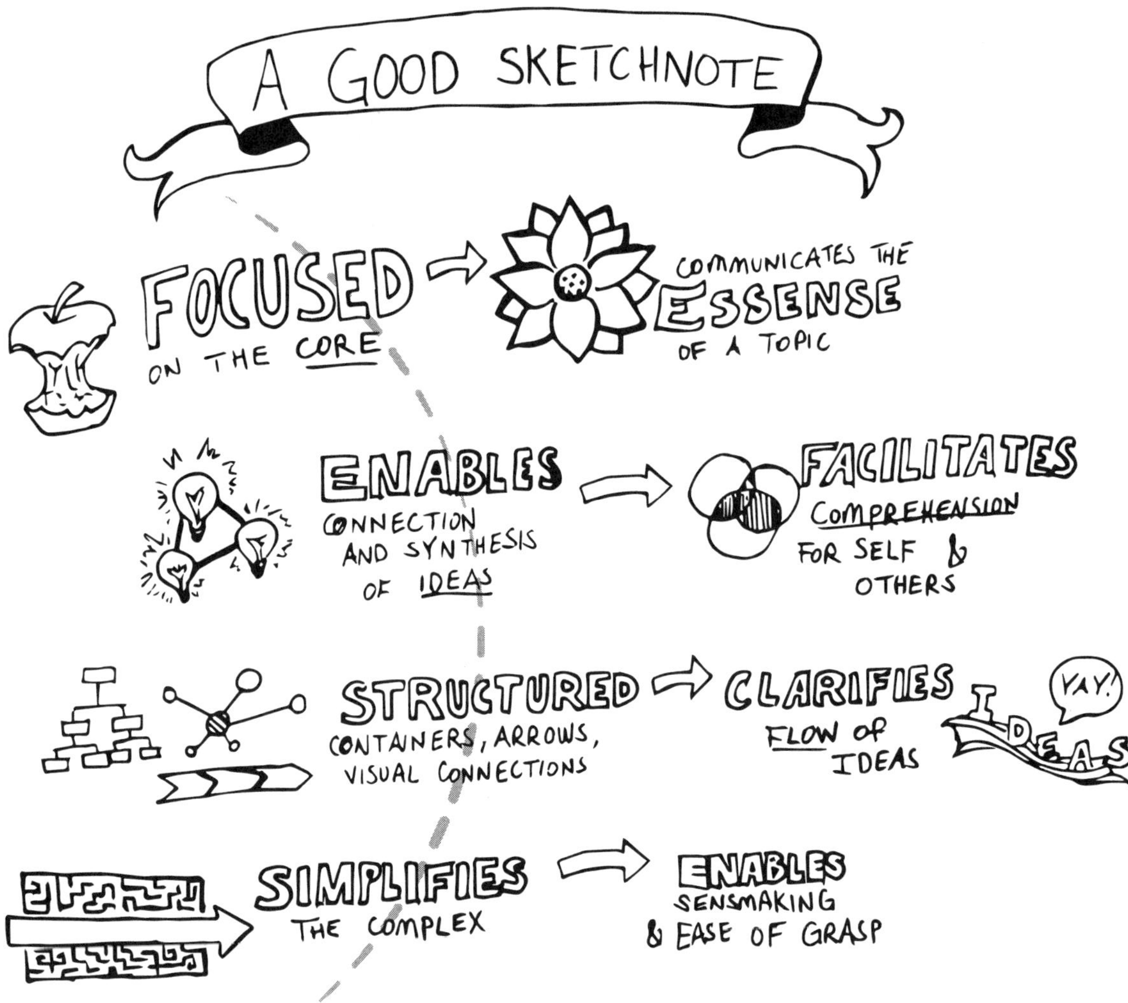

Figure 18.3 What Makes a Good *Sketch Note*

Source: Redrawing by Josh Wever of Tanmay Norva's "What Makes a Good Sketch Note" (https://twitter.com/tnvora). Used with permission.

Video Lecture	**Large Lecture**
In an online course, ask students to take notes on the video or VoIP lecture by hand. They can then transform them into *Sketch Notes.* If they draw their *Sketch Notes* by hand, they can scan or take a picture, and send them to you. There are also several online drawing tools that enable students to take notes digitally, such as Sketchbook X, Paper, and Flipink. Some students will enjoy using these, but others will likely prefer to sketch by hand.	Use this as an assignment for a single lecture, or consider having students create a single *Sketch Note* for a broad concept that connects a series of lectures. Have students submit their *Sketch Notes* as they do other assignments. If using an LMS, for example, have students scan or photograph their projects and upload them as a jpeg or PDF.

This course is a doctoral-level seminar, which in this case comprises a group of advanced students studying under a professor with each doing original research and all exchanging results through reports and discussions. The professor presents a short lecture at each session, students engage in discussion, and students do individual research between meetings.

Following are one student's *Sketch Notes* from two class sessions in which the professor lectured and the student captured the key ideas in *Sketch Notes.* The first two notes (Figures 18.4 and 18.5) were from a class session describing the knowledge teachers need for teaching and the interplay between content knowledge and pedagogical knowledge, illustrating what happens when one side is not as developed as the other. The third figure (18.6) is from a class session focused on learning that depicts surface-learning versus deep-learning approaches.

Figure 18.4 Two Types of Knowledge Needed for Teaching

Source: Used with permission of Josh Wever.

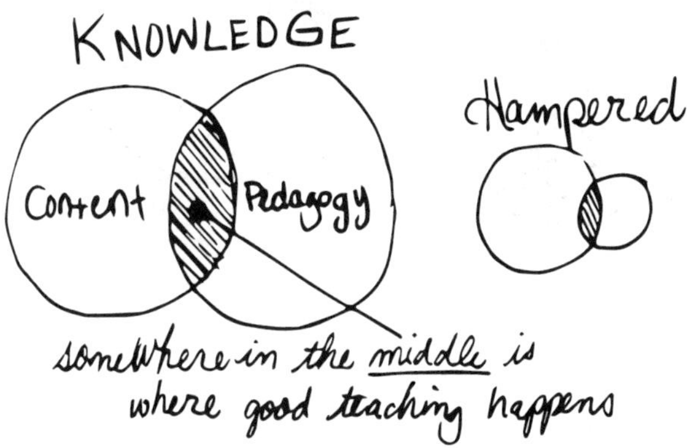

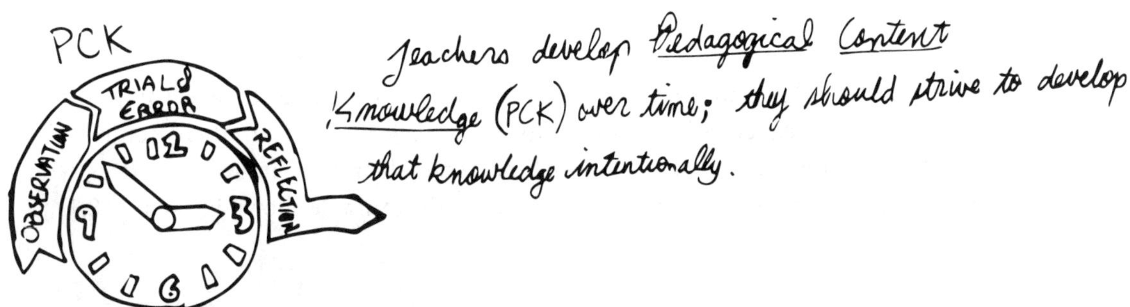

Figure 18.5 Interplay between Content Knowledge and Pedagogical Knowledge

Source: Used with permission of Josh Wever.

Figure 18.6 Surface-Learning versus Deep-Learning Approaches

Source: Used with permission of Josh Wever.

Introduction to Leadership (Large Lecture)

In this large lecture course, the two-hour course is divided into two sections, each of which meets for one hour: the first is the large lecture and the second is a learning community of eleven to twelve students each, led by an upperclass student.

During lecture presentations, the professor presents an overview of various topics related to leadership. Students are encouraged to take notes. During one of the learning community sessions, the class leaders asked students to create *Sketch Notes* from their lectures. They gave students paper and colored pens. The students recast their notes into *Sketch Notes,* which ranged in quality from elaborate to rather simple, as in the example shown in Figure 18.7.

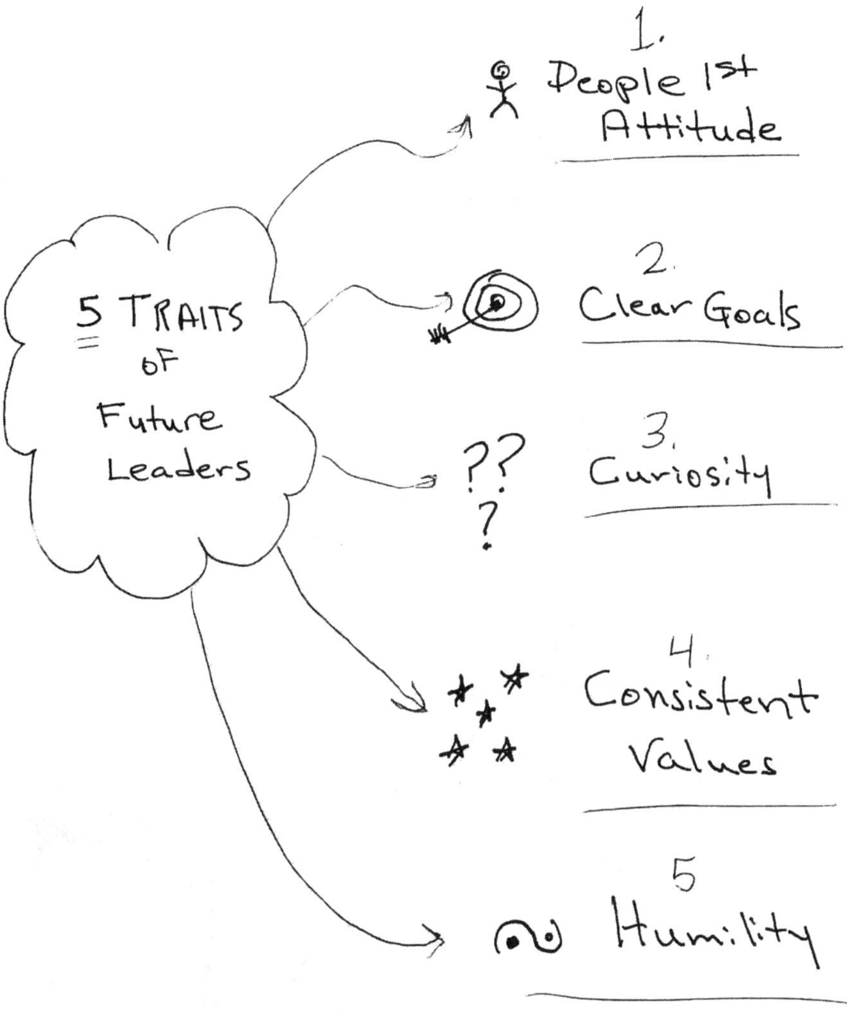

Figure 18.7 Introduction to Leadership *Sketch Note* Example

Survey of World Music (Video Lecture)

This online course is a survey of world music styles that traces various non-Western music genres from their roots in the ethnic traditions of a specific culture through their evolution into new forms that retain relevance in contemporary society. In an effort to help students identify the core concepts in the lectures, the professor assigned students to construct a *Sketch Note* on a topic of their choice. One student chose the music of South Africa (see Figure 18.8) and integrated the historical context of colonialism and apartheid with specific music styles, indicating their connection to popular music such as Paul Simon's *Graceland* and Disney's *The Lion King*. In her post-assignment reflections, the student shared how the *Sketch Note* helped her pull together these elements at a macro level that clarified and deepened her understanding. Another student chose the music of India (see Figure 18.9) and used his *Sketch Note* to compare and contrast stylistic elements between the South and North. He shared how at first he had resisted doing the assignment because he didn't have artistic skills, but that once he completed it, he was pleased with how the *Sketch Note* helped him organize the main concepts he wanted to remember regarding Indian music.

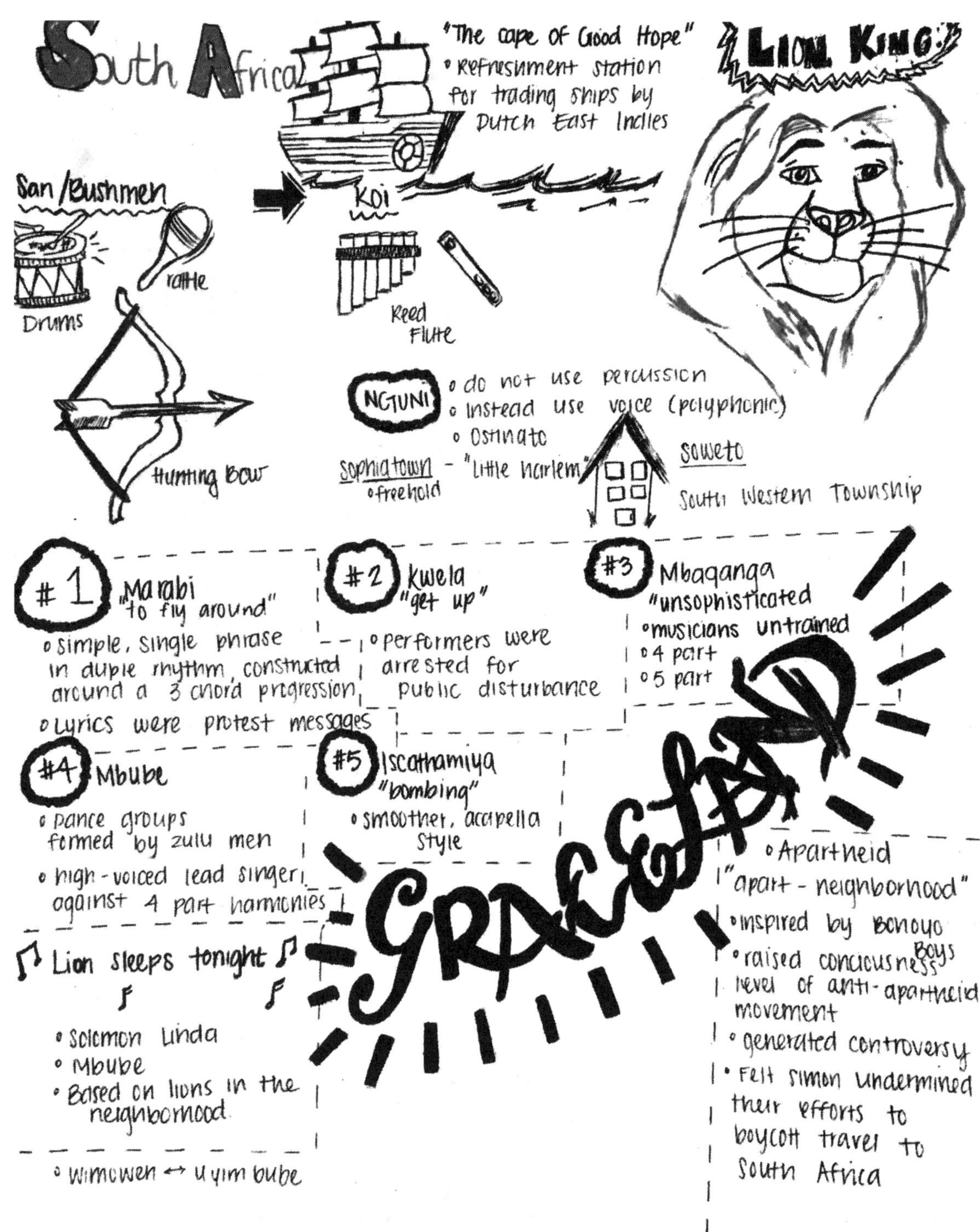

Figure 18.8 World Music *Sketch Note*: Music of South Africa

Source: Used by permission of Leilani Ortez.

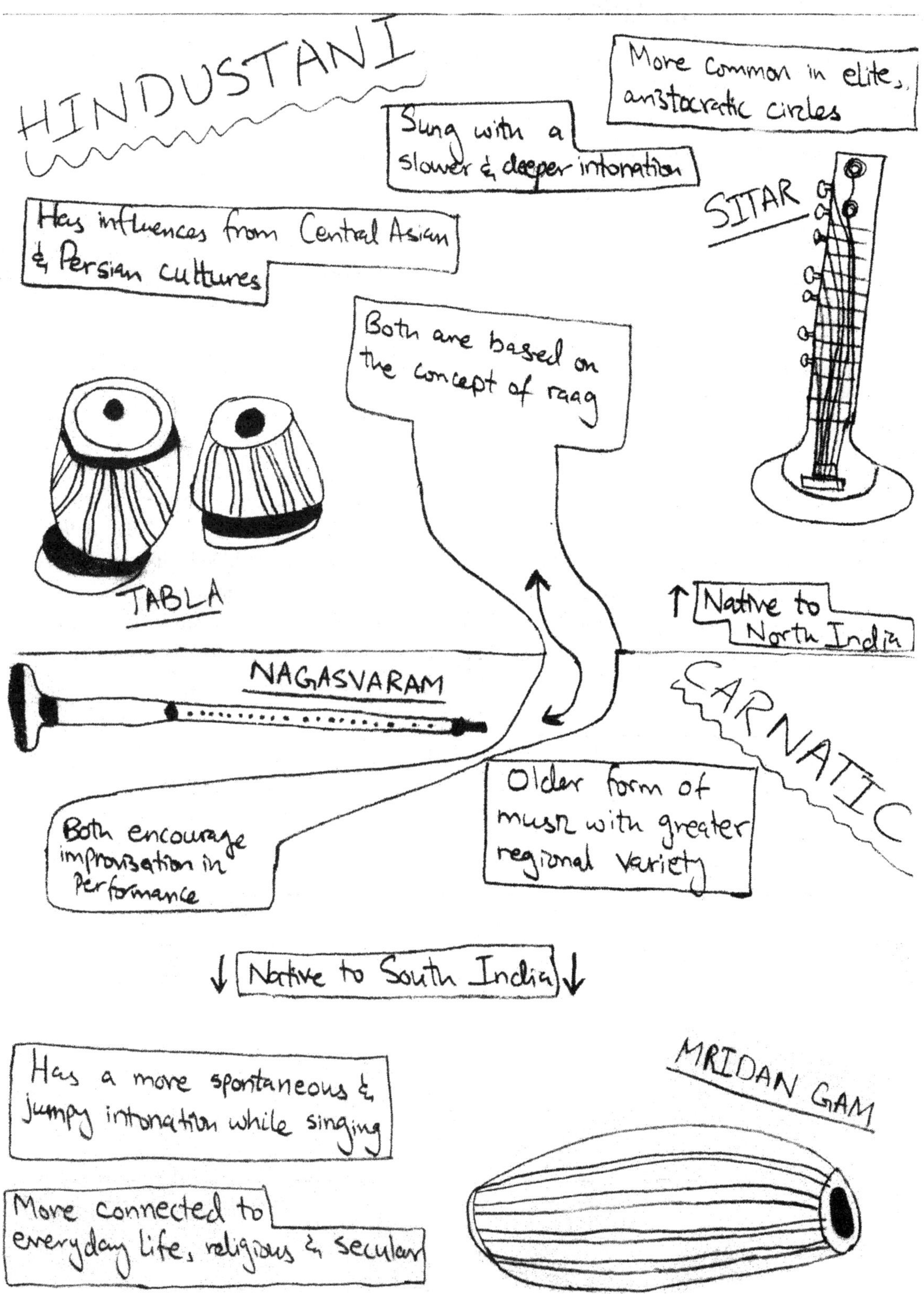

Figure 18.9 World Music *Sketch Note*: Music of India

Source: Used by permission of Syed Muhammed Masud.

Variations and Extensions

Sketch Notes can feel overwhelming for some students, particularly those who have difficulty succinctly summarizing and then organizing a substantial amount of information or alternately for those who feel that they lack artistic ability. You may want to scaffold the *Sketch Notes* activity by giving them a simple template for sketching out the main ideas.

Template for Beginning *Sketch Notes*		
	Sketch	**Main Idea**
1		
2		
3		

- You may want to ask students to start *Sketch Notes* by making a storyboard of their ideas (see Figure 18.10). This is an intermediate step between linear notes and *Sketch Notes.*
- *Sketch Notes* are at their heart a kind of mind map, so you could substitute a basic concept map with simple drawings to illustrate the main concept and connecting ideas.
- Instead of having students create the notes, provide your notes to students as *Sketch Notes* rather than as more linear notes. This variation requires students to think about your notes more than they would by receiving full copies of the lecture transcript.

Figure 18.10 Template for Storyboarding

Observations and Advice

Some students will love this technique, and others will instantly decide that it is not for them. It is often good for students to stretch to try new things, but be sure to give students plenty of space for imperfection. Stress that the idea is visual communication, which can be done with text and boxes alone, rather than artistic representation.

Key References and Resources

Barkley, E. F., & Major, C. H. (2016). *Learning assessment techniques: A handbook for college faculty.* San Francisco, CA: Jossey-Bass.

Berman, C. (2011). *Sketchnotes 101: The basics of visual note-taking.* Retrieved from www.core77.com/posts/19678/sketchnotes-101-the-basics-of-visual-note-taking-19678

Rohde, M. (n.d.). *The sketchnote handbook.* Retrieved from http://rohdesign.com/book/

CHAPTER 19

Rehearsing Information

When we hear the term *rehearsal,* we typically think of strategies that involve continually repeating information. For example, if you want to remember a person's name, you might repeat it over and over again to yourself until you have stored it in your short-term memory and can retrieve it immediately. If you have used this approach, however, you know that it is still fairly easy to forget that name, even after this "maintenance" rehearsal effort. That shows us that even with purposeful rehearsal effort, information can fade from short-term memory before it is stored in long-term memory.

There is also a second kind of rehearsal, however, called *elaboration.* This form of rehearsal involves associating new information with information existing in long-term memory. Such a rehearsal strategy is necessary to help remember information that is more complex than a name or phone number. It requires understanding the information in a way that can be retrieved later. Elaborative rehearsal strategies enrich and enhance understanding information. An example of elaborative rehearsal is trying to explain a concept to a friend so that you must communicate and thus test your own understanding. In this chapter, we offer three techniques that engage students in elaborative rehearsal. We summarize the Techniques in Exhibit 19.1.

Exhibit 19.1 Techniques for Taking Notes

This technique . . .	Helps students learn actively by having them . . .
ALT 18: *Translate That!*	Explain in their own words the fact or concept that the instructor just presented
ALT 19: *Think-Pair-Share*	Think about a prompt question, pair up to discuss, and then share with the whole class
ALT 20: *Snap Shots*	Think about and then choose a response to a multiple-choice question posed by the lecturer, and then try to convince their assigned partner that their response is correct; the instructor then provides the answer so that students can assess the accuracy of their understanding

Key Reference and Resource

Reisberg, D. (1997). *Cognition: Exploring the science of the mind.* New York, NY: Norton.

ACTIVE LEARNING TECHNIQUE 18

Translate That!

Complexity involved in	
Planning	LOW
Developing Materials	LOW
Implementing in Class	MODERATE

Description and Purpose

In *Translate That!* the instructor pauses a lecture and calls on a student at random to "translate" the recently provided information into plain English for an imagined audience that the teacher specifies. The goal is for the student to restate what he or she just heard in the lecture in a manner that remains true to the original idea but using his or her own voice. The translation should move beyond a simple reversal of the sentence structure or replacement of some of the words with synonyms to a restatement that communicates the true meaning of the original but in more accessible, easily understood language. The process repeats throughout the class session.

The activity benefits the translators by having them rethink what the instructor has just said and to express it in a new way. This action helps students to check their own comprehension and to solidify the new knowledge. Hearing information a second time in words that match their level of understanding, as opposed to the expert level of the professor, is beneficial to students. Because students may be called on at any time, it motivates them to stay involved and attentive. *Translate That!* also provides professors with a quick check of student understanding, which enables them to revisit areas that students are not fully comprehending and to feel confident moving forward when students seem to have understood.

Preparation

- Review your lecture content to identify potential opportunities for integrating this technique approximately every ten minutes. Ensure that each segment is a logical, coherent whole that students can remember and repeat.
- Identify a potential target audience so that students can modify the language of their responses accordingly; obviously their peers are an audience, but students could translate the information, for example, to a younger sibling or to someone planning to take the course next term. This small role-play can result in students feeling less self-conscious than they might if they had to explain to one another.
- Decide how you will choose students at random. You may, for example, have students count off and then draw a number from a hat, asking the student whose number was called to do the translation. The goal is for random selection so that the choice seems fair, but it is important to use an approach so that students cannot hide or pretend they were not the ones called on.

Procedures

1. Announce the activity and tell students that you will be selecting people randomly to interpret what you have said in a lecture. Explain that many students will be called on during the activity and that you are not trying to single out any one student. Also explain that after the initial translation, other students will be invited to provide additional information to support the original translation.
2. Begin your lecture. At about ten minutes, announce that it is time for a translation and provide everyone with approximately thirty seconds to one minute to organize their thoughts.
3. Randomly select a student and ask the student to translate the lecture segment for the designated role-play audience, such as students who enroll next term.
4. After the translation, if necessary, ask other students to clarify or add in missing information; you may want to continue random selection or you may at this point take volunteers.
5. Repeat the process every ten minutes or so, as time allows.

Online Lecture	Large Lecture
To use this activity in a synchronous online course, if you are using VoIP, stop a lecture and ask a student to translate the segment in chat. This provides a written rather than verbal summary, but it is still a translation that the rest of the class can review. This activity can be more challenging to implement in an asynchronous online course. An option is to post a video lecture that you break at certain segments (break 1, break 2, and so forth). Then you can post discussion threads that correspond to each break. All students must share their translations; the benefit to this approach is that students have multiple translations to help them understand the topic. Some learning management systems (LMSs) allow setting a discussion so that students must post a response before they see others' responses.	This activity can be useful in a large lecture class. The main dilemma is how to choose students to report out so that no one feels singled out. You might pull names from a hat or alternately go with geographical location in the classroom, for example, choosing a student from each quadrant of the seating area and then someone from the middle.

Examples

Geography (Lecture)

The professor of this mid-size course planned to lecture on igneous rocks, and she knew that in the past some students had trouble comprehending the information. She thought that perhaps she was providing too much information at once, without providing students sufficient time to process. She decided to use *Translate That!* to help address the issue.

She began the lecture by discussing magma, and at about ten minutes in, she stopped, allowed students time to think, and then called on a student to translate the information, with an intended audience of a friend or relative. The student translated by describing it as a rock with a high temperature that has the properties of a liquid. She then called on another student who added that magma includes not only rocks but also crystals and gas. She noticed students throughout the class augmenting their notes. The translation portion took about five minutes.

She continued her lecture on volcanic rocks. At about another ten minutes in, she stopped, gave students time to think, and then called on the next translator. The student did a good job of describing volcanic rocks as extrusive igneous rocks. The next student was able to add that this kind of rock crystallizes on the surface of the crust rather than within the earth.

She believed that students were following her and comprehending the information well. She also believed that the activity had the nice benefit of helping students to improve their lecture notes. Thus she determined that she would use *Translate That!* again.

Humanities: The Ancient World (Large Lecture)

This large lecture course is an interdisciplinary course that serves as the introduction to the humanities sequence. It starts with cultural developments of ancient civilizations and peoples and moves through major religions. It is team-taught and meets once per week for a large lecture and twice more for section meetings.

The professors wanted to be sure that students were understanding the content of their lectures, and they had an attending goal of helping students pay attention during the large lecture sessions. They decided to use *Translate That!* to help them accomplish both goals. After a professor lectured, she would stop and ask the students to translate to an imagined group of students who were planning to take the course the following semester. After lecturing on Tablet 1 in the "Epic of Gilgamesh," for example, the professor stopped the lecture and asked a student to translate the basic story line for students who planned to take the course next term. The professor continued lecturing about the tablets, stopping periodically for student translations. The professor believe that the translations helped students follow the epic story line and also helped students pay attention, in part due to the cold-calling and in part due to hearing their peers put the information into their own words.

Health: Emotional Wellness (Video Lecture)

Most of the students who took this blended course did so to learn about life and stress management. The professor taught a unit on stress that tended to be more scientific than most students anticipated, so she used *Translate That!* to scaffold the information.

In a video lecture on the body's reaction to stress, she created five ten-minute videos on stress: (1) stress defined, (2) emotional symptoms of stress, (3) physical symptoms of stress, (4) behavioral symptoms of stress, and (5) long-term consequences of stress. At the end of each segment, she told students to translate the main ideas of the lecture in the corresponding discussion board for an intended audience of students who were experiencing stress during exams. Students as a whole tended to do a good job with the translations, so there were many translations for students to read. In class, students commented on how beneficial it was to read each other's translations.

Variations and Extensions

- After presenting the lecture segment, ask students to write down their translations in their own words prior to sharing verbally. This variation takes more class time, but it provides students with adequate thinking time, so the paraphrases are likely to be better and more polished.
- To provide students with an opportunity to improve or correct their interpretations, put them in pairs or small groups to rehearse their translations prior to sharing them with the full class. Although it takes more class time, this variation of ALT 19: *Think-Pair-Share* can reduce student anxiety. The approach can be particularly useful if you prefer to stop less and have them paraphrase more content at once.

Observations and Advice

This technique is most useful for complex topics because it asks you to build in stopping points and provides repetition of complex ideas by students. This repetition should reinforce information.

Using this technique over time will provide an opportunity for students (and you) to see progress. Students' sophistication at summary should improve over the academic term. It is important to retain the step of inviting others to augment the initial translation because this step can reduce the pressure felt by any one student.

The goal of this activity is to improve student learning. The goal is *not* to catch a student who appears to be focused on a phone rather than a lecture or who otherwise looks distracted or disengaged. Keeping the goal at the forefront will improve the odds of good success with the technique because it will reduce student anxiety and improve student buy in to the activity.

Key References and Resources

Cooper, J. L., & Robinson, P. (2000). Getting started: Informal small-group strategies in large classes. *New Directions for Teaching and Learning, 81*, 17–42.

Cooper, J. L., & Robinson, P. (2014). Using classroom assessment and cognitive scaffolding to enhance the power of small-group learning. *Journal on Excellence in College Teaching, 25*(3&4), 149–161.

ACTIVE LEARNING TECHNIQUE 19

Think-Pair-Share

Complexity involved in	
Planning	LOW
Developing Materials	LOW
Implementing in Class	LOW

Description and Purpose

In *Think-Pair-Share,* the instructor develops and poses a question and gives students a few minutes to think about a response individually. The instructor then asks students to pair up with another student before sharing the information with the class.

The *Think* component requires students to stop and reflect before speaking, thus giving them an opportunity to collect and organize their thoughts before sharing with a larger group. The *Pair and Share* components encourage learners to compare and contrast their understandings with those of another and to rehearse their response first in a low-risk situation before going public with the entire class. This opportunity to practice comments first with a peer tends to improve the quality of student contributions and generally increases willingness and readiness to speak in a larger group.

Preparation

- Prior to coming to class, spend time developing an engaging question or problem that has many potential responses. Try responding to the question yourself. Decide how you are going to present the question (e.g., worksheet, presentation slide, or whiteboard) and how you are going to have students report out.

Procedures

1. Pose the question to the class, giving students a few minutes to think about the question and devise individual responses.
2. Ask students to pair up with another student nearby.
3. Ask student A to share his or her responses with student B and then student B to share ideas with student A. Suggest that if the two students disagree, they clarify their positions so that they can explain how and why they disagree. If useful, request that pairs create a joint response by building on each other's ideas.
4. Ask for volunteers to share the pair responses with the full class.

Online Lecture	Large Lecture
Implementing this technique online provides students with the opportunity to practice online communication skills and enables two students to make a direct connection with each other, which can improve their experience in online courses. Two advantages to online *Think-Pair-Share* implementation are that (1) students have a greater opportunity for reflective thought before responding to each other and that (2) archived written transcripts of students' responses to each other are readily available. However, in an online course, there is the absence of the synchronous, physical proximity that makes this technique such an easy impromptu strategy in an on-site class. Effective implementation in an online class requires preassigned peers who work together frequently and over an extended period of time. Ask students to share their initial ideas first with their work partners by way of instant messaging (IM), texting, or a telecommunications tool such as Skype. Then, one student posts the joint response to a discussion board used by the full class or a student blog.	This technique is frequently used to good effect in large lecture classes. A challenge, however, is that the noise level can get high with all of the students talking at once. Keep the sharing time short to keep the decibel level low. Also consider using Tip 39: *Silent Signals* to indicate the end of the talk time.

Examples

African Art and the Diaspora (Lecture)

In this seminar for art majors, the professor lectured on themes such as abundance, status, royalty, and prestige. To provide an engaging learning exercise as a break to her lectures, she often used a modified form of *Think-Pair-Share*. She projected an image on the screen, such as a pottery bowl, and asked student to think about what the object conveys about the lecture themes. She thus used the object as a tool to help students think about larger social and political issues. She then asked students to partner with another student sitting nearby to share their ideas. Afterward, pairs shared their thoughts with the full class. She ended the exercise with a brief discussion before her closing lecture remarks.

Inquiry in the Natural World (Large Lecture)

The professor in this large lecture class decided to use *Think-Pair-Share* to begin a lecture session. He felt that it would help students draw on their prior knowledge, focus their attention, and maintain interest in the lecture. After a few morning announcements, he asked the following question: "What is matter?" He also displayed a slide with the question so that all students could see it, and then he asked students to think about a response. After a minute, he suggested that students turn to a neighbor and share information. He used Tip 39: *Silent Signals* and clapped once, twice, and three times, with students joining in clapping as they heard him. When the class had quieted down, he asked for volunteers to share.

English Composition (Video Lecture)

An instructor of English composition to first-year students planned to have students write argument essays throughout the semester. He wanted students to work together in pairs and in larger teams, so he first formed base pairs and then combined the base pairs into base teams.

At the beginning of the term, the professor shared several passages from arguments for students to read, and he used *Think-Pair-Share* in conjunction with the writings to help students examine features of a compelling written argument. The professor began by posting the following question to the class discussion forum: "What makes a written argument effective?" He asked students to think about the assigned passages individually and to consider the features that made those arguments effective. He then asked individuals to communicate their answers with their partners in the base pair and develop a consensus answer.

Base pairs were then asked to share their answers with their base teams. The instructor called on each team to post its responses to the discussion forum. He then posted his own list of features of effective arguments against which students compared their lists. Overall, the lists were similar, and the instructor commended the students for their ability to identify qualities of a good argument. The students and the instructor then worked together to combine and refine a set of criteria, with the instructor guiding the discussion by asking questions on the forum. Together, they developed a strong set of argument evaluation criteria used by students in peer assessment of each other's writing and the instructor in grading.

Variations and Extensions

- Export the *Think* step by posing a question for students to consider outside of class. When they return to class, ask students to pair up and share their homework responses.
- Give students time to write their responses down before pairing; this variation is called *Write-Pair-Share* (Johnson, Johnson, & Smith, 2014; Lyman, 1981).
- Ask each pair to share and compare their ideas with those of another pair before, or instead of, the whole-class discussion; this variation is called *Think-Pair-Square* (Lyman, 1981).
- *Think-Tweet-Share:* Students think of a response and then generate a tweet or a 140-character representation of a tweet (Perret, 2012).
- *Think-Text-Share:* If students are allowed to use cell phones in class, they could text each other rather than verbally pairing their ideas and then share with the full group (Perret, 2012).

Observations and Advice

Give students sufficient time to think before pairing and responding; the time required will depend on the nature, scope, and complexity of the question as well as on the students' level of familiarity with the topic. For a conceptual question, allow at least a minute for individual responses.

Be sure to allow students time to formulate and rehearse ideas before sharing them. In addition to *Think* time, plan enough time for students to express and compare their responses. This *Share* time will give students the opportunity to discuss well-thought-out answers with peers and to refine their answers before speaking to the whole class.

Announce a time limit but gauge time needed by decibel levels as well. If the pairs are all still actively engaged, consider extending that limit by a minute or two. If one student seems to be dominating the other in the pair, set time limits for each student response.

The simplest reporting-out strategy is to have each pair share its most important point with the whole class. Limit the number of responses, repetition, and time required in the report out by asking each pair to share only ideas not yet mentioned. Following the reports, conclude with a synthesis to validate student responses by highlighting the good points that students brought out. Gently correct any responses that are incorrect and add any points that weren't covered. If appropriate, provide learners with an expert response, allowing them to check and revise their individual and pair responses. If time is limited or the class is large, randomly call on student pairs or collect a written version of the pair responses and review them outside of class.

To promote active listening during the report-out phase, randomly call on students and ask them to summarize what the reporting student just said. The reporting out usually provides instructors with sufficient feedback to assess student understanding. However, in cases when student pairs have exhibited a great deal of difficulty or confusion in their responses, it may be useful to do additional assessment. Consider using minute papers (Angelo & Cross, 1993, CAT 6, pp. 148–153), and ask students to write a half-sheet response to a question, such as, "What aspect of the prompt question was most difficult for you to answer?" or "On what points did you and your partner agree or disagree?"

Think-Pair-Share is typically used as an informal strategy to stimulate discussion and is not generally used for grading purposes.

Key References and Resources

Angelo, T. A., & Cross, K. P. (1993). *Classroom assessment techniques: A handbook for college teachers* (2nd ed.). San Francisco, CA: Jossey-Bass.

Barkley, E. F., Major, C. H., & Cross, K. P. (2014). CoLT 1. *Collaborative learning techniques: A handbook for college faculty* (pp. 153–158). San Francisco, CA: Jossey Bass. Adapted with permission of publisher.

Johnson, D. W., Johnson, R. T., & Smith, K. A. (2014). *Journal on Excellence in College Teaching, 25* (3–4), 85–118.

Lyman, F. (1981). The responsive classroom discussion. In A. S. Anderson (Ed.), *Mainstreaming digest.* College Park, MD: University of Maryland, College of Education.

Lyman, F. T. (1992). Think-pair-share, thinktrix, thinklinks, and weird facts: An interactive system for cooperative learning. In N. Davidson & T. Worsham (Eds.), *Enhancing thinking through cooperative learning* (pp. 169–181). New York, NY: Teachers College Press.

Millis, B. J., & Cottell, P. G. (1998). *Cooperative learning for higher education faculty.* American Council on Education. Phoenix, AZ: Oryx Press.

Perret, K. (2012, March 21). Think-pair-share variations [Web log post]. Retrieved July 27, 2017, from www.kathyperret.net/2012/03/think-pair-share-variations/

ACTIVE LEARNING TECHNIQUE 20

Snap Shots

Complexity involved in	
Planning	MODERATE
Developing Materials	LOW
Implementing in Class	LOW

Description and Purpose

Snap Shots are conceptual multiple-choice questions that help deepen student understanding while simultaneously checking it. During a lecture, the professor pauses, asks a question, and individual students choose which answer they think is correct. The questions in *Snap Shots* focus on a single concept, have a good set of multiple-choice answers, and have a moderate level of difficulty. The instructor makes a quick visual assessment of student responses. Students then discuss their answers in pairs and try to come to consensus on the answer.

When used frequently, this technique, which was originally developed by Eric Mazur (1997), encourages students to stay focused and attentive during lectures or class activities and to think about the concepts beyond a surface level. This technique also presents an opportunity for peer coaching because students participate in small-group discussions in order to determine a consensus answer.

The act of answering the question provides the teacher with an opportunity to check understanding on the spot and to make adjustments to the lesson accordingly. This technique helps teachers determine understanding or misunderstanding in the moment so that they can address misconceptions or make corrections in a timely manner. *Snap Shots* provide a simple way to collect data on how well students understand material that has just been presented, and it is particularly useful in large lecture classes where it often can be challenging to gauge student understanding in real time.

Preparation

- Develop a single conceptual question that has a multiple-choice response (a, b, c, or d).
- Determine how you will display the question(s). A slide projected on the screen is ideal, particularly for large classes so that everyone can see the questions, but writing the question(s) on the board or on a flip board are also appropriate, particularly in smaller classes.
- Determine how students will make their responses visible. Consider the following options:
  - Indicate by a show of hands. This approach has the advantage of being easy and showing you individual answers.

- Hold up color-coded response cards (for example red = A, blue = B, yellow = C, and green = D). This approach has the advantage of easy counting, but cards can be bulky and difficult to distribute and collect, particularly if you have a large number of students.
- Respond through automated response system, such as clickers or a smartphone polling system. This approach has the advantage of being easy for data collection and interesting for students. It also allows for live display of results in a slide presentation.

Procedures

1. Announce the activity and tell students how long you will lecture before a break.
2. After lecturing for approximately ten to fifteen minutes, pause.
3. Present the conceptual question and ask students to answer the question individually and to demonstrate their responses in the way that you have chosen. Give them three to five minutes to think and respond.
4. Share the overall responses to the question; don't discuss the correct answer.
5. Ask students to work in pairs for approximately five minutes to try to convince their peer as to the correctness of their answers. Ask the pairs to come to consensus if possible.
6. Repeat the question again and record student scores.
7. Go over the answer to the question and explain why one answer is the more correct or best choice.

Online Lecture	Large Lecture
Snap Shots work well in synchronous web conferencing sessions with VoIP, which many LMSs offer. As you talk, post the question. Then post the first answer (a), and ask students to signal their agreement with the answer by "raising their hands." Next, provide a different answer (b), and ask students who agree to "raise their hands." Continue until you have run out of potential answers. Alternatively, you can use a survey tool to poll students. Ask students to discuss their responses in chat rooms or on a discussion prompt. Readminister the quiz after the appropriate time has lapsed.	*Snap Shots* actually has its origins in large lecture courses, particularly in physics (Mazur, 1997), so it has documented evidence of success in this course format. Be sure to choose a method for demonstrating results that all students can see. Clickers or online polling can be useful approaches.

Examples

Introduction to Geoscience (Lecture)

The professor of this introduction to geoscience course wanted students to understand the basics of rocks and the rock cycle. To teach the concept, the professor used a fifteen-minute lecture introducing key concepts. He stopped and displayed the following questions in his presentation software (which he adapted from http://wps.prenhall.com/esm_tarbuck_earth_8/0,9073,1298259-,00.html):

- What allows us to categorize rocks into three types: igneous, sedimentary, and metamorphic?
  a. Involvement of sediment
  b. Process of deformation
  c. Process of formation
  d. Magma or weathering
  e. Process of inflation
  f. Whether or not the rock melts
- According to the rock cycle, which of the following is *incorrect*?
  a. Magma may crystallize to form igneous rocks.
  b. Sedimentary rocks may weather to become igneous rocks.
  c. Metamorphic rocks may melt to become magma.
  d. Igneous rocks may metamorphose into metamorphic rocks.

The professor asked the students for a show of hands. He noticed that most of the students had the wrong answer to both questions. He put students into working groups of four and asked the members to convince others of their responses. He polled them again after the group discussion and noticed that the number of correct responses improved dramatically.

He began to implement *Snap Shots* as a regular part of his instruction. Because he had information from tests before and after implementation of *Snap Shots,* he was able to see that student scores and attendance improved dramatically after his implementation of the quizzes.

Organizational Communication (Large Lecture)

In this large lecture course, students learn about organizations and communication patterns, from democratic bottom-up processes to managerial top-down approaches. Main content units include historical and foundational approaches to communication, culture and power problems, and processes and applications.

After offering a lecturette on the importance of effective communication on career success, the professor displayed a slide with the following question:

What percentage of workers who lose jobs do so due to their inability to communicate clearly?

a. 50
b. 65
c. 70
d. None

The professor asked students to complete an online poll. Before displaying the results, he then asked students to pair and convince each other of their answers. He asked them to answer the question for a second time. He then displayed both results and revealed the answer, citing a recent research study on the causes of job loss. More students were correct in the second poll than the first, and the professor congratulated them on their good work in pairs.

General Physics (Video Lecture)

The professor of an online course was teaching an introductory physics course. She wanted students to be able to use simple algebra in the application of physics theories to make quantitative predictions.

She met with students synchronously once per week through a collaborative tool in her institution's LMS. This particular week, she gave a brief ten-minute lecture on the laws of motion. She posted a quiz question (related to a person in an elevator and the force of the elevator floor) and had students respond by using the "raise your hand" function in the system.

Because many of the students missed the question, she formed groups and assigned students to use chat rooms for discussion. She gave the groups five minutes to discuss the question, and then she asked the students to come back to the main room, whereupon she asked the question again. Student scores improved in the second round. She explained the correct answer to the students, indicating why one answer was the better choice.

Variations and Extensions

- *Snap Shots* may be done with groups as well. Form students into teams and have the team members work together on answering the questions. Consider calling on groups to explain the rationale for their selections. This may provide you with insights into students' understandings and misunderstandings and possibly about the wording of the questions you are using.
- To learn how to use this technique to assess student-learning outcomes, see Barkley and Major (2016, LAT 8: *Snap Shots*).

Observations and Advice

One of the benefits of this technique is that students tend to perform better after the group discussions than before. This can be a particularly useful activity to establish the benefits of collaboration.

This technique is best done repeatedly and over time. Students will grow to appreciate it more and will take each other's responses more seriously as they see continual improvement in their responses.

Key References and Resources

Barkley, E. F., & Major, C. H. (2016). *Learning assessment techniques: A handbook for college faculty.* San Francisco, CA: Jossey-Bass.

Barkley, E. F., Major, C. H., & Cross, K. P. (2014). CoLT 7: Note-taking pairs. *Collaborative learning techniques: A handbook for college faculty* (2nd ed., pp. 189–194). San Francisco, CA: Jossey-Bass.

Carnegie Mellon University, Eberly Center on Teaching Excellence and Educational Innovation. (n.d.a). *Design and teach a course.* Retrieved from www.cmu.edu/teaching/designteach/design/contentschedule.html

Cottell, P. G., & Millis, B. (2010). Cooperative learning in accounting. In B. Millis (Ed.), *Cooperative learning in higher education: Across the disciplines, across the academy* (pp. 11–33). Sterling, VA: Stylus Publishing.

Larsy, N. (n.d.). *Peer instruction: Comparing clickers to flashcards.* Retrieved from http://arxiv.org/pdf/physics/0702186.pdf

Mazur, E. (1997). *Peer instruction: A user's manual.* Upper Saddle River, NJ: Prentice Hall.

CHAPTER 20

Applying Information

One of the best ways to help students develop competence in an area of inquiry is to have them apply basic facts, principles, and concepts in a new context. Application requires learners not only to acquire foundational knowledge but also to understand it within the context of a conceptual framework and also be able to transfer and use their knowledge in novel ways. The process of applying information makes it meaningful, and as learners move from novice to expert, they are able to apply information more efficiently and effectively.

Acknowledging that the ways in which knowledge is applied varies across the disciplines, Fink (2013) defines the term *application* broadly. For example, he suggests that students are engaging in application when they learn how to do some new kind of action. This action may take many forms. For example, application can mean engaging in various kinds of thinking, including critical, creative, and practical thinking. But it can also include learning special skills, such as how to communicate effectively or how to manage complex projects. Given the speed at which today's students can access information, helping students learn to apply information may actually be the true value of a college education. In this chapter, we offer several techniques that require students to apply the information they have heard in your presentation. We summarize these Techniques in Exhibit 20.1.

Exhibit 20.1 Techniques for Applying Information

This technique . . .	Helps students learn actively by having them . . .
ALT 21: *Thick and Thin Questions*	Write down two types of questions about the lecture content: *Thin Questions* that can be answered directly from the lecture and *Thick Questions* that require students to think beyond the lecture
ALT 21: *Support a Statement*	Locate in their lecture notes details, examples, or data to support a statement provided by the instructor
ALT 21: *Intrigue Journal*	List and describe the five most interesting, controversial, or resonant ideas they heard in the lecture, indicating what they would like to learn more about
ALT 21: *Real-World Applications*	Analyze a theory or concept from the lecture and then figure out how to apply it in the realm of practical or actual experience

Key Reference and Resource

Fink, L. D. (2013). *Creating significant learning experiences: An integrated approach to designing college courses*. San Francisco, CA: Jossey-Bass.

ACTIVE LEARNING TECHNIQUE 21

Thick and Thin Questions

Complexity involved in	
Planning	LOW
Developing Materials	LOW
Implementing in Class	LOW

Description and Purpose

In this technique, students keep a running record of *Thick and Thin Questions* about the lecture content. Thin questions are minimally complex and answerable by listening to the lecture for a direct answer. Answers to *Thin Questions* are usually short and close-ended, such as a quick fact. *Thin Questions* tend to ask who, what, when, where, and how many. *Thin Questions* focus on foundational knowledge, which is essential for establishing the basic understanding that is necessary for higher-order thinking. Asking such questions is useful because it helps students remember and clarify facts. Additionally, *Thin Questions* help individuals identify gaps in basic understanding.

Thick Questions are more complex. These questions tend to require students to think beyond a lecture. They prompt listening in more-complex and advanced ways. They suggest coming to terms with the big picture. *Thick Questions* deal with broader concepts, and the answers to these questions are typically long, complex, and open-ended. *Thick Questions* foster inference, connections, analysis, discussion, and debate. *Thick Questions* tend to be about why, what if, what might, how would I feel, how come, how could, and so what. They are useful because they prompt students to deeper thinking.

Deep learners ask themselves questions before a lecture (wondering or predicting what they will learn), during a lecture (questioning what they hear), and after a lecture (reflecting on what they have learned and how they might apply it or see it again in the future). Deep learners use a combination of *Thick and Thin Questions* to think about the lecture material because both are important.

The goal of this technique is to help students learn to create both types of questions from a lecture. Doing so helps them clarify meaning and to think beyond the content of a single lecture. Also, using *Thick and Thin Questions* has the potential to help students recognize the range and depth of questions one could ask and that are often asked in tests. Students begin to realize that all questions are not created equal. This in turn helps them to monitor their own comprehension and to think metacognitively.

Preparation

- Plan in some time to talk with students about *Thick and Thin Questions.* You will want to describe them and to provide examples.
- Consider how you want students to record their questions. You can simply ask them to record their questions in their notes, but you may want to create a handout similar to the one shown here so that students can keep track of their questions easily and you can collect the information efficiently if you plan to do so.

Thick and Think Questions Handout

Thin Questions		**Thick Questions**
	Lecture Topic	

Procedures

1. Announce the activity and describe the difference between *Thick and Thin Questions.* Inform students that they should record both types of questions while listening to the lecture. Tell students how you would like them to record their questions, and if you have a handout, distribute it.
2. Proceed with the lecture. Pause periodically to allow students time to think of and record their questions.
3. At the end of the lecture, ask students to form pairs or small groups to discuss their questions and allow them time to answer their own questions. Collectively they should be able to answer the *Thin Questions,* and they may be able to answer the *Thick Questions* as well.
4. Take any remaining questions. If you plan to assess the questions, ask students to hand their questions in to you.

Video Lecture	**Large Lecture**
Ask students to submit their questions after a video or VoIP lecture by way of a discussion board; post one thread for *Thin Questions* and one thread for *Thick Questions.* You may wish to set the discussion so that students must post before seeing others' responses. Allow students time to respond to each other's posts. Respond to any remaining questions in the discussion board.	After pairs discuss, either call on students randomly or ask for a few volunteers to represent the class. If you will assess the questions, ask pairs to write their questions on index cards, with a *Thin Question* on one side of the card and a *Thick Question* on the other side, both clearly labeled.

Examples

Interdisciplinary Course: 3D Printing (Lecture)

This seminar is about 3D printing and is intended to help students think through a range of issues related to the technology. The course employs critical approaches and creative ones as students learn 3D modeling and make their own 3D prints.

The course meets twice a week. The professor lectures part of the time, and the rest of the time is spent on discussions and student work. The professor decided to use *Thick and Thin Questions* to help students look past the general enthusiasm for the technology and be more critical in their considerations of it.

She told the students about *Thick and Thin Questions* during the first lecture of the course. Before she began, she asked the students to use a handout to keep a list of *Thick and Thin Questions* during the lecture. During this introductory lecture, she gave students an overview of the course. While she lectured, she could see students recording questions on their handouts. At the end of the lecture, she asked students to form pairs and work together to compile their questions. Following is a sample of the questions one pair raised:

Thin	Thick
What is 3D printing?	How will 3D printing shape culture?
Who invented 3D printing?	How will 3D printing benefit college and university students?
What types of 3D printing are there?	What are the ethical implications of bio-printing with 3D printers?
What are people printing with 3D printers?	What happens if people start printing weapons?

At the end of the pair activity, she took questions from students. This led into a good discussion session, so she determined she would continue to use *Thick and Thin Questions* throughout the term.

Statistics (Large Lecture)

The professor of this large lecture was lecturing on developing research questions and decided to adapt *Thick and Thin Questions* to help students understand the basic concept. She lectured on characteristics of effective questions (*Thick Questions*) and also characteristics of weaker questions (*Thin Questions*), such as a narrow focus, lack of focus, too simple, no need to collect data, and so forth.

At the end of her lecture, she asked students to pair and write a *Thin Question* and a *Thick Question* on the topic of obesity. Following are some sample responses:

	Thin Questions	Thick Questions
Pair 1	How are school systems currently addressing childhood obesity?	What is the relationship between intervention programs in the elementary schools and the rate of obesity in first- through fifth-grade students?
Pair 2	What are the effects of childhood obesity in the United States?	How does childhood obesity correlate with academic performance in first- through fifth-grade students?
Pair 3	What is the childhood obesity rate in Atlanta, Georgia?	What is the relationship between education level of the parents and childhood obesity rates in Atlanta, Georgia?

The instructor felt that crafting the questions helped students to apply the information from the lecture in a concrete way so that they learned the information more deeply.

History of World War II (Video Lecture)

In this course, the professor decided to use *Thick and Thin Questions* to help students focus on the video lectures. In one learning module, he focused on key leaders who had a role in starting WWII. After his video lectures, in which he introduced these people and described their various roles in the war, he asked students to create *Thick and Thin Questions* about it. To implement this technique, he posted a handout describing *Thick and Thin Questions,* with some examples. He next created two threads in the discussion board (one for *Thin Questions* and one for *Thick Questions*) and instructed students to focus specifically on the people in their questions.

Sample *Thin Questions* from the posts:

- What did Stalin do that gave him such an evil reputation?
- Where was Hitler born?
- Was Hitler really an artist?

Sample *Thick Questions* from the posts:

- Why did Stalin and Hitler create a pact?
- Would Hitler be able to come into power today?
- What would have happened if Hitler had been assassinated?

Students seemed increasingly to appreciate the post prompts, and it did not take long before they started responding to each other's questions without instructions from the professor to do so. The professor felt that the students provided each other with great responses and that the activity had accomplished what he had hoped.

Variation and Extension

- Have students keep their questions in an ongoing journal. Consider having students exchange journals to give each other responses to their questions and to suggest new questions.

Observations and Advice

This technique was originally developed as a reading strategy, but effective questioning is just as important to active participation in a lecture as it is to active reading. Students don't always know to even think of questions before, during, and after a lecture. Employing a technique that encourages them to not only question but also to evaluate the kinds of questions that they are asking is a useful skill that will extend beyond a single course.

Key References and Resources

Harvey, S., & Goudvis, A. (2007). *Strategies that work: Teaching comprehension for understanding and engagement* (2nd ed.). Portland, ME: Stenhouse.

McLaughlin, M. (2015). *Content area reading: Teaching and learning for college and career readiness.* Upper Saddle River, NJ: Pearson.

ACTIVE LEARNING TECHNIQUE 22

Support a Statement

Complexity involved in	
Planning	MODERATE
Developing Materials	LOW
Implementation in Class	MODERATE

Description and Purpose

In *Support a Statement,* the professor poses a statement to the students at the end of a lecture. Students review the statement and then gather and use evidence from their lecture notes in order to support it. They make their case by providing details, examples, or data.

Many students take a surface-level approach to learning when listening to a lecture. That is, they listen while staying at the cognitive level of identifying and memorizing key facts or being able to recall basic information for a test rather than trying to think deeply about the content. *Support a Statement* encourages and supports many professors' desire for students to take a deeper approach to learning.

With *Support a Statement,* students are given a specific task to carry out—find evidence to prove a point or support a position—which can be motivating for them. Students review their notes with intentionality and strive to understand the information they have recorded. Students select information to prove points, and in so doing, they have the opportunity to evaluate what is and is not important. In short, *Support a Statement* requires that students relate the information they have heard and recorded in their notes to the statement.

Preparation

- Craft a provocative statement related to your lecture notes. It should capture student attention and interest. The statement could be a conclusion, an inference, an opinion, or a theory.
- Review your lecture notes and ensure that there are sufficient details and examples for students to draw on to support the statement. If not, create a different statement or add examples to the lecture.
- Consider how to share the statement with students. You could show the statement on a slide or instead create a handout with room for students to add the necessary information.

Procedures

1. Tell students that they should take notes during the lecture.
2. Give the lecture.
3. Provide students with the statement you have crafted and ask them to review it.

4. Ask students to find evidence or data from their lecture notes to support the statement.
5. Ask students to organize the information into a coherent whole, such as through an organized list.
6. Ask for volunteers to share their findings. Each new student volunteer or recruit should contribute only new supporting evidence.
7. Proceed with volunteers until all potential supporting evidence has been determined.

Online Lecture	Large Lecture
At the end of a video lecture, post the lecture either as an assignment or in a discussion forum and ask students to find evidence from the lecture to *Support a Statement.* You can ask students to use their lecture notes or alternately you could suggest that they include the time stamp in the lecture at which the information is provided.	After your lecture, display the statement in a way that all students can see it, such as on a presentation slide. Give students time to work. Set an overall time limit for responses, for example, five minutes, and move quickly so that as many students as possible can respond. Alternately, ask students to do this activity regularly through journaling in class and take up the journals periodically to assess.

Examples

Geography (Lecture)

In this geography course, students were to learn about the influence of politics and political decisions on ecology. The professor wrote the following statement: "Political actions taken by a president of a major country can influence the world's environment." She announced the activity to the class and suggested that they would need good notes to complete the assignment. She then gave a lecture on the implications of politics on the environment. She paused occasionally during the lecture to ensure that students had the time they needed to craft good notes. She distributed her statement in a handout and asked students to support it. She hoped she would see responses about bomb testing, armies, and even executive actions influencing climate. At the completion of the assignment, she was pleased to see that it had resonated with students.

Energy Uses and the Environment (Large Lecture)

In this science course for students with no prior university-level physics or mathematics experience, the content focuses on energy and energy sources. The professor decided to use *Support a Statement* as an in-class active learning assignment as part of her interactive lecturing class plan. After a lecture on energy efficiency, the professor offered the following statement: "Efficiency is a clean, cost-effective, and local fuel source." The professor put students into groups of two to three students and asked them to use their notes and memories of the lecture to create a list of arguments for and against the claim. The professor was pleased with the level of engagement that the activity had fostered.

Education (Video)

In this teaching-methods class, the teacher planned a series of video lectures on learning theory, addressing one theory per video for five videos. She announced that students would use their notes to prove a position at the end of the lecture series and encouraged them to take good notes. At the end of the series, she posted the following statement in a discussion forum: "Despite innovative approaches, the theory of behaviorism has not been supplanted and can be seen in nearly every facet of today's classroom." She encouraged students to choose a side and post evidence from their notes and their own experiences to support the statement. A lively discussion ensued, ranging from the common practice of having a bell ring to start class to a range of ways to offer online learning. Students were able to pull information from the videos, and she noticed that many of the students had gone back and re-viewed segments from the videos. She felt the technique had been successful and planned to use it in the future.

Variations and Extensions

- Provide the statement ahead of the lecture to give students a reason to listen actively.
- Combine this technique with some of our note-taking techniques, such as ALT 15: *Coded Notes* or ALT 14: *Cued Notes.*
- Combine this technique with ALT 9: *Advance Organizers,* for example, by having students organize their ideas in a main idea and detail chart, an assertion and evidence chart, or a zone of relevance chart.
- Combine this with ALT 16: *Note-Taking Pairs* to ensure that students have good notes.
- Ask students to either support or refute the statement to give different perspectives. Consider using this technique in conjunction with a debate.
- Ask students to work in pairs or small groups to support the statement. If you do so, consider assigning groups different roles, with some groups trying to find affirming evidence and others trying to find negating evidence.
- Allow students to choose their own position.
- Ask students to craft their own statements and then have students work to affirm or negate.
- Ask students to generate their own ideas or experiences to support or refute the statement.
- Ask students to do outside research to come up with support or refutation, and consider using the technique in conjunction with a research paper.

Observations and Advice

Many students want to argue a position based on their beliefs or opinions, yet arguing from an informed perspective is an essential skill for college students. *Support a Statement* can be a particularly useful technique to get students into the habit of supporting their arguments with evidence. Using *Support a Statement* in pairs or small groups can encourage discussion about the lecture, which can deepen understanding and aid student memory of it.

Key References and Resources

Australian Catholic University. (2012). *Strategies for cooperative and collaborative learning in large lecture groups.* Retrieved from www.acu.edu.au/__data/assets/pdf_file/0003/405768/Large_Group_Lectures_LTC.pdf

Cooper, J. L., & Robinson, P. (2000). Getting started: Informal small-group strategies in large classes. *New Directions for Teaching and Learning, 81,* 17–42.

Cooper, J. L., Robinson, P., & Ball, D. A. (2010). The interactive lecture: Reconciling group and active learning strategies with traditional instructional formats. *Exchanges: The Online Journal of Teaching and Learning in the CSU.* Retrieved from http://web.mit.edu/jrankin/www/Active_Learning/interactive_lectures2.pdf

Los Angeles Valley College. (n.d.). *Active learning strategies: Quick thinks.* Retrieved from www.lavc.edu/profdev/library/docs/quickthinks.aspx

ACTIVE LEARNING TECHNIQUE 23

Intrigue Journal

Complexity involved in	
Planning	LOW
Developing Materials	LOW
Implementing in Class	MODERATE

Description and Purpose

With an *Intrigue Journal,* students intentionally listen during a lecture to identify what they consider to be the most-intriguing ideas presented. They record their thoughts about these interesting points in an ongoing journal.

Intrigue Journal gives students a task for listening, which helps them to focus their attention. It helps students deepen their understanding of course-related ideas and concepts. It helps them engage with the material directly because they must assign it personal meaning—they find it interesting or surprising or controversial—rather than simply recording it. In addition, it encourages students to have a positive outlook about the information. The *Intrigue Journal* is an outlet for reflection on the information presented in a lecture, which helps to solidify it and ultimately deepen student learning.

Preparation

- Decide how students will record journal entries and store their journals. Although you can use a lined table, you might consider a more high-tech solution, which can be easier to keep track of for the students and for you.
- Consider how you will assess the journal. If you give it a grade, students will take it more seriously. A good option for determining a grade is to develop a rubric.
- Consider providing students with sample journal entries—doing so can help them understand the parameters of the assignment and can alleviate some anxiety.

Procedures

1. Announce the activity and tell students how they should record entries and store their journals.
2. Tell them that at the end of each lecture they should write a journal entry about what most intrigued them by providing the following:
   a. The date and lecture topic
   b. A list of three to five points addressing what they found most interesting, resonant, or controversial
   c. A rationale for their selection

3. Consider having students report out their selections or alternately review their entries and describe their selections in the next course session to tie the information to new information to come.

Online Lecture	Large Lecture
This technique is easy to implement in most learning management systems (LMSs). If you have students blog within the LMS, you can set up preferences so that each student's blog is kept private from other students but still enables you access as the instructor. If your LMS had a journal feature, you can set up regular due dates for the assignments. Alternately you can ask students to set up their own blogs on which they can post their entries.	Because managing writing assignments in large classes can be a challenge, an approach is to review the journals periodically, assessing with a simple plus-minus system. You can review a sample of journals each time to get a sense of the effort students are putting into the assignment as well as to see what the students are finding interesting.

Examples

Behavioral Genetics (Lecture)

In this traditional lecture-based course, students learn about the field of behavioral genetics, which is focused on how individual variation can be separated into genetic and environmental components. The professor uses ongoing *Intrigue Journals* to help students think through complex material.

The class meets twice per week. Students are expected to have read a chapter from the text prior to coming to class. Each lecture focuses on a single topic, such as phenotypic variance and heritability, heritability and complex traits, population and quantitative genetics, and so forth. The professor does a brief review of the main points of the chapter to ensure that students understand it, and she provides students with the opportunity to ask clarification questions.

After each summary, the professor describes a recently published research study related to the topic of the day. She brings in articles from leading journals such as *Nature* and *Science.* The research studies are often twin studies or adoption studies. After each research presentation, she asks students to list three to five points in their *Intrigue Journals.* These points can be what students found interesting, what they found they agreed with, what they found to be particularly controversial, or a combination. She reviews the journals at the end of each month of the semester. She believes that the journals help students to focus on her lectures because it provides them a specific task to complete and to think through the main ideas of the lecture.

Sociology of the Family (Large Lecture)

In this large lecture course, students study the institution of the family from a sociological perspective. Students think about the family as a public and private social institution. The instructor uses interactive lecturing, interspersing active learning assignments and lecture segments. Each class session is focused on a specific topic, such as history of the family, social class, gender, children and parenting, cohabitation and dating, and so forth. The professor uses

Intrigue Journals to help students stay focused on the content between sessions and also to apply what they have used in informal writing.

The course meets twice per week, and she saves a few minutes at the end of each session for students to make notes in their journals. She collects journals once per month. She ensures that students have done entries for each session, assessing with a simple plus-minus. She then reviews 25 percent of the entries each time in more depth, to get feedback on her lectures, find out what students are finding interesting, and identify any misconceptions.

Grief, Death and Loss: Social Work (Video Lecture)

In this online course, social work students examine the experience of loss and subsequent grief in their personal lives, the lives of their clients, and their role as professional helpers. The professor has a series of video lectures that she encourages students to watch. She has often felt, however, that students were not taking away as much from them as they might. She decided to use *Intrigue Journals* to get students to engage with the material and to learn more about what ideas they found compelling.

She posted her lectures and set up the private journal entry function in her LMS. She asked students to watch the videos on the dates listed in the syllabus and then to post a journal entry in which they identify the five most-interesting, resonant, or controversial ideas they heard.

Students seemed to engage in the activity, and each week, she posted a list of student responses to the three prompts, which students also seemed to appreciate. One student wrote about the experience in her final journal entry for the term:

> I watched the course video lectures until there were no more. I searched them for ideas, for instructions, for ways to deal with grief and loss and to help others do the same. I have never dealt with grief—I have always buried the grief deep down, hoping it would just go away. I was intrigued by the idea that there are other, better ways. That I can help others find better ways.
>
> And I journaled about these ideas. I was able to capture these ideas in my journal. I wrote what interested me. I wrote what I agreed with. I wrote about what I didn't agree with and why. This was more than summary; it was self-interrogation and self-exploration. It was a plan for my future work with clients. I wrote my journal entries in Word before uploading them, and I plan to save my entries . . . and to continue them. This journal will be a professional resource for me.

Variations and Extensions

- You can make this a collaborative learning activity by using dialogue journals, in which peers exchange journals and read and respond to each entry with comments and questions. Journal writing can be particularly effective when writers know that someone besides the teacher will read and respond to their entries. Moreover, because reading and responding to students can be time-consuming, making this technique a collaborative activity helps ensure students receive timely and critical feedback (see Barkley, Major, & Cross, 2014) without adding too much more to your workload. You can accomplish this variation in class by simply having students journal in a notebook and then pass the notebook to a nearby peer or alternately by having students respond to each other's blog posts.

- Extend this collaborative activity by having students tie their *Intrigue Journals* to contemporary issues. Students identify what is intriguing to them and then tie the concept to an important current issue in the news. See Barkley and Major (2016, LAT 24) for additional information on this approach.

Observations and Advice

Students can procrastinate on journaling if they have the opportunity to do so. To encourage regular journaling and to help students avoid waiting until the last minute to complete their work, tell students you will be spot-checking blogs randomly throughout the term, or alternately set up a formal evaluation schedule.

Students can see journaling as a "soft" activity, so you may want to attach some points toward the final grade for the activity. If you do so, be sure to assign a sufficient number of points for students to take it seriously (for example, 10 percent of the final grade).

Key References and Resources

Barkley, E. F. (2010). SET 29: Contemporary issues journal. *Student engagement techniques: A handbook for college faculty* (pp. 276– 279). San Francisco, CA: Jossey-Bass.

Barkley, E. F., & Major, C. H. (2016). LAT 24: Dialogue journals. *Learning assessment techniques: A handbook for college faculty* (pp. 225–229). San Francisco, CA: Jossey-Bass.

Barkley, E. F., Major, C. H., & Cross, K. P. (2014). CoLT 24: Dialogue journals. *Collaborative learning techniques: A resource for college faculty* (2nd ed., pp. 283–288). San Francisco, CA: Jossey-Bass.

Finley, T. (2014). *Dipsticks: Efficient ways to check for understanding.* Retrieved from www.edutopia.org/blog/dipsticks-to-check-for-understanding-todd-finley

ACTIVE LEARNING TECHNIQUE 24

Real-World Applications

Complexity involved in	
Planning	MODERATE
Developing Materials	MODERATE
Implementation in Class	LOW

Description and Purpose

After hearing about an important principle, theory, or process, students have to develop *Real-World Applications* of what they have just learned. This activity pushes students to deeper levels of understanding of a topic by requiring them to identify the topic's underlying qualities and then generate a novel and reasonable application. Its value as an instructional activity lies in the way it challenges students to move beyond surface thinking. It is also a useful assessment because it reveals how well students understand the concept as well as how creatively they can transfer their understanding of the elements to a new context. In addition, it helps students see the relevance of what they are learning.

Preparation

- Choose a topic that is important to your course or academic discipline that students have studied in some depth.
- Reflect on the topic yourself and identify a number of ways the underlying concepts could be applied in a new context to ensure that the topic is sufficiently generative and to determine how much time to allow students to do the assignment. Choose one or two that can be used to provide models to students. (When you repeat this assignment in a subsequent class, consider using student examples as models.)
- Create a prompt such as the following:
  "Based on your understanding of the scientific process, identify at least one application for it in a novel context. Here is one example students generated last academic term: 'In the scientific process, scientists formulate a question, develop a hypothesis, predict a logical consequence of the hypothesis, then test their conjecture and draw conclusions that they share with others. This same process could be used by detectives who are investigating a crime, and the information they gather along with their findings could be judged in a court of law.' "
- Decide whether you want to assign this as an individual or group assignment.
- Create an assessment rubric that includes elements such as quantity, novelty, and appropriateness.

- Decide how long to spend on the assignment (typically three to five minutes) and how many applications students will generate (one to three is ideal).
- Determine how students will submit responses. You may want them to turn them in on index cards or you may simply want to ask for volunteers to share orally.

Procedures

1. Announce the activity, the time frame, and how students should share their responses with you.
2. Ask students to begin work.
3. Collect the responses.

Online Lecture	Large Lecture
If you have decided to use this as an individual assignment, simply create an open-ended assignment or post as a discussion. To make it a group assignment, consider forming students into groups and assign each group its own private discussion area so that members can communicate their ideas. At the deadline, have groups communicate their ideas to the whole-class discussion thread.	Limit students to one application and either choose students randomly to report out or ask for volunteers. Alternately, ask them to turn in their responses on an index card that you can assess with a simple plus-minus.

Examples

Geography and Globalization (Lecture)

The professor wanted to assess student understanding of the push-pull factor that they had been studying in relation to human migration. She organized students into small groups and challenged them to generate as many examples as they could of how the factor's underlying principles of opposing forces could be applied in non-geographical contexts.

Introduction to Inorganic Chemistry (Large Lecture)

The subject of this course is the laws, theories, and concepts of chemistry. Students also learn about methods of writing formulas and equations. The professor wanted students to understand aspects of chemistry as they take place outside of the laboratory. For a unit on atoms, electrons, and ions, he asked students to develop clicker questions designed to test the material learned in class, but set in *Real World Applications.* He asked them specifically to focus their questions on chemical bonding. To complete the assignments, students had to think about chemistry beyond the classroom and consider the *Real-World Applications* of what they had learned. Students then reviewed each other's questions to help refine them, which the professor thought exposed students to the notion of peer review.

Music History: Eighteenth-Century Classicism (Video Lecture)

A core concept in this blended course is the sonata-allegro form because this form is the basis for first movement formal organization in classical symphonies, concertos, string quartets, piano sonatas, and so forth. To ensure students fully internalized the structure of the form, the professor assigned *Real-World Applications* to the base groups she had established at the beginning of the term, presenting it as the prompt for each group's private discussion area and instructing groups to create three applications to novel contexts. At the deadline, students shared their ideas with the whole class on the public forum.

Variation and Extension

- Review the results and share the best responses with the class. This extension will enable students to learn from each other, which can be motivating for them.

Observations and Advice

Although many students will find this technique challenging and fun, those students who do not understand the underlying topic sufficiently or cannot generate an application in a novel context may find it too difficult and get frustrated. Working in small groups will help support such students, but if the assignment is graded, ensure that your assignment process and evaluation rubric address individual accountability.

This technique can help students to understand the real-word uses of the information they are studying, and thus it can improve their motivation and engagement.

Key Reference and Resource

Angelo, T. A., & Cross, K. P. (1993). *Classroom assessment techniques: A handbook for college teachers* (2nd ed.). San Francisco, CA: Jossey-Bass.

CHAPTER 21

Checking Understanding

Researchers and educators alike have lauded the beneficial outcomes of formative assessment, a type of assessment aimed at gathering data on student learning to provide prompt and frequent feedback during the learning process. Instructors can use the information they glean from formative assessment to improve their teaching because they can see where students are struggling and address the problem immediately.

Formative assessment also enables students to improve their learning by providing them with low-threat, low-stakes feedback about gaps in their learning in time to make adjustments to their studying processes; if done frequently, formative assessment can help students track their progress over time. The feedback also helps students stay involved and motivated. Guskey (2007) suggests that for assessments to become an integral part of the instructional process in ways that truly help students learn, teachers should do the following:

- Use assessments as sources of information for students *and* teachers.
- Follow assessments with high-quality corrective instruction.
- Give students second chances to demonstrate success.

In this chapter, we offer several Tips that enable faculty members to gather information on student learning that students likewise can use to gauge their own success. We summarize these Techniques in Exhibit 21.1.

Exhibit 21.1 Techniques for Checking Understanding

This technique . . .	Helps students learn actively by having them . . .
ALT 25: *Pre-Post Freewrite*	Write for about five minutes, indicating what they already know about that day's topic; students write again at the end of class, and the difference between the two writings should demonstrate what they have learned
ALT 26: *One-Sentence Summary*	Summarize a lecture in a single sentence
ALT 27: *3-2-1*	Jot down and share with a partner or in a small group three ideas or issues presented; two examples of uses of the idea or information covered; and one unresolved or remaining question or area of possible confusion
ALT 28: *RSQC2*	Follow a structured process (recall, summarize, question, comment, and connect) to pull together their understanding of a given lecture

Key References and Resources

Andrade, H., & Valtcheva, A. (2009). Promoting learning and achievement through self-assessment. *Theory into Practice, 48,* 12–19.

Guskey, T. R. (2007). Multiple sources of evidence: An analysis of stakeholders' perceptions of various indicators of student learning. *Educational Measurement: Issues and Practice, 26*(1), 19–27.

Nicol, D. J., & Macfarlane-Dick, D. (2006). Formative assessment and self-regulated learning: A model and seven principles of good feedback practice. *Studies in Higher Education, 31*(2), 199–218.

ACTIVE LEARNING TECHNIQUE 25

Pre-Post Freewrite

Complexity involved in	
Planning	LOW
Developing Materials	LOW
Implementing in Class	LOW

Description and Purpose

In a *Pre-Post Freewrite*, the instructor announces the lecture topic and asks students to write for three to five minutes, jotting down everything they know about the subject. The goal is for students to record as much information as possible without worrying about typical writing conventions such as grammar and punctuation. The instructor then lectures. At the end of the lecture, the instructor asks students to again write for five minutes, recording everything they know about the topic.

This technique is a "writing-to-learn" activity: a short, impromptu, and informal writing task done to help students think through the ideas that will be (and then were) presented in the lecture. The *Pre-Freewrite* portion of the activity requires students to focus on the topic at hand and activate their prior knowledge about a topic. They must bring this knowledge to the fore in order to write, which readies them for taking in new knowledge. Knowing they will write again at the end of the lecture helps them to focus their attention on what the lecturer is saying.

The *Post-Freewrite* activity enables students to generate new information and then compare their first writing to their second. Thus, students are able to see progress from the first iteration to the last iteration, which gives them a sense of the value of the lecture to their learning. *Pre-Post Freewrite* is also a useful assessment technique for instructors who can use the initial *Pre-Freewrite* to identify misconceptions and their comparison of the pre- and post-versions to assess knowledge gains.

Preparation

- Determine the main topic of your lecture. Craft a writing prompt for that topic; your prompt may be a single word (e.g., *teaching*), or it may be a statement about the topic that you wish for students to explore more fully (e.g., "Teachers are currently encouraged to use technology in their teaching.").
- Determine how students will record their writing samples. You might provide them with a template in the form of a handout, such as the following (which you gather at the end of

class), you may have them write on index cards (which you gather before and after a lecture), or you may ask them to record their responses in a journal, which you gather periodically.

Student name: ______________________ Date: ______________________	
***Pre-Freewrite*:** **What I know about the topic already**	***Post-Freewrite*:** **What I learned from the lecture**
______________________ ______________________ ______________________ ______________________ ______________________ ______________________ ______________________ ______________________	______________________ ______________________ ______________________ ______________________ ______________________ ______________________ ______________________ ______________________

- Consider how you will end the *Pre-Post Freewrite* activity. You may want to ask students to review both writings to consider their gains and then ask them to rate their improvement. You may also hold a conversation about the most important learning gains they made during the lecture.

Procedures

1. Announce the *Pre-Post Freewrite* activity, and tell students that they are to write about the lecture topic for a specified amount of time (e.g., three minutes). Tell them that they should write continuously without stopping and without worrying about punctuation or grammar. Assure them that you will not assess their work on the basis of writing conventions, such as spelling, grammar, or punctuation. Let students know as well that they will freewrite about the topic before *and* after the lecture.
2. Announce the time limit, and let students know how you will signal that time has ended, whether by using a bell, flashing the lights, or simply calling time.
3. Announce the prompt and ask students to begin writing.
4. When you see students stopping before time has ended, prompt them to continue writing, even if they think they do not have anything more to say. Prompt with "just keep writing."
5. Announce the end of the activity; if you have planned to do so, gather student *Pre-Freewrites.*
6. Give your lecture.
7. Announce the *Post-Freewrite* activity, telling students that they are to again write about the lecture topic for five minutes. Tell them again that they should write continuously, without stopping, and without worrying about punctuation or grammar. Assure them that you will not assess their work on the basis of writing conventions, such as spelling, grammar, or punctuation.
8. Remind students of the prompt and ask students to begin writing.
9. When you see students stopping, prompt them to continue writing, with "just keep writing."
10. Announce the end of the activity and gather student *Post-Freewrites.*

Video Lecture	Large Lecture
Ask students to freewrite as an assignment prior to a video lecture. You can make pre-lecture writing a prerequisite for viewing the video. After the lecture, ask them to freewrite again. They may submit their work as an assignment.	The challenge of this technique for the large lecture is the amount of content students can create. Consider having students keep their *Freewrites* in a journal that you assess periodically.

Examples

Health and Wellness (Lecture)

In this mid-size course, the professor teaches several different topics related to health and wellness, with the goal of helping students to learn about, adopt, and maintain healthy lifestyles after college. One of the topics she addresses is nutrition and its relation to health and wellness.

At the beginning of her lecture on this topic, she asks students to freewrite everything they know about the recommended Dietary Guidelines for Americans for approximately five minutes. She next asks them to spend one minute describing the last meal they ate at a restaurant, including fast food restaurants, and assessing how well it meets the dietary guidelines.

Next she lectures on the topic of the dietary guidelines. She asks students to again freewrite as much as they know about the guidelines for five minutes and again assess their most recent meal experience dining out. She holds a discussion about their results prior to dismissing class. Students often note how much they have learned about the guidelines, and they suggest they are better prepared to choose healthy restaurant meals in the future.

Media History and Culture (Large Lecture)

The professor of this very large lecture course was a proponent of requiring students to engage in extensive written discourse. Indeed, one of the course goals was to help improve student writing skills and critical capacity for evaluating the roles played by the media in American history. The professor regularly asked students to create short lists or quickly written responses to a central question to help begin a class discussion. The professor also used *Pre-Post Freewrites* as a way to help students engage with lecture content.

The professor began each lecture segment by asking students to freewrite about the topic. The professor ended each lecture segment by asking students to freewrite again. He required students to keep a regular journal of their *Freewrites* and then submit them twice during the term for evaluation. He found that allowing students to express themselves informally through journal writing gave him the opportunity for a more complete assessment of each student's writing ability than he would have gotten through a combination of formal papers and examinations.

Spanish (Video Lecture)

The professor of a flipped intermediate Spanish course uses *Pre-Post Freewrite* regularly to complement his video lectures. Prior to a video lecture on the film *La Familia,* which is about a second-generation Mexican immigrant and his family, he asks students to freewrite about one of their own family members who is important to them; he also allows students to use fictional family members if they prefer. He asks them to write for five minutes without stopping, using no English words except for proper nouns (specifically names) when appropriate. He suggests that they keep it simple, but he encourages them to use as many adjectives as possible. He tells them to spell as accurately as they can, but he advises them not to get bogged down by it.

After students have submitted their assignments to the course learning management system (LMS), they are able to watch the film *La Familia* and his video lecture on the topic of the family in which he describes the various family members and tells how they are often featured in Hispanic culture and media.

At the end of his video lecture, he asks students to again freewrite about their own family members. He says they can use the initial *Pre-Freewrite* as a basis but should use what they learned in the film and in his video lecture in their augmented *Post-Freewrite* descriptions. He notices that the writing is always dramatically improved, and he believes this helps students feel a sense of accomplishment in their language learning. This also serves as a springboard for in-class discussion.

Variations and Extensions

- A variation of the *Pre-Post Freewrite* is a "shotgun" exercise. In this activity, students are instructed not to lift their pens or pencils from the paper (or fingers from the keyboard) while they are writing. If they believe they are out of things to say, they write "I have run out of things to say" until they think of something else to include.
- Another more structured variation is the *4-2-1 Freewrite.* In this approach, students receive the prompt and write four big ideas. They pair and share ideas and select the two most important. They pair again, creating teams of four, and together they select the one idea that is the most important. They then write freely for five minutes.
- For a final variation, you may ask students to read their *Freewrites* to each other in pairs when they have completed it. They may hear interesting ideas in their own writing that they had not fully processed, or they may learn something from their peer's papers.

Observations and Advice

Some students may find the *Pre-Post Freewrite* to be challenging at first, particularly those who are not fond of writing, but they may appreciate it as they gain time and experience. It may take telling the students why they are doing it, and it may take more than one attempt for them to begin to feel comfortable and to see the value of the exercise.

The *Pre-Post Freewrite* makes a useful assessment tool, and you can gauge student progress by assessing the writing and counting the number of valid or interesting points they make. A simple check system, with a plus for a good point and minus for inaccuracies, can make for a quick count.

Key References and Resources

Berkenkotter, C. (n.d.). *Writing and problem solving.* Retrieved from http://wac.colostate.edu/books/language_connections/chapter3.pdf

TEAL. (2011). *Just Write! guide.* Retrieved from https://lincs.ed.gov/sites/default/files/TEAL_JustWriteGuide.pdf

Tompkins, G. E. (1997). *Literacy for the 21st century: A balanced approach.* Upper Saddle River, NJ: Prentice Hall. Retrieved from https://hatrc.org/library/eoQl3/tompkins-literacy-21st-century-pdf.pdf

ACTIVE LEARNING TECHNIQUE 26

One-Sentence Summary

Complexity involved in	
Planning	LOW
Developing Materials	LOW
Implementing in Class	LOW

Description and Purpose

In *One-Sentence Summary,* the instructor asks students to summarize the most important ideas from a lecture by crafting them into a single sentence. This variation of Angelo and Cross's (1993) classroom assessment technique of the same name is intended to provide students with practice summarizing information by using a predetermined structure to help guide their work.

The *One-Sentence Summary* offers students an opportunity to practice concisely synthesizing the main point of a lecture that covers a large amount of information. When students have to translate information into their own words, they understand it better. The technique requires students to organize information, and it requires them to think critically and creatively about the lecture content. When used over time, it helps focus student attention on the main points, giving students support as they learn to distinguish between what is central and what is ancillary information. The *One-Sentence Summary* also provides teachers with immediate information about whether students understood the key takeaway message of a talk; thus, it is useful as an assessment technique.

Preparation

- Try crafting a *One-Sentence Summary* of the content you intend to cover yourself before assigning it to students. Plan to allow for twice as much time as it takes you for students to do the activity in class.
- Provide an example summary for students on a different lecture topic prior to having students write *One-Sentence Summaries* independently.
- Provide a specific structure or guiding questions for students to use, particularly the first time, to help them organize their thoughts. The following list provides some sample structures.

One-Sentence Summary Structures

Description

A __________ is a kind of _________ that ______________.

Sequence

_______ begins with, continues with _______, and ends with _______.

Compare-Contrast
____ and ____ are similar in that both ____, but ______ while _____.
Cause-Effect
________________ causes ________________.
Problem-Solution
__________ wanted _______ but ______ so ____________.

- The following questions also provide a useful structure: "Who does what to whom, when, where, how, and why?"

Procedures

1. Announce the activity, and tell students what kind of sentence they will write to summarize the main points of the lecture.
2. Proceed with your lecture.
3. Conclude your lecture and ask students to freewrite for approximately two minutes about the key points of the lecture.
4. Ask students to turn their ideas into a single sentence of the type you have identified.
5. Ask for student volunteers to share their summaries or take back the summaries so that you can review them later.

Video Lecture	Large Lecture
To use online, ask students to post their summaries of a VoIP or video lecture in a discussion forum. You can set the discussion to require a response before students can see others' responses to reduce the temptation to borrow from others' summaries. Alternately, create an essay assignment. In addition, social media (such as Twitter) provides a viable option for having students post their summaries.	Explain the task to students and allow them time to complete it. Consider having them report out orally, selecting students randomly or asking for volunteers. If you want to collect written information to assess student understanding, ask them to write their responses on index cards and submit them. Or consider combining this with a more-substantive assignment, such as an in-class lecture journal that you collect and assess once or twice during the term. For example, each student's journal could include his or her *Pre-Post Freewrites,* lecture notes, and a concluding *One-Sentence Summary* for each lecture attended.

Examples

Immunology (Lecture)

The students in this mid-size course on immunology typically plan to work in medical fields on graduation. The instructor believes that it is critical that they are able to understand the core of various concepts in order to be able to apply them. She uses *One-Sentence Summaries* to help students develop skill in this area.

After a lecture on the common cold, for example, the professor gave students five minutes to write a *One-Sentence Summary* explaining causes and effects associated with the common cold. She provided them with the following structure to use to guide their work:

_______________, __________________, and _________________ cause the common cold, and effects are __________________, _______________, and __________________________.

She stipulated that only the three viruses she had mentioned had to be the subject or cause of the summary sentence. Students were also to list at least three symptoms of the common cold as effects. She gave students five minutes to work, and then she collected their responses. The quality of responses ranged from excellent to poor. Thus, she selected three well-written summaries and read them to the class as examples. She continued to use this assignment with lectures throughout the term, and she believed that students' summaries improved over time.

Fundamentals of Oral Communication (Large Lecture)

Students in this large lecture course learn the theory and practice of oral communication. The course meets twice per week and is team-taught. The professors use *One-Sentence Summaries* after lecture segments to ensure that students have grasped the foundational concepts they would need for success in future courses. After a lecture on visual aids, for example, the professors ask students to write a *One-Sentence Summary* about the key point and submit it on an index card. The professors reviewed the cards to gauge student understanding of the lecture content. They sort them into excellent, fair, and poor. The professors reach out to struggling students, and if they see larger issues, they discuss them in the next day's lecture to correct misconceptions and supply information to fill gaps they identify.

Modern British Literature (Video Lecture)

In this blended creative writing course, the professor had recently posted a video lecture on Virginia Woolf's *Mrs. Dalloway.* The professor wanted to know whether students understood the main points she was making about the novel, which she felt went beyond a simple summary into a more nuanced critique and analysis.

She posted an assignment asking students to freewrite for five to ten minutes about the following aspects from her lecture:

- The setting
- The central characters
- Their choices, conflicts, or goals
- What was at stake
- Which actions, or inactions, are the most critical

The assignment next asked students to craft a *One-Sentence Summary* that distilled the key ideas of the lecture. The professor gave the students three days to complete the assignment. She was pleased with the responses she saw, so she used the assignment text to create a word cloud through Wordle, which she shared with the class during their next on-site session.

Variations and Extensions

- Rather than doing this activity at the end of the lecture, do it at the start of class. Students can recall and summarize the previous class lecture so that they activate prior knowledge and connect it to the new incoming information.
- Students can work in groups to share their *Summaries* with each other and to help each other improve them.
- Students can use their *One-Sentence Summaries* as a beginning for creating concise and informative two- or three-sentence summaries.
- Students may journal a sequence of *Summaries* over time. Take back the journal periodically to review progress and development over time.
- Students can write slogan-like bumper stickers to illustrate a particular concept from a lecture.
- Students can write a single text message to summarize the key point of the lecture.
- Students can respond to and complete a sentence stem that you create that requires the lecture material.

Observations and Advice

Students who are new to the topic area or to college generally may not be proficient at crafting good summaries. If this is the case, you will need to spend time helping them develop this skill. It also will likely be a better-received activity if initially it is ungraded or not graded until students become more adept at the skill.

If the content of your lecture is particularly complicated or dense, you will want to consider stopping your lecture periodically, approximately every fifteen minutes, to allow students time to write. They can either freewrite several times in preparation for writing a final summary sentence, or alternately, they can write several *One-Sentence Summaries* in a single class session.

Students may be disappointed in their sentence crafting initially and may find this to be demotivating. Particularly with new students, you may want to specify that the sentences are to be accurate and complete but that they do not have to be beautifully written. The idea is that it is a writing-to-learn activity, not a formal writing activity. You may also want to advise students that they will get better over time.

Key References and Resources

Angelo, T. A., & Cross, K. P. (1993). *Classroom assessment techniques: A handbook for college teachers* (2nd ed.). San Francisco, CA: Jossey-Bass.

Nilson, L. B. (2010). *Teaching at its best: A research-based resource for college instructors* (3rd ed.). San Francisco, CA: Jossey-Bass.

Santa, C., Havens, L., & Valdes, B. (2004). *Project CRISS: Creating independence through student-owned strategies.* Dubuque, IA: Kendall Hunt.

University of North Carolina, Charlotte. (n.d.). *Classroom assessment technique examples.* The Center for Teaching and Learning. Retrieved from http://teaching.uncc.edu/learning-resources/articles-books/best-practice/assessment-grading/assessment-technique-examples

University of South Florida. (n.d.). *Classroom assessment techniques: Academy for teaching and learning excellence.* Retrieved from www.usf.edu/atle/teaching/interactive-techniques.aspx

ACTIVE LEARNING TECHNIQUE 27

3-2-1

Complexity involved in	
Planning	LOW
Developing Materials	LOW
Implementing in Class	LOW

Description and Purpose

In the *3-2-1* technique, students write about three things they learned in the lecture, two things they found particularly interesting in the lecture, and one question they still have about the lecture. This technique provides students with an opportunity to summarize, evaluate, and question key ideas and information. It is an effective approach for having students consolidate and reformulate information they have just received in a lecture.

Being able to summarize key points from a lecture is a sign of effective listening, and a *3-2-1* activity provides a scaffold for helping students think through the information they have just heard. It helps them to reconsider the key concepts you have covered and sort through them to identify which of those are the most important. This technique also provides an efficient way for teachers to check for understanding and to gauge interest in a topic.

Preparation

- To prepare for this technique, review your lecture to ensure that you will be introducing a sufficient number of new concepts or facts for the activity to be effective.
- Create a *3-2-1* template such as the following to distribute as a handout.
- Practice completing the form yourself to ensure that it can be done and to get a rough gauge of the time it will take students to complete. Plan for about twice as long as it takes you.

<table>
<tr><td colspan="3">3
Three new things I learned from the lecture:</td></tr>
<tr><td>1</td><td>2</td><td>3</td></tr>
<tr><td colspan="3">2
Two things in the lecture I found particularly interesting:</td></tr>
<tr><td>1</td><td colspan="2">2</td></tr>
<tr><td colspan="3">1
One thing from the lecture that I still have a question about:</td></tr>
<tr><td colspan="3">1</td></tr>
</table>

Procedures

1. Announce the activity and distribute the handout.
2. Proceed with the lecture.
3. Conclude the lecture and ask students to fill out their *3-2-1* charts, which should contain the following prompts:
   a. Three things you just learned
   b. Two things you found particularly interesting
   c. One question you still have
4. Collect the responses and review them. Consider whether you need to review concepts that students still had questions about and how you will do so.

Video Lecture	Large Lecture
To use this technique in an online class, post the *3-2-1* chart as an assignment, and ask students to submit their responses through the LMS. Alternately, if there is value in having students see each other's responses, post the prompt in a discussion thread. The advantage to this approach is that students can help to answer each other's questions.	In large lectures, it is still possible to use a handout or alternately to have students write *3-2-1* on a sheet of notebook paper. In very large lectures, you will likely want to shift to an online form, such as a survey, which allows you to sort the results and quickly review.

Examples

Science Fiction (Lecture)

In this seminar focused on science fiction readings, the professor was concerned that discussions were often falling flat. She decided to have students do a *3-2-1* activity following her lectures to ensure that they had understood the lecture and to give them time to process their thoughts and ideas. For example, after reading and attending her lecture on *Ender's Game,* she asked students to take out a sheet of paper and write *3* at the top third of the page leaving at least three lines for responses, *2* toward the middle third of the page leaving at least two lines for responses, and *1* toward the bottom third, leaving a line for responses. She then asked students to fill in the *3* area with three things they just learned, the *2* area with two things they found interesting, and the *1* area with one question they still had. She then opened the class for a discussion and found students had much more to contribute.

Psychology (Large Lecture)

The professor of a large lecture psychology course was planning a lecture on Maslow's hierarchy of needs. The lecture was intended as an introduction, and the class would spend several additional sessions talking about Maslow's work and his model.

The professor wanted to check for understanding on the basic concept of the hierarchy immediately after the first session. Additionally, he wanted to be able to answer any student questions at the next class session. He decided to use *3-2-1* charts to provide him with this information.

The professor created a handout with the three main prompts and then proceeded with the introductory lecture. At the end of the lecture, he passed out the handout and asked students to spend five minutes working on it and to hand it in as they left class. Following is an example response:

3 **Three new things I learned from the lecture:**		
1 The five stages	2 That each step must be met before moving to the next level up the hierarchy	3 That transcendence was added later on
2 **Two things in the lecture I found particularly interesting:**		
1 Certain behaviors can lead to self-actualization.	2 That people can have some bad habits and still be self-actualized	
1 **One thing from the lecture that I still have a question about:**		
1 How accurate is this theory?		

The professor was pleased with the responses and planned to respond to the questions in the next class session.

Chemistry (Video Lecture)

In this online introduction to chemistry class, the professor planned to give a short video lecture on chemical and physical properties of matter. The professor believed that having students summarize information after hearing it would help them better understand and retain the material. The professor also wanted to ensure that the students were understanding the key points from the lecture, so he decided to use a *3-2-1* chart to collect information about their understanding.

The professor proceeded with the lecture, and at the end he announced that he had posted a prompt in the discussion forum. He asked students to post their responses there and to respond to each other's posts in two ways: (1) to acknowledge they learned similar things or found similar things interesting or (2) to respond to questions if they believed they knew the answers. Following is a sample response:

3 **Three new things I learned from the lecture:**		
1 What matter is on earth	2 What a chemical property is in relation to the earth	3 What a physical property is in relation to the earth
2 **Two things in the lecture I found particularly interesting:**		
1 That there is an intensive physical property	2 That there is an extensive physical property	
1 **One thing from the lecture that I still have a question about:**		
1 Why is the formation of gas bubbles a chemical change? Is it the same with water bubbles?		

Variations and Extensions

- Use a *3-2-1* chart as a prompt to review the lecture from the previous class session.
- Create a content-specific *3-2-1*. For example, in teaching grammar, you might ask for the following:
  - Three ways to join two independent clauses
  - Two ways to punctuate two independent clauses
  - One way to rewrite two independent clauses so that you have a dependent clause followed by an independent clause
- Use the activity to help students identify main ideas and details from the lecture. For example, ask students to record three of the most important ideas from the lesson, to provide supporting detail for each idea, and to pose one question for each idea.
- Extend the activity by having students research answers to the questions they still have.

Observations and Advice

This technique is best used when the information is fairly foundational. More complex information can be difficult to summarize and can leave students feeling frustrated and constrained.

Students may have trouble completing the "one question" portion of the activity, particularly if they are new to the topic area. At times, they will be tempted to write "I have no questions." You may want to walk around the room to ensure that students are responding to the questions. If you have novice students and are introducing a new topic, you may wish to have students work in pairs or small groups so that they can support each other as they seek to create questions.

Key References and Resources

Alsamadani, H. A. (2011). The effects of the 3-2-1 reading strategy on EFL reading comprehension. *English Language Teaching, 4*(3), 184–191. Retrieved from http://files.eric.ed.gov/fulltext/EJ1080738.pdf

Lipton, L., & Wellman, B. (1999). *Pathways to understanding: Patterns and practices in the learning focused classroom.* Guildford, VT: Pathways Publishing.

Van Gyn, G. (2013). The little assignment with the big impact: Reading, writing, critical reflection, and meaningful discussion. *Faculty Focus.* Retrieved from www.facultyfocus.com/articles/instructional-design/the-little-assignment-with-the-big-impact-reading-writing-critical-reflection-and-meaningful-discussion/

Zygouris-Coe, V., Wiggins, M. B., & Smith, L. H. (2004). Engaging students with text: The 3–2–1 strategy. *The Reading Teacher, 58*(4), 381–384.

ACTIVE LEARNING TECHNIQUE 28

RSQC2

Complexity involved in	
Planning	LOW
Developing Materials	LOW
Implementing in Class	LOW

Description and Purpose

RSQC2 (Recall, Summarize, Question, Connect, and Comment) provides a structure that encourages students to rehearse, organize, and evaluate information from a lecture and to comprehensively assess how it applies to the overall foundation of the course. In this adaptation of Angelo and Cross's (1993) classroom assessment technique, students do the following:

R. *Recall* key points from the lecture.
S. *Summarize* the lecture's main purpose in a single sentence.
Q. Ask an unanswered *question* they have about the lecture material.
C. *Connect* the lecture material to the goals of the course.
C. Write an evaluative *comment* about their confidence with lecture material.

This technique helps students achieve several educational objectives. In particular, the *Recall, Summary,* and *Question* sections require students to consider their basic knowledge and comprehension. In addition, the *Connect* and *Comment* sections require students to move beyond knowledge and comprehension to application, integration, and evaluation of the information they have just heard. The technique encourages students to continually review, reconsider, and integrate the major points from a lecture. It invites students to engage in self-reflection and self-regulation. Students must consider what the relationship of this topic is to the overall course plan and why the material is important. When students see the relevance of the information and articulate where they may be falling short in learning it, it may motivate them to learn more. This process reflects processes students will be expected to use in their future employment, and that can also be motivational for students. This technique helps build an understanding of course goals, objectives, and content that all students share.

RSQC2 also enables teachers to assess student learning. It provides the teacher with immediate feedback on what students learned, remembered, or valued from the lecture. Student feedback through *RSQC2* can help an instructor identify where students need the most help. Their responses also inform the teacher of student questions and comments that require timely responses. Finally, *RSQC2* enables professors to compare students' perspectives against their own.

Preparation

- Determine when to employ this technique and plan for students to work for approximately five to ten minutes.
- Consider creating a handout to help them efficiently capture the information, such as the following sample.
- Respond to the prompts yourself using the day's lecture material so that you can later gauge how closely the student responses match yours.

Sample Handout: *RSQC2*

Lecture date and topic________________________________
Student name________________________________

Recall. What were the main points of the lecture?

Summarize. State the lecture's main purpose in a single sentence.

Question. Ask an unanswered question you have from the lecture.

Connect. Explain how the concepts in today's lecture connect to the learning goals of this course.

Comment. Evaluate how confident you feel regarding your understanding of this lecture's material.

Procedures

1. Announce the activity and the time frame and give students an overview of what *RSQC2* stands for.
2. Pass out the handout if you've made one or ask students to record each prompt word on their own paper.

3. Provide students with time to respond to the prompts:
   a. **Recall.** Ask students to remember and rank the three most important points from the lecture.
   b. **Summarize.** Ask students to write down a one-sentence summary of the day's lecture.
   c. **Question.** Ask students to generate one question they have about the lecture content.
   d. **Connect.** Ask students to identify connections from the most-important concepts they have identified to the overall goals for the course.
   e. **Comment.** Ask students to comment on their understanding of the concepts from the lecture.
4. Collect and compare students' responses to each other and to your own responses to the prompts.
5. Bring an overview of what you learned from the responses to the beginning of the next class and tell the class what you plan to do with the information in order to close the loop on the activity.

Video Lecture	Large Lecture
In an online course, have students submit their *RSQC2* documents as a quiz or a Word document. You can also create a thread for each prompt word in a discussion board and ask students to respond there. You can also set the discussion to require students to respond prior to seeing others' responses.	Although the basic procedure for this technique calls for written responses, collecting and analyzing these in a large lecture course can be daunting. Consider asking students to write responses and call on a few students in class to report out; you'll be able to get a sense of whether they understand the materials. Alternately, ask them to keep journals of in-class writing and collect those periodically to assess, selecting a sample of responses. Finally, it is not necessary to gather the responses; instead, you can call on students randomly or ask for volunteers for oral report-outs.

Examples

German for Business (Lecture)

This course enrolled students who had good German language skills but needed more focused preparation for doing business with Germany-based companies. The instructor used *RSQC2* several times throughout the semester to help them develop those skills. For example, at the end of a lecture and discussion on German tax reform, the professor asked students to summarize important changes in new tax rates, provide comments on the consequences for the Deutschland AG, describe a connection between the topic and Standort Deutschland, and formulate a question about the topic.

She noted that many students were able to identify important rate changes, that a couple of students had difficulty understanding specific terms, and that other students did not understand the meaning of an important concept. She was able to correct students' lack of information and understanding.

The professor reported that the activity was useful. Indeed, she noted that the activity became a student favorite and that students requested that they be tested in a similar fashion to *RSQC2* so that they could make connections and comments on the learning units. (For additional information see Daines, 2001.)

Introduction to Engineering Fields (Large Lecture)

In this first-year, large-lecture course, students learn about different engineering fields. On an end-of term survey of the students in the course from the previous term, the professor found out that as many as 20 percent of the students change their engineering field as a result of participation in this course and about 70 percent felt they had chosen correctly. She also learned, however, that approximately 10 percent of the students did not feel they had learned a sufficient amount about the various fields to determine whether they were in the appropriate majors. She believed that at least some of these students were not paying sufficient attention to the lecture information or alternately were not processing the information at a deep-enough level to make the decision.

She determined that for each lecturette on an engineering field, she would use *RSQC2.* For example, for the class session on civil engineering, she asked students to do the following:

R. *Recall* key points from the lecture about civil engineering.
S. *Summarize* the field's main branches in a single sentence.
Q. Ask an unanswered *question* you have about civil engineering.
C. *Connect* the lecture material to your professional career goals.
C. Write an evaluative *comment* about your confidence in determining whether civil engineering would be a good choice of major and profession for you.

After the students had completed the activity, the professor held a discussion about the different elements of the *RSQC2,* asking for volunteers to share thoughts on each letter. She felt that students engaged in the discussion, and she believed that the number of students who could not determine if civil engineering was the best choice for them would decrease on the next survey administration.

College Algebra (Video Lecture)

In this online course, students watch a series of video lectures in addition to other course activities. In one lecture on graphing, beginning with the Cartesian coordinate system, the professor decided to use *RSQC2.*

The professor posted the lecture. At the end of a lecture, he posted prompts to a discussion board. In these prompts, he asked students to recall the key points about the Cartesian structure from the lecture, to summarize the main point of the lecture, and to craft one question about it. He then asked students to connect the information to a previous lecture and to comment on their understanding of the Cartesian system.

Students then posted their responses on the discussion board. The instructor noticed that several students were missing important background knowledge about graphing, key ideas about graphing, and the interrelations between ideas. He had assumed students would know about basic graphing prior to entering the course, and when the *RSQC2* activity helped him discover that this was not the case, he added a review module to ensure all students had this baseline knowledge before proceeding.

Variations and Extensions

- Using all components of this activity may be too advanced for novice students. You can choose from the prompts. Indeed, starting with the *Recall* and *Summarize* steps can be a good way to scaffold this technique before adding some of the later steps.
- However, with advanced students, using *Comment* and *Connect* enabled students to demonstrate their ability to synthesize information and connect ideas.

Observations and Advice

Students who are less skilled at organizing information and applying it are the most likely to benefit from this technique. The technique is structured enough for students to carry out the task relatively quickly. *RSQC2* can be time-consuming to evaluate, however, particularly in large classes. Be sure you have sufficient time to review student responses and to report back to students. If it is overused or used poorly, *RSQC2* can become a mindless, pro-forma activity.

Key References and Resources

Angelo, T. A., & Cross, K. P. (1993). *Classroom assessment techniques: A handbook for college teachers* (2nd ed.). San Francisco, CA: Jossey-Bass.

Daines, E. (2001). Classroom assessment techniques in the German-for-business course. *Global Business Languages, 6*(2). Retrieved from http://docs.lib.purdue.edu/gbl/vol6/iss1/2

CHAPTER 22

Reflecting and Metacognition

Today's students will be better prepared to succeed in today's complex and quickly changing world if they understand how they learn and manage their own learning. Students can develop these insights and skills through metacognition. *Metacognition* is a higher-order thinking process that involves active control over mental processes. It can be simply defined as "thinking about thinking" or as a "person's cognition about cognition" (Wellman, 1985, p. 1). To give a concrete example, when an instructor asks a student to solve a problem, the student engages in a cognitive process to come up with an answer to the problem. The student's awareness of the problem-solving process and understanding of the rationale for solving it a certain way is metacognition (Flavell, 1979).

Researchers and instructors have recognized the need to intentionally weave metacognitive strategies into teaching and learning activities. Metacognitive reflection activities guide students through the process of reflecting on what they have learned, comparing intended learning to actual outcomes, evaluating the efficacy of their own learning strategies, and synthesizing the meaning of not only what they have learned but also how well they learned it. Metacognitive reflection activities encourage students to produce personal insight and learn from their learning experiences. In this chapter, we offer four metacognitive reflection techniques. We summarize these Techniques in Exhibit 22.1.

Exhibit 22.1 Techniques for Reflecting and Metacognition

This technique . . .	Helps students learn actively by having them . . .
ALT 29: *Punctuated Lecture*	Answer questions about what they are doing at a given moment during a class
ALT 30: *Post-Lecture Knowledge Survey*	Review questions and rate their confidence in answering them
ALT 31: *Lecture Wrapper*	Write what they think the three most-important ideas of the lecture were on an index card, hand the cards in, and then compare their responses to the ideas the instructor shares were the most important
ALT 32: *Lecture Engagement Logs*	Keep running logs of their preparation, participation, and reflection in lecture courses

Key References and Resources

Flavell, J. H. (1979). Metacognition and cognitive monitoring: A new area of cognitive-developmental inquiry. *American Psychologist, 34,* 906–911.

Wellman, H. (1985). *The child's theory of mind: The development of conscious cognition.* San Diego, CA: Academic Press.

ACTIVE LEARNING TECHNIQUE 29

Punctuated Lecture

Complexity involved in	
Planning	MODERATE
Developing Materials	MODERATE
Implementing in Class	LOW

Description and Purpose

During a *Punctuated Lecture,* students listen to the lecture for approximately twenty minutes. At the end of the lecture segment, the lecturer pauses and asks students to answer questions about what they are doing at that particular moment.

Punctuated Lectures help to promote student engagement during a lecture through the process of asking students to be more self-aware of their own involvement (Angelo & Cross, 1993). The activity also can help students refocus attention if their minds have wandered, which can help to improve active listening. Over time and with practice, students can develop skills as self-monitoring listeners. In short, *Punctuated Lectures* can help student develop metacognitive skills, or the ability to think about their own thinking and learning.

Punctuated Lectures also are a useful method of providing instructors with information about what learning strategies students use during the lecture. In turn, instructors can use the information to help guide students during lectures, such as directing students to attend to important content or reviewing a concept for understanding.

Preparation

- Before deciding to use this *Punctuated Lectures,* consider exactly what you want to know, such as the following:
  - How much students were focused on the lecture content at a given point
  - How distracted students were by technology or by each other
  - What students were physically doing, whether listening or taking notes or doing something unrelated
- Next consider your question format. You might ask students to respond to an item based on a scale (5 = extremely high, 1 = extremely low) with prompts such as "How would you describe your level of focus on the lecture?" "How would you describe your level of distraction from the lecture?" Or you also might ask an open-ended question such as "Describe what you were doing when the lecture paused."
- Finally, consider how you will have students respond. You might have them respond on an index card or you could use an automated response system (clickers) or an online survey.

Procedures

1. Tell students that you will lecture and stop every so often to ask them to record what they are doing.
2. Tell them how they should record their responses.
3. Begin the first section of the lecture, which should last approximately fifteen to twenty minutes.
4. Stop the lecture and ask students to think about what they were just doing.
5. Ask students to answer the question(s) you have developed.
6. Resume the lecture and repeat every fifteen to twenty minutes for the duration of the class.

Video Lecture	Large Lecture
When lecturing through video online, stop the content portion of your lecture periodically and ask students to record what they are doing at that time. They can submit their work as a quiz during the lecture or as an assignment.	For large lecture courses, consider developing a multiple-choice stem (e.g., 1. What is your current attention level for the lecture: a. very high, b. high, c. low, d. very low) and administering electronically through an automatic personal response system (clickers).

Examples

Nursing as a Profession (Lecture)

In this seminar course, the professor felt that students were always engaged when they were taking about their past experiences. However, the professor felt that the students "checked out" as soon as she started talking. She had important content to share, however. She didn't believe that the students had ill intentions; indeed, she didn't believe that they knew that they were checking out at all. She wanted to help them learn to self-monitor their own attention levels.

She decided to use a *Punctuated Lecture.* She told students that she had some information to share with them that would take roughly fifteen minutes and noted that she would be using a slide deck because some of the information was visual. She asked students to take notes on the information. About ten minutes into her lecture, she showed a slide that read "on a scale of 5 to 1, with 5 being the highest level and 1 being the lowest level, rate your current level of attention to the lecture." She noted some uncomfortable shuffling as students began to look up and read the question. Several acknowledged after class that they had not been paying as much attention as they should have been and stated their determination to do better in the future.

Sociology (Large Lecture)

In this course on sociology, the professor believed that students were being distracted by personal technology. He noticed that some students were checking social media sites as well as their personal texts during class. He knew that this habit distracted them from learning and believed that it distracted other students around them. He decided to use *Punctuated Lecture* to help draw student attention to the issue. During a lecture on inequality and stratification by social class, he paused the lecture for a minute and asked students to use their clickers to respond to a series of items:

When the lecture paused, what were you looking directly at (check all that apply):

☐ The professor
☐ Your notes (handwritten)
☐ Your notes (typed in laptop)
☐ The ceiling
☐ The floor
☐ Your cell phone
☐ Your neighbor's cell phone
☐ Your neighbor's laptop (off-course topic)

When the lecture paused, what were you specifically doing (check all that apply):

☐ Taking notes on the lecture
☐ Checking texts
☐ Checking social media
☐ Watching your neighbors checking their texts or social media

Because students responded with clickers, their responses were anonymous. He thought this anonymity coupled with the large class size allowed for fairly honest responses. He noted that most students believed that they were listening to the lecture and looking at the lecturer when the lecture paused; his visual scan of the room did not confirm this assessment, however, so although he believed they thought they were paying attention, their multitasking was contributing to a lack of self-awareness. A few students acknowledged checking social media and texts. However, many students noted that they were distracted by other students' technology.

The professor used his own assessment as well as the survey results as an opportunity to discuss the importance of paying attention to the lecture for learning and for course success. He also described some of the recent research on multitasking that suggests that it detracts from learning. Finally, he talked about course citizenship and reviewed the course policy on technology use during class.

He began to implement the activity regularly. He alerted students when it seemed that they had not accurately self-assessed, and he congratulated them when they had and when their attention seemed to be at high levels. He noticed improvement in attention and fewer technological distractions over time.

Microeconomics (Video Lecture)

The professor of this online microeconomics course used the *Punctuated Lecture* to help students pay attention to the course video lectures. During a lecture on pricing, he discussed the factors that went into developing the pricing of the iPod. At about ten minutes in, he asked students to stop the video and respond to a quiz in the learning management system (LMS). The quiz asked students to rate their level of engagement in the lecture on a scale of 5 to 1, with 5 being the highest and 1 being the lowest. He also asked students to reflect in their course journals on what they were doing during the lecture. He was surprised with several students' candor. Some reported caring for small children, others folding laundry, and others surfing the Internet. He sent a note to the class thanking them for their honest disclosures but also stressed the importance of giving full attention to the lecture. He continued using the activity and noted a decrease in reporting of distracting activities that coincided with an increase in quiz scores. These results helped him conclude that students were learning to better self-manage in his online course, and he shared this insight and the evidence of their improvement with them.

Variation and Extension

- Ask students to journal their responses over time. Take up their journals to assess them periodically. This variation will enable them, and you, to see changes over time.

Observations and Advice

Students new to higher education may find this activity particularly beneficial because it teaches them self-monitoring, which is a skill that can help them in other courses as well. This activity can be effectively scaffolded. You can begin by using it at each class session and then reduce to using it during half of the class meetings. Also, you can start by breaking every fifteen to twenty minutes and move to longer lecture segments.

Key References and Resources

Angelo, T. A., & Cross, K. P. (1993). *Classroom assessment techniques: A handbook for college teachers* (2nd ed.). San Francisco, CA: Jossey-Bass.

Cashin, W. E. (2010). *IDEA paper #46: Effective lecturing.* Retrieved from http://ideaedu.org/wp-content/uploads/2014/11/IDEA_Paper_46.pdf

Duke University, Center for Instructional Technology. (n.d.). *Lecture busters: Keeping students engaged.* Retrieved from https://mclibrary.duke.edu/sites/mclibrary.duke.edu/files/public/research/lecturebusters.pdf

ACTIVE LEARNING TECHNIQUE 30

Post-Lecture Knowledge Survey

Complexity involved in	
Planning	LOW
Developing Materials	MODERATE
Implementing in Class	LOW

Description and Purpose

In a *Post-Lecture Knowledge Survey,* the professor presents students with a set of questions or problems related to the knowledge and skills just shared. Students respond to the survey by rating their perceived ability to answer the questions or solve the problem. *Post-Lecture Knowledge Surveys* require students to self-assess their understanding of the lecture content and their readiness to respond to questions related to it.

This technique promotes student reflection on course content. Coming to terms with their confidence levels can provide students with motivation to ask questions and to review the material. Completing a *Post-Lecture Knowledge Survey* also points students to areas for improvement prior to testing. The questions on the test can serve as a learning guide for students. *Post-Lecture Knowledge Surveys,* then, provide students with a sense of control over their own learning by making the learning more visible.

A *Post-Lecture Knowledge Survey* provides the instructor with valuable information about students' state of knowledge and confidence abilities. It can lead the instructor to revisit any points in which students lack confidence. Moreover, *Post-Lecture Knowledge Surveys* prompt professors and students to think ahead to the next quiz or test.

Preparation

- Create a survey in which you use questions that are like the ones students may see on a future quiz or exam. Previous exams or quizzes are a great place to look for such questions. Present the questions and provide students with a scale where they rate their confidence in being able to respond. Following are four samples of questions and rating scales.

Sample *Post-Lecture* Questions and Rating Scales

Sample 1

Review the question and respond to indicate how well you can answer it:

4. I cannot answer the question.
3. I understand the question, and I think I have a good chance of answering it correctly.
2. I am confident I can answer the question to earn a baseline passing grade.
1. I am confident I can answer the question well enough to earn a high grade.

Sample 2

Review the question and respond to indicate how confident you are that you can answer it correctly:

4. Highly confident
3. Fairly confident
2. Slightly confident
1. Not confident

Sample 3

Review the question and respond to indicate how likely you are to answer it correctly:

4. Highly likely
3. Fairly likely
2. Slightly likely
1. Unlikely

Sample 4

Review the question and identify which of the following are true:

4. I can answer this question with full confidence.
3. I can get most of the credit for this question.
2. I can get some partial credit for this question.
1. I cannot begin to answer this question right now.

Procedures

1. Complete the lecture and announce the *Post-Lecture Knowledge Survey* activity.
2. Distribute the handout and ask students to complete it.
3. Consider revealing the correct answers to the quiz questions so that students can gauge how accurately they responded in the survey questions.

Video Lecture	Large Lecture
After watching a video or VoIP lecture, students can take a *Post-Lecture Knowledge Survey* as a quiz.	Use an online quiz or survey tool to collect the information quickly and efficiently.

Examples

Oceanography (Lecture)

The overall learning goal for this course was to help students acquire foundational knowledge regarding the geological, physical, chemical, and biological processes in the world's oceans and their interactions with the earth as a system. One of the course's learning modules focuses on Wegener, Pangaea, and continental drift. The professor decided to use a *Post-Lecture Knowledge Survey* to help students understand how well they had attended to the lecture content.

After a lecture on the module's topic, the professor passed out the *Post-Lecture Knowledge Survey* handout shown here and asked students to complete it.

Post-Lecture Knowledge Survey Handout	
Review the following questions and circle the correct answers.	**Review the questions and your answers. Circle the response to indicate how likely you are to have answered it correctly.**
1. The notion that continents move over the earth's surface slowly is called a. Pangaea b. Continental drift c. Plate tectonics d. Landmass movement	4. Highly likely 3. Fairly likely 2. Slightly likely 1. Unlikely
2. Plates move because of a. Wind b. Convection in the mantle c. Ocean currents d. Convection in the core	4. Highly likely 3. Fairly likely 2. Slightly likely 1. Unlikely
3. Wegener's hypothesis suggests that a. The landmasses have always been in the same places b. The landmasses were joined together as Pangaea but have since drifted apart c. The continents do not move d. Earthquakes have caused the landmasses to move	4. Highly likely 3. Fairly likely 2. Slightly likely 1. Unlikely
4. Evidence for Pangaea was that a. The same fossilized organism was found on two different continents b. Part of an organism was found on one landmass and the other part on another landmass c. A land bridge was found d. People are found on all landmasses	4. Highly likely 3. Fairly likely 2. Slightly likely 1. Unlikely
5. Pangaea existed a. About 100 thousand years ago b. About 5 million years ago c. About 250 million years ago d. In the past and still exists today	4. Highly likely 3. Fairly likely 2. Slightly likely 1. Unlikely

After the students completed the *Post-Lecture Knowledge Survey,* the professor shared the correct answers with students. He encouraged them to look at not only what they answered correctly and incorrectly but also at their confidence ratings to help them better prepare for the upcoming exam.

Film Studies (Large Lecture)

In this large lecture course, the professor was worried that students were overconfident in their knowledge of basic concepts and vocabulary. They seemed to think just watching the film was sufficient studying and were failing to review their lecture notes. She developed a nongraded quiz on several films students had watched and asked them to rate their confidence in their responses. The quiz consisted of a content question followed by a confidence question. For example:

1. A cinematographer's decision about how to frame a shot would influence the scene's
   a. Montage
   b. Mise-en-scène
   c. Duration
   d. Lighting
2. Rate your confidence level in the accuracy of your response:
   a. Very high
   b. High
   c. Low
   d. Very Low

Despite fairly low scores on the content questions, students had high levels of confidence in their responses. The professor reviewed the results with the class and was able to demonstrate to students the importance of studying the lecture notes before the exam.

Pathophysiology (Video Lecture)

The professor for a nursing course used *Post-Lecture Knowledge Surveys* throughout the term. At the end of each online lecture, the professor administered the surveys through the course LMS. On each survey, she included questions that met each level of Bloom's taxonomy. Some questions were baseline knowledge questions whereas others moved students into analysis, synthesis, and evaluation. She counted completion of the surveys as 5 percent toward the total grade.

The professor noted that student self-confidence was relatively low across the board during the first few administrations of the surveys. Toward the middle of the semester, students raised their self-confidence on the knowledge and comprehension questions. She noticed, however, that their scores were not improving on the higher-order questions. This prompted her to include more case studies in the course activities that required students to use these higher-order skills. Eventually, student confidence in these areas also improved.

Variations and Extensions

- Give the survey before and after the lecture. Students can see change in their knowledge and confidence, which can contribute to their understanding of the lectures as important learning tools. In turn, this understanding can motivate students to pay better attention in future lectures.
- Ask students to compare their assessments of the state of their knowledge on *Post-Lecture Knowledge Surveys* with their performance on actual exams. To do this, collect the surveys, and in addition to the exam, also give them their survey responses.

Observations and Advice

Some instructors express concerns about the reliability of the surveys as valid measures of student understanding. It is true that students can overestimate or underestimate their knowledge and abilities. The real value of this technique lies in helping students become more accurate assessors of their knowledge, which can be a valuable learning moment for them.

Key References and Resources

Clauss, J., & Geedey, K. (2010). Knowledge survey: Students ability to self-assess. *Journal of the Scholarship of Teaching and Learning, 10*(2), 14–24.

Nilson, L. B. (2013). *Creating self-regulated learners: Strategies to strengthen students' self-awareness and learning skills.* Sterling, VA: Stylus Publishing.

Nuhfer, E. B., & Knipp, D. (2003). The knowledge survey: A tool for all reasons. *To Improve the Academy, 21,* 59–78. Retrieved from http://pachyderm.cdl.edu/elixr-stories/resource-documents/knowledge-survey/KS_a_too_for_all_reasons.pdf

ACTIVE LEARNING TECHNIQUE 31

Lecture Wrapper

Complexity involved in	
Planning	LOW
Developing Materials	MODERATE
Implementing in Class	LOW

Description and Purpose

Lecture Wrappers enable students to listen to a lecture to identify its key points and then compare their judgments to what the instructor identifies as the most-important points. Through this process, students self-assess their ability to listen actively and identify salient information as well as their understanding of the lecture content.

This technique helps students identify gaps in their understanding. It focuses their concentration on important ideas, reducing emphasis on extraneous details. A *Lecture Wrapper* allows for self-assessment, but it is less subjective than some self-assessment measures because it is grounded in actual performance, so students can gauge the accuracy of their assessment. Through this process, the technique can help students to improve their judgment skills. *Lecture Wrappers* are also techniques for helping students learn to think like an expert in the field. In addition, they help students to become more responsible for their own learning.

Lecture Wrappers help instructors assess student understanding of key content and concepts. Instructors can use the information gleaned from this technique to correct student misunderstandings and gaps in comprehension as well as to shape the direction and layout of future lectures.

Preparation

- Decide how students will record their responses. Index cards are particularly useful for this activity because they help focus student responses by limiting the amount of information they can record, but you can also ask students to record the main points on their own paper.
- Prior to class, identify the three to five most-important points of your lecture.

Procedures

1. Inform students that they should listen actively to the information in the lecture. Tell them that in addition to taking their regular notes, they should listen for the three most-important points. Inform them that you will collect their responses but that you will not grade them—indicate that the goal of the activity is for them to self-assess and improve their listening skills.

2. Proceed with the lecture.
3. Pass out the index cards, or tell students that they will record the main points on their own paper, and ask students to record the three most-important points.
4. Collect their responses.
5. Reveal what you see as the three most-important points.
6. Ask students to compare their main points with yours.
7. Consider reporting out at the next session on the full-class responses or alternately having a discussion about the differences in student responses and yours.

Video Lecture	Large Lecture
After a VoIP or video lecture, ask students to respond to a quiz on what they believe to be the three main points. Reveal your points and ask students to compare their responses to yours.	Index cards can be a useful way to collect information on the three main points. If it is a very large lecture, consider using survey or polling software.

Examples

Organizational Theory (Lecture)

In this medium-sized lecture course, the goal was to have students develop a comprehensive understanding of what organizations are and how they work. The professor was worried that students were becoming so bogged down in the details of different theories that they were not getting the bigger picture. The professor decided to use *Lecture Wrappers* at the end of each lecturette on a specific theory.

For example, after a lecturette that focused on systems theory, the professor asked students to write down the three major domains of systems theory inquiry. Students recorded their responses on index cards. He then revealed his main areas: philosophy, science, and technology. Several students had at least two of the three responses, and they were able to discuss all three are major areas of inquiry. Several students had also written *cybernetics,* which he had mentioned in the lecture, and they had a discussion about whether the terms are synonymous or whether one is a subset of the other. All in all, he felt the exercise had been productive, particularly in its influence on the quality of course discussion.

Music Appreciation (Large Lecture)

This music course intends to help students understand the elements of music and apply knowledge of musical styles to composer and composition identification across several historical periods. The professor knew that in previous courses, students had had difficulty grasping the main themes of the historical and social context for each period, so she decided to use *Lecture Wrappers* to help the new group of students do a better job of this task.

Before her lecture on the historical and social context of the medieval period, she told students that they should take notes as usual but that they should also try to identify the three main points of her lecture about the period. At the end of her lecture, she handed out index cards and asked students to record what they believed to be the three main points. She collected the cards and then told students what she believed were the three main points. She provided her rationale for the importance of her points.

She opened up class for discussion about what clues there might have been to signal the three main points. Students correctly noted that her presentation slides had a different format for the main points. They also noted that she paused when summarizing a point and asked for questions before starting in on a new one. And they noted that she used language such as "up next" or "another important aspect of this period" to signal a new idea. Students believed that they would be able to pay attention to the cues and identify the key points more accurately in the next session. She planned to use the technique in each of the lectures to follow.

JavaScript for Programmers (Video Lecture)

In this online course, the professor teaches a unit to introduce model-view-controller architecture. The professor had noticed that students did not do as well on their exams on this topic as she would have liked, and she believed that the main reason for this was that they got bogged down in the details rather than paying attention to the main ideas. She decided to use *Lecture Wrappers* to help students intentionally focus on the key points.

The professor posted a video lecture and then posted an ungraded quiz that asked students to rate the three main points from the lecture. She reviewed their responses. She then posted a follow-up video explaining what she believed to be the three main points from the lecture were and her rationale for identifying the ones she did. In her lecture, she encouraged students to compare their responses to hers, and she described techniques for identifying key points, such as looking for what is the main idea and what is elaboration.

Variations and Extensions

- Present some tips on active listening prior to the activity. For example:
    - Come prepared for the new topic (e.g., look over notes from the last class, read the assignments, and so forth).
    - Face the speaker and strive to maintain eye contact within limits (when live) or stay focused on the screen (when video).
    - Listen to the words and attempt to understand what the speaker is saying.
    - Listen for main ideas and relevant details.
    - Pay close attention when the speaker is analyzing, synthesizing, or processing information (e.g., when the speaker makes lists, notes cause and effect, or spends time on a specific topic or issue).
    - When live, wait for the speaker to pause before asking clarification questions.
    - Ask questions that will help understanding.
- Ask students to provide a rationale for why the three points were the most important; doing so will help you to evaluate their logical reasoning skills.
- Ask students to pair up to discuss the main concepts prior to turning in their cards or handouts.
- Present a list of approximately ten potential main points and ask students to identify the top

three or alternately rank them. Collect their responses through either a polling system (e.g., clickers or phone-in poll) or alternately through a handout.

- Ask students to do a top-ten important points list. Put students into pairs or small groups and ask them to rank them in order from least important to most important.

Observations and Advice

This technique is at its best when used repeatedly over time. It enables students to have practice at identifying important concepts and to see improvement. Lovett (2008), the originator of this technique, noted that fewer than half of the students (45 percent) were able to identify the most-important points accurately on the first try. Seventy-five percent were able to identify them correctly by the third try.

This technique is typically ungraded, but for some classes, it may be important to provide some extrinsic motivation incentive for students to take the assignment seriously and to turn in their responses. In such cases, assign a few points for the grade, possibly as participation points.

Key References and Resources

Lovett, M. C. (2008, January 29). *Teaching metacognition.* Presentation at Educause Learning Initiative Conference. Retrieved from https://net.educause.edu/upload/presentations/eli081/fs03/metacognition-eli.pdf

Nilson, L. B. (2013). *Creating self-regulated learners: Strategies to strengthen students' self-awareness and learning skills.* Sterling, VA: Stylus Publishing.

ACTIVE LEARNING TECHNIQUE 32

Lecture Engagement Logs

Complexity involved in	
Planning	LOW
Developing Materials	LOW
Implementing in Class	LOW

Description and Purpose

Lecture Engagement Logs are records that students keep to document the various academic activities they engage in for a particular class. One challenge of lecture classes is that students do not often know what they need to do in order to be good participants. They don't always fully understand that they need to read ahead and think of questions about the content. They don't know that they need to actively listen and ask themselves questions during a lecture. Additionally, they don't always know that they need to spend time thinking and reflecting on the lecture content after the session is over. *Lecture Engagement Logs* help students become more aware of the various activities that go into being an active participant in a lecture course. Students gain valuable information about their own study habits so that they have a better chance of making changes to improve them.

Lecture Engagement Logs are also a useful way for faculty members to gauge student participation. This technique provides information about the quality of the activities students use to prepare, attend, and follow up on lecture content. Professors can determine whether students' activities are in line with their expectations and can make suggestions accordingly.

Preparation

- Decide what students should do and notice about their engagement in the lectures. For example, do you want to know what they do to prepare or know how many hours they study before class overall? Should they think about what they do for each class or activities over the course of the semester in general? What about when and where they study? Should they log what else they do while studying or sit in class (do they check phones, laptops, Facebook, Twitter, and so forth)?
- Create a *Lecture Engagement Log* with the activities you hope students will carry out before, during, and after a lecture along with the details you are most interested in learning about and having them consider. Following are four samples that can be adapted.

Lecture Engagement Log Sample 1: Full-Course Term

<table>
<tr><th colspan="2">Lecture Engagement Log</th></tr>
<tr><td colspan="2">Name____</td></tr>
<tr><td colspan="2">1. Lecture Preparation. Log approximately ten specific examples describing how you prepared for that date's lecture. Ensure that your log entries are spread out over the course of the semester.</td></tr>
<tr><td>Date</td><td>Report what you read, whether and how you developed questions ahead of the lecture, and so forth.</td></tr>
<tr><td></td><td></td></tr>
<tr><td></td><td></td></tr>
<tr><td></td><td></td></tr>
<tr><td colspan="2">2. Participation During Lecture. Your entries in this log should be referring to comments you made that were heard by the entire class. Please log approximately ten specific examples and ensure that they are spread out over the course of the semester.</td></tr>
<tr><td>Date</td><td>Describe how you contributed to the lecture. Report what you shared specifically and your perception of how, if at all, your contribution aided the flow of the lecture or discussion, as well as your contribution's relevance to the lecture or large-class discussion.</td></tr>
<tr><td></td><td></td></tr>
<tr><td></td><td></td></tr>
<tr><td></td><td></td></tr>
<tr><td colspan="2">3. Participation in Small-Group Activities. Log at least ten specific examples and ensure that they are spread out over the course of the semester.</td></tr>
<tr><td>Date</td><td>Describe your contribution to the small-group activities, including participating in pairs and in small-group projects. Summarize how you participated and your perception of how, if at all, your participation aided the interaction.</td></tr>
<tr><td></td><td></td></tr>
<tr><td></td><td></td></tr>
<tr><td></td><td></td></tr>
<tr><td colspan="2">4. Self-Assessment, Reflection, and Improvement. Log two self-assessments of your performance as a participant in this class, focusing on your strengths and how you can improve. Reflect on the participation expectations outlined in the syllabus as well as the quality and quantity of your participation in class. The first self-assessment should be completed between weeks three and seven, and the second should be completed between weeks eight and twelve. Each self-assessment should be at least five sentences in length.</td></tr>
</table>

Date	Reflection

Source: Adapted from Docan-Morgan (2015).

***Lecture Engagement Log* Sample 2: Weekly Log**

Weekly Lecture Engagement Log			
Name_______________ Week_______			
Please use the following scale to rate your engagement: 4 Fully engaged 3 Fairly engaged 2 Minimally engaged 1 Not engaged			
Day	**Start and Stop Time**	**Type of Engagement**	**Self-Rating on Engagement**
Monday			
Wednesday			
Friday			

***Lecture Engagement Log* Sample 3: Full-Course Term on Multiple Activities**

Learning Log						
Name_______________						
Date	**Assignment or Test**	**Time Spent Studying or Meeting with Instructor**	**Time Spent in Class Lecture**	**Time Spent Working on Assignments**	**Grade on Test**	**Total Time**

Create a sample completed sheet to show students. Decide how often you will check the logs. You should do so often enough to ensure that students are completing them, but not so frequently as to be overwhelming. For example, once a month can be sufficient.

Procedures

1. Explain the process and show students the sample.
2. Ask students to complete the logs and let them know the due dates.
3. At the due date, review their submitted logs.

Video Lecture	Large Lecture
To use this technique online, provide students with the log as a worksheet. Have them complete it and submit it electronically, according to your preference for student submissions. Alternately have them complete regular quizzes through a course management system.	Ask students to keep their logs in a journal format and turn in periodically. Alternately, similar to video lectures, you can have them complete regular quizzes through a course management system.

Examples

Business Law (Lecture)

The professor of this mid-size business law lecture course recognized that students were having difficulty on the examinations. He felt that students were not studying sufficiently and they did not realize that. He decided to use *Lecture Engagement Logs* to help students start documenting their own work.

Sample *Lecture Engagement Log*		
Module 1: Legal History and Legal Systems		
Name:______________________ Grade on test: ________		
	Dates	**Minutes**
Sample response	January 15 January 17 January 20	20 minutes 15 minutes 15 minutes
Time spent reading homework assignments		
Time spent attending class lecture sessions		
Time spent studying for the test		
Time spent in contact with peers about course-related issues		
Total time studying		

Introduction to Communication Studies (Large Lecture)

The professor of this large lecture course knew the benefits of student participation to student learning and wanted to encourage it. He also wanted to recognize and grade the participation. Over time, however, he realized the difficulty of assessing their participation. He could review documented attendance, and he could see pairs working when he gave assignments. However, he could not listen in on all the groups to assess the quality of individual contribution. Moreover, he did not know what students were doing outside of class. He wanted a better way to assess student engagement and therefore decided to create and use a *Lecture Engagement Log.*

He determined that participation in lecture and discussion, participation in small-group activities, and self-reflection were the most-important components to him. His log focused on these activities and he asked students to log a specific number and kind of engagements across the term. He felt that the log helped him be a better assessor and that it changed his view of students. Rather than seeing a mass of anonymous faces looking at him as he lectured, he started to see students as engaged learners.

Finite Mathematics (Video Lecture)

The professor of this online course believed that students were trying to multitask while working on course activities. During one synchronous session, he even saw a student folding her laundry. The professor knew that trying to multitask was not an efficient or effective way to study. He also believed that some students were not even aware that they were doing it. He suspected, for example, that while watching video lectures, students would also check e-mail or try to shop online. He wanted to alert students of their actions so that they could adjust their own behaviors. He assigned a *Lecture Engagement Log.*

For each lecture that students watched, they were to record how much time they spent reading ahead and how much time they spent thinking of questions. He also asked them to record what other windows were open on their computer while they watched the lectures. Finally he asked them to report how much time they spent reflecting on the activity after class.

Name:
Date:
Record the time spent (rounding to the nearest quarter hour) to prepare for the lecture: _____
Record the activities you engaged in preparing for the lecture:

1.
2.
3.
4.
5.

Record what time you watched video 5: __________________
Record what technology you had access to while watching the lecture. Check all that apply:

__Radio
__MP3
__Phone
__Television
__Social media
__E-mail
__Text

Record the activities you engaged in after the lecture:

____
____

After the first logs came in, the professor noticed a few things that confirmed his suspicions about student engagement behavior:

- Students read assignments, but they did little advanced additional preparation for lectures.
- Students watched the videos very late night or early morning.
- Students had access to many technologies during the lecture.
- Students on the whole did no reflections after the lecture.

The professor decided to add assignments to the next lecture, including a pre-lecture assignment that asked questions to access prior knowledge and helped students focus and also a guided reflection activity for students to complete following the lecture. He also shared with students an article on multitasking and requested that they turn off all but technology necessary for emergency situations during a lecture (i.e., e-mail notifications and phones, unless the student had a child in day care and needed the phone in case of emergency).

He continued implementing the activity throughout the semester and noticed continued improvement. A couple of students even mentioned on the evaluations that drawing their attention to their study habits had been helpful.

Variation and Extension

- Ask students to pair up so that they can compare their participation. Seeing what others are doing can help students improve or augment their own preparation and participation.

Observations and Advice

Learning about the ways in which students do or do not engage in class lectures may be an unwelcome surprise. Think through your response before you report back to the class. Unsupervised, students may forget to complete logs and could be tempted to wait until the last minute. It can be beneficial to check logs periodically.

Key References and Resources

Angelo, T. A., & Cross, K. P. (1993). *Classroom assessment techniques: A handbook for college teachers* (2nd ed.). San Francisco, CA: Jossey-Bass.

Docan-Morgan, T. (2015). The participation log: Assessing students' classroom participation. *Assessment Update, 27*(2). Retrieved from http://catl.typepad.com/files/tdm-f15-cotl.pdf

REFERENCES

Abrams, M. (2012). *Death of the lecture*. Retrieved from www.asme.org/career-education/articles/undergraduate-students/the-death-of-the-lecture/

Aebel, I., & Lund, B. (2013). *Teaching with Twitter*. Retrieved from www.tamuk.edu/cehp/hkn/docs/Twitter.pdf

Aguilar-Roca, N. M., Williams, A. E., & O'Dowd, D. K. (2012). The impact of laptop-free zones on student performance and attitudes in large lectures. *Computers & Education, 59*(4), 1300–1308.

Allain, R. (2017). *The traditional lecture is dead. I would know—I'm a professor*. Retrieved from www.wired.com/2017/05/the-mechanical-universe/

Alsamadani, H. A. (2011). The effects of the 3-2-1 reading strategy on EFL reading comprehension. *English Language Teaching, 4*(3), 184–191. Retrieved from http://files.eric.ed.gov/fulltext/EJ1080738.pdf

Ambrose, S. A., Bridges, M. W., DiPietro, M., Lovett, M. C., & Norman, M. K. (2010). *How learning works: Seven research-based principles for smart teaching*. San Francisco, CA: Jossey-Bass.

American Institutes for Research. (2012). *Teaching excellence in adult literacy: Just write*. Retrieved from https://teal.ed.gov/documents/TEAL_JustWriteGuide.pdf

Andersen, E. (2012). *Leading so people will follow*. San Francisco, CA: Jossey-Bass.

Anderson, L. W., & Krathwohl, D. R. (2001). *A taxonomy for learning, teaching and assessing: A revision of Bloom's taxonomy of educational outcomes* (Complete edition). New York, NY: Longman.

Andrade, H., & Valtcheva, A. (2009). Promoting learning and achievement through self-assessment. *Theory into Practice, 48*, 12–19.

Angelo, T. A., & Cross, K. P. (1993). *Classroom assessment techniques: A handbook for college teachers* (2nd ed.). San Francisco, CA: Jossey-Bass.

Austin, J. L., Lee, M., & Carr, J. P. (2004). The effects of guided notes on undergraduate students' recording of lecture content. *Journal of Instructional Psychology, 31*, 314–320.

Australian Catholic University. (2012). *Strategies for cooperative and collaborative learning in large lecture groups*. Retrieved from www.acu.edu.au/__data/assets/pdf_file/0003/405768/Large_Group_Lectures_LTC.pdf

Ausubel, D. P. (1963). *The psychology of meaningful verbal learning*. New York, NY: Grune & Stratton.

Ausubel, D. P. (1968). *Educational psychology: A cognitive view*. New York, NY: Holt, Rinehart, and Winston.

Axelrod, J., Bloom, B. S., Ginsburg, B. E., O'Meara, W., & Williams, J. C. (1949). *Teaching by discussion in the college program*. Chicago, IL: College of the University of Chicago.

Bajak, A. (2014). *Lectures aren't just boring, they're ineffective too, study finds*. Retrieved from www.sciencemag.org/news/2014/05/lectures-arent-just-boring-theyre-ineffective-too-study-finds

Balch, W. R. (2012). A free-recall demonstration versus a lecture-only control: Learning benefits. *Teaching of Psychology, 39*(1), 34–37.

Barkley, E. F. (2010). *Student engagement techniques: A handbook for college faculty*. San Francisco, CA: Jossey-Bass.

Barkley, E. F., & Major, C. H. (2016). *Learning assessment techniques: A handbook for college faculty*. San Francisco, CA: Jossey-Bass.

Barkley, E. F., Major, C. H., & Cross, K. P. (2014). *Collaborative learning techniques: A resource for college faculty* (2nd ed.). San Francisco, CA: Jossey-Bass.

Barnett, J. E. (2003). Do instructor-provided online notes facilitate student learning? *The Journal of Interactive Online Learning, 2*(2), 1–7. Retrieved from www.ncolr.org/jiol/issues/pdf/2.2.4.pdf

Bartsch, R. A., & Cobern, K. M. (2003). Effectiveness of PowerPoint presentations in lectures. *Computers and Education, 41*(1), 77–78.

Bates, S., & Lister, A. (2013, September 23). Acceptable technology in the classroom. Let the students decide [Web log post]. Retrieved from www.pedagogyunbound.com/tips-index/2013/9/23/acceptable-technology-in-the-classroom-let-students-decide

BBC Active. (2010). *Ten ways to make lectures more dynamic*. Retrieved from www.bbcactive.com/BBCActiveIdeasandResources/Tenwaystomakelecturesmoredynamic.aspx

Berkenkotter, C. (n.d.). *Writing and problem solving*. Retrieved from http://wac.colostate.edu/books/language_connections/chapter3.pdf

Berkun, S. (2013, December 19). How to present well without slides [Web log post]. Retrieved August 31, 2016, from http://scottberkun.com/2013/how-to-present-well-without-slides/

Berman, C. (2011). *Sketchnotes 101: The basics of visual note-taking*. Retrieved from www.core77.com/posts/19678/sketchnotes-101-the-basics-of-visual-note-taking-19678

Beyond Bullets. (2012). *Seeing the speaker's face improves communication*. Retrieved from www.beyondbullets.com/2005/01/face.html

Birnholtz, J., Hancock, J., & Retelny, D. (2013). *Tweeting for class: Co-construction as a means for engaging students in lectures*. Retrieved from http://socialmedia.northwestern.edu/files/2012/09/twitternote_revision_CHI13_130123_camready_a2.pdf

Bligh, D. A. (1999). *What's the use of lectures?* San Francisco, CA: Jossey-Bass.

Bolkan, S., Goodboy, A. K., & Kelsey, D. M. (2016). Instructor clarity and student motivation: Academic performance as a product of students' ability and motivation to process instructional material. *Communication Education, 65*(2), 129–148.

Bonwell, C. C. (1996). Enhancing the lecture: Revitalizing a traditional format. *New Directions for Teaching and Learning, 1996*(67), 31–44.

Bonwell, C. C., & Eison, J. A. (1991). *Active learning: Creating excitement in the classroom*. ASHE-ERIC Higher Education Report No. 1. Washington, DC: The George Washington University, School of Education and Human Development.

Bowen, J. A. (2012). *Teaching naked: How moving technology out of your college classroom will improve student learning*. San Francisco, CA: Jossey-Bass.

Bowman, S. (2001). *Preventing death by lecture! Terrific tips for turning listeners into learners*. Glenbrook, NV: Bowperson.

Boyce, T. E., & Hineline, P. N. (2002). Interteaching: A strategy for enhancing the user-friendliness of behavioral arrangements in the college classroom. *The Behavior Analyst, 25,* 215–226.

Bransford, J., & Johnson, M. (1972). Contextual prerequisites for understanding: Some investigations of comprehension and recall. *Journal of Verbal Learning and Verbal Behavior, 11,* 717–726.

Brassard, M. (1989). *The memory jogger II.* Methuen, MA: Goal/QPC Press.

Braxton, J. M., Bray, N. J., & Berger, J. B. (2000). Faculty teaching skills and their influence on the student departure process. *Journal of College Student Development, 41*(2), 215–226.

Brazeau, G. (2006). Handouts in the classroom: Is note taking a lost skill? *American Journal of Pharmaceutical Education, (70)*2, 1–2.

Broadwell, M. M. (1980). *The lecture method of instruction.* Englewood Cliffs, NJ: Educational Technology.

Brookfield, S. D. (2006). *The skillful teacher: On technique, trust, and responsiveness in the classroom* (2nd ed.). San Francisco, CA: Jossey-Bass.

Brown, G., & Atkins, M. (1988). *Effective teaching in higher education.* London, UK: Routledge.

Bruff, K. (2009). *Teaching with classroom response systems: Creating active learning environments.* San Francisco, CA: Jossey-Bass.

Bruff, D. (2015, September 15). In defense of continuous exposition by the teacher [Web log post]. Retrieved July 11, 2017, from http://derekbruff.org/?p=3126

Bui, D. C., & Myerson, J. (2014). The role of working memory abilities in lecture note-taking. *Learning and Individual Differences, 33,* 12–22.

Bunce, D. M., Flens, E. A., & Neiles, K. Y. (2010). How long can students pay attention in class? A study of student attention decline using clickers. *Journal of Chemical Education, 87*(12), 1438–1443.

Cacciamani, S., Cesareni, D., Martini, F., Ferrini, T., & Fujita, N. (2012). Influence of participation, facilitator styles, and metacognitive reflection on knowledge building in online university courses. *Computers & Education, 58*(3), 874–884.

Carnegie Mellon University, Eberly Center on Teaching Excellence and Educational Innovation. (n.d.a). *Design and teach a course.* Retrieved from www.cmu.edu/teaching/designteach/design/contentschedule.html

Carnegie Mellon University, Eberly Center on Teaching Excellence and Educational Innovation. (n.d.b). *Recognize who your students are.* Retrieved from www.cmu.edu/teaching/designteach/design/yourstudents.html

Cashin, W. E. (2010). *IDEA paper #46: Effective lecturing.* Retrieved from http://ideaedu.org/wp-content/uploads/2014/11/IDEA_Paper_46.pdf

Chen, B., Hirumi, A., & Zhang, N. J. (2007). Investigating the use of advance organizers as an instructional strategy for web-based distance education. *Quarterly Review of Distance Education, 8*(3), 223–231.

Chen, Z., Stelzer, T., & Gladding, G. (2010). Using multimedia modules to better prepare students for introductory physics lecture. *Physical Review Special Topics—Physics Education Research, 6*(1).

Clauss, J., & Geedey, K. (2010). Knowledge survey: Students ability to self-assess. *Journal of the Scholarship of Teaching and Learning, 10*(2), 14–24.

Cohn, E., Cohn, S., & Bradley, J. J. (1995). Note-taking, working memory, and learning in principles of economics. *Research in Economic Education, 26*(4), 291–307.

Cooper, J. L., & Robinson, P. (2000). Getting started: Informal small-group strategies in large classes. *New Directions for Teaching and Learning, 81,* 17–42.

Cooper, J. L., & Robinson, P. (2014). Using classroom assessment and cognitive scaffolding to enhance the power of small-group learning. *Journal on Excellence in College Teaching, 25*(3&4), 149–161.

Cooper, J. L., Robinson, P., & Ball, D. A. (2010). The interactive lecture: Reconciling group and active learning strategies with traditional instructional formats. *Exchanges: The Online Journal of Teaching and Learning in the CSU.* Retrieved from http://web.mit.edu/jrankin/www/Active_Learning/interactive_lectures2.pdf

Cottell, P. G., & Millis, B. (2010). Cooperative learning in accounting. In B. Millis (Ed.), *Cooperative learning in higher education: Across the disciplines, across the academy* (pp. 11–33). Sterling, VA: Stylus Publishing.

Cotton, G. (2013). *Gestures to avoid in cross-cultural business: In other words, keep your fingers to yourself!* Retrieved from www.huffingtonpost.com/gayle-cotton/cross-cultural-gestures_b_3437653.html

Crawford, C. C. (1925). The correlation between college lecture notes and quiz papers. *Journal of Educational Research, 12*(4), 282–291.

Cross, K. P. (1998). *Opening windows on learning: Cross paper number 2.* Mission Viejo, CA: League for Innovation in the Community College.

Crouch, C. H., & Mazur, E. (2001). Peer instruction: Ten years of experience and results. *American Journal of Physics, 69,* 970–977.

Dachner, A. M., & Saxton, B. M. (2014). If you don't care, then why should I? The influence of instructor commitment on student satisfaction and commitment. *Journal of Management Education, 39*(5), 549–571.

Daines, E. (2001). Classroom assessment techniques in the German-for-business course. *Global Business Languages, 6*(2). Retrieved from http://docs.lib.purdue.edu/gbl/vol6/iss1/2

Dallimore, E. J., Hertenstein, J. H., & Platt, M. B. (2006). Nonvoluntary class participation in graduate discussion courses: Effects on grading and cold calling. *Journal of Management Education, 30*(2), 354–377.

Davidson, N., & Major, C. H. (2014). Boundary crossing: Cooperative learning, collaborative learning, and problem-based learning. *Journal on Excellence in College Teaching, 25*(3&4), 7–55.

Davis, B. G. (1993). *Tools for teaching.* San Francisco, CA: Jossey-Bass.

Davis, B. G. (2009). *Tools for teaching* (2nd ed.). San Francisco, CA: Jossey Bass.

Dawson, P. (2016). *Are lectures a good way to learn?* Retrieved from www.theedadvocate.org/lectures-good-way-learn/

Deslauriers, L., Schelew, E., & Wieman, C. (2011). Improved learning in a large enrollment physics class. *Science, 33,* 862. Retrieved from www.math.umn.edu/mctp/gstts/science.pdf

DiVesta, F. J., & Smith, D. A. (1979). The pausing principle: Increasing the efficiency of memory for ongoing events. *Contemporary Educational Psychology, 4,* 288–296.

Dlugan, A. (2012). *What is the average speaking rate?* Retrieved from http://sixminutes.dlugan.com/speaking-rate/

Docan-Morgan, T. (2015). The participation log: Assessing students' classroom participation. *Assessment Update, 27*(2). Retrieved from http://catl.typepad.com/files/tdm-f15-cotl.pdf

Doran, G. T. (1981). There's a S.M.A.R.T. way to write management's goals and objectives. *Management Review, 70*(11), 35–36.

Doymus, K., Karacop, A., & Simsek, U. (2010). Effects of jigsaw and animation techniques on students' understanding of concepts and subjects in electrochemistry. *Educational Technology Research and Development, 58*(6), 671–691.

Dubas, J. M., & Toledo, S. A. (2015). Active reading documents (ARDs): A tool to facilitate meaningful learning through reading. *College Teaching, 63*(1), 27–33.

Duffelmeyer, F. (1994). Effective anticipation guide statements for learning from expository prose. *Journal of Reading, 37,* 452–455.

Duke University, Center for Instructional Technology. (n.d.). *Lecture busters: Keeping students engaged.* Retrieved from https://mclibrary.duke.edu/sites/mclibrary.duke.edu/files/public/research/lecturebusters.pdf

Dunbar, K. N., Fugelsang, J. A., & Stein, C. (2007). Do naïve theories ever go away? Using brain and behavior to understand changes in concepts. In M. C. Lovett & P. Shah (Eds.), *Thinking with data: 33rd Carnegie Symposium on Cognition* (pp. 193–205). Mahwah, NJ: Erlbaum.

Duncan, D. K. (2005). *Clickers in the classroom*. New York, NY: Pearson/Addison-Wesley.

Eagan, M. K., Stolzenberg, E. B., Berdan Lozano, J., Aragon, M. C., Suchard, M. R., & Hurtado, S. (2014). *Undergraduate teaching faculty: The 2013–2014 HERI faculty survey*. Retrieved from http://heri.ucla.edu/monographs/HERI-FAC2014-monograph.pdf

Ebert-May, D., Derting, T. L., Hodder, J., Momsen, J. L., Long, T. M., & Jardeleza, S. E. (2011). What we say is not what we do: Effective evaluation of faculty professional development programs. *BioScience, 61*(7), 550–558. Retrieved from https://bioscience.oxfordjournals.org/content/61/7/550.full.pdf

Edgerton, R. (2001). *Education white paper*. Washington, DC: Pew Charitable Trusts, Pew Forum on Undergraduate Learning.

Edutopia. (2016). Using the rule of three for learning [Web log post]. Retrieved August 22, 2016, from www.edutopia.org/blog/using-rule-three-learning-ben-johnson

Eison, J. (2010). *Using active learning instructional strategies to create excitement and enhance learning*. Retrieved from www.cte.cornell.edu/documents/presentations/Eisen-Handout.pdf

El-Shamy, S. (2004). *How to design and deliver training for the new and emerging generations*. San Francisco, CA: Pfeiffer.

Evans, C. (2013). Twitter for teaching: Can social media be used to enhance the process of learning? *British Journal of Educational Technology, 45*, 902–915.

Exley, K., & Dennick, R. (2004). *Giving a lecture: From presenting to teaching*. New York, NY: Routledge Falmer.

Fagen, A., Crouch, C. H., & Mazur, E. (2003). Peer instruction: Results from a range of classrooms. *The Physics Teacher, 40*, 206–209.

Farley, J., Risko, E. F., & Kingstone, A. (2013). Everyday attention and lecture retention: The effects of time, fidgeting, and mind wandering. *Frontiers in Psychology, 4*, 619.

Feeney-Hart, A. (2014). *Top 10 tips for being a weather presenter*. Retrieved from www.bbc.com/news/entertainment-arts-30180596

Felten, P. (2014). *Is there a place for lecture in engaged learning?* Retrieved from www.centerforengagedlearning.org/is-there-a-place-for-lecture-in-engaged-learning/

Fengjuan, Z. (2010). The integration of the know-want-learn (KWL) strategy into English language teaching for non-English majors. *Chinese Journal of Applied Linguistics, 33*(4), 77–127. Retrieved from http://218.4.189.15:8090/download/9b1c7bc7-e2b2–40ea-b8b6–42be6b38f911.pdf

Fink, L. D. (2013). *Creating significant learning experiences: An integrated approach to designing college courses*. San Francisco, CA: Jossey-Bass.

Finley, T. (2014). *Dipsticks: Efficient ways to check for understanding*. Retrieved from www.edutopia.org/blog/dipsticks-to-check-for-understanding-todd-finley

Fisher, D., & Frey, N. (2011). *Improving adolescent literacy: Strategies at work* (3rd ed.). Upper Saddle River, NJ: Pearson.

Fitch, M. L., Drucker, A. J., & Norton, J. A. (1951). Frequent testing as a motivating factor in large lecture classes. *The Journal of Educational Psychology, 42(*1), 1–20.

Fjortoft, N. (2005). Students' motivations for class attendance. *American Journal of Pharmaceutical Education, 69*, 107–112.

Flavell, J. H. (1976). Metacognitive aspects of problem solving. In L. B. Resnick (Ed.), *The nature of intelligence* (pp. 231–236). Hillsdale, NJ: Erlbaum.

Flavell, J. H. (1979). Metacognition and cognitive monitoring: A new area of cognitive-developmental inquiry. *American Psychologist, 34*, 906–911.

Ford, N., McCullough, M., & Schutta, N. T. (2012). *Presentation patterns: Techniques for crafting better presentations*. Boston, MA: Addison Wesley.

Fowler, M. (2012a). *The future is not just NoSQL, it's polyglot persistence*. Retrieved from https://dzone.com/articles/polyglot-persistence-future

Fowler, M. (2012b). *Infodeck*. Retrieved from http://martinfowler.com/bliki/Infodeck.html

Fraser, B. J., Treagust, D. F., & Dennis, N. C. (1996). Development of an instrument for assessing classroom psychosocial environment at universities and colleges. *Studies in Higher Education, 11*(1), 43–53.

Frederick, P. (1981). The dreaded discussion: Ten ways to start. *College Teaching, 29,* 109–114.

Freeman, S., Eddy, S. L., McDonough, M., Smith, M. K., Okoroafor, N., Jordt, H., & Wenderoth, M. P. (2014). Active learning increases student performance in science, engineering, and mathematics. *Proceedings of the National Academy of Sciences, 111*(23). Retrieved from www.pnas.org/content/111/23/8410

Freire, P. (1968). *Pedagogy of the oppressed.* New York, NY: Continuum.

Friedman, M. C. (n.d.). *Notes on note-taking: Review of research and insights for students and instructors.* Retrieved from http://hilt.harvard.edu/files/hilt/files/notetaking_0.pdf

Furnham, A., & Yazdanpanahi, T. (1995). Personality differences and group versus individual brainstorming. *Personality and Individual Differences, 19,* 73–80.

Gabriel, Y. (2008). Against the tyranny of PowerPoint: Technology-in-use and technology abuse. *Organization Studies, 29*(2), 255–276.

Garside, C. (1996). Look who's talking: A comparison of lecture and group discussion teaching strategies in developing critical thinking skills. *Communication Education, 45,* 212.

Gasper-Hulvat, M. (2017). Active learning in art history: A review of formal literature. *Art History Pedagogy & Practice, 2*(1). Retrieved from http://academicworks.cuny.edu/ahpp/vol2/iss1/2

Gaynor, J., & Millham, J. (1976). Student performance and evaluation under variant teaching and testing methods in a large college course. *Journal of Educational Psychology, 68,* 312–317.

Gillet, A. (2015). Using English for academic purposes: A guide for students in higher education. Retrieved from www.uefap.com/listen/struct/liststru.htm#emphasis

Glass, A. L. (2009). The effect of distributed questioning with varied examples on exam performance on inference questions. *Educational Psychology, 29,* 831–848.

Glonek, K. L., & King, P. E. (2014). Listening to narratives: An experimental examination of storytelling in the classroom. *International Journal of Listening, 28*(1), 32–46.

Godin, S. (2001). *Really bad PowerPoints.* Retrieved from www.sethgodin.com/freeprize/reallybad-1.pdf

Goffe, W. L., & Kauper, D. (2014). A survey of principles instructors: Why lecture prevails. *Journal of Economic Education, 45*(4), 360–375.

Goldsmith, P. (2006). Learning to understand inequality and diversity: Getting students past ideologies. *Teaching Sociology, 34,* 263–277.

Gooblar, D. (2013a, August 13). Give your students a pause button [Web log post]. Retrieved August 31, 2016, from www.pedagogyunbound.com/tips-index/?category=Effective+Lecturing

Gooblar, D. (2013b, September 13). Help your students stay awake in class [Web log post]. Retrieved August 31, 2016, from www.pedagogyunbound.com/tips-index/2013/9/12/help-your-students-stay-awake-in-class?rq=truck

Gooblar, D. (2013c). Lecture map. *Pedagogy Unbound.* Retrieved from www.pedagogyunbound.com/tips-index/2013/8/23/make-a-lecture-map-to-help-students-follow

Gooblar, D. (2014). *Smartphones in the classroom? Let students decide.* Retrieved from https://chroniclevitae.com/news/289-smartphones-in-the-classroom-let-students-decide

Good, C. V., & Merkel, W. R. (1959). *Dictionary of education* (2nd ed.). New York, NY: McGraw-Hill.

Grabowski, P. (2016, January 28). How to deliver an unforgettable pitch by finding your presentation style [Web log post]. Retrieved August 18, 2016, from https://attach.io/blog/deliver-an-unforgettable-pitch-by-finding-your-presentation-style/

Grant Thornton International. (2015). *Women in business: The value of diversity.* Retrieved from www.grantthornton.global/globalassets/wib_value_of_diversity.pdf

Gross-Loh, C. (2016). Should colleges really eliminate the college lecture? *The Atlantic*. Retrieved from www.theatlantic.com/education/archive/2016/07/eliminating-the-lecture/491135/

Guskey, T. R. (2007). Multiple sources of evidence: An analysis of stakeholders' perceptions of various indicators of student learning. *Educational Measurement: Issues and Practice, 26*(1), 19–27.

Hackathorn, J., Solomon, E. D., Blankmeyer, K. L., Tennial, R. E., & Garczynski, A. M. (2011). Learning by doing: An empirical study of active teaching techniques. *The Journal of Effective Teaching, 11*(2), 40–54.

Hackathorn, J., Solomon, E. D., Tennial, R. E., Garczynski, A. M., Blankmeyer, K., Gebhardt, K., & Anthony, J. N. (2010). You get out what you put in: Student engagement affects assessment. Poster presented at Best Practices in Assessment Conference, Atlanta, GA.

Hake, R. R. (1998). Interactive-engagement versus traditional methods: A six-thousand-student survey of mechanics test data for introductory physics courses. *American Journal of Physics, 66*(1), 64–74. doi: 10.1119/1.18809

Harp, S. F., & Maslich, A. A. (2005). The consequences of including seductive details during lecture. *Teaching of Psychology, 32*(2), 100–103.

Harvard Magazine. (2013). Chapter and verse. Correspondence on not-so-famous lost words. Retrieved from http://harvardmagazine.com/2013/01/chapter-and-verse

Harvey, S., & Goudvis, A. (2007). *Strategies that work: Teaching comprehension for understanding and engagement* (2nd ed.). Portland, ME: Stenhouse.

Hattenberg, S. J., & Steffy, K. (2013). Increasing reading compliance of undergraduates: An evaluation of compliance methods. *Teaching Sociology, 41*(4), 346–352.

Hattie, J. (2011). *Visible learning: A synthesis of over 800 meta-analyses relating to achievement*. New York, NY: Routledge.

Hattie, J. (2016). *Learning strategies: A synthesis and conceptual model*. Retrieved from www.nature.com/articles/npjscilearn201613

Health Education and Training Institute. (2012). *The learning guide: A handbook for allied health professionals facilitating learning in the workplace*. Sydney, Australia: HETI. Retrieved from www.heti.nsw.gov.au/

Heller, R. (2002). *High-impact speeches: How to create and deliver words that move minds*. London, UK: Prentice Hall Business.

Hembrooke, H., & Gay, G. (2003). The laptop and the lecture: The effects of multitasking in learning environments. *Journal of Computing in Higher Education, 15*, 1–19.

Henningsen, D. D., & Henningsen, M. L. M. (2013). Generating ideas about the uses of brainstorming: Reconsidering the losses and gains of brainstorming groups relative to nominal groups. *Southern Communication Journal, 78*(1), 42–55.

Heuston, S. (2013). Trucker tips: Helping students stay awake in class. *College Teaching, 61*(3), 108.

Heward, W. L. (2001). *Guided notes: Improving the effectiveness of your lectures*. Columbus, OH: The Ohio State University Partnership Grant for Improving the Quality of Education for Students with Disabilities. Retrieved from http://ada.osu.edu/resources/fastfacts/

Hirschy, A. S., & Braxton, J. M. (2004). Effects of student classroom incivilities on students. *New Directions for Teaching and Learning, 2004*(9), 67–76.

Historical Scene Investigation. (n.d.). *Interactive notation system for effective reading and thinking*. Retrieved from www.hsionline.org/cases/anthony/InsertReadngActivity%20.pdf

Hodgson, V. (1984). Learning from lectures. In F. Marton, D. Hounsell, & N. Entwistle (Eds.), *The experiences of learning* (pp. 90–102). Edinburgh, Scotland: Scottish Academic Press.

Hora, M. (2015). Toward a descriptive science of teaching: How the TDOP illuminates the multidimensional nature of active learning in postsecondary classrooms. *Science Education, 99*(5), 783–818. Retrieved from http://onlinelibrary.wiley.com/doi/10.1002/sce.21175/abstract

Hrepic, Z. (2007). Utilizing DyKnow software and pen-based, wireless computing in teaching introductory modern physics. In *Proceedings of 30th Jubilee International Convention MIPRO, Conference on Computers in Education,* May 22–26, Opatija, Croatia.

Hrepic, Z., Zollman, D., & Rebello, N. (2007). Comparing students' and experts' understanding of the content of a lecture. *Journal of Science Education and Technology, 16*(3), 213–224.

Hrynchak, P., & Batty, H. (2012). The educational theory basis of team-based learning. *Medical Teacher, 34,* 796–801.

Huffman, L. E. (1998). Combine focus questions (5 W and 1 H) with K-W-L. *Journal of Adolescent & Adult Literacy, 41*(6), 470–472.

Hunter, M. (1982). *Mastery teaching: Increasing instructional effectiveness in secondary schools, colleges, and universities.* El Segundo, CA: TIP Publications.

Illinois State University, College of Education. (n.d.). *Revised Bloom's taxonomy question starters.* Retrieved from https://education.illinoisstate.edu/downloads/casei/5-02-Revised%20Blooms.pdf

Jensen, E. (2008). A call for professional attire. *Inside Higher Ed.* Retrieved from www.insidehighered.com/views/2008/02/08/call-professional-attire

Jensen, E., & Davidson, N. (1997). 12-step recovery program for lectureholics. *College Teaching, 45,* 102–103.

Johnson, A. (n.d.). *Good handout design: How to make sure your students are actually learning from your lecture notes.* Retrieved from www.pcc.edu/resources/tlc/cascade/documents/PCCHandouts_handout.pdf

Johnson, D. W., Johnson, R., & Smith, K. (1998). *Active learning: Cooperation in the college classroom.* Edina, MN: Interaction Book Company.

Johnson, D. W., Johnson, R. T., & Smith, K. (2014). Cooperative learning: Improving university instruction by basing practice on validated theory. In N. Davidson, C. Major, & L. Michaelsen (Eds.), Small-group learning in higher education: Cooperative, collaborative, problem-based and team-based learning. *Journal on Excellence in College Teaching, 25*(3–4), 85–118.

Jones, J. M. (2014). Discussion group effectiveness is related to critical thinking through interest and engagement. *Psychology Learning and Teaching, 13*(1), 12–24.

Kamanetz, A. (2015). How to get students to stop using their cellphones in class. *National Public Radio.* Retrieved from www.npr.org/sections/ed/2015/11/10/453986816/how-to-get-students-to-stop-using-their-cellphones-in-class

Karacop, A., & Doymus, K. (2013). Effects of jigsaw cooperative learning and animation techniques on students' understanding of chemical bonding and their conceptions of the particulate nature of matter. *Journal of Science Education and Technology, 22*(2), 186–203.

Karen L. Smith Faculty Center for Teaching and Learning. (n.d.). *Interactive techniques.* Retrieved from www.fctl.ucf.edu/teachingandlearningresources/coursedesign/assessment/content/101_tips.pdf

Kauffman, D. F., Ge, X., Xie, K., & Chen, C. (2008). Prompting in web-based environments: Supporting self-monitoring and problem solving skills in college students. *Journal of Educational Computing Research, 38*(2), 115–137.

Keough, S. M. (2012). Clickers in the classroom: A review and replication. *Journal of Management Education, 36*(6), 822–847.

King, A. (1993). From sage on a stage to guide on the side. *College Teaching, 41*(1), 3–35.

King, R. (1989). *Hoshin planning: The developmental approach.* Methuen, MA: Goal/QPC Press.

Kirschner, P. A., Sweller, J., & Clark, R. E. (2006). Why minimal guidance during instruction does not work: An analysis of the failure of constructivist discovery, problem-based, experiential, and inquiry-based teaching. *Educational Psychologist, 41*(2), 75–86.

Kobayashi, K. (2006). Combined effects of note-taking/-reviewing on learning and the enhancement through interventions: A meta-analytical review. *Educational Psychology, 26,* 459–477.

Komarraju, M., & Karau, S. J. (2008). Relationships between the perceived value of instructional techniques and academic motivation. *Journal of Instructional Psychology, 35*(1), 70–82.

Kraushaar, J. M., & Novak, D. C. (2010). Examining the affects of student multitasking with laptops during the lecture. *Journal of Information Systems Education, 21*(2), 241–251.

Lambert, C. (2012). *Twilight of the lecture*. Retrieved from http://harvardmagazine.com/2012/03/twilight-of-the-lecture

Lang, J. M. (2005). Looking like a professor. *Chronicle of Higher Education, 51*(47). Retrieved from http://old.biz.colostate.edu/mti/tips/pages/LookingLikeaProfessor.aspx

Larsy, N. (n.d.). *Peer instruction: Comparing clickers to flashcards*. Retrieved from http://arxiv.org/pdf/physics/0702186.pdf

Lemov, D. (2010). *Teach like a champion: 49 strategies that put students on the path to success*. San Francisco, CA: Jossey-Bass.

Lewis, A., & Thompson, A. (2010). *Quick summarizing strategies for use in the classroom*. Retrieved from www.gcasd.org/Downloads/Summarizing_Strategies.pdf

Light, G., & Cox, R. (2001). *Learning and teaching in higher education: The reflective professional*. London, UK: Paul Chapman.

Linkedin Slide Share. (2014). *TED Talk takeaways: 8 ways to hook your audience*. Retrieved from https://blog.slideshare.net/2014/07/30/set-your-hook-to-capture-your-audience

Lipton, L., & Wellman, B. (1999). *Pathways to understanding: Patterns and practices in the learning focused classroom*. Guildford, VT: Pathways Publishing.

Loes, C. N., & Pascarella, E. T. (2015). The benefits of good teaching extend beyond course achievement. *Journal of the Scholarship of Teaching and Learning, 15*(2), 1–13.

London Deanery. (2012). *Improve your lecturing*. Retrieved from www.faculty.londondeanery.ac.uk/e-learning/improve-your-lecturing-1/structure

Longfield, J. (2009). Discrepant teaching events: Using an inquiry stance to address students' misconceptions. *International Journal of Teaching and Learning in Higher Education, 21*(2), 266–271.

Los Angeles Valley College. (n.d.). *Active learning strategies: Quick thinks*. Retrieved from www.lavc.edu/profdev/library/docs/quickthinks.aspx

Lovett, M. C. (2008, January 29). *Teaching metacognition*. Presentation at Educause Learning Initiative Conference. Retrieved from https://net.educause.edu/upload/presentations/eli081/fs03/metacognition-eli.pdf

Luo, L., Kiewra, K. A., & Samuelson, L. (2016). Revising lecture notes: How revision, pauses, and partners affect note taking and achievement. *Instructional Science: An International Journal of the Learning Sciences, 44*(1), 45–67.

Lyman, F. (1981). The responsive classroom discussion. In A. S. Anderson (Ed.), *Mainstreaming digest*. College Park, MD: University of Maryland, College of Education.

Lyman, F. T. (1992). Think-pair-share, thinktrix, thinklinks, and weird facts: An interactive system for cooperative learning. In N. Davidson & T. Worsham (Eds.), *Enhancing thinking through cooperative learning* (pp. 169–181). New York, NY: Teachers College Press.

Macdonald, R. H., Manduca, C. A., Mogk, D. W., & Tewksbury, B. J. (2005). Teaching methods in undergraduate geoscience courses: Results of the 2004 On the Cutting Edge Survey of U.S. faculty. *Journal of Geoscience Education, 53*(3), 237–252.

Maden, S. (2010). The effect of jigsaw IV on the achievement of course of language teaching methods and techniques. *Educational Research and Reviews, 5*(12), 770–776.

Magnan, R. (1990). *147 practical tips for teaching professors*. Madison, WI: Atwood.

Maier, M. H. (2016). Rotating note taker. *College Teaching, 64*(3), 148.

Major, C. H., Harris, M., & Zakrajsek, T. (2015). *Teaching for learning: 101 techniques to put students on the path to success*. New York, NY: Routledge.

Marrs, K. A., & Novak, G. (2004). Just-in-time teaching in biology: Creating an active learner classroom using the internet. *Cell Biology Education, 3*(1), 49–61.

Marzano, R., Pickering, D., & Pollock, J. (2001). *Classroom instruction that works: Research-based strategies for increasing student achievement.* Alexandria, VA: Association for Supervision and Curriculum Development.

Mathematics Association of America. (2013). *Insights and recommendations.* Retrieved from www.maa.org/sites/default/files/pdf/cspcc/InsightsandRecommendations.pdf

Mayer, R. E. (2017). *Principles for learning from multimedia with Richard Mayer.* Retrieved from https://hilt.harvard.edu/blog/principles-multimedia-learning-richard-e-mayer

Mazur, E. (1997). *Peer instruction: A user's manual.* Upper Saddle River, NJ: Prentice Hall.

McDaniel, M. A., Anderson, J. L., Derbish, M. H., & Morrisette, N. (2007). Testing the testing effect in the classroom. *European Journal of Cognitive Psychology, 19,* 494–513.

McDaniel, M. A., Roediger, H. L., & McDermott, K. B. (2007). Generalizing test-enhanced learning from the laboratory to the classroom. *Psychonomic Bulletin & Review, 14,* 200–206.

McDaniel, R. (n.d.). *Wireless in the classroom.* Retrieved from https://cft.vanderbilt.edu/guides-sub-pages/wireless/

McDermott, L. C., & Redish, E. F. (1999). Resource letter: PER-1: Physics education research. *American Journal of Physics, 67*(9), 755–767.

McLaughlin, M. (2015). *Content area reading: Teaching and learning for college and career readiness.* Upper Saddle River, NJ: Pearson.

McLean, S. (2012). Emphasis strategies. *Communications for business success.* Retrieved from https://2012books.lardbucket.org/pdfs/communication-for-business-success-canadian-edition.pdf

Mello, D., & Less, C. A. (2013). Effectiveness of active learning in the arts and sciences. *Humanities Department Faculty Publications and Research,* Paper 45.

Michael, J. (2006). Where's the evidence that active learning works? *Advances in Physiology Education, 30,* 159–167.

Michaelsen, L. K., Davidson, N., & Major, C. H. (2014). Team-based learning practices and principles in comparison with cooperative learning and problem-based learning. *Journal on Excellence in College Teaching, 25*(3/4), 57–84.

Middendorf, J., & Kalish, A. (1996). The "change-up" in lectures. *National Teaching and Learning Forum, 5*(2), 1–5.

Millis, B. J., & Cottell, P. G. (1998). *Cooperative learning for higher education faculty.* American Council on Education. Phoenix, AZ: Oryx Press.

MindTools. (n.d.). *Brainstorming: Generating many radical, creative ideas.* Retrieved from www.mindtools.com/brainstm.html

Mintz, S. (n.d.). *Gender issues in the college classroom.* Retrieved from www.columbia.edu/cu/tat/pdfs/gender.pdf

Missouri State University. (2014). *Cornell note-taking* [brochure]. Retrieved from www.missouristate.edu/assets/busadv2014/p.22–23.pdf

Mitkis, J. (2009). *The use of classroom handouts.* Retrieved from www.westpoint.edu/cfe/Literature/Mikits_09.pdf

Moravec, M., Williams, A., Aguilar-Roca, N., & O'Dowd, D. K. (2010). Learn before lecture: A strategy that improves learning outcomes in a large introductory biology class. *CBE—Life Sciences Education, 9*(4), 473–481.

Morgan, N. (2011). 10 things to do instead of PowerPoint. *Forbes.* Retrieved from www.forbes.com/sites/nickmorgan/2011/06/13/10-things-to-do-instead-of-power-point/#39f7ad182ca7

Morgan, N. (2013). How to avoid disaster: Six rules for what to wear when giving a speech. *Forbes.* Retrieved from www.forbes.com/sites/nickmorgan/2013/12/05/how-to-avoid-disaster-six-rules-for-what-to-wear-when-giving-a-speech/#2c5dd6022dce

Morrow, J. (2012). *Do guided notes improve student performance?* Retrieved from www.westpoint.edu/cfe/Literature/Morrow_12.pdf

Moukperian, S., & Woloshyn, V. (2013). The learning strategist teaches first-year undergraduates: Embedding learning strategies and metacognitive dialogue into course content. *Universal Journal of Educational Research, 1*(2), 96–103.

Mueller, P. A., & Oppenheimer, D. M. (2014). The pen is mightier than the keyboard: Advantages of longhand over laptop note taking. *Psychological Science, 25*(6), 1159.

Murray, M. H. (1997). Better learning through curricular design at a reduced cost. *The Research Journal for Engineering Education, 86*(4), 309–313.

National Survey of Student Engagement. (2015). *Annual results.* Retrieved from http://nsse.indiana.edu/html/annual_results.cfm

Nevid, J. S., & Mahon, K. (2009). Mastery quizzing as a signaling device to cue attention to lecture material. *Teaching of Psychology, 36*(1), 29–32.

Newman, J. H. (1852). Discourse 6: Knowledge viewed in relation to learning. *Idea of the University.* Retrieved from www.newmanreader.org/works/idea/discourse6.html

New York University. (n.d.). *Twitter explained.* Retrieved from www.nyu.edu/content/dam/nyu/studentAffairs/images/Explained/twitter/pdf

Nicol, D. J., & Macfarlane-Dick, D. (2006). Formative assessment and self-regulated learning: A model and seven principles of good feedback practice. *Studies in Higher Education, 31*(2), 199–218.

Nilson, L. B. (2010). *Teaching at its best: A research-based resource for college instructors* (3rd ed.). San Francisco, CA: Jossey-Bass.

Nouri, H., & Shahid, A. (2008). The effects and PowerPoint lecture notes on student performance and attitudes. *The Accounting Educators' Journal, 18,* 103–107.

Novak, G. M., Patterson, E. T., Gavrin, A. D., & Christian, W. (1999). *Just-in-time-teaching: Blending active learning with web technology.* Upper Saddle River, NJ: Prentice Hall.

Nuhfer, E. B., & Knipp, D. (2003). The knowledge survey: A tool for all reasons. *To Improve the Academy, 21,* 59–78. Retrieved from http://pachyderm.cdl.edu/elixr-stories/resource-documents/knowledge-survey/KS_a_too_for_all_reasons.pdf

Ogle, D. M. (1986). K-W-L: A teaching model that develops active reading of expository text. *Reading Teacher, 39*(6), 564–570.

Osborn, A. F. (1963). *Applied imagination: Principles and procedures of creative problem solving* (3rd ed.). New York, NY: Charles Scribner's Sons.

Oxford Dictionary. (n.d.). Lecture. Retrieved from https://en.oxforddictionaries.com/definition/lecture

Paff, L., Weimer, M., Haave, N., & Lovitt, C. (2016). *The lecture vs. active learning debate.* Plenary Panel Presentation. Teaching Professor Annual Conference, Washington, DC.

Page, M. (1990). *Active learning: Historical and contemporary perspectives* (Unpublished doctoral dissertation). University of Massachusetts, Amherst, MA.

Parry, D. (2008, January 23). Twitter for academia [Blog post]. Retrieved from http://academhack.outsidethetext.com/home/2008/twitter-for-academia/

Pascarella, E. T., Edison, M., Nora, A., Hagedorn, L. S., & Terenzini, P. T. (1996). Influences on student's openness to diversity and challenges in the first year of college. *Journal of Higher Education, 67*(2), 178–195.

Pastötter, B., & Bäuml, K. H. (2014). Retrieval practice enhances new learning: The forward effect of testing. *Frontiers in Psychology: Cognitive Science, 5,* Article 286.

Pate, A. G. (2015). *Tweeting during lectures/tutorials: Engaging learners-not clipping their wings.* Retrieved from www.gla.ac.uk/media/media_309215_en.pdf

Pauk, W. (2001). *How to study in college* (7th ed.). Boston, MA: Houghton Mifflin.

Paul, A. M. (2015). Are college lectures unfair? Sunday Review. *New York Times.* Retrieved from www.nytimes.com/2015/09/13/opinion/sunday/are-college-lectures-unfair.html?_r=0

Perret, K. (2012, March 21). Think-pair-share variations [Web log post]. Retrieved July 27, 2017, from www.kathyperret.net/2012/03/think-pair-share-variations/

Piskurich, G. M. (2015). *Rapid instructional design: Learning ID fast and right.* Hoboken, NJ: John Wiley & Sons.

Presenter News. (2014). *Use a blank slide for a powerful presentation.* Retrieved from https://presenternews.wordpress.com/2014/06/16/use-a-blank-slide-for-a-powerful-presentation/

Prince, M. (2004). Does active learning work? A review of the research. *Journal of Engineering Education, 93*(3), 223–231.

Pundak, D., Herscovitz, O., Shacham, M., & Wiser-Biton, R. (2009). Instructors' attitude towards active learning. *Interdisciplinary Journal of E-Learning and Learning Objects, 5,* 215–232.

Raver, S. A., & Maydosz, A. S. (2010). Impact of the provision and timing of instructor-provided notes on university students' learning. *Active Learning in Higher Education, 11*(3), 189–200.

The Regents of the University of Minnesota. (2006). *Effective lecture preparation and delivery.* Reprinted by Washington State University Graduate School. Retrieved from https://gradschool.wsu.edu/effective-lecture-preparation-and-delivery/

Reisberg, D. (1997). *Cognition: Exploring the science of the mind.* New York, NY: Norton.

Resnick, L. B. (1983). Mathematics and science learning: A new conception. *Science, 220,* 477–478.

Reynolds, G. (2005, February 3). Keep the lights on [Web log post]. Retrieved August 31, 2016, from www.presentationzen.com/presentationzen/2005/02/keep_the_lights.html

Reynolds, G. (2009, May 12). Making presentations in the TED style [Web log post]. Retrieved August 31, 2016, from www.presentationzen.com/presentationzen/2009/05/making-presentations-in-the-ted-style.html

Reynolds, G. (2016). *Top ten delivery tips.* Retrieved from www.garrreynolds.com/preso-tips/deliver/

Reynolds, G. (n.d.). *Presentation zen: How to design & deliver presentations like a pro.* Retrieved from www.garrreynolds.com/Presentation/pdf/presentation_tips.pdf

Risko, E. F., Anderson, N., Sarwal, A., Engelhardt, M., & Kingstone, A. (2012). Everyday attention: Variation in mind wandering and memory in a lecture. *Applied Cognitive Psychology, 26,* 234–242.

Robinson, S. (2013). *Beware of the SLIDEUMENT!* Retrieved from www.slideshare.net/SheilaBRobinson/unconventional-wisdom-26429659/43-Beware_the_SLIDEUMENT_This_is

Roediger, H. L., Putnam, A. L., & Smith, M. A. (2011). Ten benefits of testing and their applications to educational practice. In J. Mestre & B. Ross (Eds.), *Psychology of learning and motivation: Cognition in education* (pp. 1–36). Oxford, UK: Elsevier.

Rohde, M. (n.d.). *The sketchnote handbook.* Retrieved from http://rohdesign.com/book/

Ronchetti, M. (2010). Using video lectures to make teaching more interactive. *International Journal of Emerging Technologies in Learning, 5*(2). doi: 10.3991/ijet.v5i2.1156

Rosegard, E., & Wilson, J. (2013). Capturing students' attention: An empirical study. *Journal of the Scholarship of Teaching and Learning, 13*(5), 1–20.

Rowe, M. B. (1987). Wait time: Slowing down may be a way of speeding up. *American Educator, 11*(1), 38–43.

Santa, C., Havens, L., & Valdes, B. (2004). *Project CRISS: Creating independence through student-owned strategies.* Dubuque, IA: Kendall Hunt.

Santa Clara University, Office of the Provost. (n.d.). *Mini-lectures.* Retrieved from www.scu.edu/provost/teaching-and-learning/digital-resources-for-teaching-drt/teaching/mini-lectures/

Sarma, R. (2015). *Guest lecture to biomed department.* Retrieved from http://slideplayer.com/slide/4716954/

Saville, B. K., Bureau, A., Eckenrode, C., Fullerton, A., Herbert, R., Maley, M., Porter, A., & Zombakis, J. (2014). Interteaching and lecture: A comparison of long-term recognition memory. *Teaching of Psychology, 41,* 325–329.

Saville, B. K., Zinn, T. E., & Elliott, M. P. (2005). Interteaching versus traditional methods of instruction: A preliminary analysis. *Teaching of Psychology, 32,* 161–163.

Saville, B. K., Zinn, T. E., Neef, N. A., Norman, R. V., & Ferreri, S. J. (2006). A comparison of interteaching and lecture in the college classroom. *Journal of Applied Behavior Analysis, 39,* 49–61.

Scerbo, M. W., Warm, J. S., Dember, W. N., & Grasha, A. F. (1992). The role of time and cuing in a college lecture. *Contemporary Educational Psychology, 17,* 312–328.

Schwartz, D., & Bransford, J. (1998). A time for telling. *Cognition and Instruction, 16*(4), 475–522.

Segal, J., Smith, M., & Boose, G. (2017). *Nonverbal communication: Improving your nonverbal skills and reading body language.* Retrieved from www.helpguide.org/articles/relationships/nonverbal-communication.htm

Segesten, A. D. (2012). Death of the lecture. *Inside Higher Education.* Retrieved from www.insidehighered.com/blogs/university-venus/death-lecture

Short, F., & Martin, J. (2011). Presentation vs. performance: Effects of lecturing style in higher education on student preference and student learning. *Psychology Teaching Review, 17*(2), 71–82.

Sidman, C. L., & Jones, D. (2007). Addressing students' learning styles through skeletal PowerPoint slides: A case study. *Journal of Online Learning and Teaching, 3*(4). Retrieved from http://jolt.merlot.org/vol3no4/sidman.htm

Silberman, M. (1995). *101 ways to make training active.* Johannesburg, South Africa: Pfeiffer.

Silberman, M. (1996). *Active learning: 101 strategies to teach any subject.* Upper Saddle River, NJ: Pearson.

Silver, H. F., & Perini, M. J. (2010). *The interactive lecture: How to engage students, build memory, and deepen comprehension.* Alexandria, VA: Association for Supervision and Curriculum Development .

Singh, C. (2006). *Introduction to educational technology.* Darya Ganj, New Delhi, India: Lotus Press.

Slide Comet. (n.d.). *Presentation design techniques.* Retrieved from http://journaux.cegep-ste-foy.qc.ca/educenligne/public/Fichiers_attaches/presentationdesigntechniques-130510022136-phpapp02.pdf

Slide Genius. (2016). *Five effective PowerPoint delivery methods for presentations.* Retrieved from www.slidegenius.com/blog/5-effective-powerpoint-delivery-methods-for-presentations/

Smith, D. J., & Valentine, T. (2012). The use and perceived effectiveness of instructional practices in two-year technical colleges. *Journal on Excellence in College Teaching, 23*(1), 133–161.

Smith, K. A. (2000). Going deeper: Formal small-group learning in large classes. In J. MacGregor, J. L. Cooper, K. A. Smith, & P. Robinson (Eds.), *New Directions for Teaching and Learning: Strategies for Energizing Large Classes; From Small Groups to Learning Communities, 81,* 25–46.

Smith, K. A., Sheppard, S. D., Johnson, D. W., & Johnson, R. T. (2005). Pedagogies of engagement: Classroom-based practices. *Journal of Engineering Education,* pp. 1–16.

Sokoloff, D., & Thornton, R. K. (1997). Using interactive lecture demonstrations to create an active learning environment. *The Physics Teachers, 35,* 340–346.

Sproat, E., Driscoll, D. L., & Brizee, A. (2013, March 1). *Purposes.* Retrieved from https://owl.english.purdue.edu/owl/resource/625/06/

Stafford, K., & Kelly, M. (1993). An introduction to lecturing (Workshop Series No. 10, pp. 5–6). City Polytechnic of Hong Kong, Professional Development Unit (now City University of Hong Kong, Centre for the Enhancement of Learning and Teaching). Retrieved from http://teaching.polyu.edu.hk/datafiles/r18a.doc

Stahl, R. (1994). Using "think-time" and "wait-time" skillfully in the classroom. *ERIC Digest.* Retrieved from http://files.eric.ed.gov/fulltext/ED370885.pdf

Staley, C. (2003). *Fifty ways to leave your lectern.* Belmont, CA: Wadsworth/Cengage Learning.

Stanford Teaching Commons. (n.d.). *Lecture guidelines.* Retrieved from https://teachingcommons.stanford.edu/resources/teaching-resources/teaching-strategies/checklist-effective-lecturing/lecturing-guidelines

Steinert, Y., & Snell, L. S. (1999). Interactive lecturing: Strategies for increasing participation in large group presentations. *Medical Teacher, 21*(1), 37–42.

Strauss, B. (2009). *Big is beautiful.* Retrieved from www.mindingthecampus.org/2009/12/big_is_beautiful/

Strevler, R. A., & Meneske, M. (2017). Taking a closer look at the active learning. *Journal of Engineering Education, 106*(2), 186–190.

Strauss, V. (2017). It puts kids to sleep—but teachers keep lecturing anyway. Here's what to do about it. Washington Post. Retrieved from www.washingtonpost.com/news/answer-sheet/wp/2017/07/11/it-puts-kids-to-sleep-but-teachers-keep-lecturing-anyway-heres-what-to-do-about-it/?utm_term=.83ecfe701101

Szpunar, K. K., McDermott, K. B., & Roediger, H. L. (2008). Testing during study insulates against the buildup of proactive interference. *Journal of Experimental Psychology: Learning, Memory, and Cognition, 34,* 1392–1399.

Talbert, R. (2016a). Lecture reality check. Part 1 [Web log post]. Retrieved September 15, 2016, from http://rtalbert.org/blog/2016/lecture-reality-check

Talbert, R. (2016b). Lecture reality check. Part 2 [Web log post]. Retrieved September 15, 2016, from http://rtalbert.org/blog/2016/lecture-reality-check-2

TEAL. (2011). *Just Write! guide.* Retrieved from https://lincs.ed.gov/sites/default/files/TEAL_JustWriteGuide.pdf

Teteak, J. (2013, October 21). *Find your presentation style.* Retrieved from http://ruletheroom.com/find-your-presentation-style/

Tiscone, R. (2006). *Aristotle's tried and true recipe for argument casserole.* Retrieved from https://info.legalsolutions.thomsonreuters.com/pdf/perspec/2006-fall/2006-fall-9.pdf

Titsworth, B. (2004). Student note taking: The effects of teacher immediacy and clarity. *Communication Education, 53,* 305–320.

Titsworth, B. S., & Kiewra, K. A. (2004). Spoken organizational lecture cues and student. Notetaking as facilitators of student learning. *Contemporary Educational Psychology, 29*(4), 447–461.

Tompkins, G. E. (1997). *Literacy for the 21st century: A balanced approach.* Upper Saddle River, NJ: Prentice Hall. Retrieved from https://hatrc.org/library/eoQl3/tompkins-literacy-21st-century-pdf.pdf

Tsou, T. (2015). *Geographic and spatial reasoning.* Retrieved from http://map.sdsu.edu/geog104/lecture/unit-2.htm

Umbach, P. D., & Wawrzynski, M. R. (2004). Faculty do matter: The role of college faculty in student learning and engagement. *Research in Higher Education, 46*(2), 153–184.

University of British Columbia. (n.d.). *Physics 101.* Retrieved from https://docs.google.com/document/d/1mK02XpvB7JUMWd7cp_1iYJvk8H1j1gvCWl2StKORvCY/pub

University of California, Davis. (n.d.). *Effective presentation and visuals for PowerPoint.* Faculty Support for Technology in Teaching and Research. Retrieved from http://facultysupport.ucdavis.edu/techtip/powerpoint/Effective%20presentation/index.html

University of Central Florida, University Writing Center. (2011). *Annotated bibliography.* Retrieved from https://uwc.cah.ucf.edu/wp-content/uploads/sites/9/2016/10/Annotated_Bibliography_MLA.pdf

University of Hawaii. (n.d.a). *Specific purpose statements.* Retrieved from www.hawaii.edu/mauispeech/html/your_purpose.html

University of Hawaii. (n.d.b). *Using connectives.* Retrieved from www.hawaii.edu/mauispeech/pdf/connectives.pdf

University of Leicester. (n.d.). *Signposts.* Retrieved from www2.le.ac.uk/offices/eltu/presessional-course-information/downloads/sl-materials-week-2/signposts-doc

University of Maine, Fort Kent. (n.d.). *Cornell note-taking method.* Retrieved from www.umfk.edu/learning-center/studying-tips/notes/

University of Michigan, Center for Research on Learning and Teaching (2016). *Active learning*. Retrieved from www.crlt.umich.edu/tstrategies/tsal

University of Michigan, Center for Research on Learning and Teaching. (n.d.a). *Breaking the ice with your students*. Retrieved from www.crlt.umich.edu/node/816

University of Michigan, Center for Research on Teaching and Learning. (n.d.b). *Classroom challenge: Handing wrong answers*. Retrieved from www.crlt.umich.edu/node/712

University of North Carolina, Chapel Hill. (2014). *Brainstorming*. The Writing Center. Retrieved from http://writingcenter.unc.edu/handouts/brainstorming/

University of North Carolina, Charlotte. (n.d.). *Classroom assessment technique examples*. The Center for Teaching and Learning. Retrieved from http://teaching.uncc.edu/learning-resources/articles-books/best-practice/assessment-grading/assessment-technique-examples

University of Northern Colorado. (2015). *Monfort College of Business classroom technology guidelines*. Retrieved from http://studylib.net/doc/13960385/monfort-college-of-business-classroom-technology-guidelines

University of Pittsburg. (2008b). *Verbal delivery tips*. Retrieved from www.speaking.pitt.edu/student/public-speaking/suggestions-verbal.html

University of South Florida. (n.d.). *Classroom assessment techniques: Academy for teaching and learning excellence*. Retrieved from www.usf.edu/atle/teaching/interactive-techniques.aspx

University of Southern California, Center for Excellence in Teaching. (n.d.). *Preparing and structuring lecture notes*. Retrieved from http://cet.usc.edu/resources/teaching_learning/docs/teaching_nuggets_docs/3.1_Preparing_and_Structuring_Lecture_Notes.pdf

University of Virginia. (n.d.). *Cubing and think dots*. Retrieved from curry.virginia.edu/uploads/resourcelibrary/magc_cubing_think_dots.pdf

University of Waterloo. (n.d.). *Lecturing effectively*. Centre for Teaching Excellence. Retrieved from https://uwaterloo.ca/centre-for-teaching-excellence/teaching-resources/teaching-tips/lecturing-and-presenting/delivery/lecturing-effectively-university

University of Wisconsin. (2014). Thesis or purpose statements. *Writers handbook*. Retrieved from http://writing.wisc.edu/Handbook/Thesis_or_Purpose.html

Vanderbilt University. (2016). *Building vocabulary and conceptual knowledge using the Frayer model*. IRIS Center. Retrieved from https://iris.peabody.vanderbilt.edu/module/sec-rdng/cresource/q2/p07/#content

Van Gyn, G. (2013). The little assignment with the big impact: Reading, writing, critical reflection, and meaningful discussion. *Faculty Focus*. Retrieved from www.facultyfocus.com/articles/instructional-design/the-little-assignment-with-the-big-impact-reading-writing-critical-reflection-and-meaningful-discussion/

Vaughan, J. L., & Estes, T. H. (1986). *Reading and reasoning beyond the primary grades*. Boston, MA: Allyn and Bacon.

Vygotsky, L. S. (1978). *Mind in society: The development of higher psychological processes*. Cambridge, MA: Harvard University Press.

Walker, J. (n.d.). *Emerging trends and technologies*. Retrieved from http://slideplayer.com/slide/6321152/

Walker, J. D., Cotner, S. H., Baepler, P. M., & Decker, M. D. (2008). A delicate balance: Integrating active learning into a large lecture course. *CBE—Life Sciences Education, 7*(4), 361–367.

Wang, J., Pascarella, E. T., Nelson-Laird, T. F., & Ribera, A. K. (2015). How clear and organized classroom instruction and deep approaches to learning affect growth in critical thinking and need for cognition. *Studies in Higher Education, 40*(10), 1786–1807.

Weimer, M. (2008). Ways of responding to wrong or not very good answers. *Faculty Focus*. Retrieved from www.facultyfocus.com/articles/teaching-and-learning/ways-of-responding-to-a-wrong-or-not-very-good-answers/

Weimer, M. (2010). Classroom climates. *Faculty Focus*. Retrieved from www.facultyfocus.com/articles/effective-classroom-management/classroom-climates/

Weimer, M. (2015). Step away from the lectern. *Faculty Focus*. Retrieved from www.facultyfocus.com/articles/teaching-professor-blog/step-away-from-the-lectern/

Weimer, M. (2016). Note-taking strategies to improve learning. *Faculty Focus*. Retrieved from http://bit.ly/2bY1RTc

Weisskirch, R. S. (2009). Playing bingo to review fundamental concepts in advanced courses. *International Journal for the Scholarship of Teaching and Learning, 3*(1). Retrieved from http://digitalcommons.georgiasouthern.edu/cgi/viewcontent.cgi?article=1142&context=ij-sotl

Wellman, H. (1985). *The child's theory of mind: The development of conscious cognition*. San Diego, CA: Academic Press.

Weltman, D., & Whiteside, M. (2010). Comparing the effectiveness of traditional and active learning methods in business statistics: Convergence to the mean. *Journal of Statistics Education, 18*(1).

Wentzel, K. R., & Brophy, J. (2014). *Motivating students to learn* (4th ed.). New York, NY: Routledge.

Westervelt, E. (2016, April 14). *Nobel laureate: College lectures are about as effective as bloodletting*. Retrieved from www.wbur.org/hereandnow/2016/04/15/college-lecture-overdue-for-revision

Wieman, C. E. (2014). Large-scale comparison of science teaching methods sends clear message. *Proceedings of the National Academy of Sciences, 111*(23), 8319–8320.

Wiggins, G., & McTighe, J. (1998). *Understanding by design*. Alexandria, VA: Association for Supervision and Curriculum Development.

Williams, J.B.W. (2006). *How to give a sensational scientific talk*. Retrieved from http://chem.virginia.edu/wp-content/uploads/2009/05/talk_in_pdf

Williams, R. (2010). *The non-designer's presentation book: Principles for effective presentation design*. Berkeley, CA: Peachpit Press.

Winter, R. (2003). Alternative to the essay. *The Guardian*. Retrieved from www.guardian.co.uk/education/2003/jun/10/highereducation.uk

Wood, E., Zivcakova, L., Gentile, P., Archer, K., Pasquale, D. D., & Nosko, A. (2011). Examining the impact of off-task multi-tasking with technology on real-time classroom learning. *Computers & Education, 58*, 365–374.

Worthen, M. (2015). Lecture me: Really. *New York Times*. Retrieved from www.nytimes.com/2015/10/18/opinion/sunday/lecture-me-really.html

Yip, D. Y. (1998). Identification of misconceptions in novice biology teachers and remedial strategies for improving biology learning. *International Journal of Science Education, 20*(4), 461–477.

Youdas, J. W., Krouse, D. A., Hellyer, N. J., Hollman, J. H., & Rindflesh, A. B. (2007). Perceived usefulness or reciprocal peer teaching among doctor of physical therapy students in the gross anatomy laboratory. *Journal of Physical Theory Education, 21*, 30–38.

Zaremba, A. J. (2011). *Speaking professionally: Influence, power and responsibility at the podium*. New York, NY: Routledge.

Zhao, N., Wardeska, J. G., McGuire, S. Y., & Cook, E. (2014). Metacognition: An effective tool to promote success in college science learning. *Journal of College Science Teaching, 43*(4), 48–54.

Zygouris-Coe, V., Wiggins, M. B., & Smith, L. H. (2004). Engaging students with text: The 3-2-1 strategy. *The Reading Teacher, 58*(4), 381–384.

NAME INDEX

SUBJECT INDEX

Page references followed by *fig* indicate an illustrated figure; followed by *t* indicate a table.

D

E

T

U

V